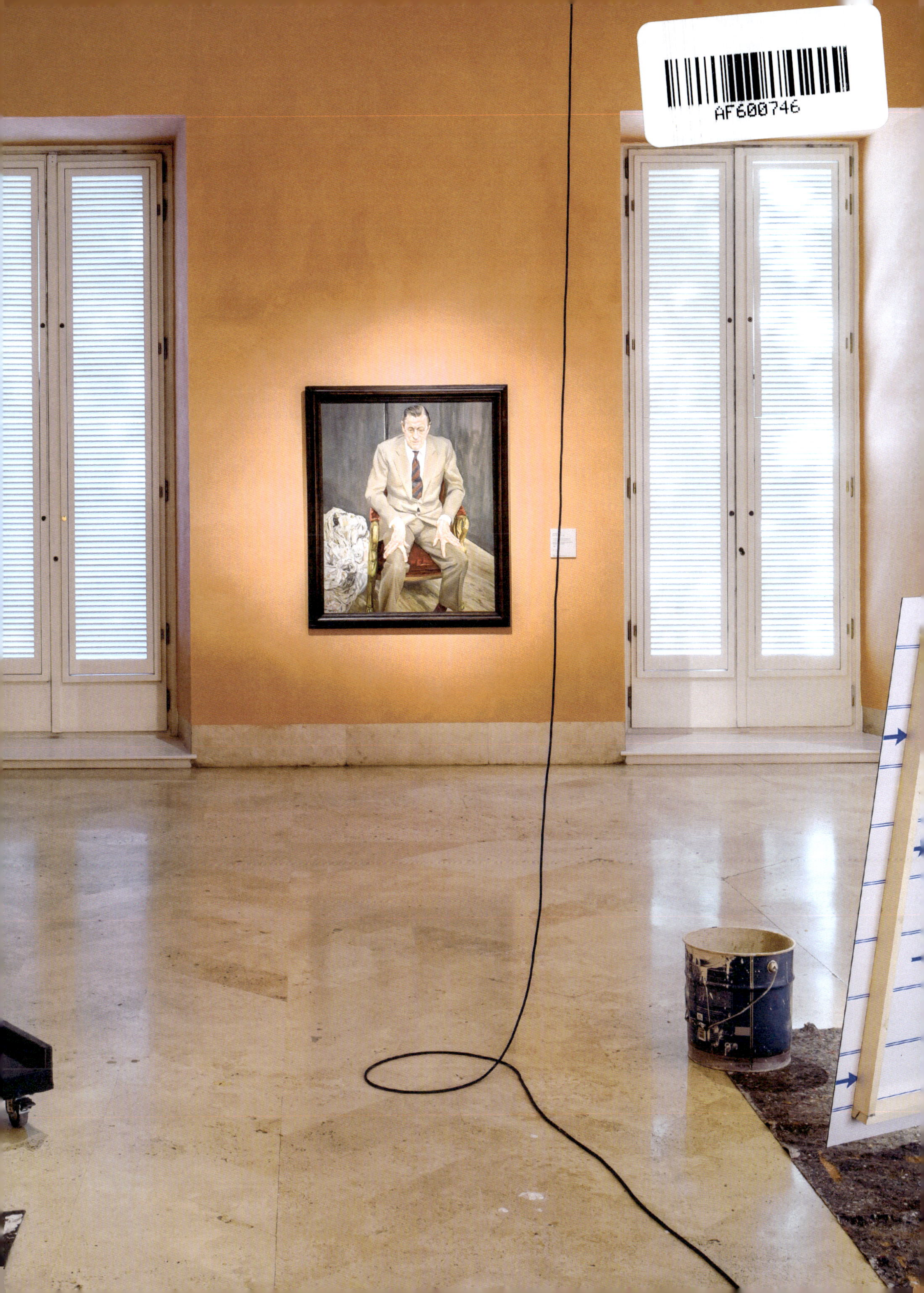

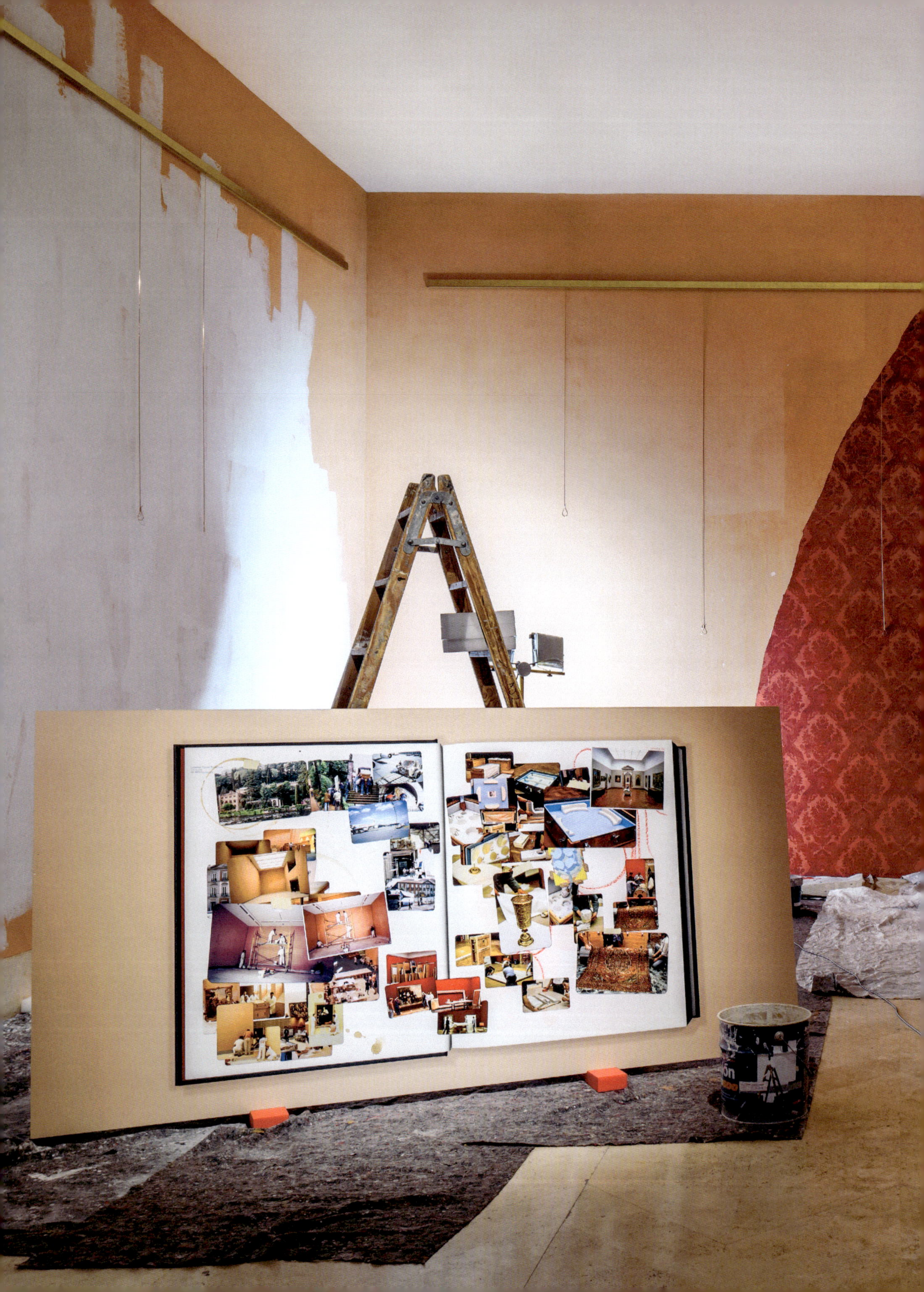

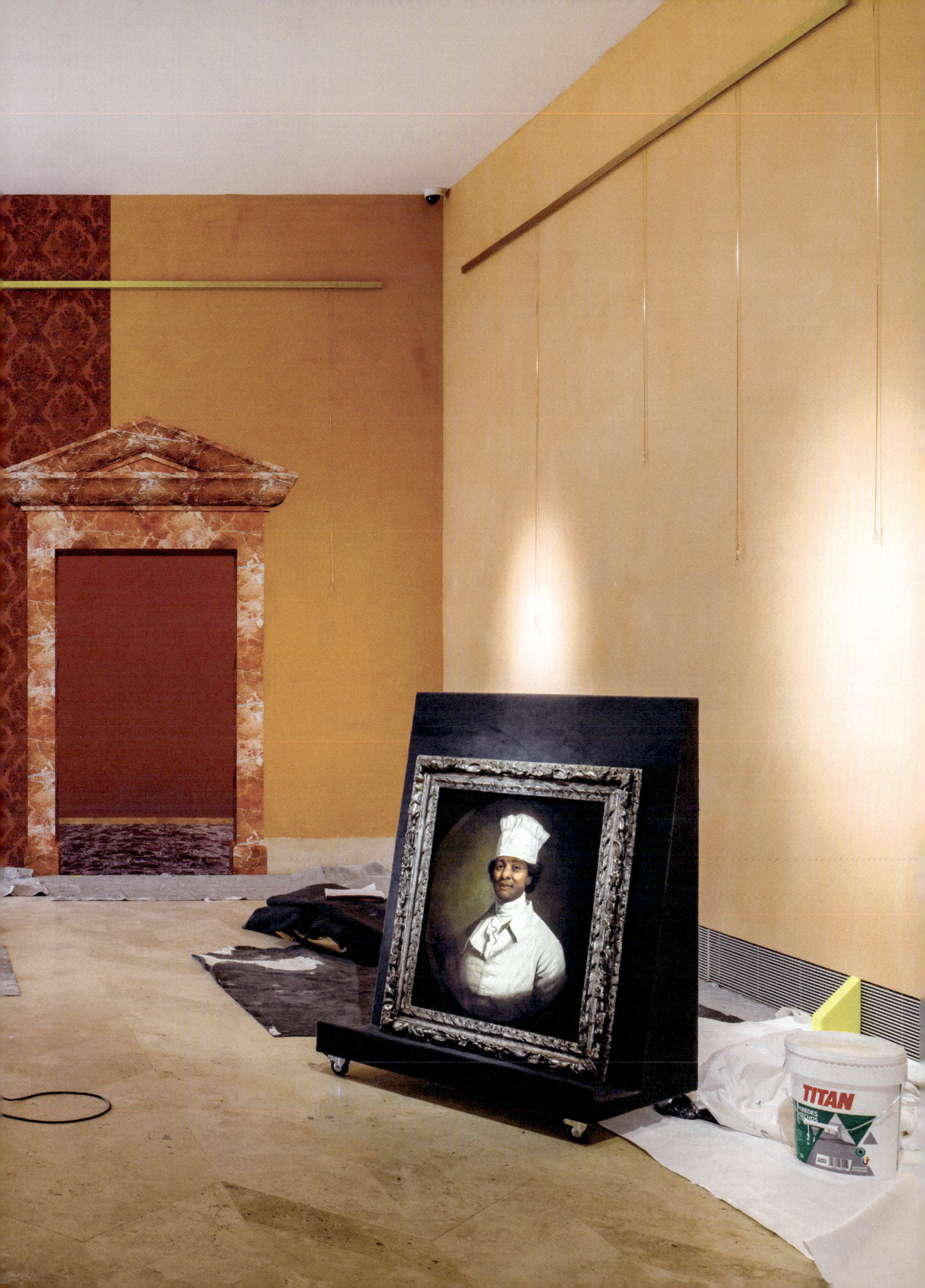
TITAN

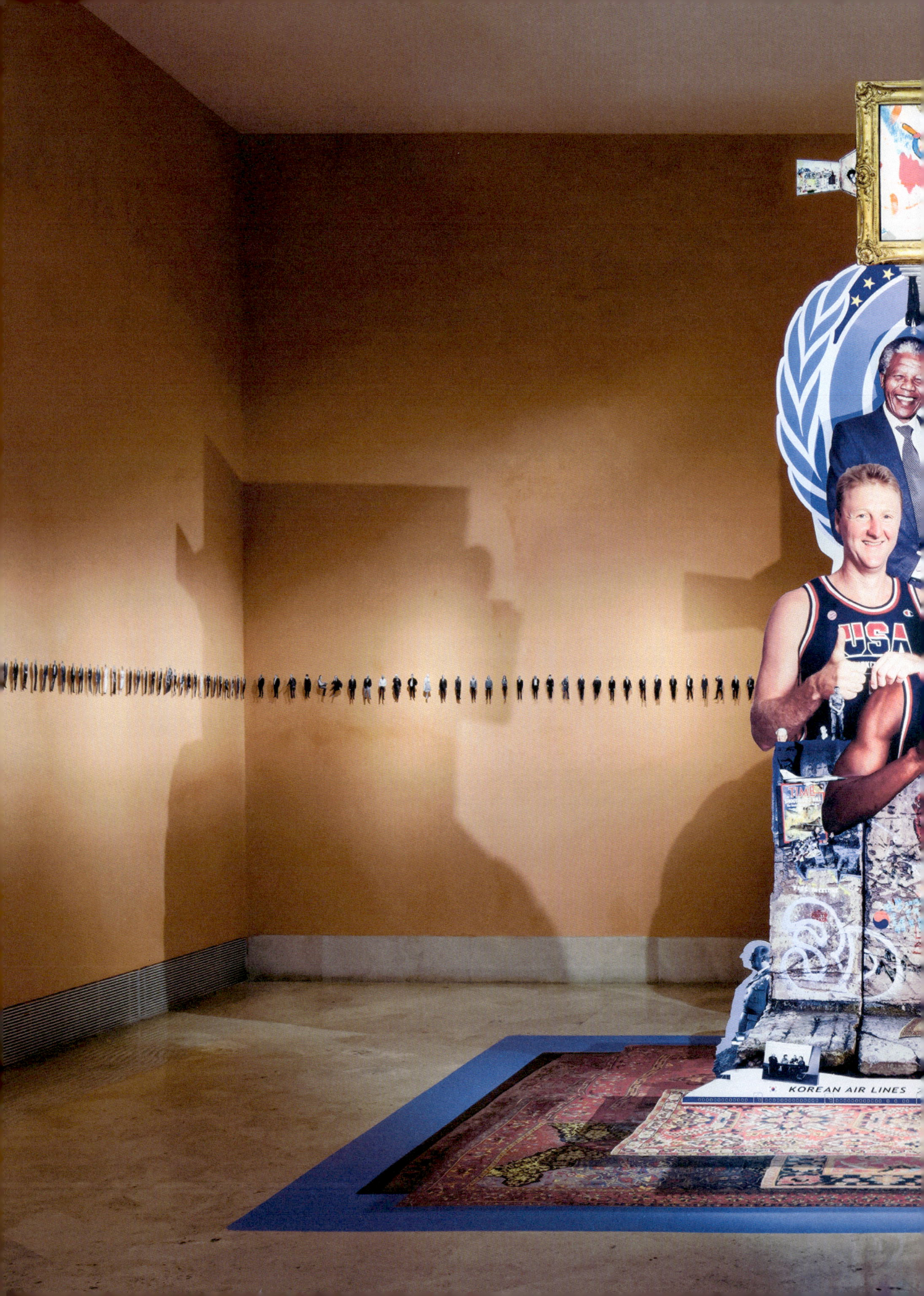
USA
KOREAN AIR LINES

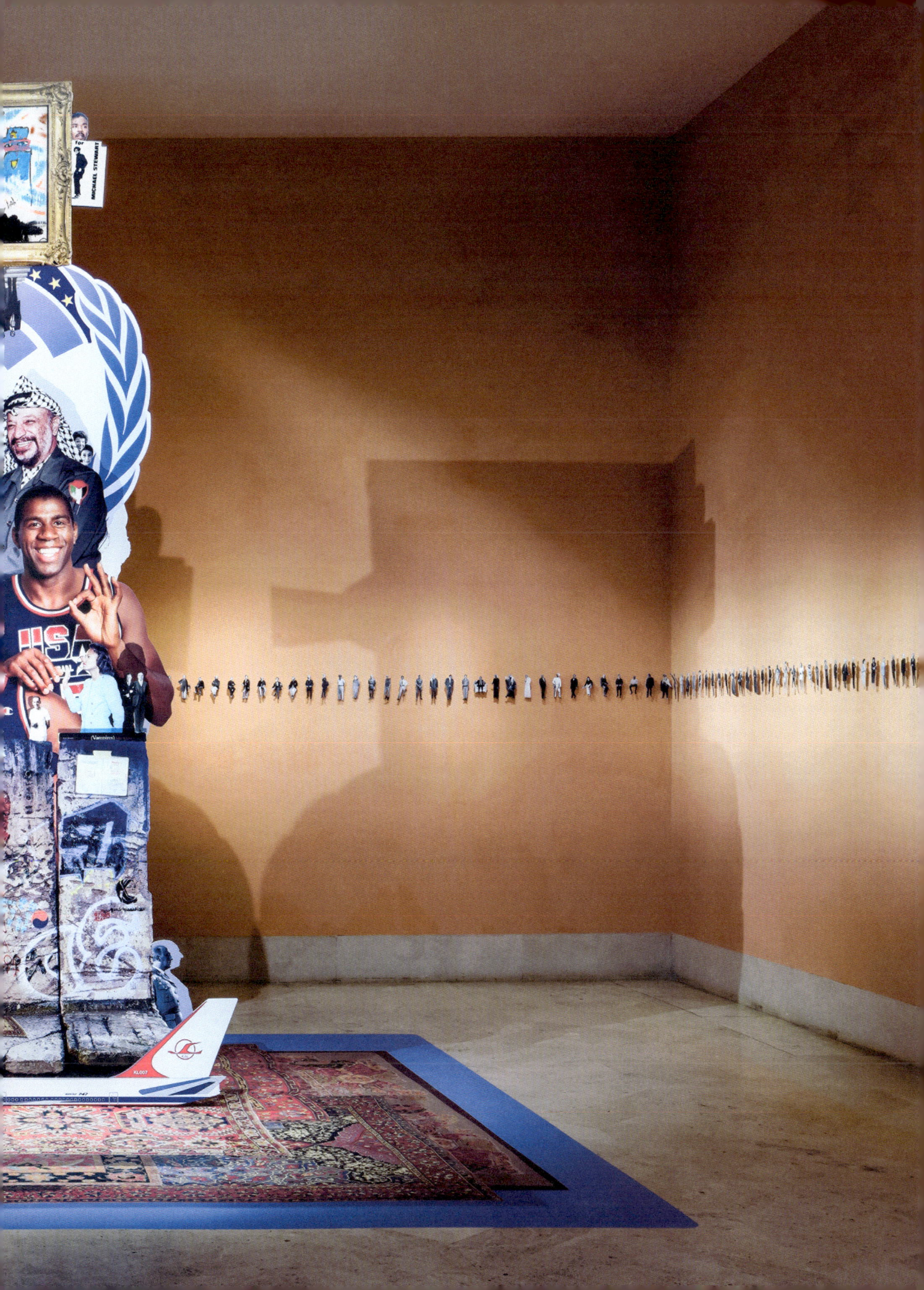

for
MICHAEL STEWART
USA

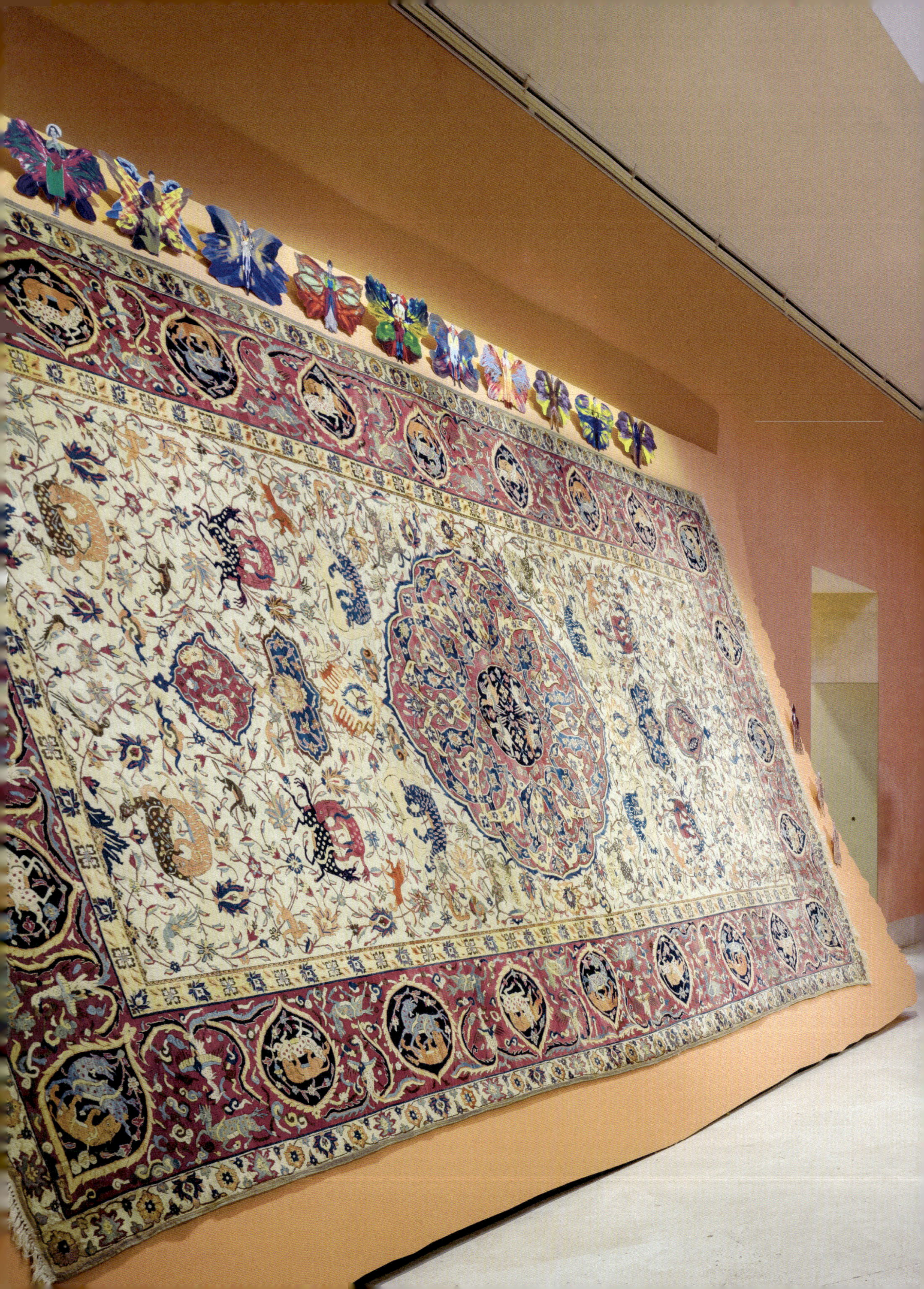

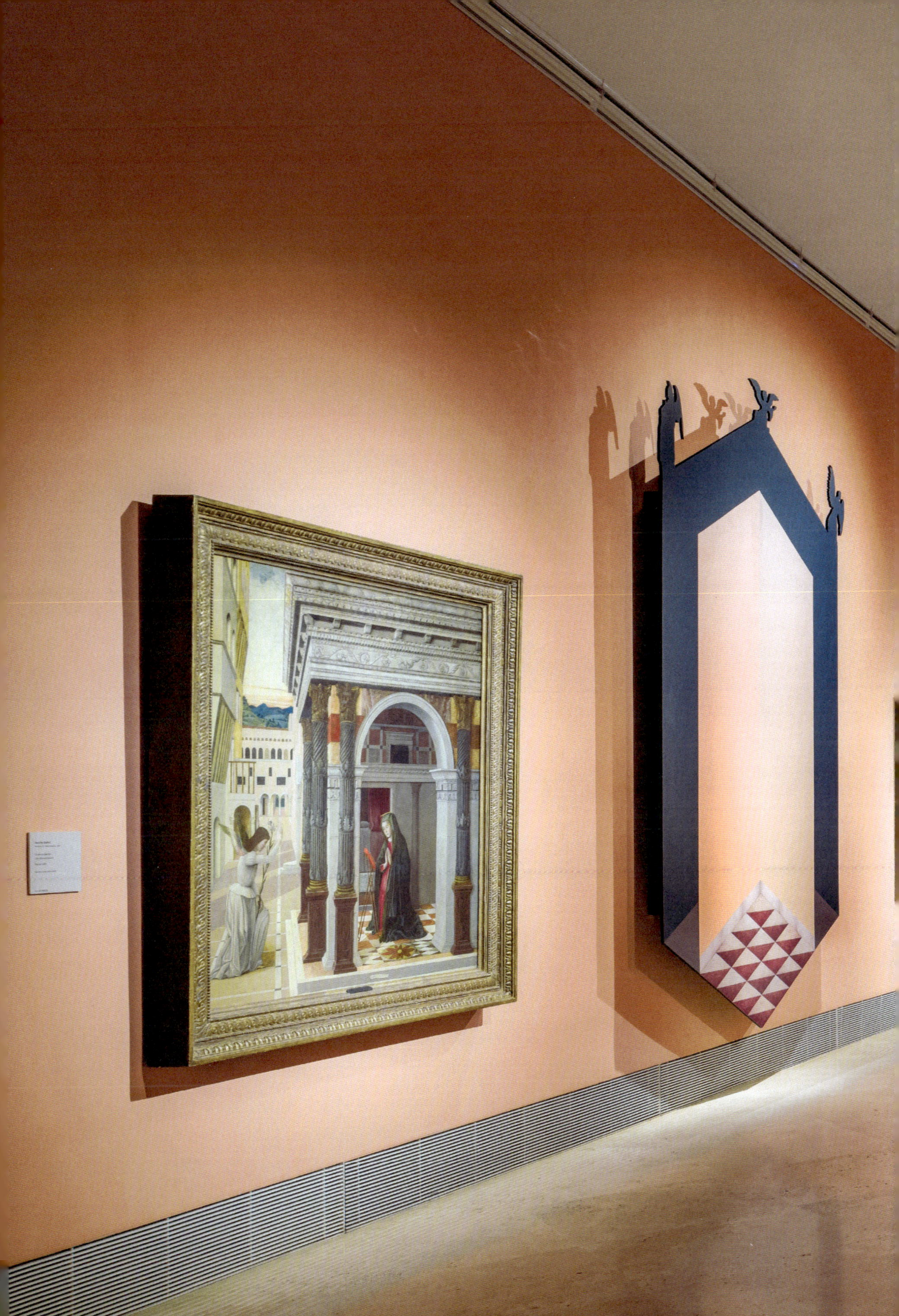

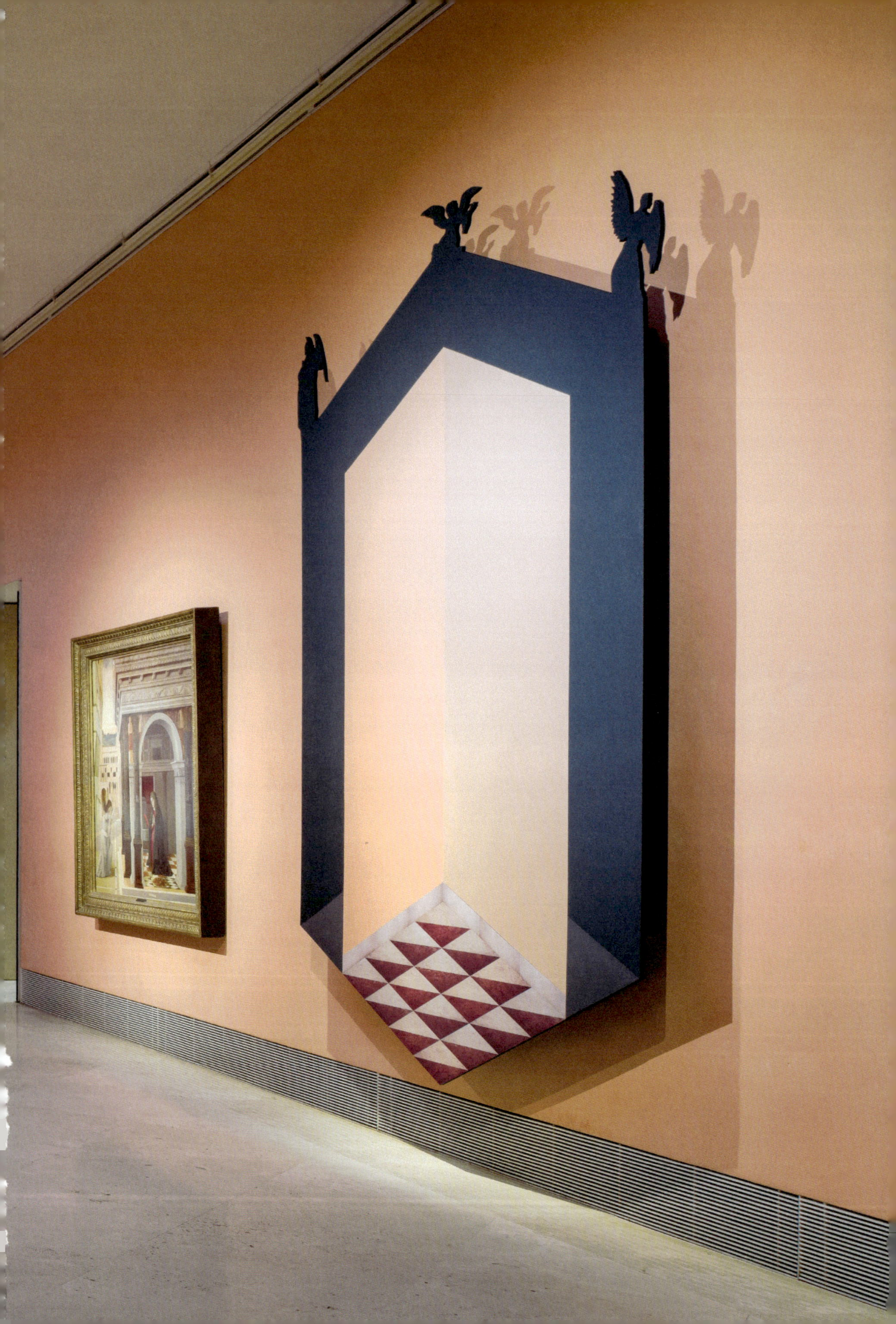

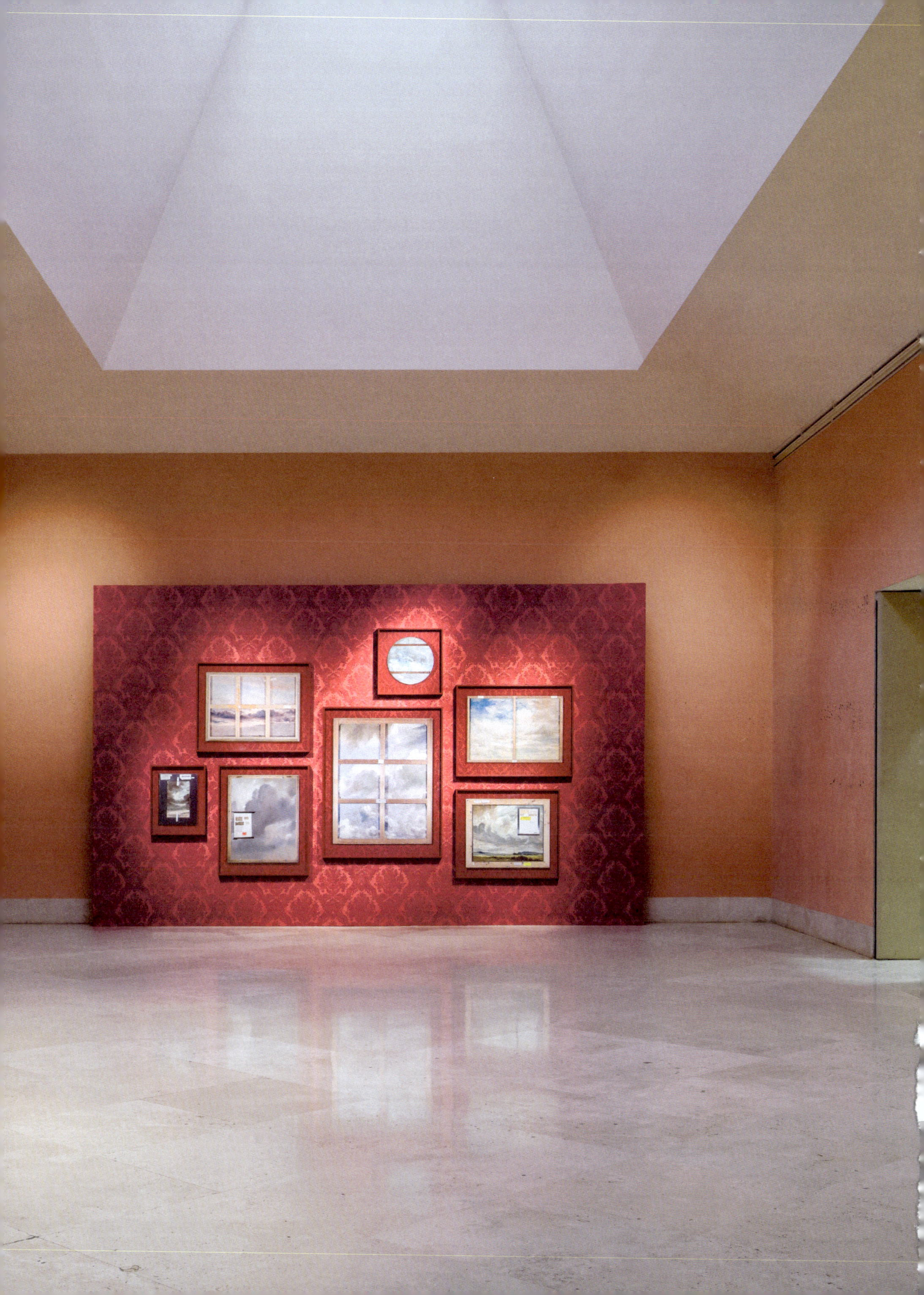

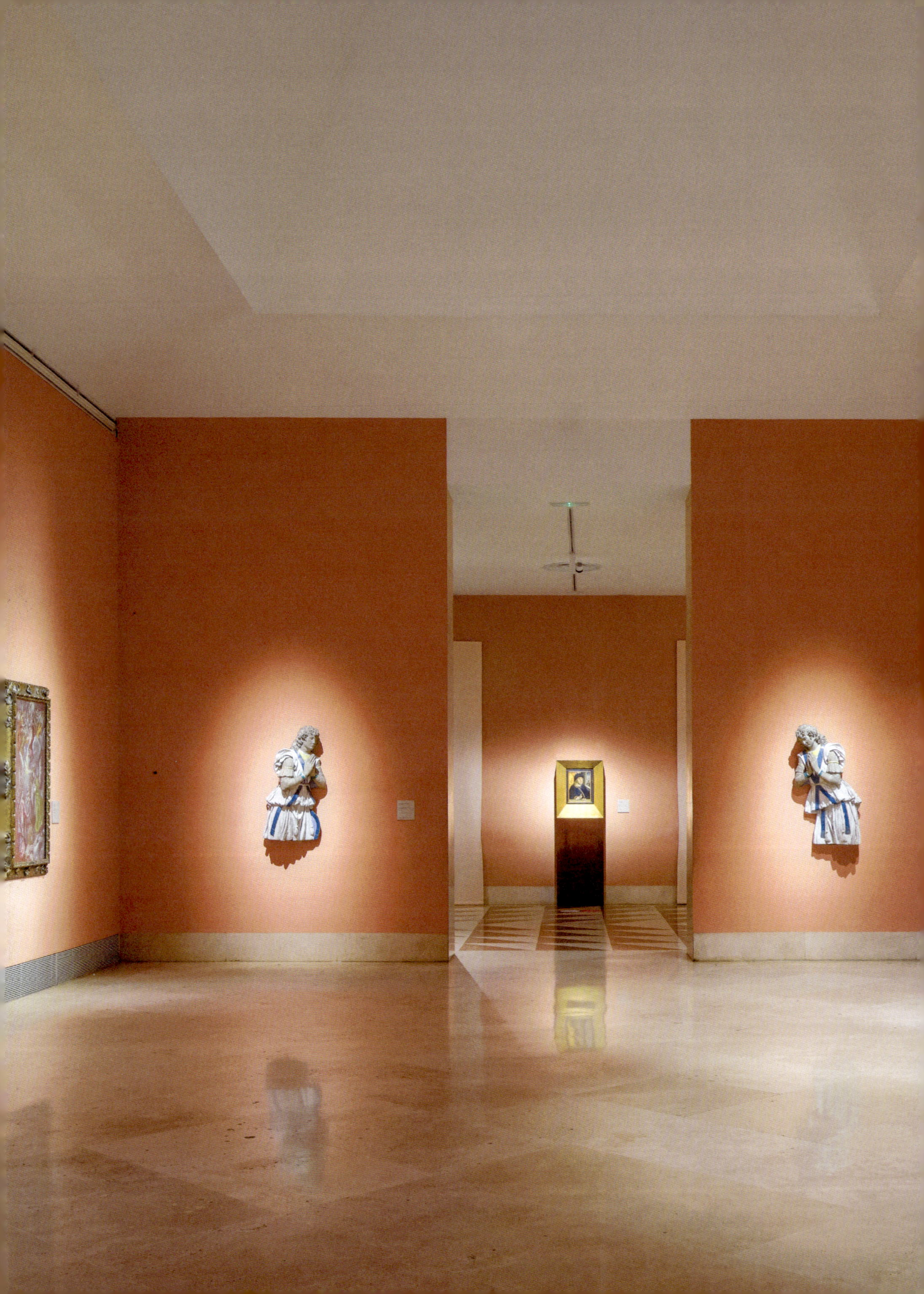

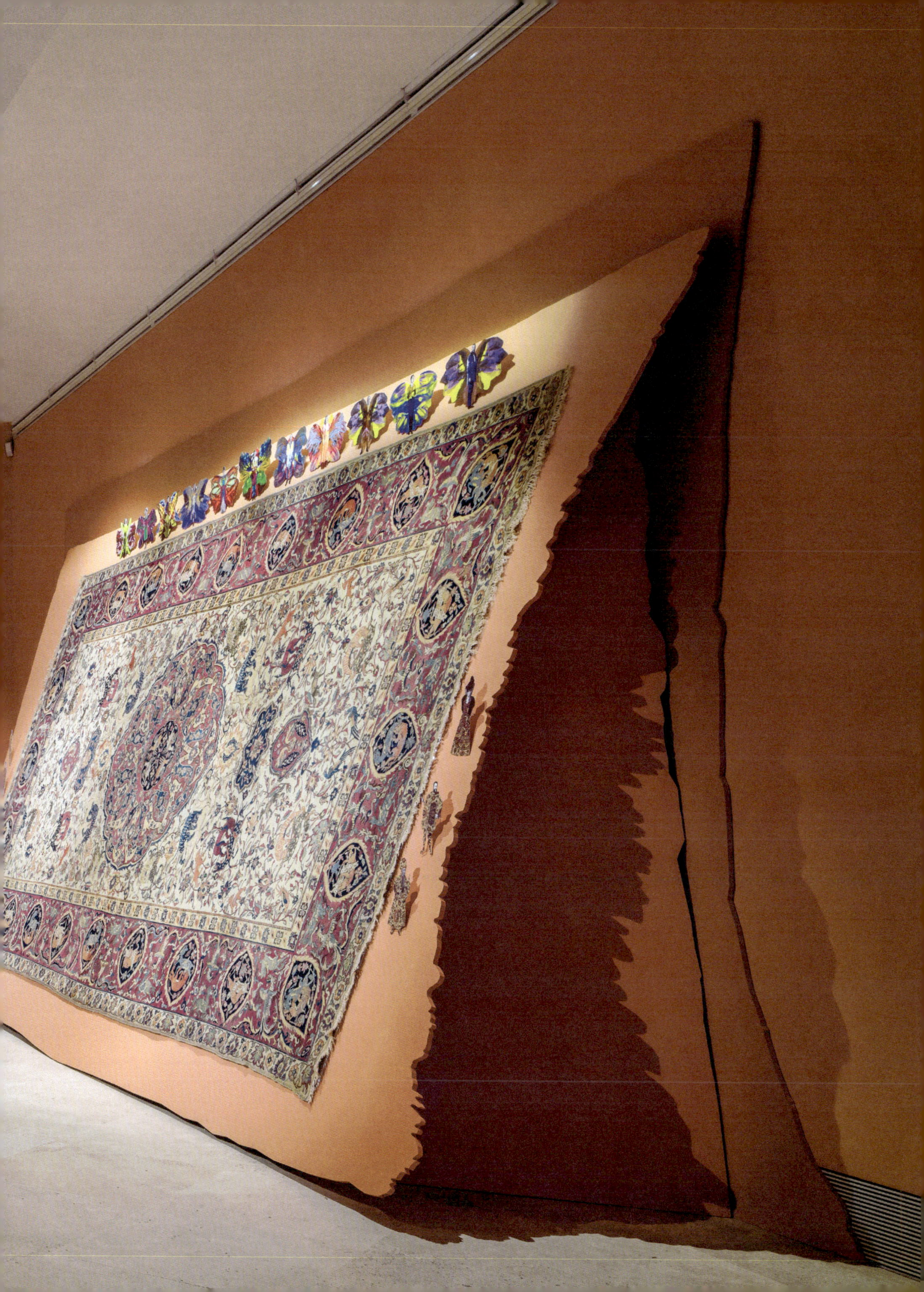

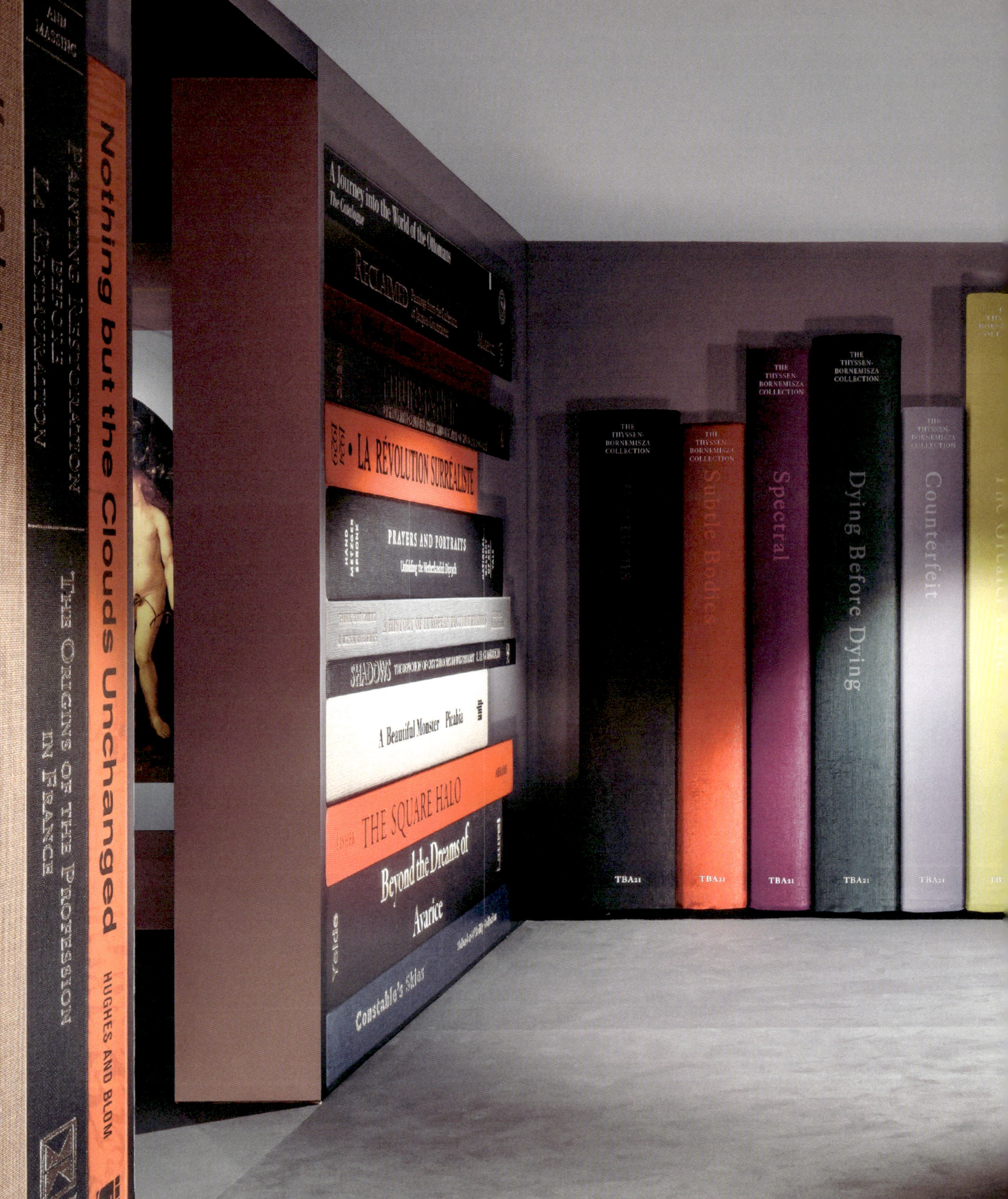
Nothing but the Clouds Unchanged
HUGHES AND BLOM
Painting Restoration Before La Restauration
The Origins of the Profession in France
A Journey into the World of the Ottomans
The Catalogue
RECLAIMED
LA RÉVOLUTION SURRÉALISTE
PRAYERS AND PORTRAITS
Unfolding the Netherlandish Diptych
SHADOWS
A Beautiful Monster Picabia
THE SQUARE HALO
Beyond the Dreams of Avarice
Constable's Skies
THE THYSSEN-BORNEMISZA COLLECTION
Subtle Bodies
Spectral
Dying Before Dying
Counterfeit
TBA21

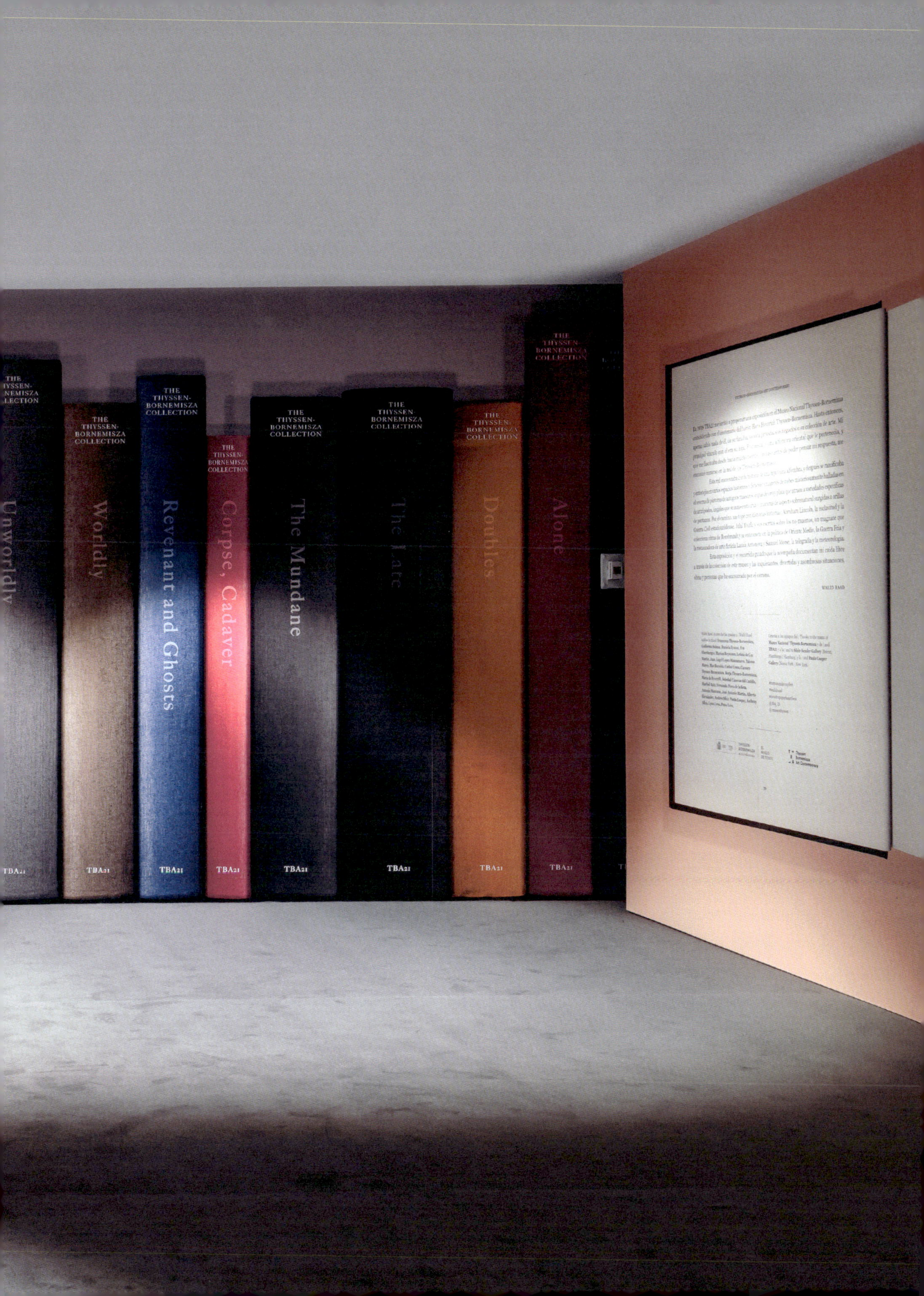

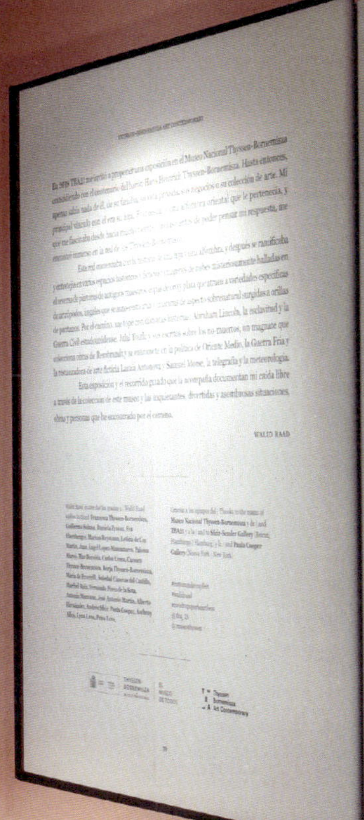

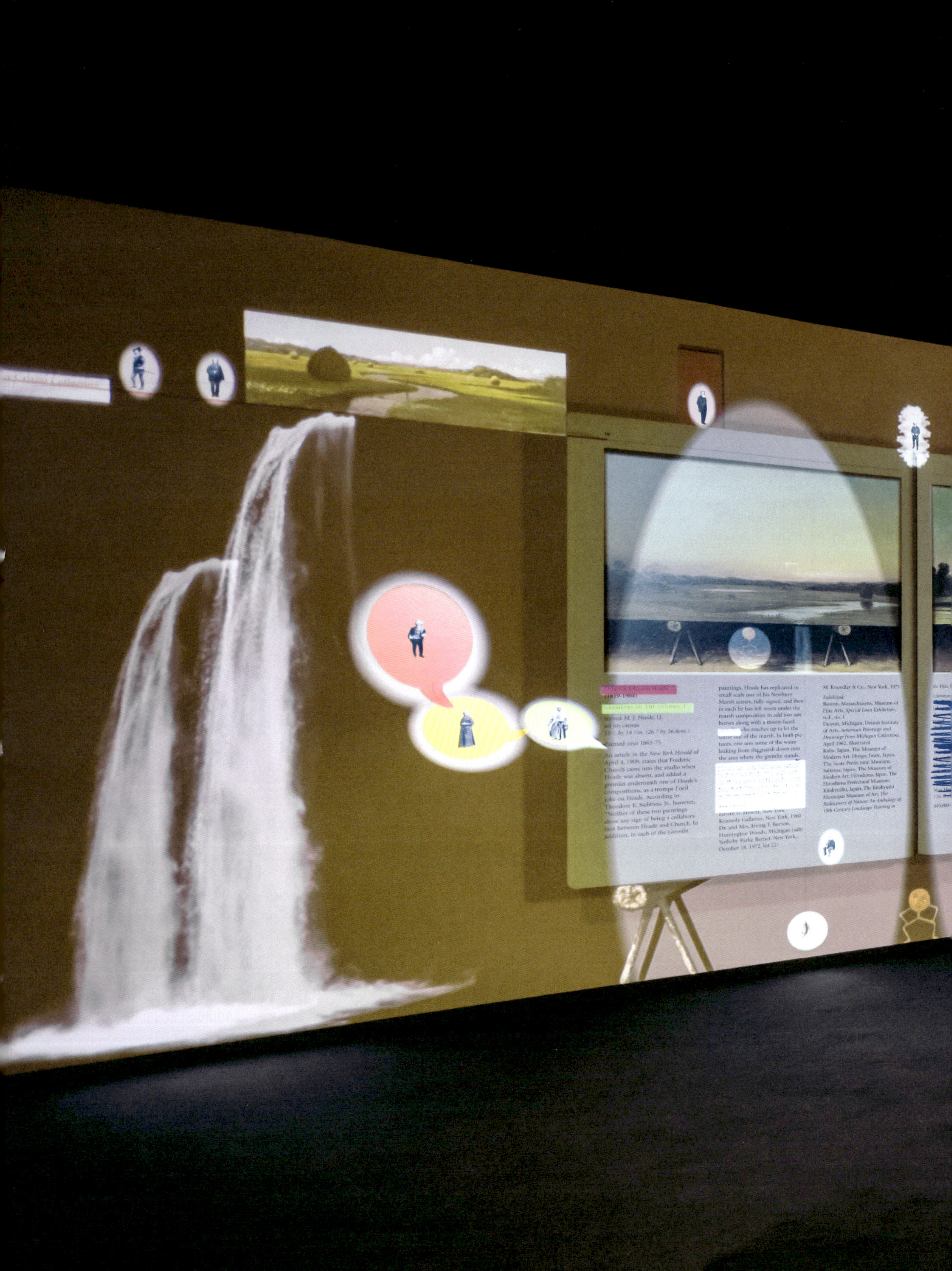

(1819-1904)
Painted circa 1863-75.
An article in the New York Herald of April 4, 1909, states that Frederic Church came into the studio when Heade was absent, and added a gremlin underneath one of Heade's compositions, as a trompe l'oeil joke on Heade. According to Theodore E. Stebbins, Jr., however, "Neither of these two paintings show any sign of being a collabora-tion between Heade and Church. In addition, in each of the Gremlin
paintings, Heade has replicated in small scale one of his Newbury Marsh scenes, fully signed, and then in each he has left room under the marsh composition to add two saw horses along with a moon-faced
water out of the marsh. In both pic-tures, one sees some of the water leaking from the marsh down into the area where the gremlin stands.
Kennedy Galleries, New York, 1960
Dr. and Mrs. Irving F. Burton, Huntington Woods, Michigan (sale: Sotheby Parke Bernet, New York, October 18, 1972, lot 22)
M. Knoedler & Co., New York, 1973
Exhibited
Boston, Massachusetts, Museum of Fine Arts, Special Loan Exhibition, n.d., no. 1
Detroit, Michigan, Detroit Institute of Arts, American Paintings and Drawings from Michigan Collections, April 1962, illustrated
Kobe, Japan, The Museum of Modern Art, Hyogo; Iwate, Japan, The Iwate Prefectural Museum; Saitama, Japan, The Museum of Modern Art; Hiroshima, Japan, The Hiroshima Prefectural Museum; Kitakyushu, Japan, The Kitakyushu Municipal Museum of Art, The Rediscovery of Nature: An Anthology of 19th Century Landscape Painting in

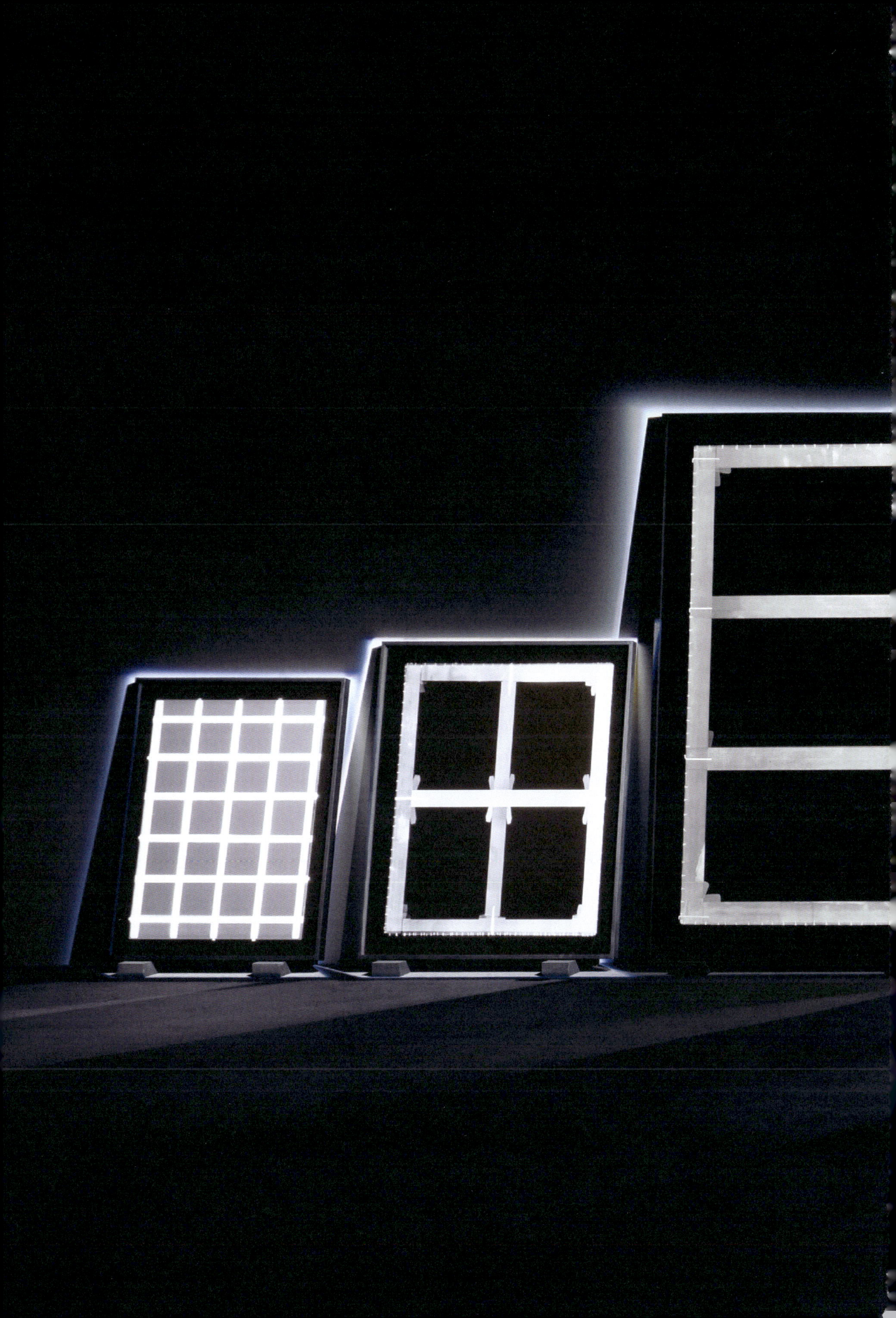

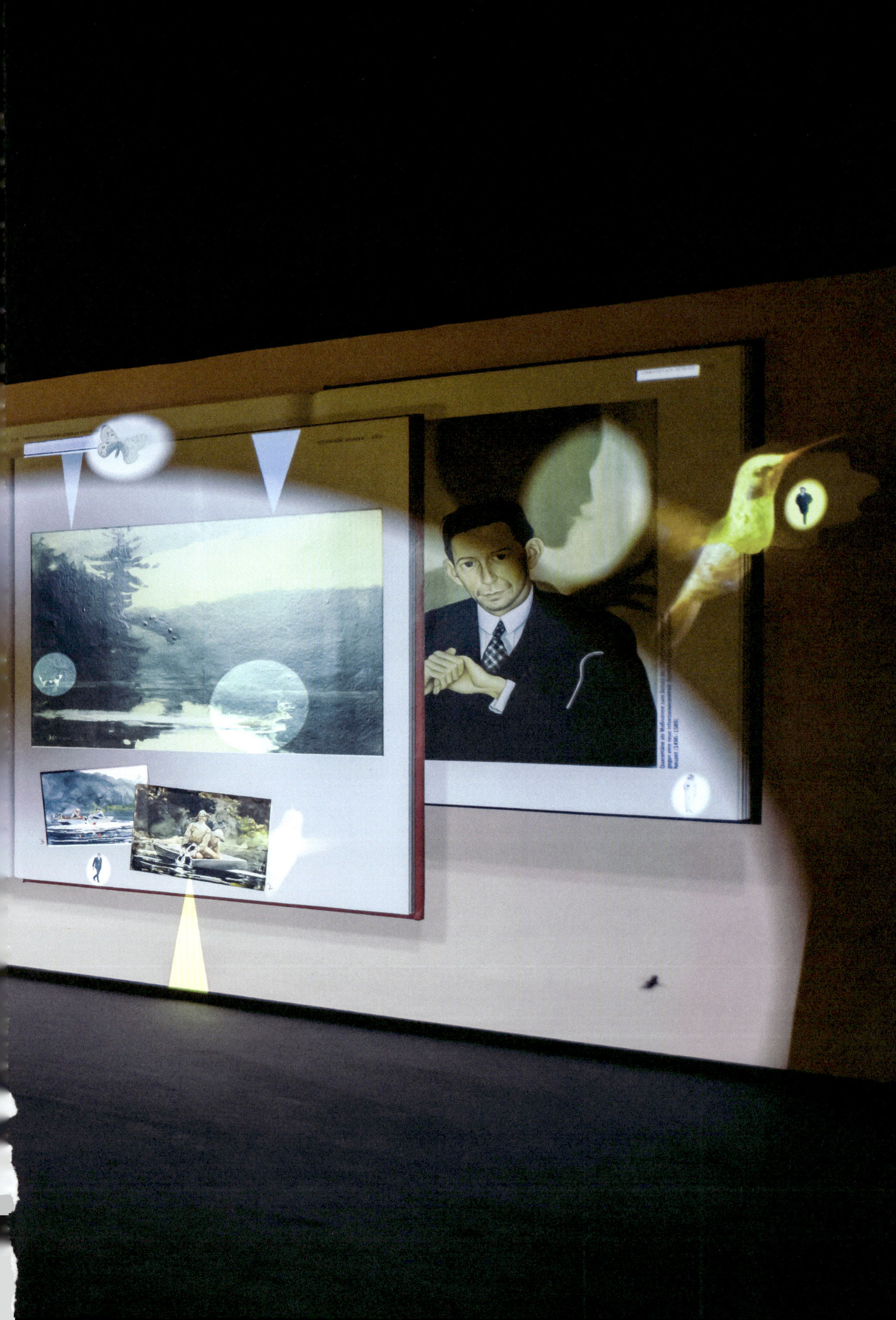

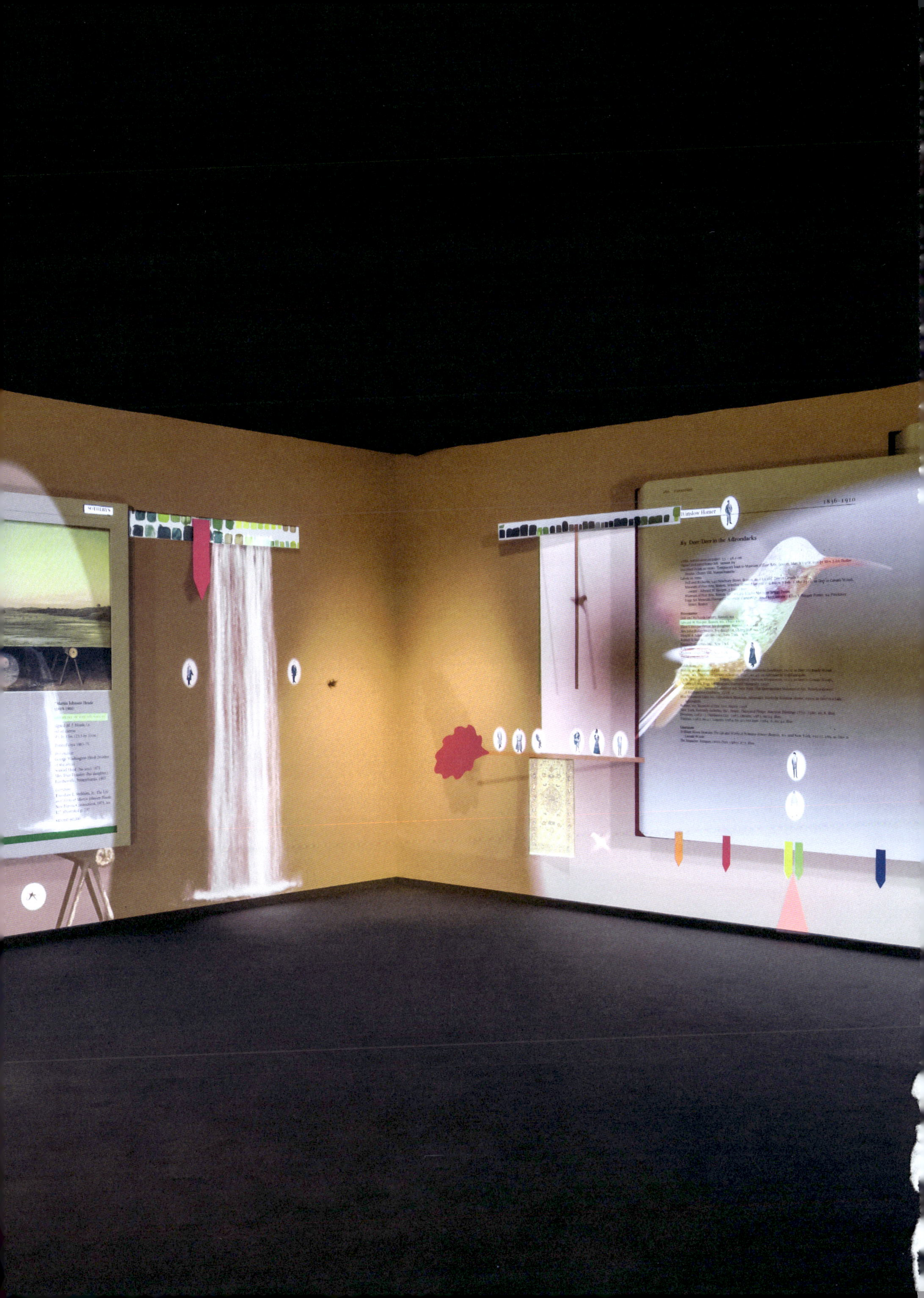

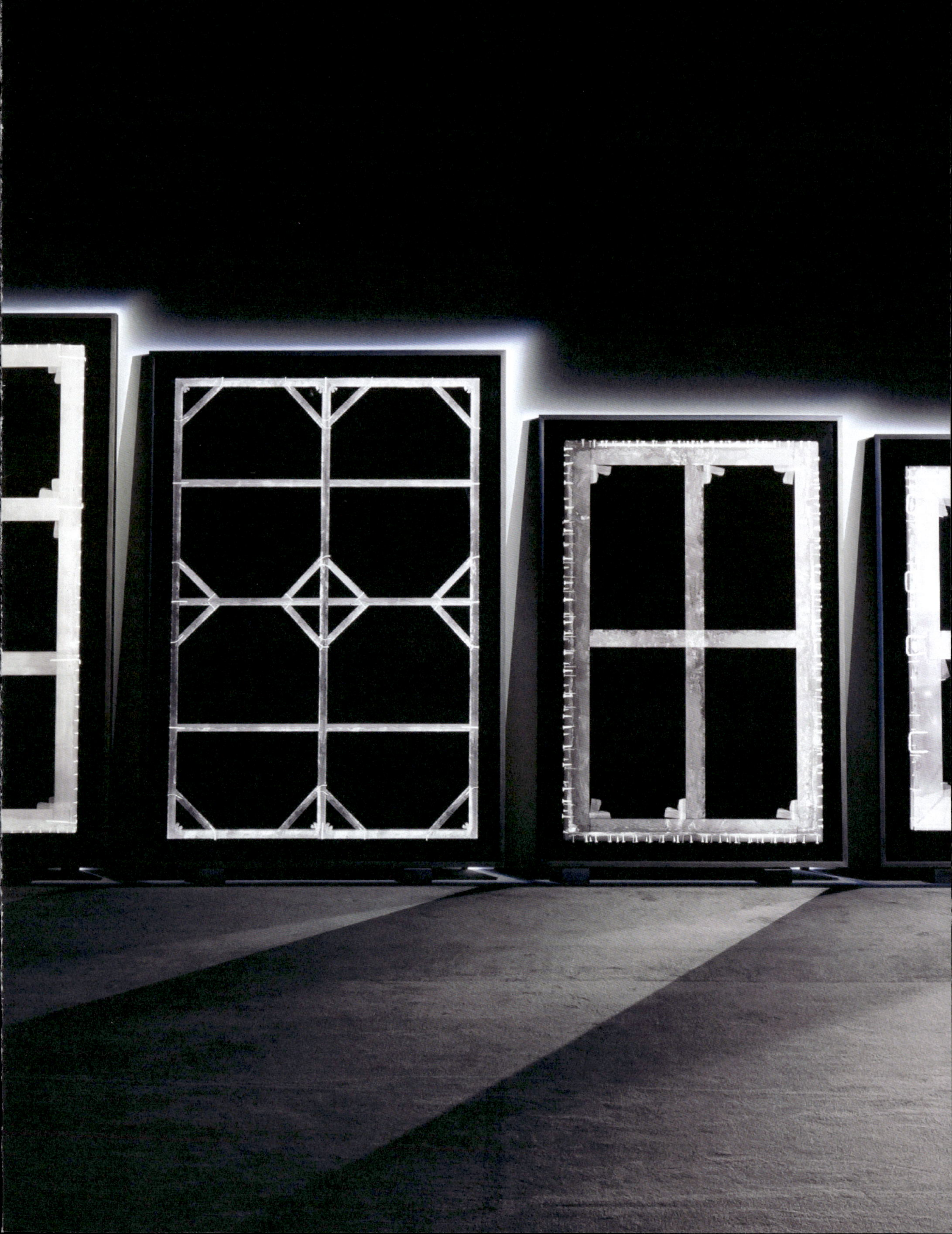

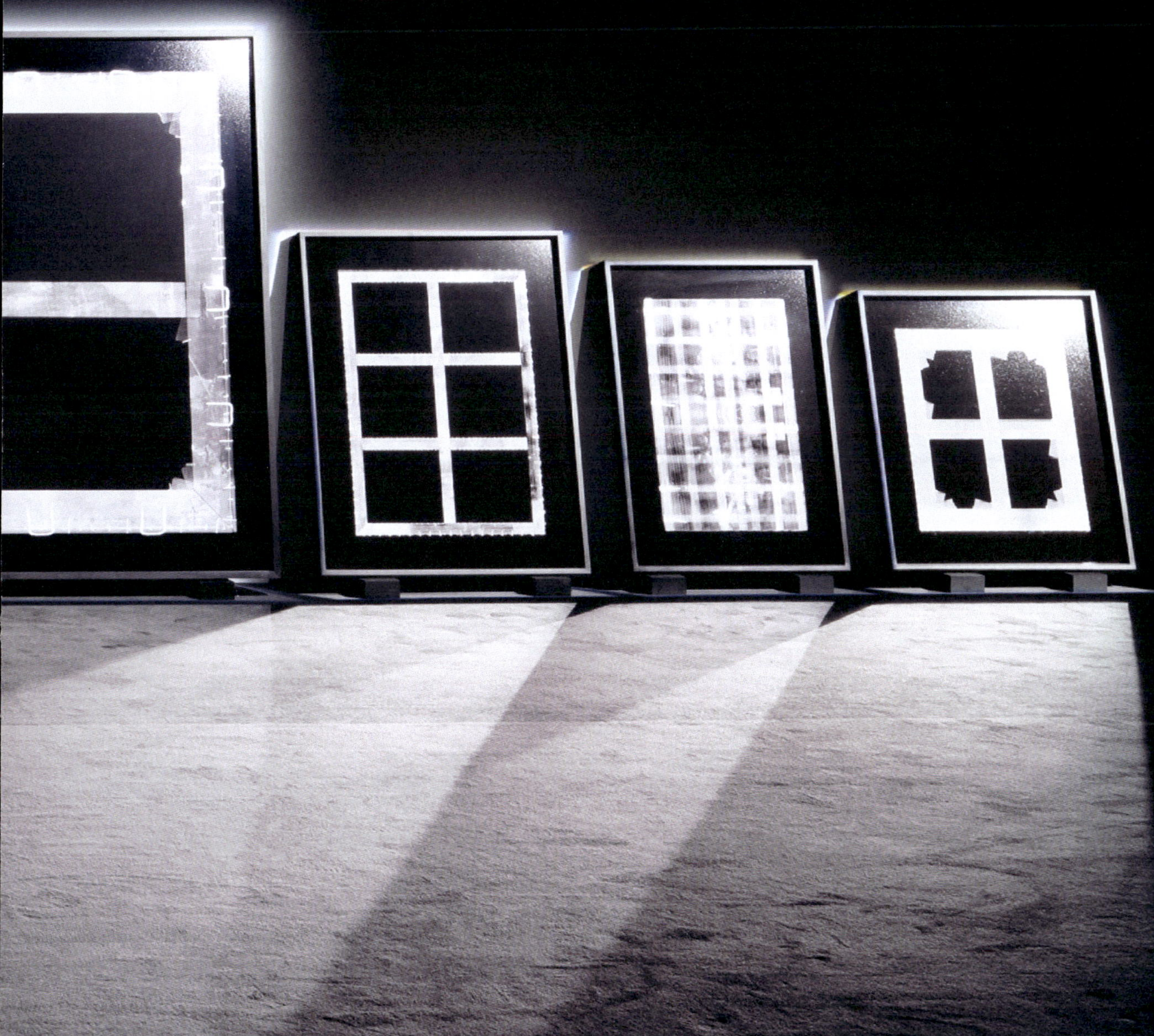

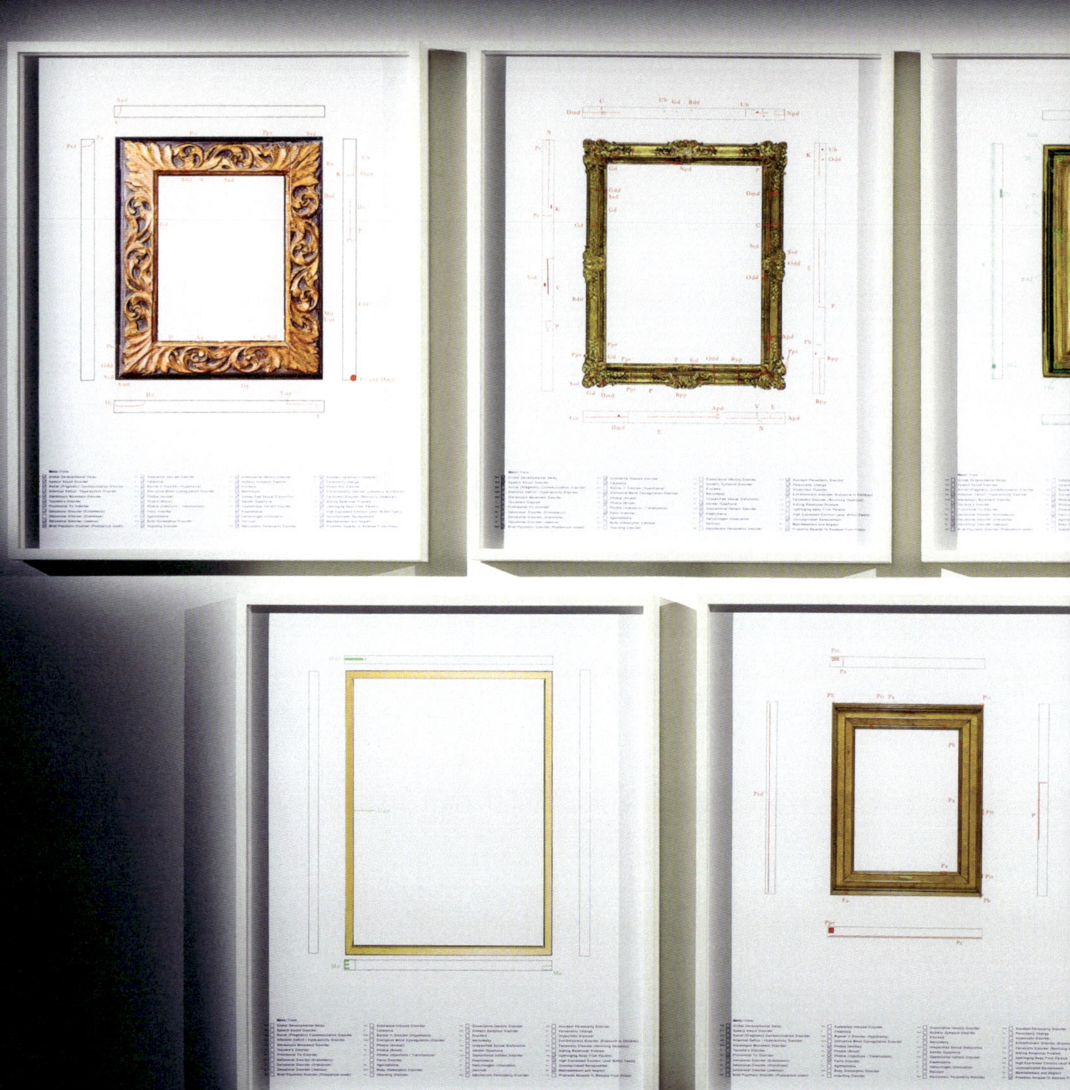

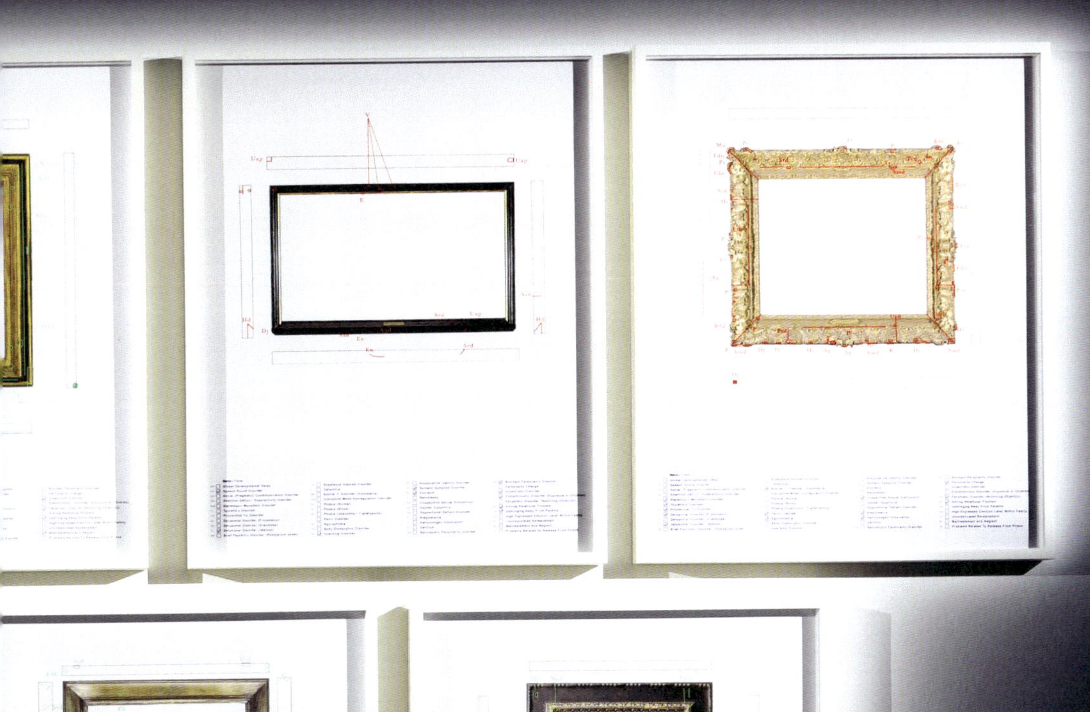

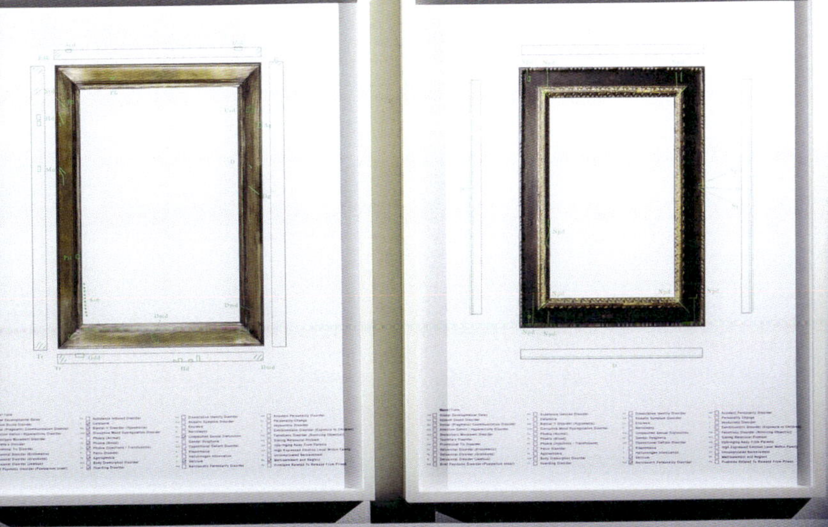

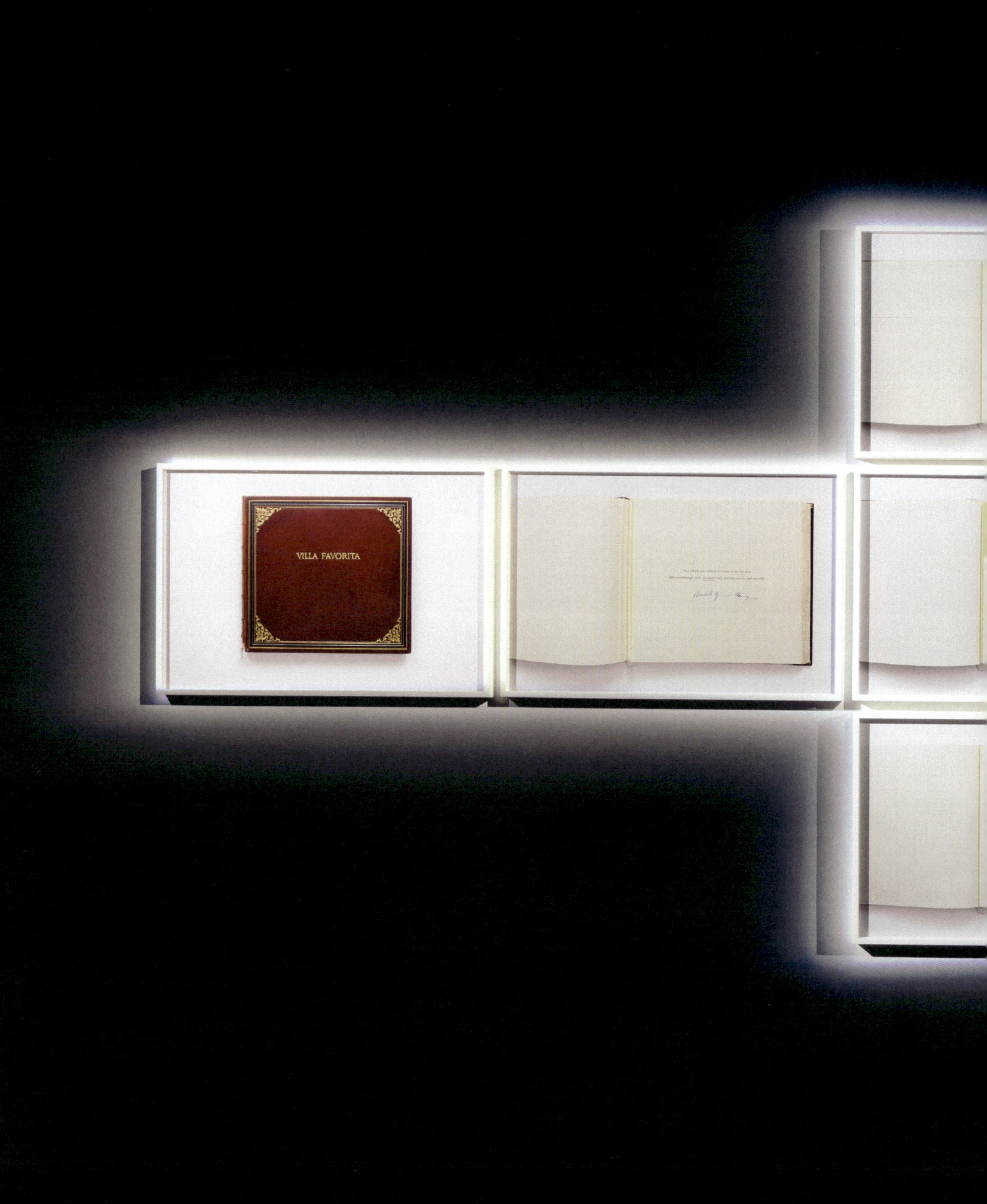
VILLA FAVORITA

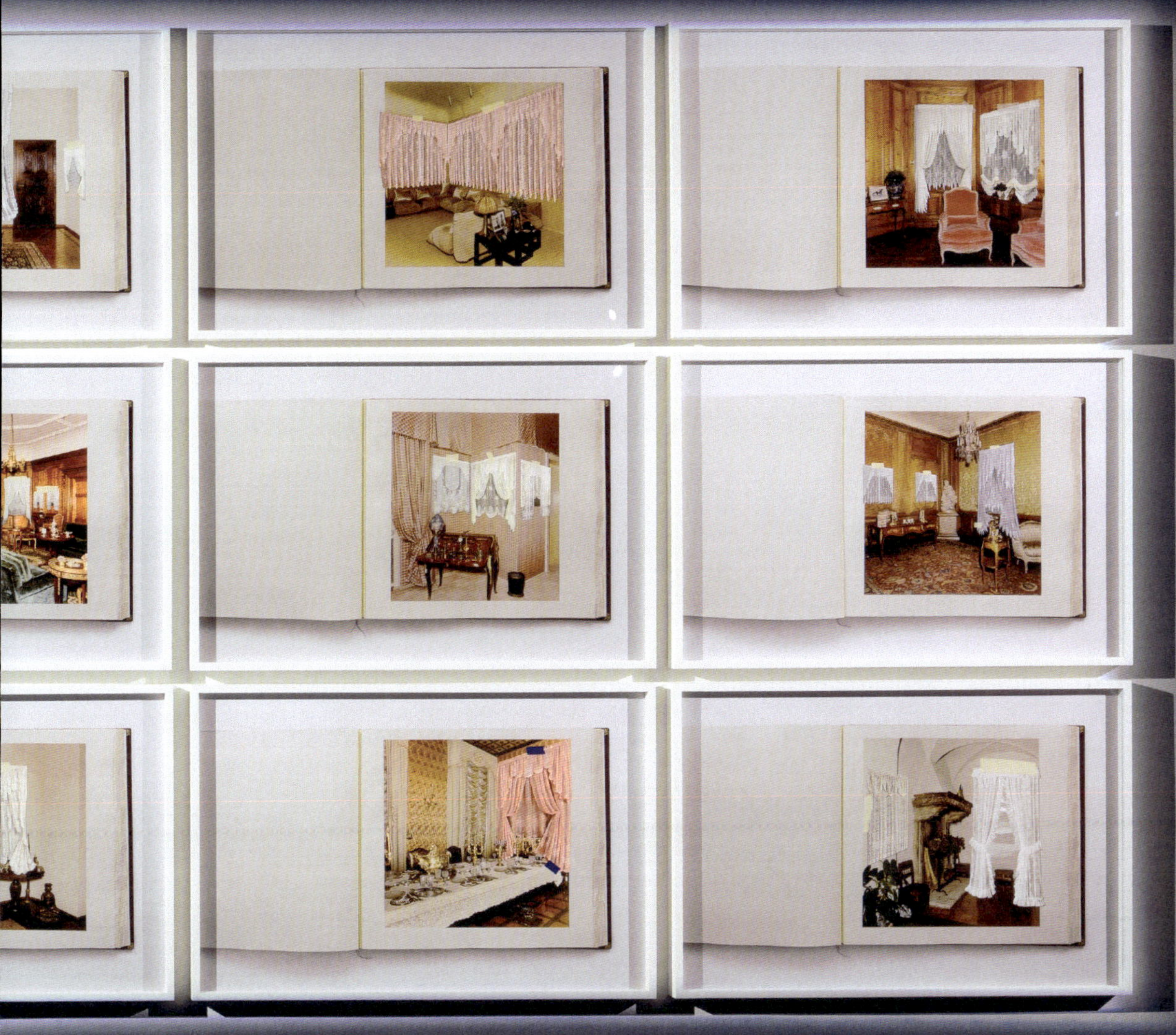

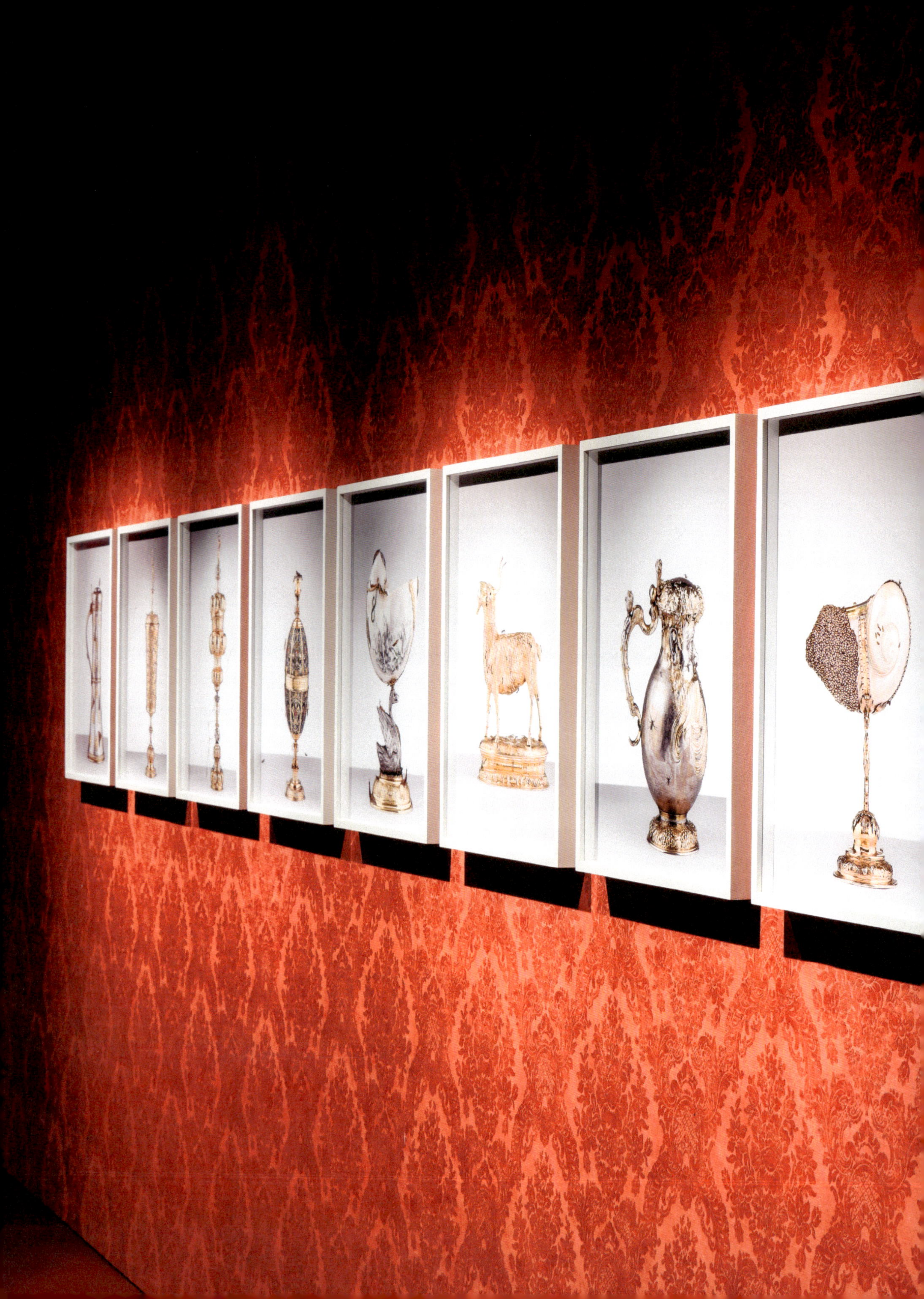

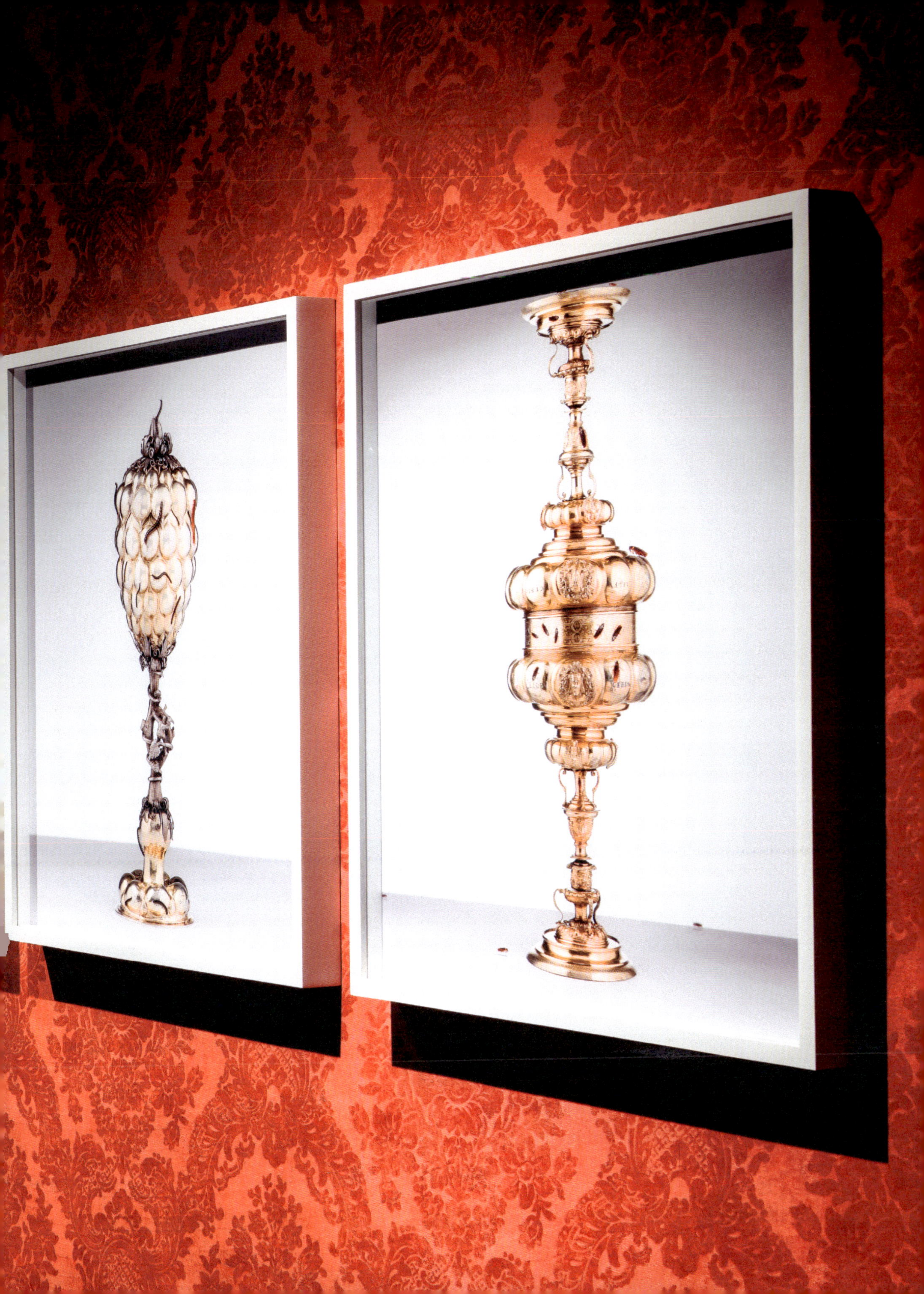

Verlag der Buchhandlung Walther und Franz König

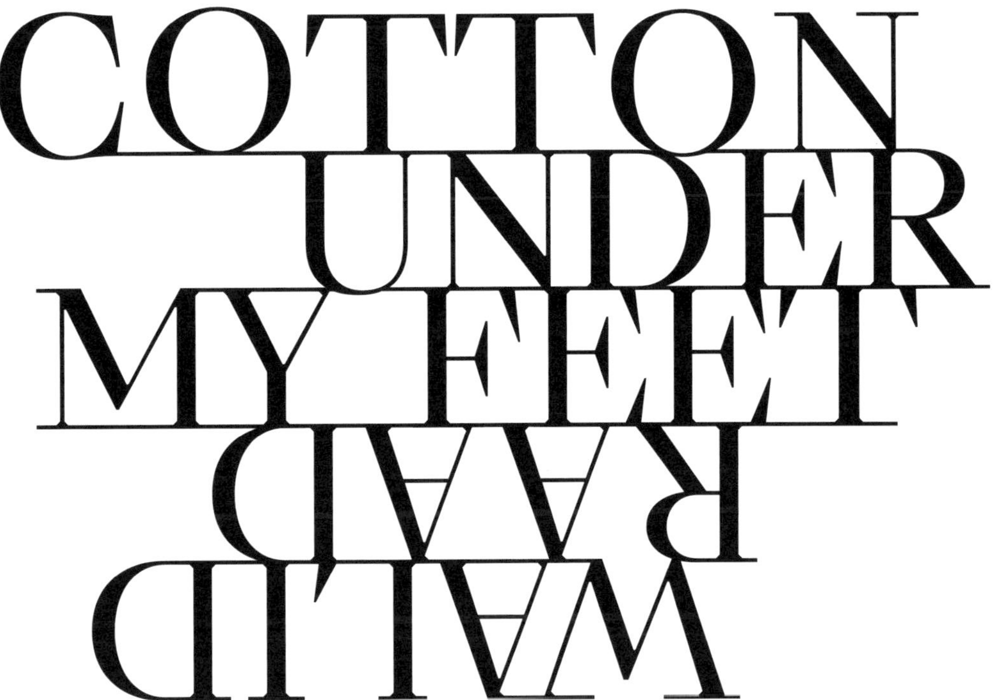

Edited by Daniela Zyman and Eva Ebersberger

Thyssen-Bornemisza Art Contemporary

Table of Contents

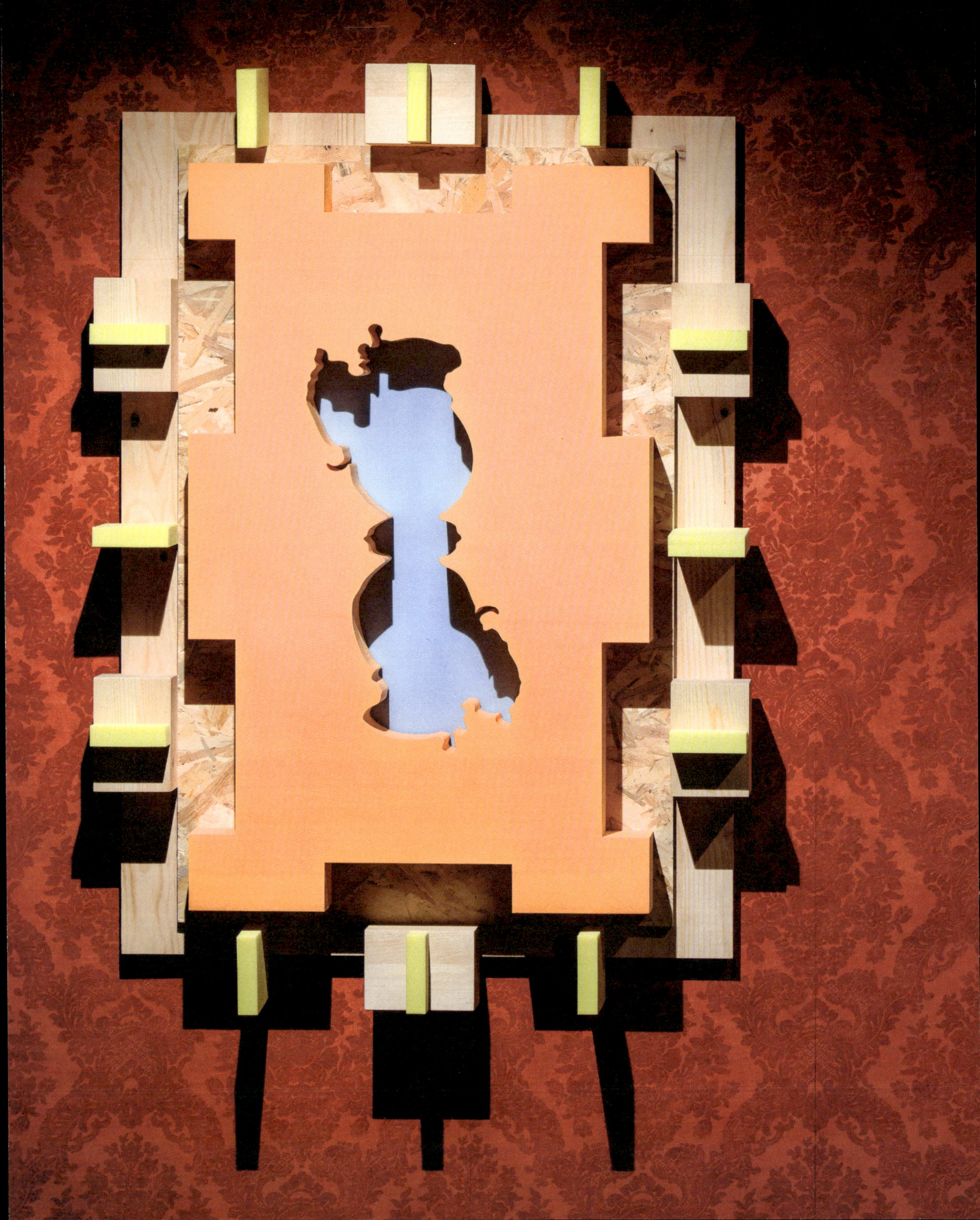

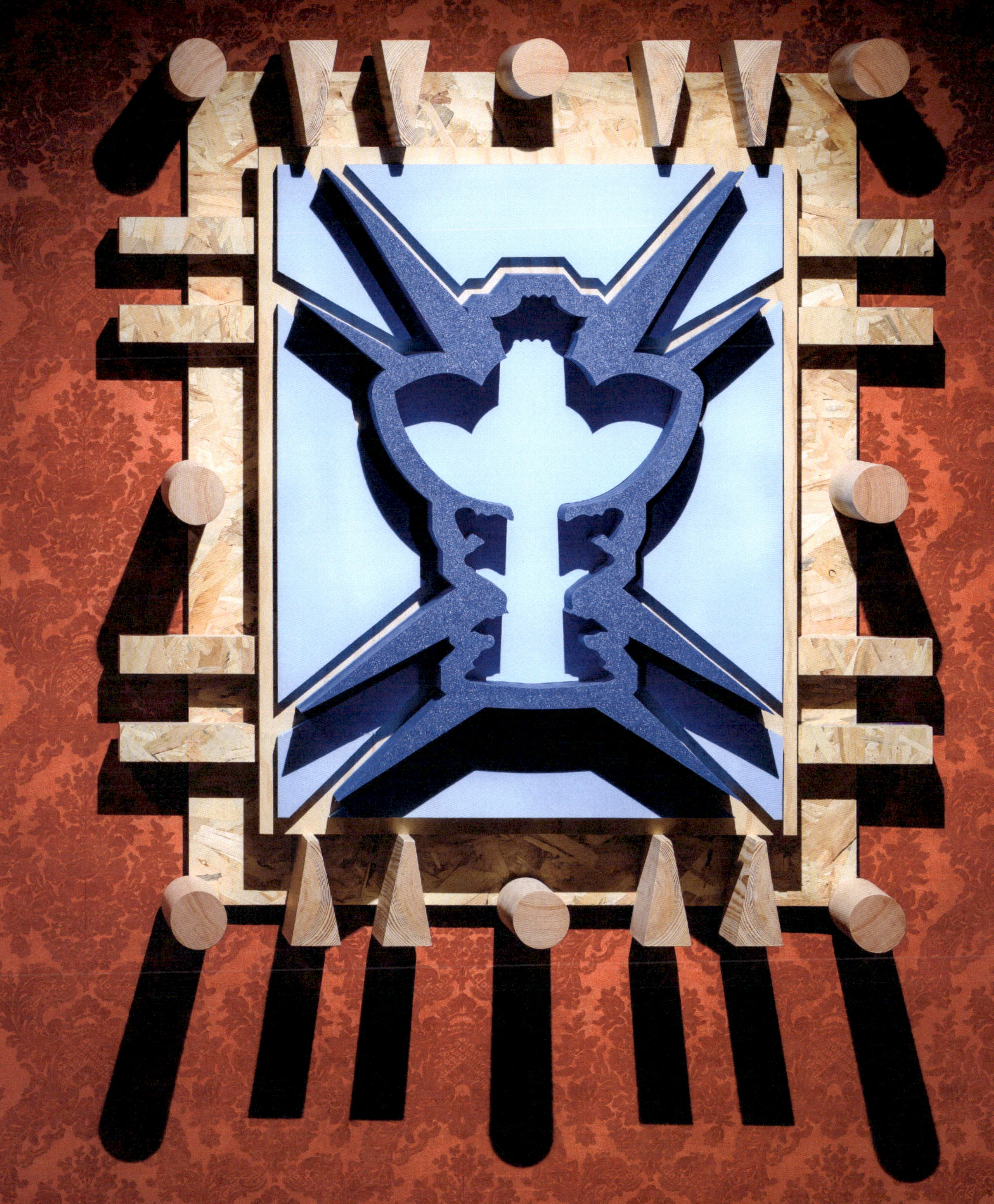

Foreword

Guillermo Solana

Museums frame, mount, label, analyze, and interpret works of art. Until recently it was assumed that the role of the artists, who created those artworks was to submit meekly to the museum as a hospital patient surrenders to treatment by medical staff. Walid Raad represents a different approach. His work involves him being the one who comes to examine and diagnose the museum. His pieces simulate the discursive genres typical of the museum, from the collection catalog to technical studies for restorations, which he creates fictional versions of. In addition to these, Raad's performances parody the central genre of the museum experience, the guided tour.

For this year's celebrations of the centenary of Hans Heinrich Thyssen-Bornemisza's birth, Raad has created the most imaginative tribute to the museum's founder. Three years of archival research and in-depth interviews with the collectors in the Thyssen-Bornemisza family and the professionals at the museum have produced a web of stories in which, as always in Raad's work, fact and fiction are interwoven and real characters are mingled with fabricated ones. The work of the restorers inspires some of Raad's most fascinating inventions: the painted angels that self-restore, the insects and spiders that invade gold and silver objects, psychiatric complaints registered on condition reports, the anomaly of stretchers revealed by X-rays.

The museum thus appears to be a totally different world, a planet ruled by undecipherable laws. But if the museum lacks windows, like Gottfried Wilhelm Leibniz's monads, it also has the ability, like the monads, to reflect the whole universe inside itself. In the collections of the Museo Nacional Thyssen-Bornemisza, Raad has found revealing clues to the political and social history of the modern world, from slavery in North America to the Cold War and the tortured history of the Middle East.

I wish to express my gratitude to Francesca Thyssen-Bornemisza, the founder and chairwoman of TBA21; to its director, Carlos Urroz; to Daniela Zyman, the exhibition's curator; to Araceli Galán and Leticia de Cos, the coordinators of the show; to the whole team at TBA21 and at the museum; and above all to Walid Raad himself for his enthralling work.

Cotton Under My Feet and Clouds in My Head

Francesca Thyssen-Bornemisza

I have been following Walid Raad's work for some time now, mesmerized by it, drawn in by the narratives Raad builds, and seduced by his charm and humor. Over the years, I have attended several of Raad's performances, and over that time we also enjoyed some casual conversations fueled by our mutual passion for good gin. These conversations were about the world, his world, and mine. We discussed families, more often mine, and I was intrigued to see if he would consider a commission based on my family's relationship to art. Like all families, we have things everyone knows, then there is all that we don't even know ourselves, or have forgotten as our selective memory protects us from deep wounds that we all carry. Then there are the things we love to embellish, or alternatively preserve in a well-sealed vacuum. There are people we enshrine and put on pedestals, and others who are demonized it seems forever. There are the ancestors, the elders, whose voices and stories become part of lives and are passed on to younger generations. However, I think we can all agree that we exist beyond our own individual and ancestral histories, be it via stories remembered or not. Our image of ourselves can be as constructed as one pieced together by historians with all the hypotheses put forward by researchers. "Cotton Under My Feet" takes us all through a complex web of entanglements embedded in social structures, ideologies, and economies that include but also exceed us. We are all linked to futures, not just pasts, and to other versions of ourselves that possibly dwell in other realms and metaphysical conditions. It takes us through quite a lot of the history of the collection and its move from the Villa Favorita to the Villahermosa Palace in Madrid. I sincerely hope that you enjoy it, are provoked by it, and that you also learn something about yourself through it.

My father dedicated a great deal of his life to "continuity," a challenge left to him by his father and his ever-present art advisor Rudolf Heinemann. He worked to rebuild his father's collection after it was split up through inheritance. It fed my father's passion to learn more and more about art. He was not by any means a scholar, but all those who knew him remember him well for his extraordinary eye for great paintings both old and modern, and his thirst for knowledge. As a teenager, I watched in awe as my father developed a path of his own, ultimately quite different from that of his father's. He chose to open up what had for a long time been kept as one of the world's greatest art secrets. His conviction that collections must be shared and not hoarded was very important to him. In 1948, he opened the doors of the Villa Favorita in Lugano for two days a week, under the watchful eye of the Hungarian guardian Sándor Berkes, and put the Thyssen-Bornemisza collection on public view. The gallery itself remained unchanged from his father's time, with its red damask silk walls and deep-green marble or polished terracotta floors. References of which you will discover in this exhibition. The upper gallery had a natural lighting system that beautifully lit the old master works, as opposed to today's more sensationally lit museums. In the back of the gallery, through a secret door, there was storage space and restoration laboratory which was always occupied by a restorer in residence, as my father was passionate about discovering lost or hidden treasures that needed to be brought back to life. All of this was reached through a large stone staircase, where a stunning painting by Tiepolo depicting *The Death of Hyacinthus* hung. It was overlooked by two majestic white Baroque angels that beckoned one to enter what was indeed a magical space. The entrance alone promised all visitors an exceptional experience. The visitor needed to climb two flights of stairs before reaching the gallery, and that's after a kilometer walk along a pink cobbled driveway lined with tall cypresses and beautiful gardens boasting trees that were over a hundred years old. It was not for the faint hearted! It separated the art lovers from the casual tourists. My father never let anyone drive in, except for very special guests. And there were many interesting people who were invited to share a meal and exchange ideas about art with my father. I enjoyed many of these conversations: I learned more about art from the company my father kept than the extraordinary collection that lined the relatively austere exhibition halls designed by his father. Somehow time stood still in the gallery, but the private house was another story altogether.

The main force driving my father was to take the art collection across political boundaries in the hope that it would contribute to world peace. The way he went about that fascinated me and inspired the journey that I subsequently followed. Those few passionate art lovers who made the pilgrimage to the Villa Favorita on weekends, were replaced in the 1980s by huge queues of hundreds of thousands of people who came to see the treasures of Soviet collections inaccessible in the West, when my father embarked on a five-year exchange of art between his collection and the Soviet museums at the height of the Cold War. The same thing happened in Moscow, Leningrad, and Novosibirsk, as Russians discovered the treasures from his wonderful collection. The terms and conditions of those loans were quite extraordinary at a time when US President Ronald Reagan and Soviet Union leader Leonid Brezhnev were deep into a nuclear arms race. World peace was on the agenda and my father hoped art would transform the way the two sides of the Iron Curtain truly received each other. Having been born in 1921, my father saw how his family was divided over World War II and he was determined to do whatever he could not to give into the political divide that we all lived with at the time. He was a fighter for peace.

I learned something really important from him at that time, during the numerous trips we took together to the Soviet Block, exploring Ukraine, the Baltic states, Moscow, and Leningrad. I learned that the practice of peace is active, not passive. Raad is also close to this concept, with his hugely important project The Atlas Group (1989–2004). Raad was born in Lebanon and left it at the very same time of these expeditions to the Soviet Union. His struggle for his homeland torn up by civil war, Israeli invasions, and civil unrest, which sadly has reached a point of total collapse just recently, is a very important part of his legacy. This work is also about the construct of legacy. We all leave a trace. We all cut down trees even though we know we shouldn't. Is it not peace that we all dream of?

Raad's performance, the script of which is included in this book, reflects his truth, much researched. This is not a disclaimer in any way, as it is my absolute priority not to meddle with the artistic license. Let the experience become your own journey through some of the collection, and let the facts and fictions that interweave themselves through different metaphysical realities bring to light some of the strangest coincidences, or should I say synergies, that Raad describes in this extraordinary narrative. The access he was given to family and museum archives leaves him in the position of knowing far more about my family than I ever will. The way he has constructed this incredible work that has taken him four years to create reminds me a little of that wonderful story "The Aleph" by Jorge Luis Borges, where the protagonist tumbles down the staircase to the basement of his home, bumps his head, and sees his whole life and the whole history of the world and its future in one single tiny drop, as it reflects all truths simultaneously.

Entertainment for Angels[1]: Walid Raad's "Cotton Under My Feet"

Daniela Zyman

A freestanding structure wallpapered with pastoral scenes marks the final sequence of Walid Raad's exhibition at the Museo Nacional Thyssen-Bornemisza. Small-format paintings adorn each side of the wall: Martin Johnson Heade's *The Marshes at Rhodes Island* (1866) and *Jersey Marshes* (1874). Upon close inspection, viewers will recognize that the wallpaper renders doubled and mirrored images of each of the paintings. When Raad walks groups of visitors through the exhibition in a seventy-minute-long performance titled *Two Drops Per Heartbeat*, he grabs one corner of the painting and peels it off from its support. The painting dangles, Magritte-like, on the wall. "I mean, look at them," he instructs the visitors and points at the painting behind the painting. "Standing in the shadows, we find this cartoonish figure that Martin Johnson Heade himself called a gremlin..." he explains. A gremlin? The stick figure seemingly appeared "out of nowhere," mischievously grinning at the scene it is in the course of spoiling. Who is this gremlin, and where is nowhere? The installation *Epilogue IX: The Gremlins*, while at the very end of the parcours through the exhibitionary labyrinth Raad has devised for "Cotton Under My Feet," coinciding with the centennial of the museum's founder, Hans Heinrich Thyssen-Bornemisza, is key to the whole project. The attempt to resolve the apparition of a gremlin out of nowhere on a painting behind a painting, installed on a wall of mirrored doubles, takes us on a circuitous route through the museum and into a quagmire of art historical, political, and mystical narratives.

1.

To unpack Raad's visionary quest into Hans Heinrich Thyssen-Bornemisza's collection and its many enigmas, I propose to start by tracking what is (hidden) in the name "Cotton Under My Feet," and discuss how the project compels us to see stories and their material manifestations not as "mere stories" but as more powerful pathways to retell the world. Raad has dedicated a significant part of his artistic labor both under the project The Atlas Group (1989–2004)[2] and in his practice as Walid Raad to the creation of archival records. Not burying photographs, files, and documents in the "cemetery" of the archive, Raad's cross-referenced record-keeping and archiving impulse are fractious, often proleptic, and profoundly subversive of what Peter Osborne calls "the memory model." His artworks-as-records are not created to rest in a depository but made for public presentation. They deal with the historical and yet trouble history and remembrance, as they do not represent actual events as they are remembered, but rather point to incidences withdrawn from the world. Raad's recent works borrow their structuring principle from books and the literary and are assigned to chapters, sections, indexes, appendixes, and prefaces. A book, after all, is a narrative

1 "An entertainment for angels, rather than men" was how one observer described electricity, the new scientific development in the age of Enlightenment. See Patricia Fara, *An Entertainment for Angels* (New York: Columbia University Press, 2002).

2 See The Atlas Group Archive, https://www.theatlasgroup1989.org.

device and can contain many things, often overflowing with a wealth of details and facts, including those unwritten, withheld, marginalized, and anticipated. "Cotton Under My Feet" thus heralds a good number of Frontispieces, Epilogues, and two Appendixes. Notably, the work lacks a middle, center, or body.

As Raad refuses to surrender to the methodic imperatives of the archive, the historian trying to follow his lead will appreciate the inventive flexibility in the artist's assignments, naming conventions, and dating systems. Thus, it comes as no surprise that "Cotton Under My Feet," attributed to the calendar year 2007, features as an extant record in Raad's oeuvre. I vividly remember seeing the installation of ninety-six inkjet prints identifying the colors of the New York sky between 8:46 a.m. and 9:03 a.m., precisely at the respective times when flights AA11 and UA175 crashed into the North and South Towers of the World Trade Center on September 11, 2001. The short note on the wall next to the neatly ordered depictions read: "For months after 9/11, I could not remember the color of the sky over New York on that day. For some reason, I needed to see that blue again, desperately looking for it in photo and video archives, and on color swatches in paint stores." Not remembering the color of the sky over New York that day indicates the scope of a traumatic event that masks the underlying conflict and displaces its memory.

A cursory search into the work's title also led me to the cover page of the *New York Times* from April 18, 1993. On that day, the newspaper reported the conviction "of a police sergeant and the officer who delivered the most blows to Rodney G. King in a beating two years ago and acquitted two other officers." Describing the sense of relief after "two years of convulsions, racial turmoil and fear" that reigned over Los Angeles, Robert Reinhold writes: "'It's like I've got cotton under my feet,' Jimmy Simon, a black retired mechanic, said as he flashed a toothy smile on a street in South-Central Los Angeles. 'Everybody can go home-nothing will happen now.'"[3]

Mr. Simon's words, "It's like I've got cotton under my feet," uttered after the conviction of the police officers responsible for excessive brutality during King's arrest in 1991, posit a historical and immaterial connection between the events of the 1992 LA riots, the opening of the Thyssen-Bornemisza Museum in Madrid in the same year, and the civil unrest in the summer of 2020 sparked by the extrajudicial killing of George Floyd. This conjunction of events might have caused "Cotton Under My Feet" to reappear after a long hiatus. Or not. Other itineraries are possible and emerging.

3 Robert Reinhold, "Calm Where Rage Once Ruled," *The New York Times* (April 18, 1993), https://www.nytimes.com/1993/04/18/us/verdict-in-los-angeles-calm-relief-where-rage-once-ruled.html.

2.

Let's enter Raad's forking tunnels of braided and imaginary histories more deeply. The exhibition's title gestures at residual histories of violence that Raad's inquiries lay bare. Violence and conflict are inseparably connected to peace-making; peace is related to failure and contestation; politics are linked to science and invention; nineteenth-century landscape painting to clouds, marshes, and enslavement; marshes and unfree labor to terraforming and extractivism—and before we know we are short-circuited in another network of possible references. Indeed, in the quest for an untold (art) history, Raad's project rubs against the official histories of slavery, US sugar politics, silver speculation, and weather forecasting, among other unexpected traces hidden under an extremely rare Oriental carpet. These all-too-worldly histories reinvigorate the discussion of what a museum stands for or whose history it represents.

While historical exegesis complicates narratives about the political, economic, or scientific circumstances under which artworks were created, this research method only offers a certain kind of reading. Complementary to this approach, Raad's works in "Cotton Under My Feet" function as "attractors" and opalescent mirrors of phenomena that surpass mundane reality. They irritate the paradigms that for the longest time have locked viewers and researchers into expectations about the physical and aesthetic world of art. They reveal manifestations that have reached the artist from a different source, namely from the "undead realm." This realm has been described by Jalal Toufic, an artist and writer deeply invested in developing a complex theory of art, culture, and tradition that radically departs from the tenets of art history or Western philosophy. In Toufic's writing, the undead realm is a domain that dialogs with the common world yet is separate from it and marked by a threshold ostensibly leading to the unworldly.[4] When a human is "dead while still physically alive,"[5] things start shifting significantly. He/she gets drawn into the labyrinth. "A labyrinth has no entry and no exit. No up. No down. No right. No left. No past. No present. No future," clarifies Raad.

So, let's suppose some masterpieces in Hans Heinrich Thyssen-Bornemisza's collection disclosed some kinds of indications—omens, warnings, sentiments—relevant to the contemporary moment, but originating from that other realm and its visionary potentials. Sensing that they would be on public display, they demanded to be attended to not only physically but also immaterially. What if Hans Heinrich Thyssen-Bornemisza and his hypersensitive conservator, a fictional figure called Lamia Antonova, intuited that some of the following works had to be handled in ways hitherto unknown to museum conservators and restorers?

4 Jalal Toufic, "Labyrinth," *What Was I Thinking?* (Berlin: e-flux journal and Sternberg Press, 2007), 107.

5 Toufic, "Labyrinth," 106.

- Objects in need of arthropods (*Epilogue VII: The Gold and Silver*)
- Paintings immaterially abandoning their canvases and thus requiring special fixtures and extra material support (*Epilogue IV: The X-Rays*)
- Artworks wishing for another form of display, feeling as though they are being strangled by being hung (*Frontispiece IV: The Hangs*)
- Artifacts cohabiting with their doubles when out of sight (*Epilogue VIII: The Crates*)
- Paintings that leak when pulled by gremlins in a space where there is no up or down, right or left (*Epilogue IX: The Gremlins*)
- Paintings producing and projecting one or more doubles to collaborate with (*Epilogue IX: The Gremlins*)
- Artworks intended for a beholder who can see through veils (*Epilogue VI: The Curtains*)
- Frames requiring psychological condition reports, specifically registering delusional disorder, brief psychotic disorder, catatonia, phobia of animals, agoraphobia, hoarding disorder, narcolepsy, delirium, narcissistic personality disorder, maltreatment, and neglect (*Epilogue V: The Frames*)
- Prototype of a device that attracts figures of damaged angels to self-repair (*Epilogue III: The Flat Corner*)
- Forms that take refuge on the backs of artworks (*Epilogue II: The Constables*)
- A carpet, the source of tears and sweat, that is heavier than its weight (*Frontispiece II: The Carpet*)

For each of these mysterious revelations, Raad has fashioned series of photographs, sculptures, and elaborate immersive installations. The works serve to ground his arguments in proof and provide numerous archival records to verify matters of conjectural truth. Modified collection catalogs and other annotated publications offer an obtuse road map into the historiographical maze. These altered archival and bibliographic exhibits contain means and tools for testing and falsifying the artist's claims: images and documents that can be revisited, details and comparisons that can be verified or contested. "Reality is opaque," states the historian Carlo Ginzburg, "but there are certain points—clues, symptoms—which allow us to decipher it."[6] Some clues and symptoms lead to the world of mere mortals, others to the unworldly. Certain conditions find their expression in reality, while others seek their manifestation in fiction.

With everything noted thus far, the kinds of afflictions and distress these artworks have endured might no longer feel arbitrary, nor fantastic. Perturbed and destitute[7] legacies have set them on trajectories to otherworldly and disjointed realms. By resituating the possibility of revelation within a larger cultural project, the works of art in "Cotton Under My Feet" reveal themselves to hypersensitive mortals

6 Carlo Ginzburg, "Clues: Morelli, Freud, and Sherlock Holmes," *The Sign of Three: Dupin, Holmes, Peirce*, eds. Umberto Eco and Thomas. A. Sebeok. (Bloomington: Indiana University Press, 1988), 109.

7 Walter D. Mignolo, "The Logic of the In-Visible: Decolonial Reflections on the Change of Epoch," *Theory, Culture & Society* vol. 37, no. 7–8 (December 2020): 215, https://doi.org/10.1177/0263276420957741.

through their ostensibly whimsical needs and desires. They would remain repressed and banished, literally suspended in a state of worldlessness, were it not for the exceptional care they command. The rituals devised for their preservation permit them to guard the secrets and mysteries they behold, even while the works are exposed to the public's eyes. Beyond the economic, political, and eco-social framings that Raad supplies, the exhibition supports claims with arguments and evidence for the vital import of the undead realm.

3.

Raad's attraction to Hans Heinrich Thyssen-Bornemisza's collecting foible for American landscape paintings of the nineteenth century is shared today by many admirers of this long-overlooked era. Indeed, the Museo Nacional Thyssen-Bornemisza has one of the most noted and extensive repositories of nineteenth-century American paintings in Europe. The baron began collecting American paintings in 1979, at a time when his business relations brought him more frequently to the US. "I am very attracted by all American artists," described the baron, "mainly because of the artists' profound love for nature, space and perfection."[8]

Hans Heinrich Thyssen-Bornemisza was also very attracted to the writings of the eminent scholar Barbara Novak. Originally published in 1969, *American Painting of the Nineteenth Century: Realism, Idealism, and the American Experience* sought to identify continuous American traditions and trace their emergence and legacy. But it was her subsequent 1980 tome, *Nature and Culture: American Landscape and Painting, 1825–1875*, that would have a lasting influence on the collector. Taking a complementary approach, Novak states: "Here, I stress ideas, and attempt to show how the history of ideas flows freely through the membranes that compartmentalize the various disciplines comprising a culture."[9] We know that the baron was deeply enthralled by Novak's interdisciplinary thesis and indeed had commissioned her in 1986 to work on the catalog of nineteenth-century art in the Thyssen-Bornemisza collection.

8 Hans Heinrich Thyssen-Bornemisza in John I. H. Baur, "Introduction," *American Masters: The Thyssen-Bornemisza Collection* (exhibition catalogue, the International Exhibitions Foundation, Washington, DC, 1984–86. Milan: Electa, 1984), 11.

9 Barbara Novak, *Nature and Culture: American Landscape and Painting, 1825-1875* (Oxford: Oxford University Press: 2007), 11.

For personal reasons, not least having moved to Upstate New York only a few years prior to working on this project, a handful of the American landscapists in the collection captured Raad's attention. Novak's groundbreaking work, enriched with detailed descriptions of American culture and religion, did not go unnoticed. In her account, as well as in the writings of several other art historians, nineteenth-century culture and history of ideas are deeply rooted in specific lineages of morality, faith, liberalism, business acumen, and dedication to hard work, as well as an interest in elemental phenomena (rock, clouds, plants) and scientific innovation. Strikingly, the topics of enslavement and plantation labor are rarely discussed, not even for their blatant absence in American landscape paintings. Nor is the genocide of Native American peoples. Seemingly, it did not trouble historians to describe the high moral imperatives in the nineteenth century as the common destiny of a chosen people united under God and nature without reckoning with those excluded and banished from their lands.[10] American society of that period (neither united nor unified) wrote out of history the millions who were disenfranchised and enslaved, substantially contributing to the accumulation of wealth and prosperity in protoindustrial America. But given that the antebellum period was marked by the polarization between abolitionists and defenders of slaveholding, as well as by the Indian Removal Act of 1830, the obliviousness to America's Black and Indigenous history is disconcerting, certainly from today's point of view and for an artist of Raad's sensibility.

10 Novak, *Nature and Culture*, 13.

11 Novak, *Nature and Culture*, 111.

Three areas of concern surface from the nineteenth-century paintings in the Thyssen-Bornemisza collections: the interest in liquid landscapes and the supernatural figures they produce, the afflictions on culture caused by slavery and its aftermath, and meteorology and communication technologies that revolutionized both the nineteenth and the twenty-first centuries. I will touch on all three, as they offer different narratives to those explored by Novak and many other art historians.

The baron's first acquisitions of American landscape paintings were Martin Johnson Heade's *Jersey Marshes* (1874) and *Orchid and Hummingbird near a Mountain* (1902). What might have drawn him to Heade's New Jersey and Rhodes Island marshes is the painter's persistent dedication to a landscape form that must have been familiar to the collector, who grew up in the Low Countries. Marshes are essentially wet landscapes that sit between water and land, the product of complex hydro-morphological dynamics. Heade painted over 120 of these small-format, horizontal canvases depicting innumerable salt-hay meadows crowned by perfectly shaped haystacks. Perhaps, it is precisely for their "so classically and mathematically controlled"[11] compositions and execution that these paintings so adequately render the regulated landscapes of the marshes. The tireless variations and repetitions of seemingly very similar vistas, capturing the changing lights, skies, and meteorological conditions make this series seem like an almanac.

Were it not for two exceptional paintings, *Gremlin in the Studio I* (1871–1875) and *Gremlin in the Studio II* (1865–1875), Raad might have overlooked Heade's oeuvre. In these two studio paintings, a gremlin, a fictive being of folklore and imagination, has entered the scene from below the painter's easel. The gremlin is pulling down the edge of the canvas to allow water from the painted marsh to gush onto the floor. The liquid of the artifact penetrates and soaks the space of the studio. Heade, who also used the pen name Didymus, the twin, claimed, according to Raad, that the supernatural figure appeared "out of nowhere." Is the gremlin's deus ex machina apparition an indication of the metaphysical order called to unravel the predicaments of humans? "A monster," writes Jacques Derrida in a much-cited passage, "is a species for which we do not yet have a name [...]. Simply, it *shows* itself [*elle* se montre]—that is what the word monster means—it shows itself in something that is not yet shown and that therefore looks like a hallucination, it strikes the eye, it frightens precisely because no anticipation had prepared one to identify this figure."[12] Is nowhere a special chronotope, to use Mikhail Bakhtin's neologism describing the confluence of time and space constitutive of specific contexts and realities? If nowhere is the labyrinth space, which doubles for the ordinary world, has Heade knowingly produced analog pairs so they could communicate with each other across time and space? The gremlin-as-monster disturbs norms and normality because it is a messenger between worlds, a portent.

The pastoral luminosity of Heade's paintings could not be in starker contrast to a different scene of liquid recuperation. After 1830, following the forced displacement of Native Americans from their lands in the Southwest, alluvial soils around the Mississippi Delta were carved out of swamps and forests. Here, soil and enslaved labor were resignified as original capital. This fertility of the alluvium, paired with the availability of enslaved labor, gave rise to the "Southern cotton plantation empire [which] became the pillar of the textile-driven British industrial revolution" as well as Yankee wealth.[13] Plantations were built on malarial swamps, "described as both factories in the fields and death camps."[14] The plantation system produced a distinctly violent regime of political, ethnic, and economic regulation along with the massive terraforming of the environment.

According to the Jamaican theorist Sylvia Wynter, the atrocities of plantation slavery can be traced back to 1452. The first plantations on the Portuguese island of Madeira initiated the "sugar-slave" complex, which would massively reform autochthonous ecologies and initiate the forced relocation of people in subsequent centuries.[15] In the eighteenth and nineteenth centuries, the so-called sugar islands—Jamaica, eighteenth-century Haiti (Saint Domingue), Cuba,

12 Jacques Derrida, "Passages – From Traumatism to Promise," *Points...: Interviews, 1974-1994*, trans. by Peggy Kamuf, ed. Elisabeth Weber (Stanford: Stanford University Press, 1995), 385–386.

13 Clyde Woods, *Development Arrested* (London: Verso, 2017), 6. By the middle of nineteenth century, New York had effectively become the "capital of the South" because of its dominant role in cotton and other colonial trades.

14 Woods, *Development Arrested*, 6.

15 Sylvia Wynter, "Black Metamorphosis: New Natives in a New World" (unpublished manuscript, 1970).

Grenada, Barbados and Antigua, the British Leeward Islands, Martinique, and Guadeloupe—were massively terraformed to become significant sugar producers, exporting the much-coveted molasses to a new class of imperial consumers.

While sugar became an indispensable condiment for the affluent consumers of exotic cash crops in Europe and the United States, the discourse around its consumption gradually transformed and acquired new meanings. By the end of the eighteenth century, the "blood sugar" topos signaled the complicity of sweetened drinks with slave labor and the plantation system. "Tea, coffee and chocolate were suddenly rendered nauseating by the notion that they contained the blood of slaves," writes Timothy Morton.[16] Among abolitionist circles, sugar and the rum derived from its production were substituted by other sweeteners such as honey and maple syrup. To refrain from sugar implied moral superiority over luxury and injustice.

16 Timothy Morton, "Blood Sugar," *Romanticism and Colonialism: Writing and Empire, 1780-1830*, eds. Tim Fulford and Peter J. Kitson (Cambridge: Cambridge University Press, 1998), 87–88.

In the United States, maple syrup was thus promoted as a consumable substance free from the politics spawned by slave-produced sugar in the colonies and the wealth it generated. Harvested only in the Midwest, New York, New England, and southeastern Canada, wild sugar could be divorced from the atrocities of the South. The small-format painting by Eastman Johnson, *The Maple Sugar Camp-Turning Off* from c. 1865–1873 in the Carmen Thyssen collection memorializes the arduous communal labor of sugaring, set in the snowy landscape of Maine. The sugaring off celebrates the end of the maple season, usually in February, with bonfires, music, whiskey, and sugar-on-snow. More than a party, it marked the end of winter and "the community's spirit of egalitarian union" and became "a symbol of Yankee independence."[17] Johnson, an ardent abolitionist, painted a series of twenty-five small sketches on this subject around the time of the American Civil War, sketches that he never completed.

17 "Sugaring Off: The Maple Sugar Paintings of Eastman Johnson," The Clark Art Institute website, see http://tfaoi.org/aa/4aa/4aa53.htm.

In the nexus established between marshes, cotton plantations, chattel slavery, blood sugar, maple tapping, and the foolish gremlins appearing out of nowhere, Raad's assertion that Johnson would refuse the "hanging" of his completed paintings is fully in line with the latter's abolitionist convictions. Paintings as metonymized hangings are chained to lynching, just as sugar links to colonial power and stands for the blood of enslaved laborers. The unfinished installation *Frontispiece IV: The Hangs* effectively gestures to the uncomfortable intimacies between atrocity and art, nation-building and slavery, extreme unfreedom and the promises of Enlightenment. A room that can only remain unfinished, just as the time of racial injustice and discrimination finds no end.

Turning from questions on landscape, sugar politics, and slavery to clouds and meteorology in Raad's chronotopical tale ushers in the figure of the conservator Lamia Antonova. Palestinian-born, Soviet-trained, and the closest collaborator to Hans Heinrich Thyssen-Bornemisza for nearly two decades, Antonova clairvoyantly recognized and identified the many anomalies in the collection. A fine connoisseur of art history but equally versed in the phenomenology of the undead realm, she enters the tunnels, reads the clues, and resolves the riddles posed by unruly artworks. Antonova suffers from (or is endowed with) an extreme extension of the sensitive spectrum; she is the one who discovers the series of cloud paintings on the backs of canvases and motivates the baron to impose a moratorium on viewing their fronts; she also devises a set of condition reports to specify the psychological afflictions of frames. While diagnosing the paintings, she realizes that some of them are set to depart on otherworldly trajectories, yet could not be held back by nails and reinforced armatures. She also intuits that some paintings could not be hung, while others needed to cohabit with their doubles. Furthermore, Antonova discovers a special device she calls the Angel-Attractor. The device not only anticipates the exact choice of color to be used in the future museum in Madrid but also serves as a healing prosthesis for damaged angels. But it seems that not only angels, but also the painter-inventor Samuel Morse led Antonova to believe that other forces must be reckoned with when dealing with the undead realm.

Morse painted in the Salon Carré in the Louvre throughout the cholera winter of 1831. In those Parisian months, the aspiring artist painted Rembrandt's *The Angel Leaving the Family of Tobias* twice. One copy was commissioned by his friend James Fenimore Cooper. The other version is a tiny miniature that forms part, along with thirty-seven other miniaturized masterpieces, of his most ambitious work, the *Gallery of the Louvre*. At this juncture, another narrative vortex gapes. One pathway connects Rembrandt's angel to the attractor panel, the self-repairing of damaged angels, and the Rembrandt-collecting silver magnate Thomas Kaplan, known to befriend dodgy political figures and mess with US nuclear politics. Another branches away from Morse's telegraph apparatus and its unforeseen significance for meteorology to John Constable's cloud paintings and is latched to a series of recent corporate mergers and acquisitions. These corporate coalescences converge around contemporary weather prediction technologies devised for so-called risk assessment and performance optimization in anticipation of massive climate disruption.

4.

We have barely skimmed the surface of "Cotton Under My Feet," just entered a few of the tunnels of conjectures without thoroughly vetting the initial questions posed. We wanted to inquire how the project intervened in the practices of collecting and philanthropy, while propagating viable explanations for hyper-strange aesthetic phenomena. Returning once more to the nineteenth century throws into relief the purview of our investigation. This period, very much in the crucible of Raad's argument, introduces a ritualization of viewing that is still practiced today in museums and exhibitions. The art historian Dorothea von Hantelmann specifies the social role of museums in mapping out an evolutionary art history as follows: "By collecting artifacts from the past, the museum gives shape and presence to history, inventing it, in effect, by defining the space for a ritual encounter with the past. It marks time into a series of stages that comprises a linear path of evolution; it organizes these stages into an itinerary that the visitor's route retraces; and it projects the future as a course of limitless development."[18] By virtue of this ritual, the museum singularizes the individual viewer and consolidates his or her relationship to objects framed by a culture that values possession. Just around the time of the invention of photography and film, the museum projected a space of purity against the media of reproduction that threatened to subvert and rupture the singularity of art. But photography and film were not the only threats to the epistemologies enshrined in museums. Things had to be separated on a larger scale, against the unclean, the unruly, magical, mechanical, technical, natural, and the "other." They had to be refigured as objects of different kinds, separate from art: the magical object, the natural object, the technical object.

18 Dorothea von Hantelmann, *How to Do Things with Art: What Performativity Means in Art* (Zurich: JRP/Ringier, 2010), 11.

This purification, as effective as it might have been, could never be achieved fully. As Raad powerfully demonstrates, residual and emergent traces remain. And what has been banished can be made to return. Insects and arthropods, the horror of conservators, find their ways through invisible cracks. Technical inventions, such as the Morse apparatus, ambiguously hover between divine and secular telecommunication. The bond with the metaphysical and otherworldly was never permanently severed. The entangled realms of the here and now and the spiritual (or call it fictional, visionary, metaphysical) remain the attractors of unstable occurrences that exceed normality and disrupt normalization. And lastly, the museum's male whiteness started to foment mistrust of the encyclopedic collection. Originary violence has crept permanently into the museum's epistemological ambitions. The collection's narratives were to be critically remade, not the least through a refusal of whiteness.

"Cotton Under My Feet" and the accompanying walkthrough *Two Drops Per Heartbeat* inscribe themselves into the very spaces dedicated to the presentation of museum masterpieces and into their canonical narratives. Exhibition and performance propose a new ritual of encounters that intermediates between history, its actualization, and the fictional. This ritual both visualizes and narrativizes the fragile, always discontinuous process of art making and collecting, concurring with the failure of rational order and coherence. Attempting to give a more adequate account of the complexities of our opaque and precarious realities through the lens of art, Raad proposes a heuristic that draws from and oscillates between the factual, fictive, and fictional. The irritatingly fragmented and wondrous experience offered to viewers exposes spaces for refusal, contestation, and enchantment. Likewise, the work instigates a "performative collection,"[19] that can only be fully experienced as a temporal event, staged in a set dramaturgy. Thereby Raad establishes a specific form of social interaction in which the audience becomes a public, tasked with verifying and testing the artist's assertions while passing on the narrative thread from body to body. Just as the undead realm from which Raad receives his cues and warnings is a space that can never be fully occupied, the collection in its performative dynamism refuses ontological stability. In the field of tension between celebration and contestation, it escapes its condition frozen in linear time to negotiate between the poles of preservation, transience, and reimagination.

19 Stefanie Lorey, *Performative Sammlungen: Begriffsbestimmung eines neuen künstlerischen Formats* (Bielefeld: Transcript, 2020).

Two Drops Per Heartbeat: A Free Fall Through the Thyssen-Bornemisza Collections in Madrid and Elsewhere

Walid Raad

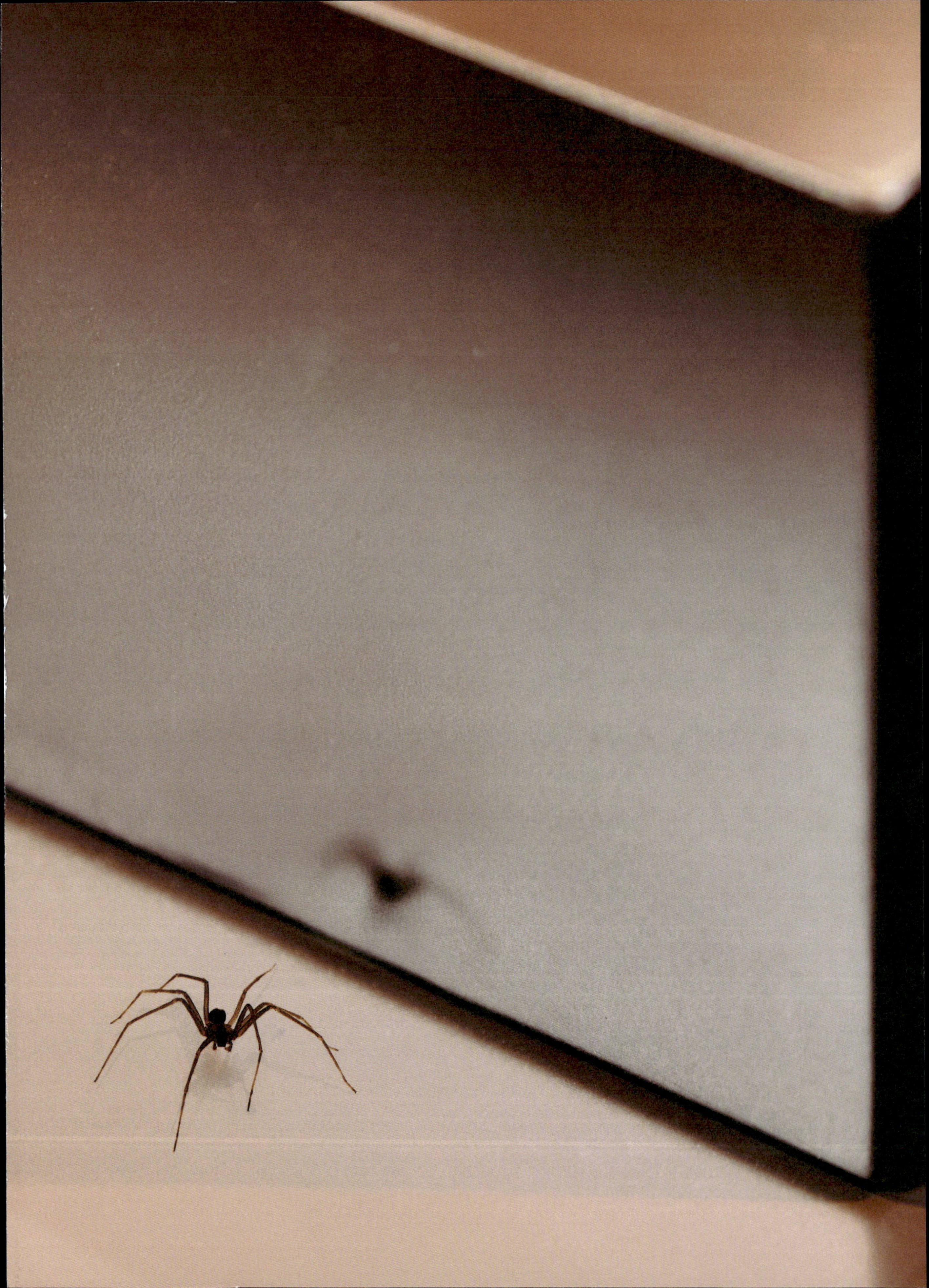

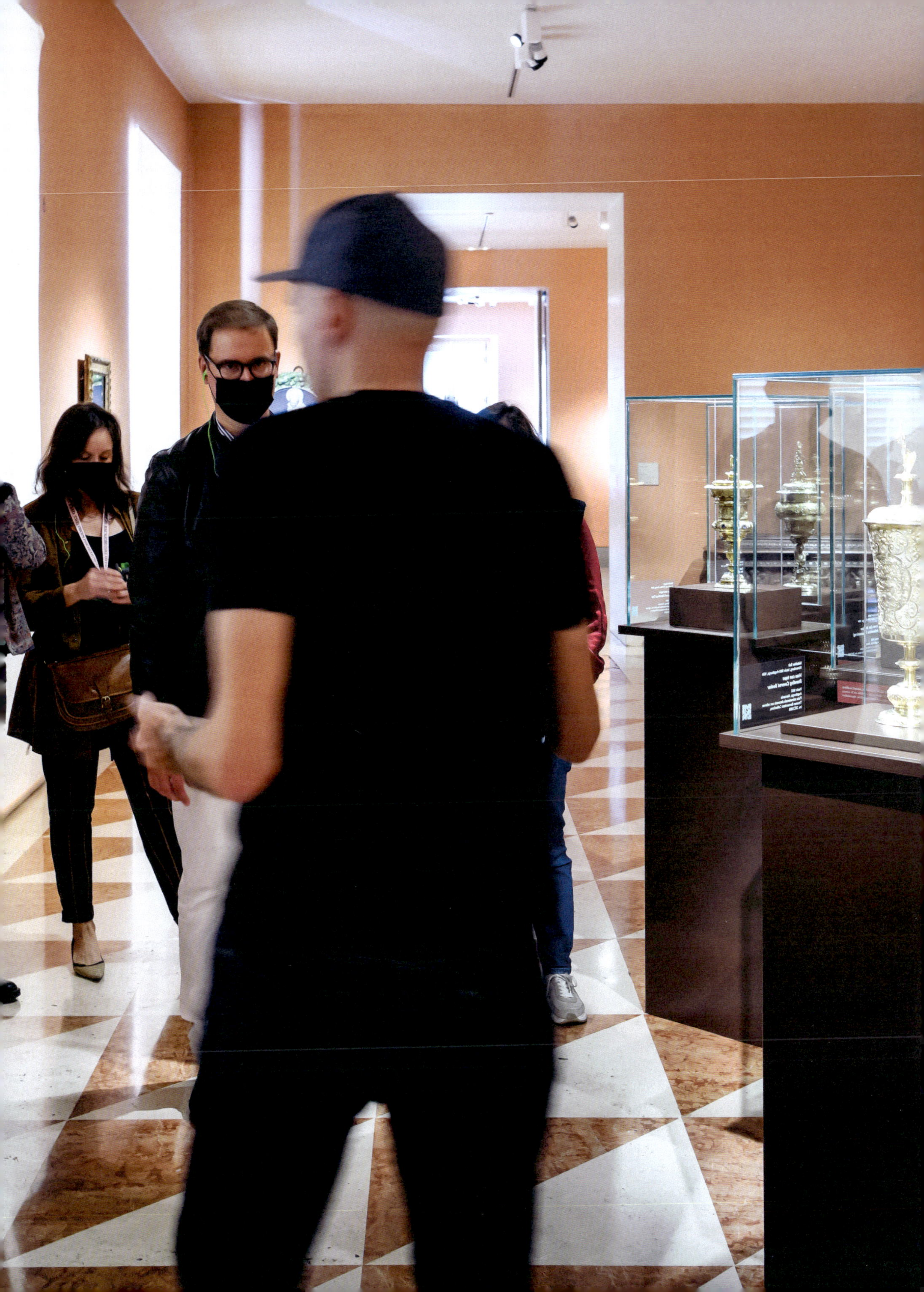

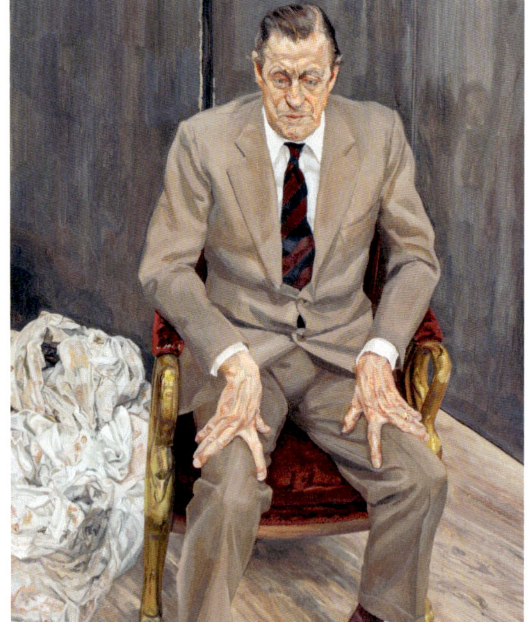

Lucian Freud, *Man in a Chair (Portrait of Baron H.H. Thyssen-Bornemisza)*, 1985
Thyssen-Bornemisza Collections

Jordi Solé Tura and Baron Hans Heinrich Thyssen-Bornemisza signing the acquisition agreement, June 18, 1993

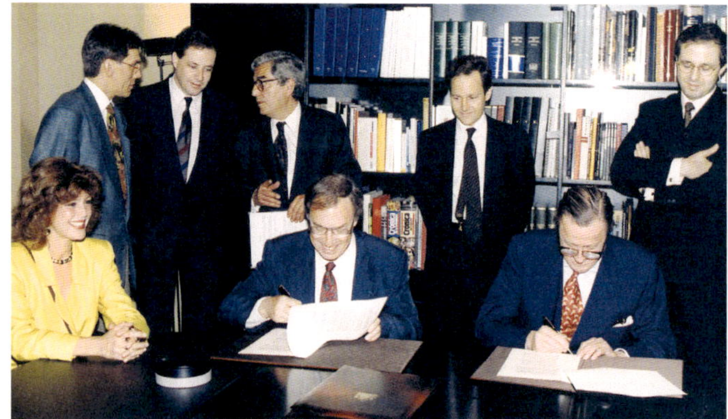

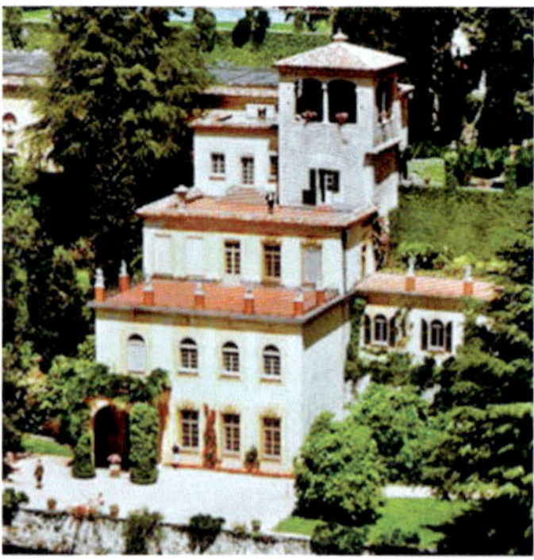

Villa Favorita, Lugano, Switzerland

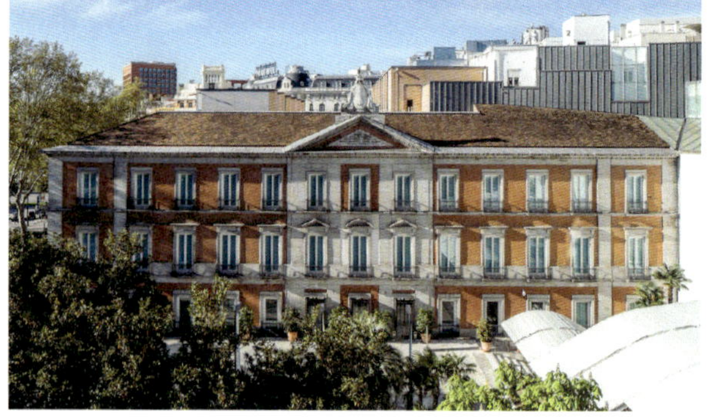

Museo Nacional Thyssen-Bornemisza, Madrid

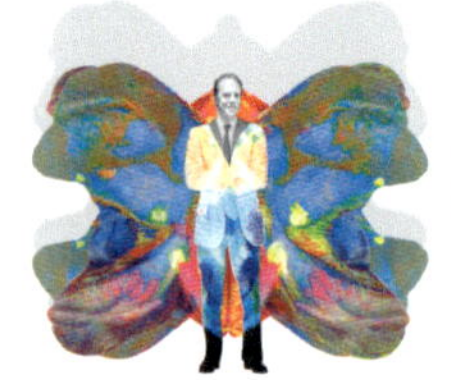

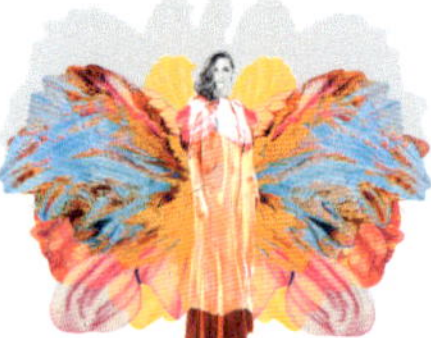

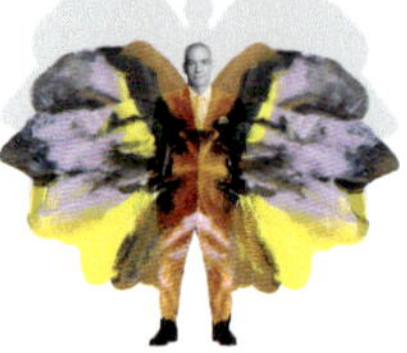

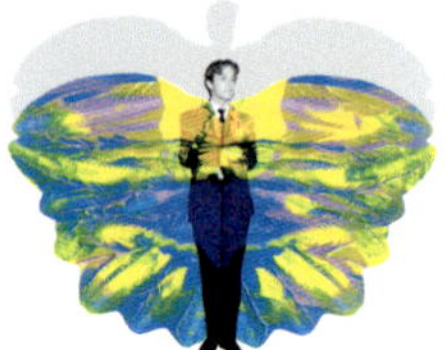

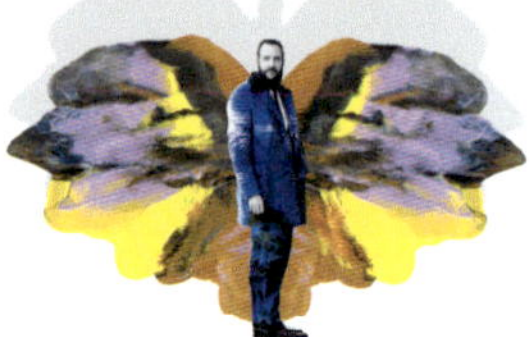

From left to right: Georg Heinrich, Francesca, Lorne, Alexander, and Borja Thyssen-Bornemisza.
Detail from **Walid Raad**, *Frontispiece II: The Carpet*, 2021

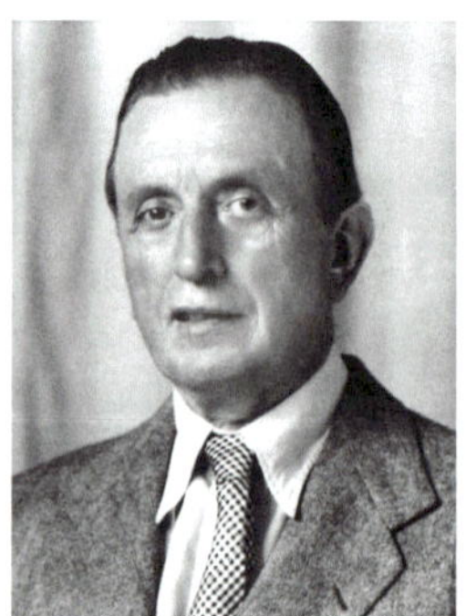

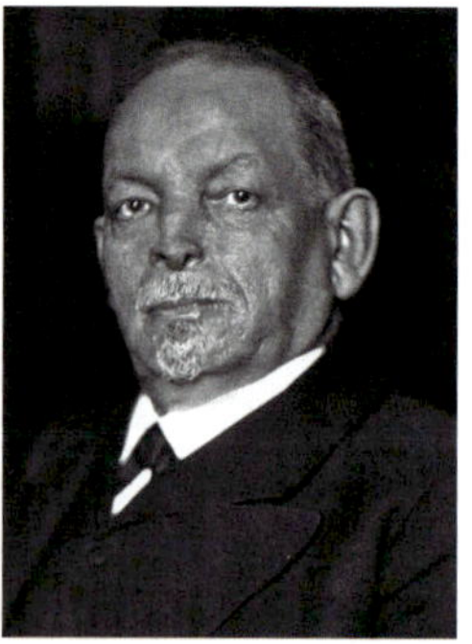

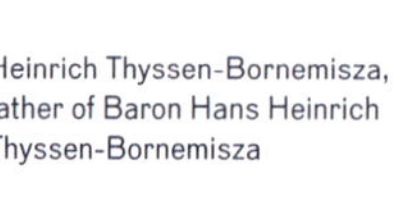

Heinrich Thyssen-Bornemisza, father of Baron Hans Heinrich Thyssen-Bornemisza

August Thyssen, grandfather of Baron Hans Heinrich Thyssen-Bornemisza

Baroness Carmen Thyssen-Bornemisza

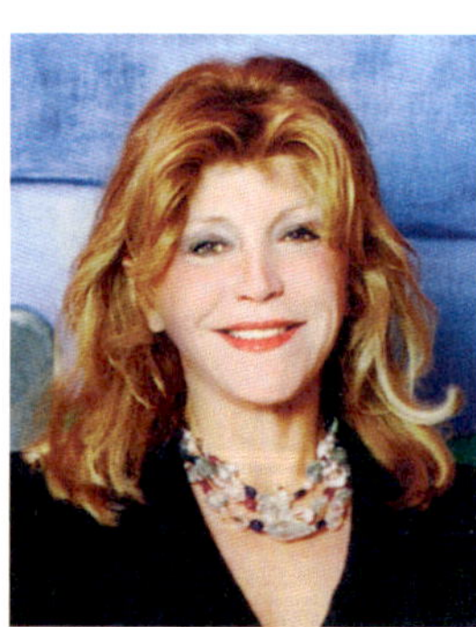

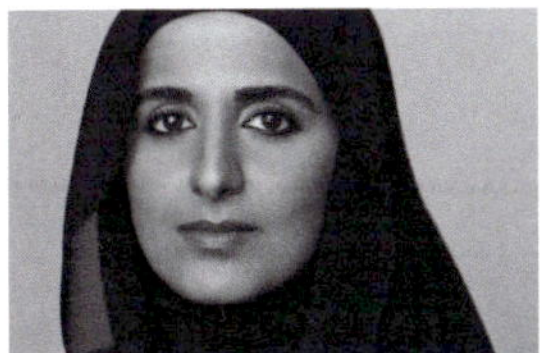

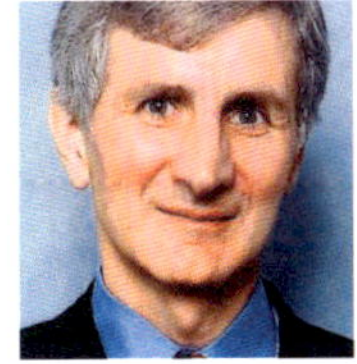

Sheikha Al-Mayassa bint Hamad bin Khalifa Al Thani

Michael Franses

The Schwarzenberg "Paradise Park" carpet, c. 1550 Museum of Islamic Arts, Doha

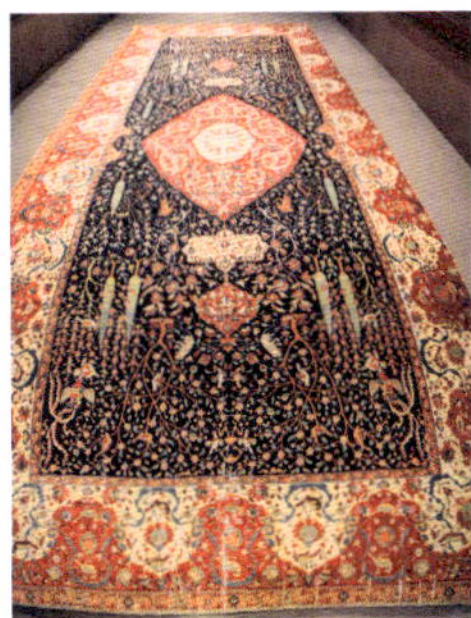

The Museum of Islamic Art, Doha, Qatar, opened 2008

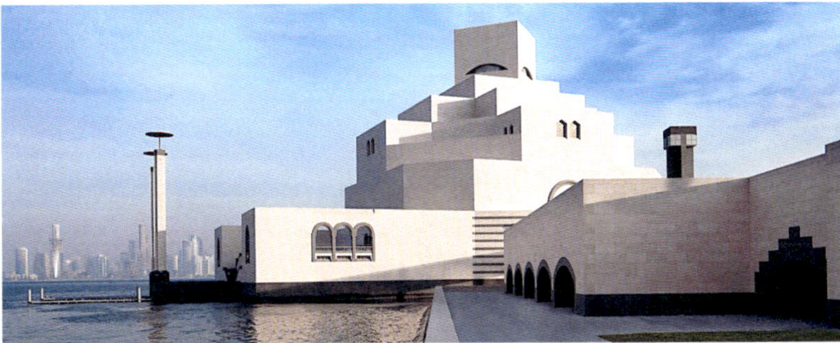

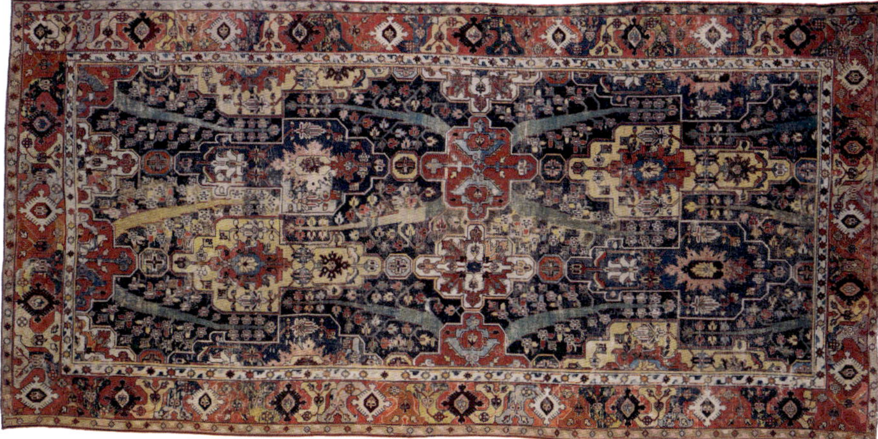

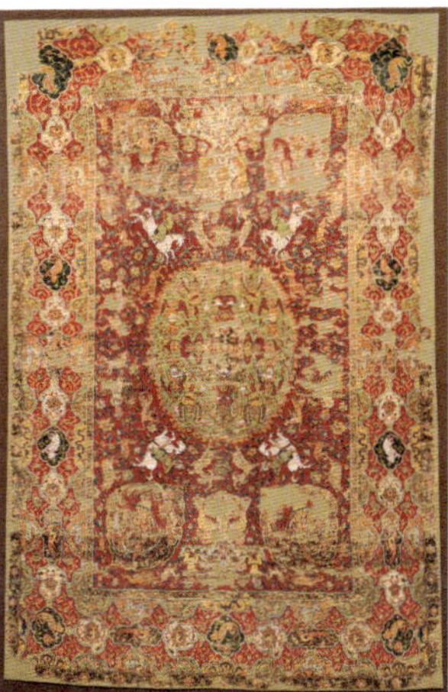

The Lamm Tree Carpet, c. 1700. The Béarn Hunting Carpet, c. 1650. Thyssen-Bornemisza Collections

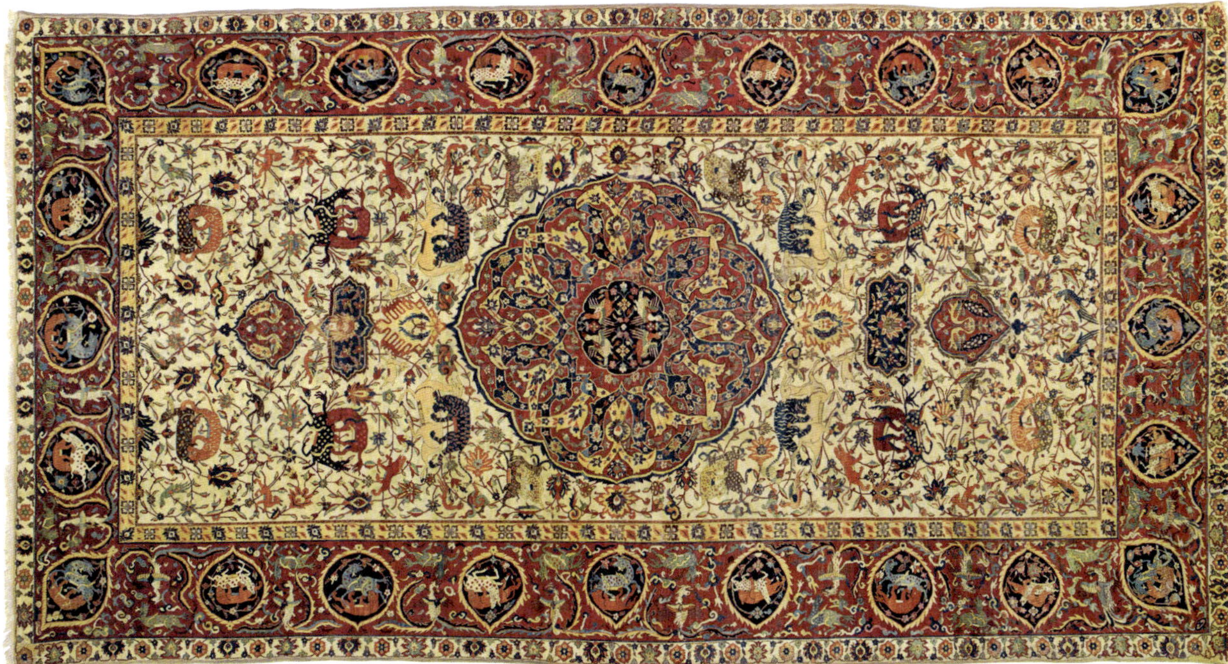

The Béhague-Sanguszko carpet, late sixteenth century. Thyssen-Bornemisza Collections

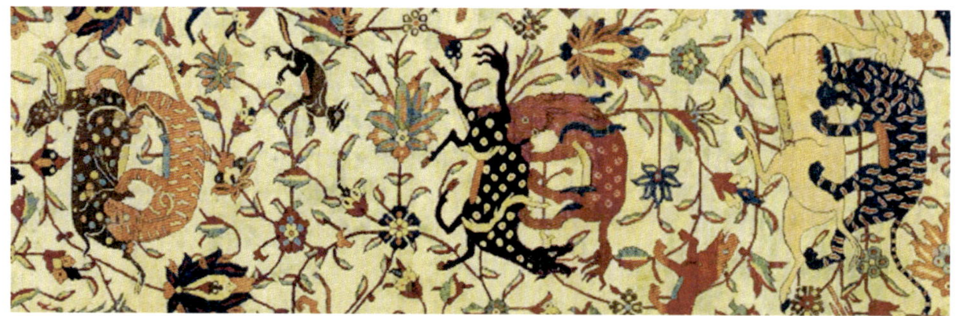

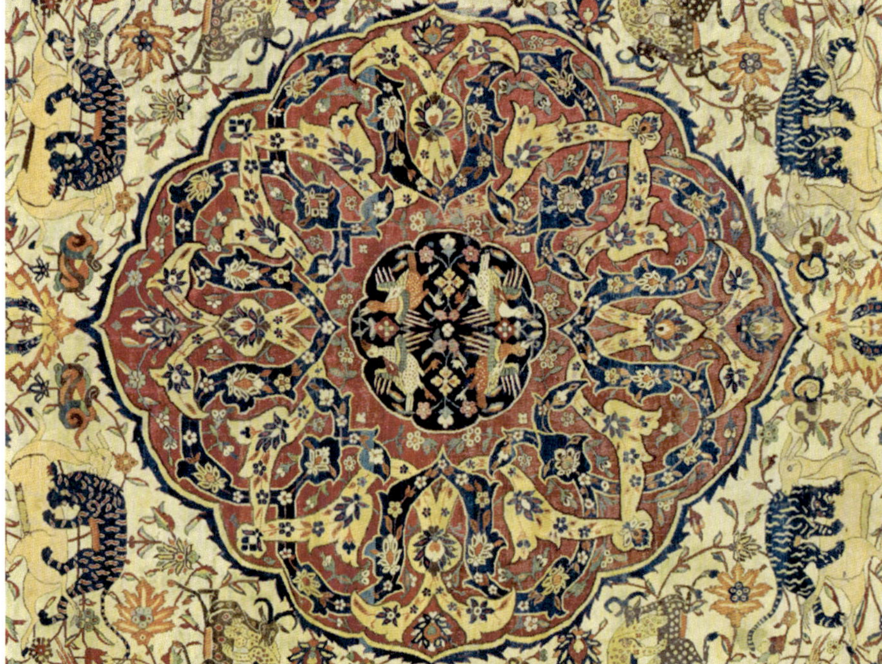

The Béhague-Sanguszko carpet, details

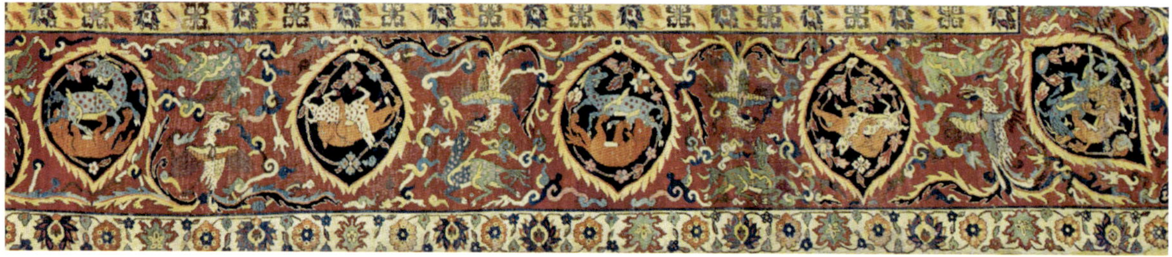

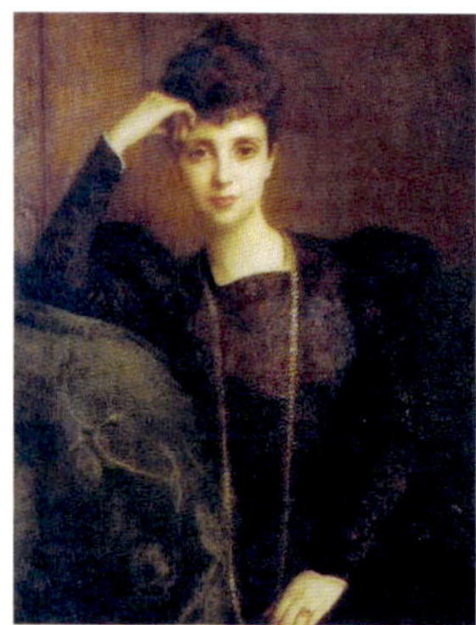

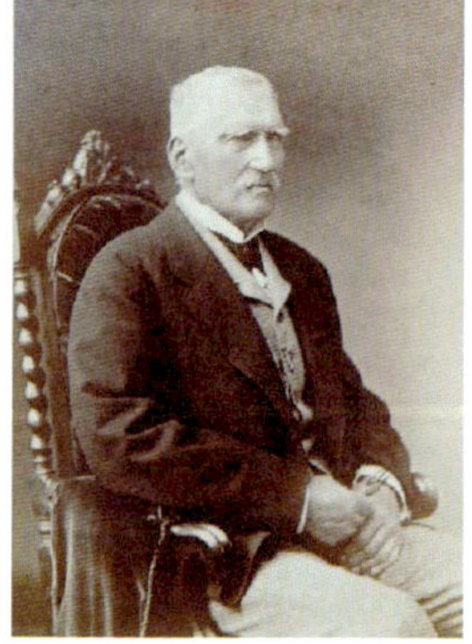

Portrait of Martine de Béhague, late nineteenth century

Roman Sanguszko, c. 1880

It is beautiful, right? Five hundred and thirty-one centimeters long. Two hundred and seventy-five centimeters wide. It has these incredible hunting scenes. An exquisite medallion. Incredible borders. It is a late sixteenth- or early seventeenth-century Persian carpet called the Béhague-Sanguszko. Its estimated value? Around $39 million (even if it is insured at €7.5 million), making it, if it ever sells at that price, the most expensive carpet in the world. This carpet is world renowned and so valuable for a very specific reason: it is known to be extremely heavy, but not in the usual sense. The carpet's weight, twenty-one kilograms, is not unusual for its size. But everyone who has tried to lift it will tell you that there is no way this carpet weighs only twenty-one kilograms, because it feels like it weighs a ton or more. And it remains unclear to this day, after dozens of technical studies, why this carpet feels as heavy as it does, why its heaviness is not proportional to its weight. And this is precisely the reason why Qatar wanted to buy it. But Francesca had no intention of selling it. In fact, she outright offered the carpet as a gift to Qatar.

I should say that as part of my own research, I read story after story about this carpet. In fact, I have been trying to find and see it for years and I had no idea that it was with Francesca. As soon as I found out that she had the carpet, I started to harass Francesca to let me spend time with it. But Francesca did not need much harassment, and about four years ago, I was allowed to spend as much time as I wanted with the carpet. I started to study it closely, to look at it and around it, and I would like to say to look under it, but I could not lift it to look at what's underneath. And that's how I found myself in a very deep tunnel. It started with Francesca and the carpet, and then it just kept going and going and going.

>
Walid Raad
Frontispiece II: The Carpet, 2021
Installation view, Museo Nacional Thyssen-Bornemisza, Madrid, 2021

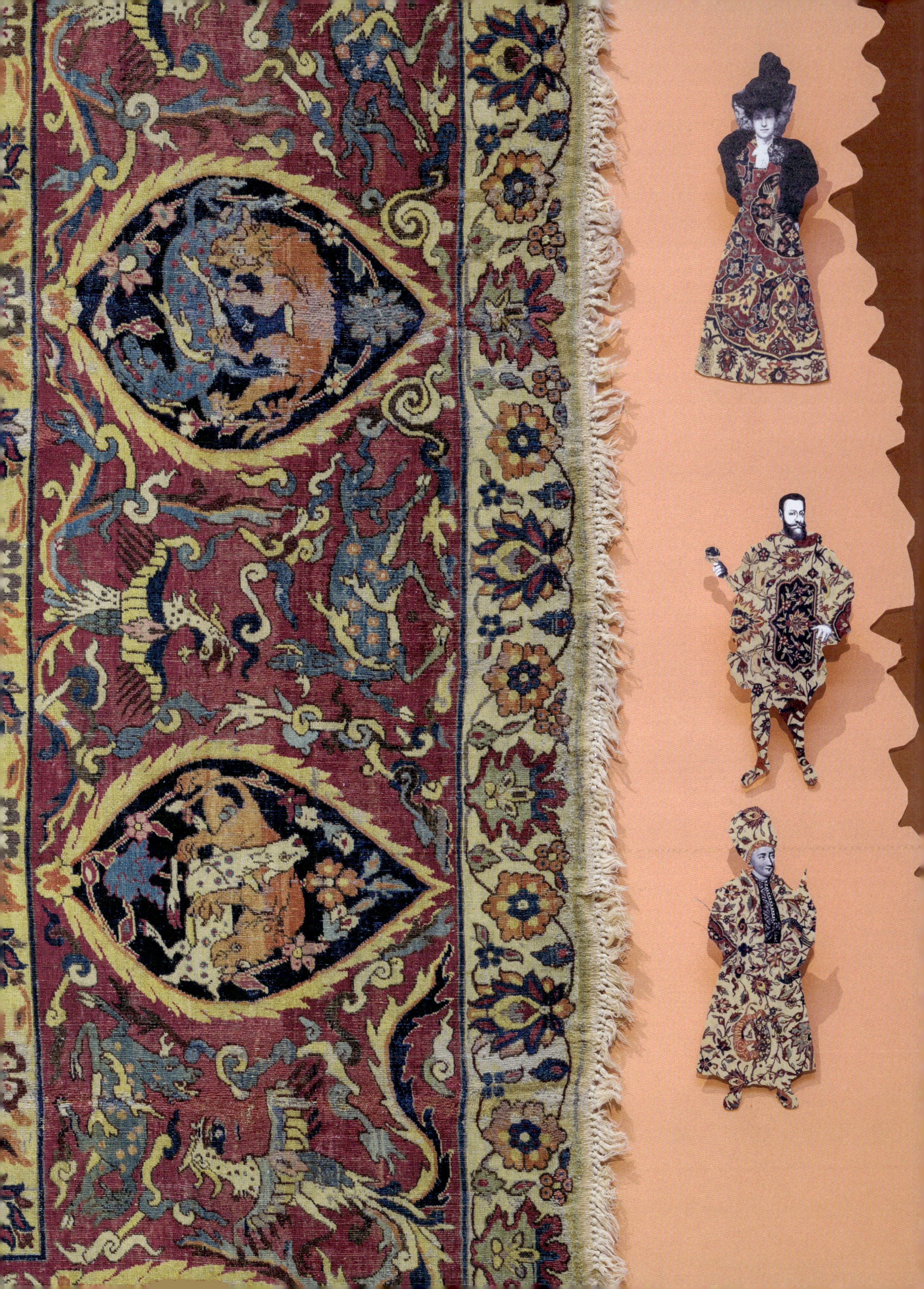

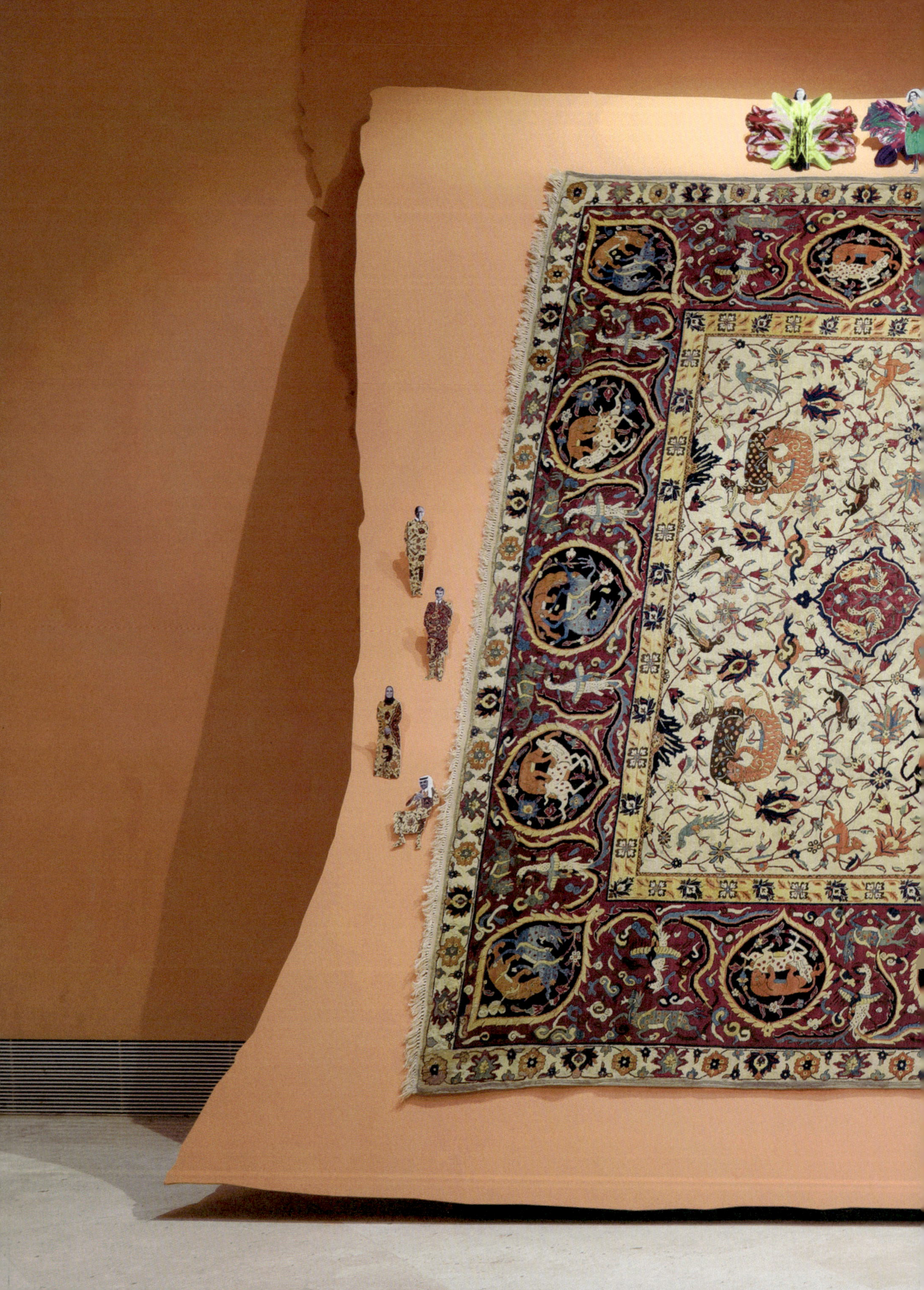

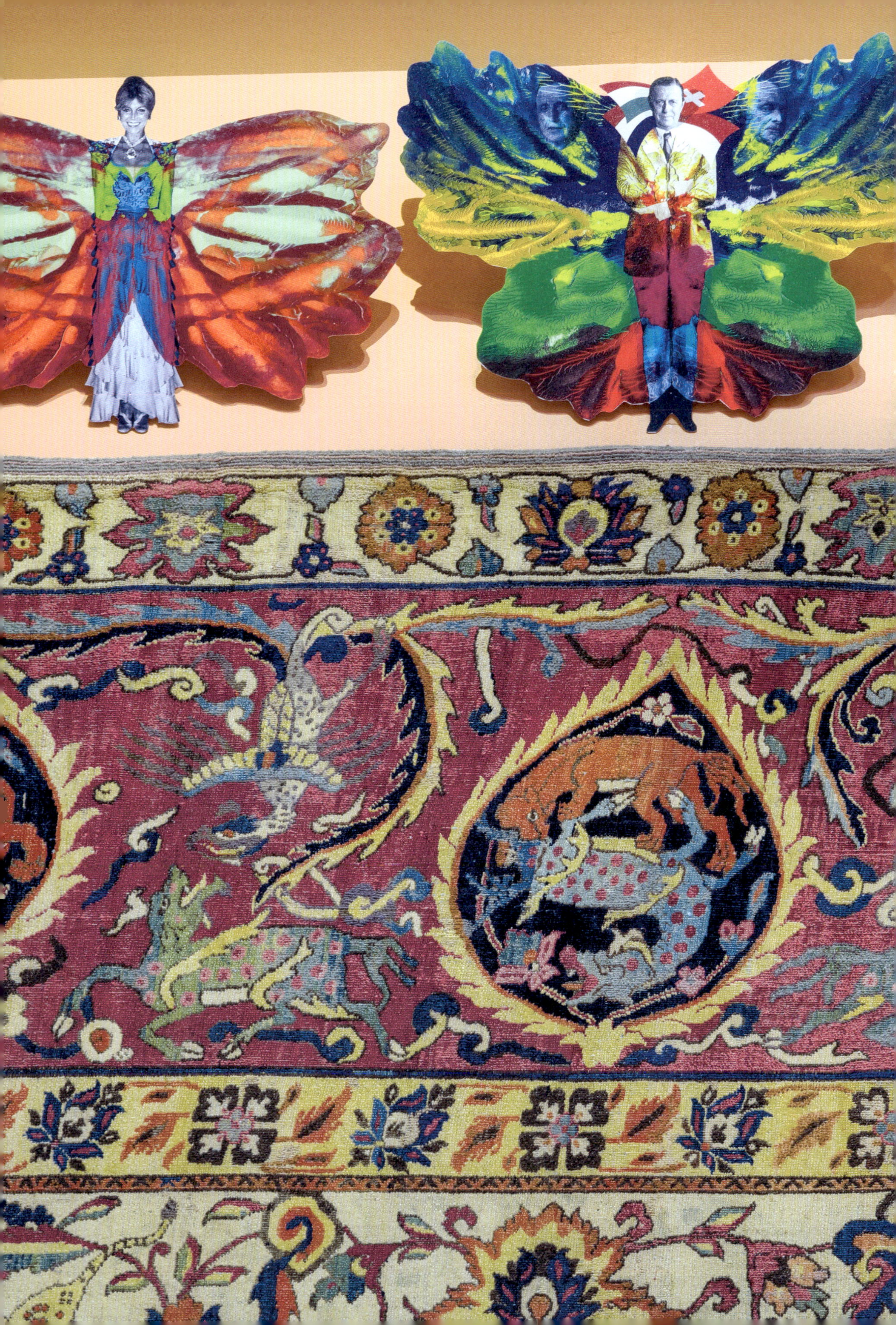

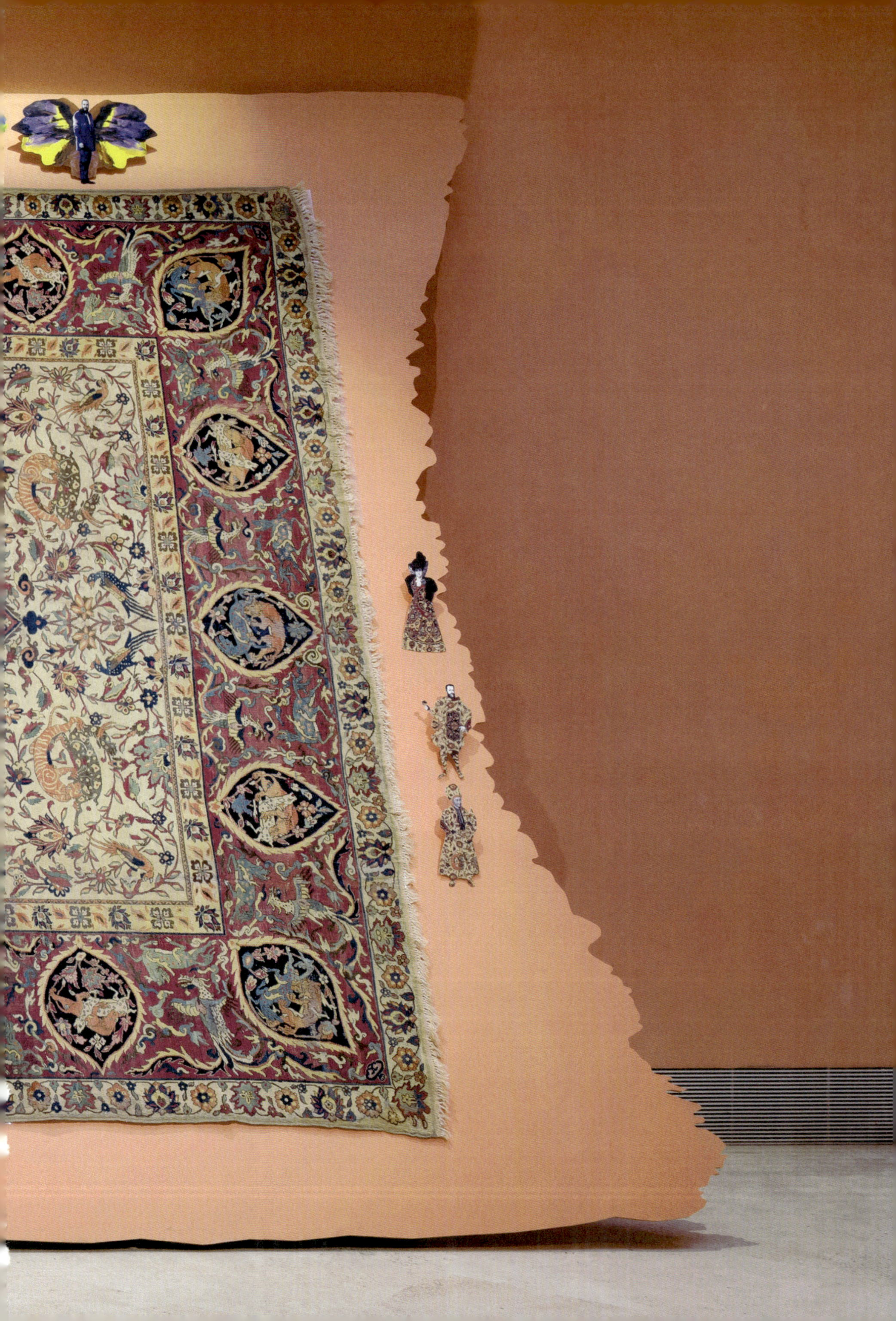

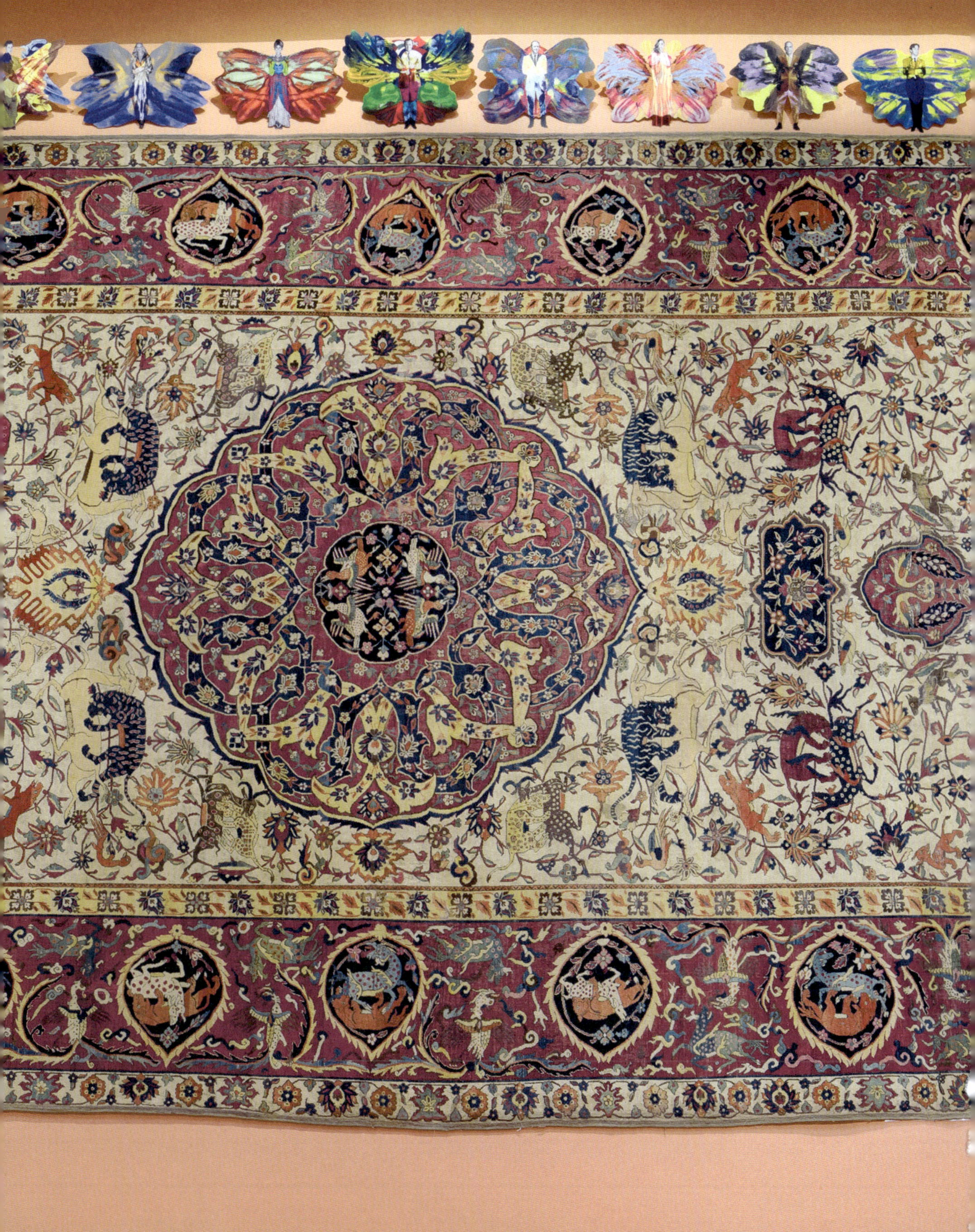

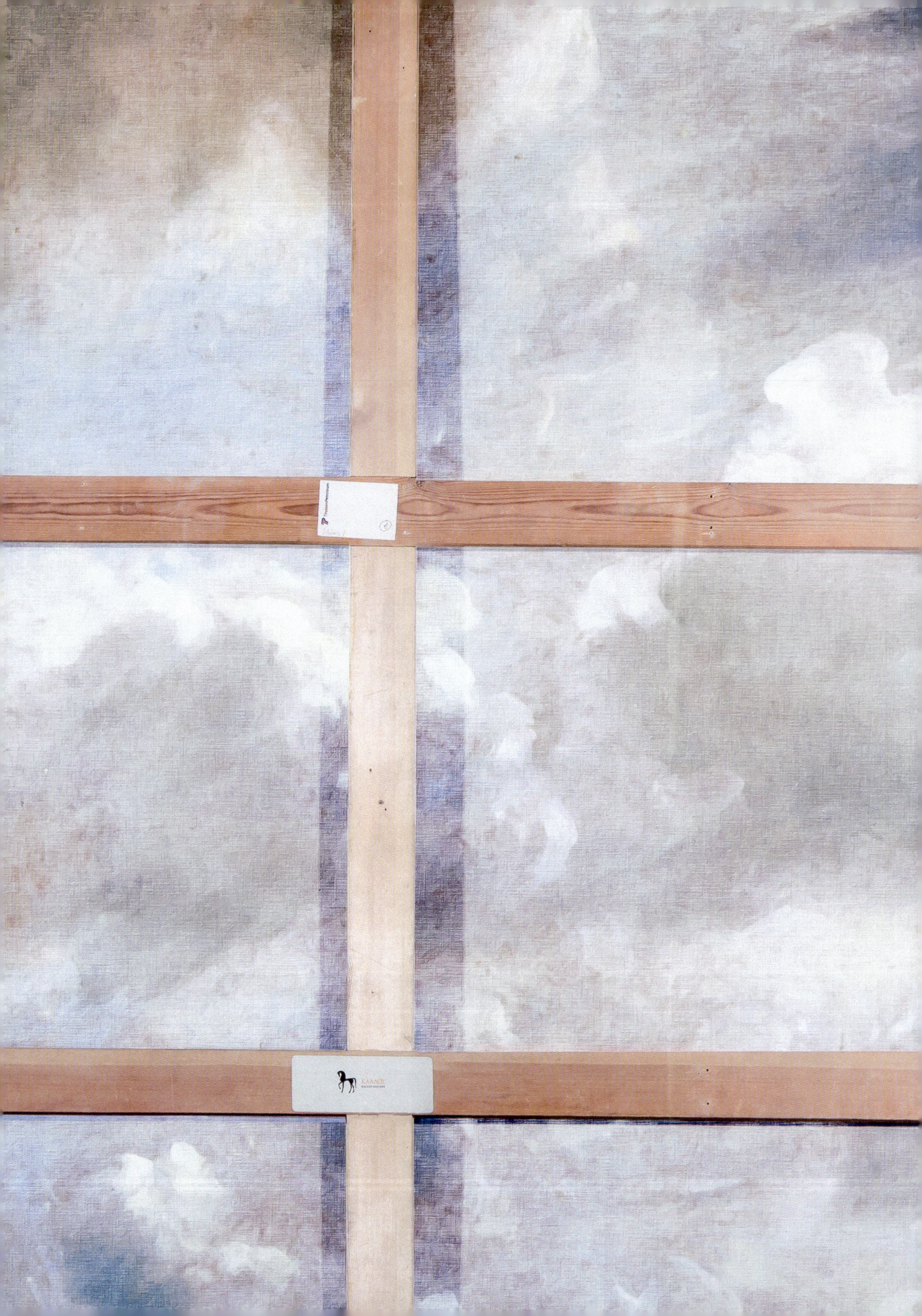

Epilogue II: The Constables

So, beginning, or tunnel #1: a carpet that's heavier than its weight.

Tunnel #2.

After a few months with the carpet, I decided to come to this museum to look at the Thyssen-Bornemisza archives, to see if there were any documents here about the carpet. It was here that I discovered these seven photographs. Seven color photographs of the backs of seven paintings. I immediately asked the museum's staff about this, and was told that seven of the 775 paintings that Hans Heinrich Thyssen-Bornemisza sold to Spain had other paintings on their backs. They were double-sided paintings, as art people say, and these back paintings were all paintings of clouds.

What is also strange here is that today no one at the museum has any idea what is on the other side of these clouds, on the fronts. Is it a Rembrandt? A Hans Memling? An Artemisia Gentileschi?

The museum staff also told me that these back paintings were discovered in 1983, when the collection was still in Switzerland, in Villa Favorita. They were discovered by a person whose name you will hear me mention a lot, a woman named Lamia Antonova.

In 1983, when she started working for Hans Heinrich Thyssen-Bornemisza, Antonova was known as the best art restorer of her generation. She was originally from Palestine but grew up, married, and was trained in the Soviet Union.

When she discovered these back paintings, Antonova immediately showed them to Hans Heinrich Thyssen-Bornemisza, thinking he would know what this is about. But the baron had no idea the clouds were even there because up until then, the backs were covered by wooden panels. Antonova discovered them when she x-rayed the artworks. But ever since he was shown the backs, the baron has forbidden anyone from looking at the fronts. Moreover, in his negotiations with the Spanish state, the baron insisted that these seven paintings travel to Madrid with the rest of the collection, but he never told the museum what is on the fronts. By contract, the museum is not allowed to look at the fronts; nor to x-ray the paintings or show the backs of the paintings. They are only allowed to show these photographs.

As you can imagine, there are many rumors about the backs and the fronts. And this is Spain, so I am certain that some people actually know what's on the fronts, but no one is talking, at least not so far.

What we do know about the back paintings today is that they were painted in 1821, and they look exactly like the cloud studies made by the nineteenth-century British painter John Constable. Constable was an early meteorologist, and he wanted the clouds in his paintings to look real, not like puffy cotton balls. Between 1820 and 1822, he spent two years sky-ing, as he called it, and made over 100 beautiful sketches of clouds. But, as far as we know, he painted on the backs of other paintings only once and that painting is in the Tate. So, who did this? We don't know. Are they Constables? We don't know. What's on the fronts? We don't know.

>>
Walid Raad
Epilogue II: The Constables, 2021
Installation view, Museo Nacional Thyssen-Bornemisza, Madrid, 2021

John Constable, *Self-portrait*, 1799–1804
National Portrait Gallery, London

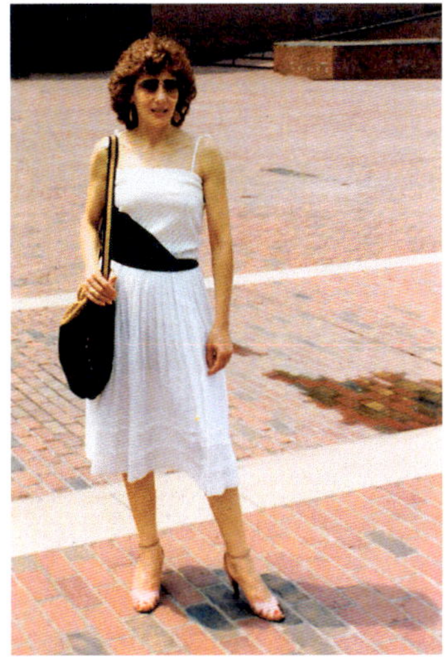

Lamia
Antonova

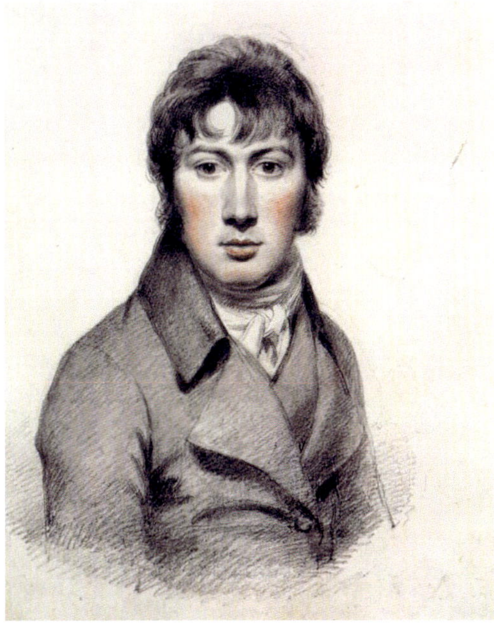

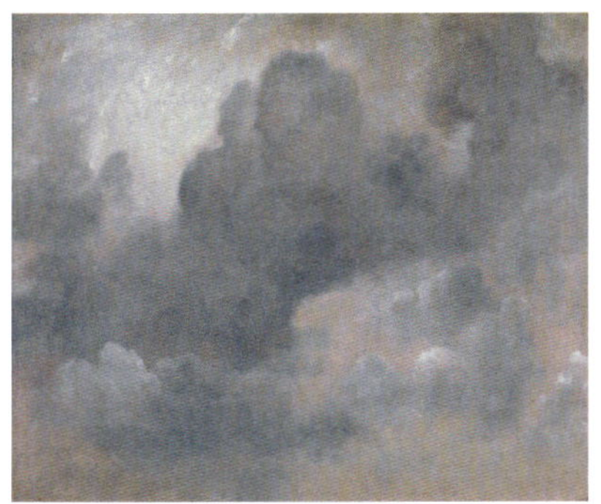

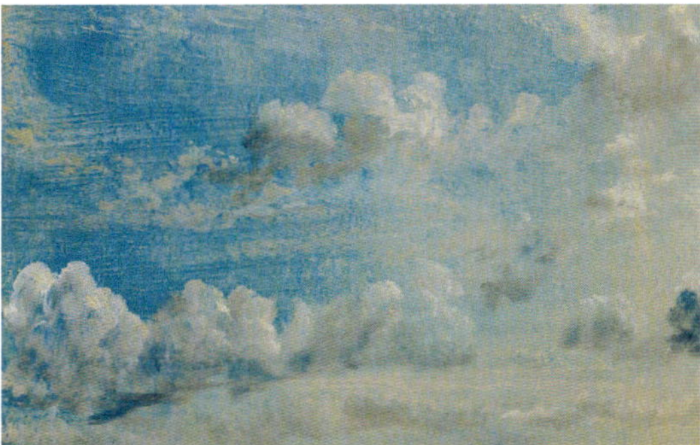

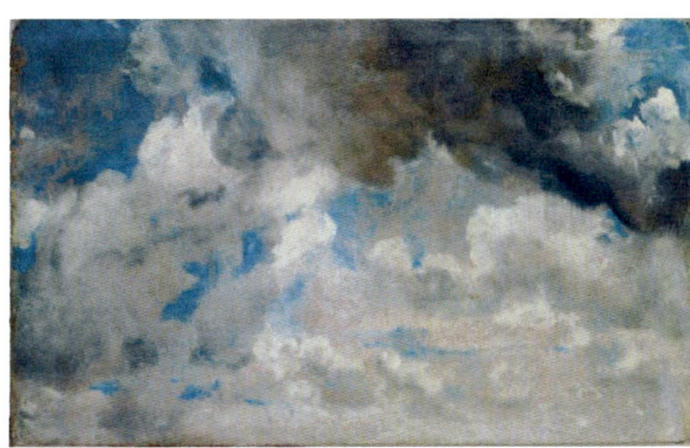

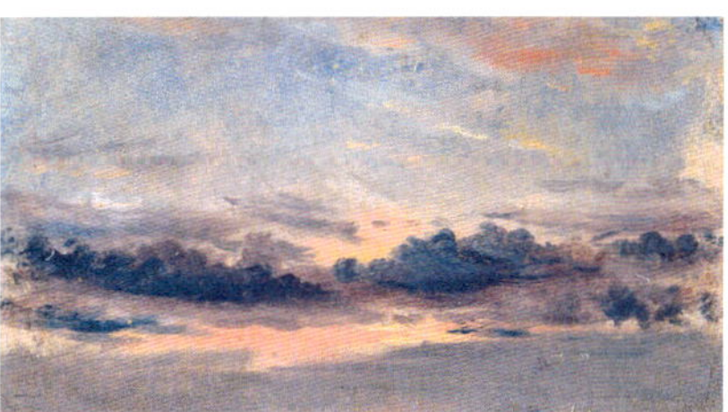

From left to right:

John Constable

Cloud Study, 1822. Tate

Cloud Study, 1822. Yale Center for British Art, Paul Mellon Collection, New Haven, CT

Cloud Study, c. 1822. The Frick Collection, New York

A Cloud Study, Sunset, c. 1821. Yale Center for British Art, Paul Mellon Collection, New Haven, CT

Cloud Study, 1822. National Gallery of Victoria, Melbourne

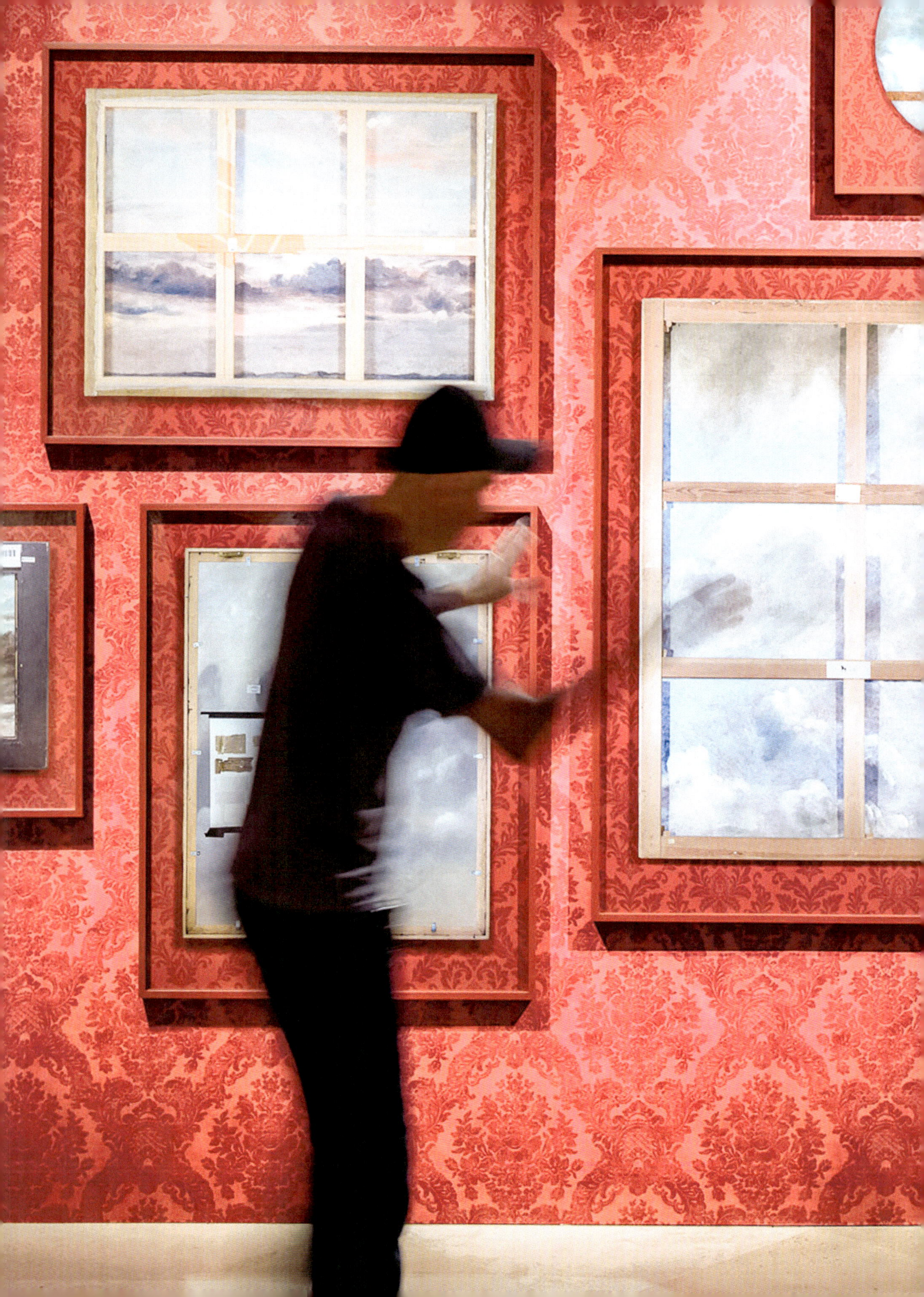

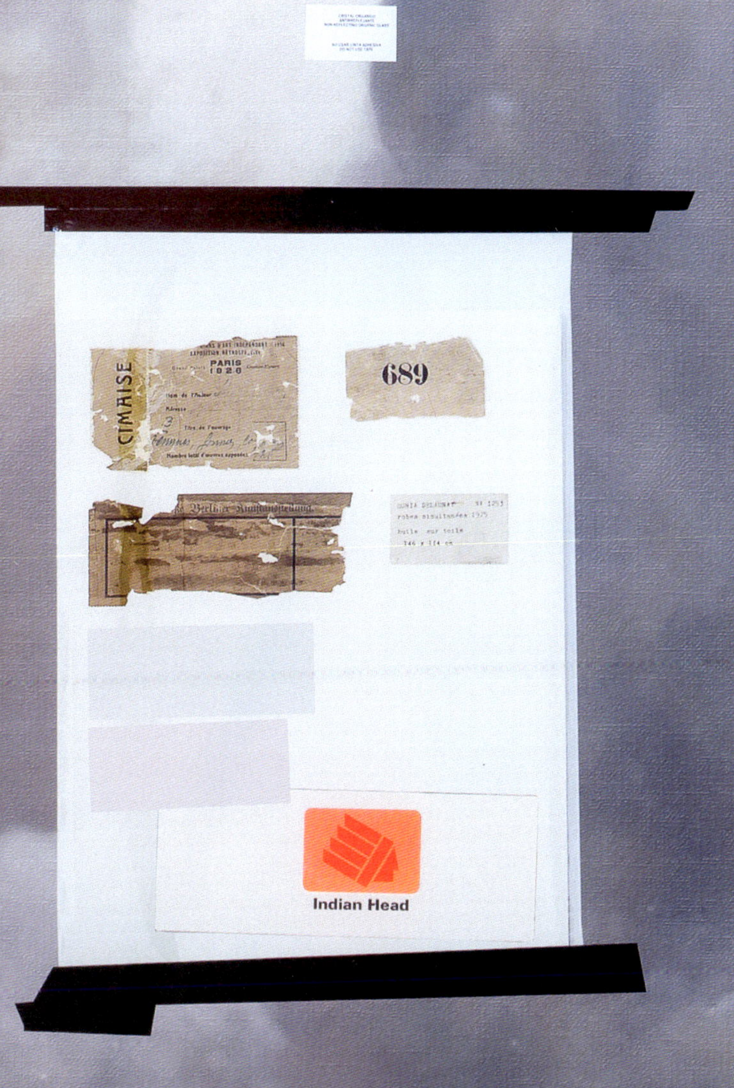
CIMAISE
PARIS
1920
689
robes simultanées
huile sur toile
Indian Head

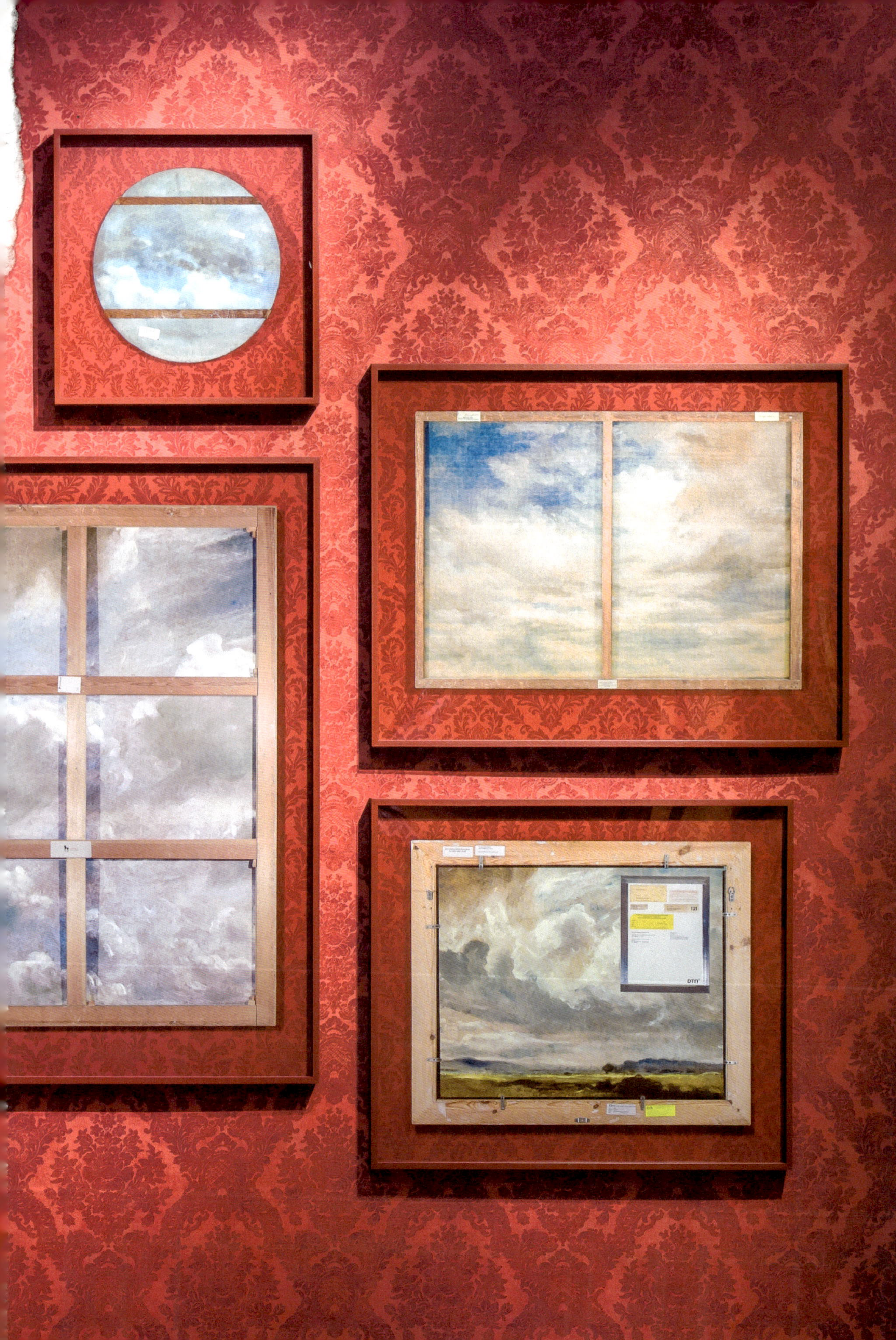

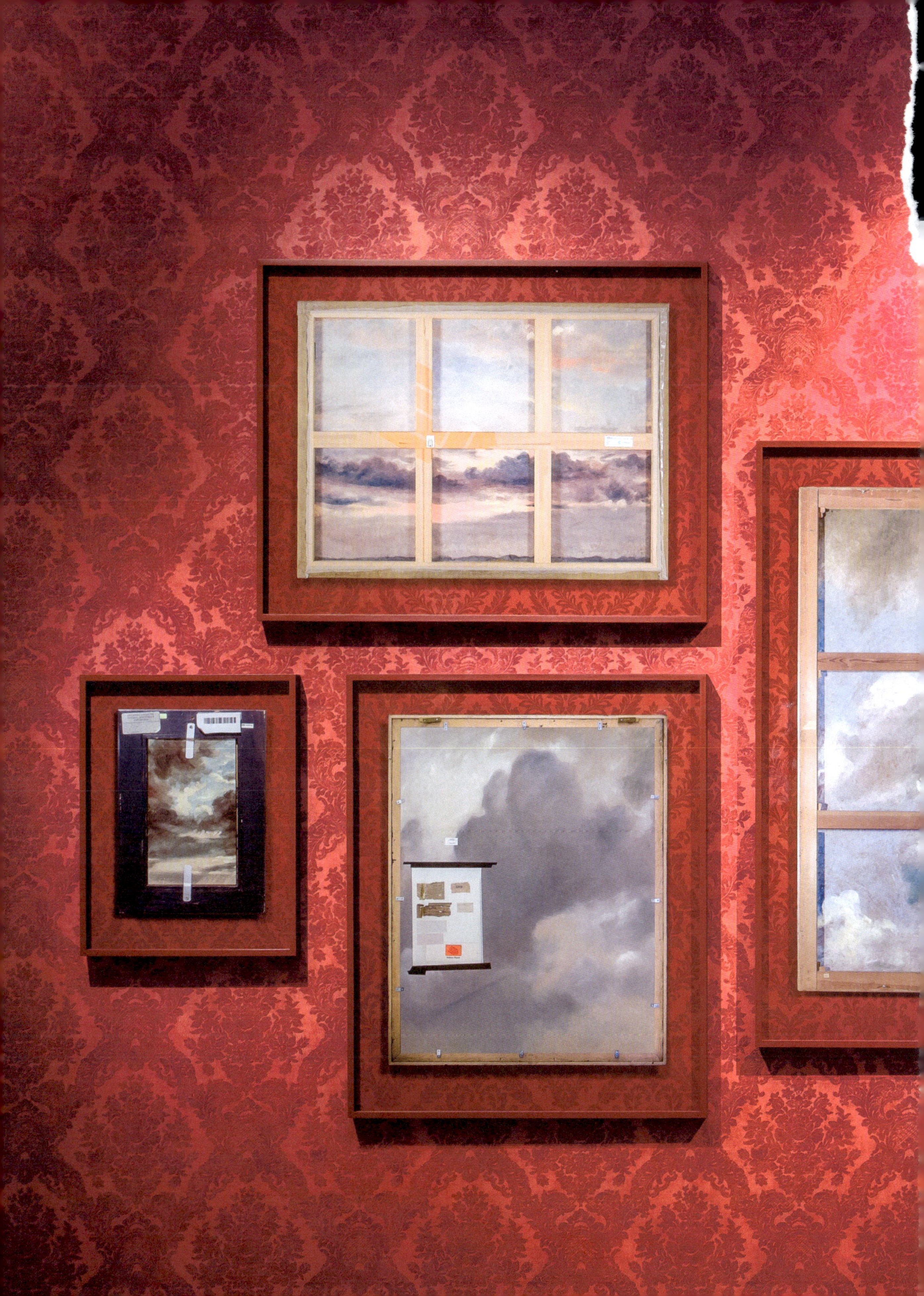

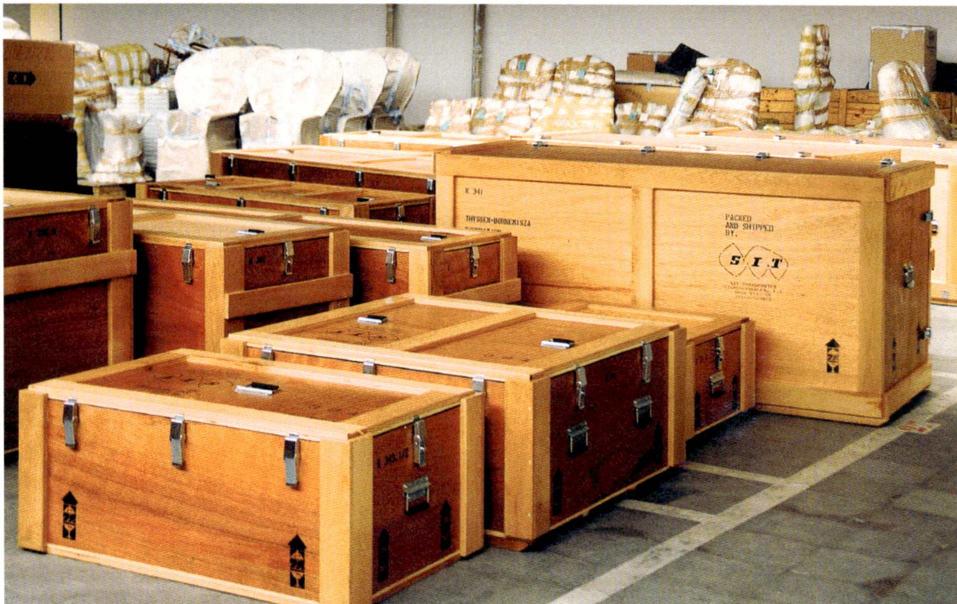

Storage space at the Museo Nacional Thyssen-Bornemisza, Madrid

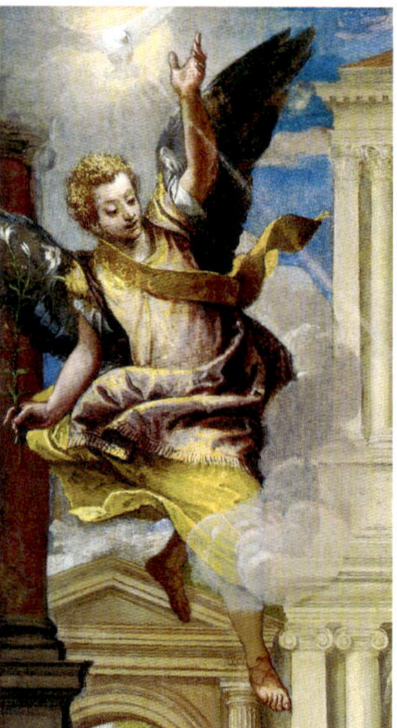

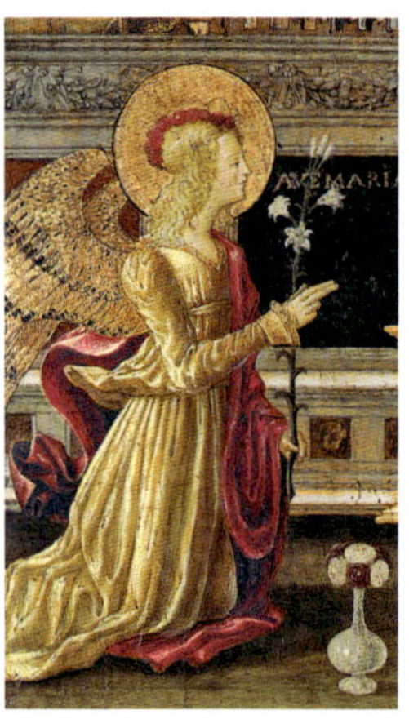

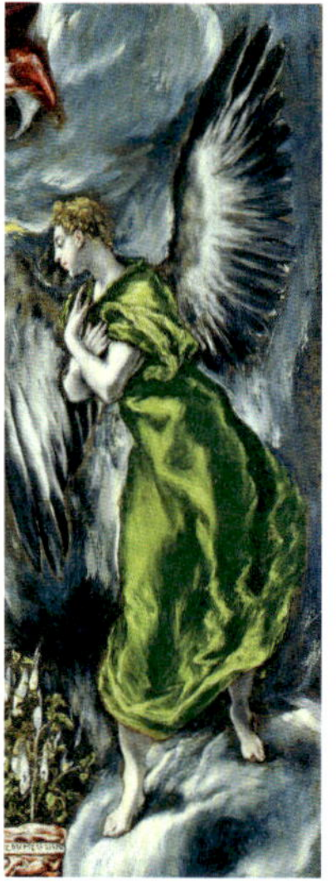

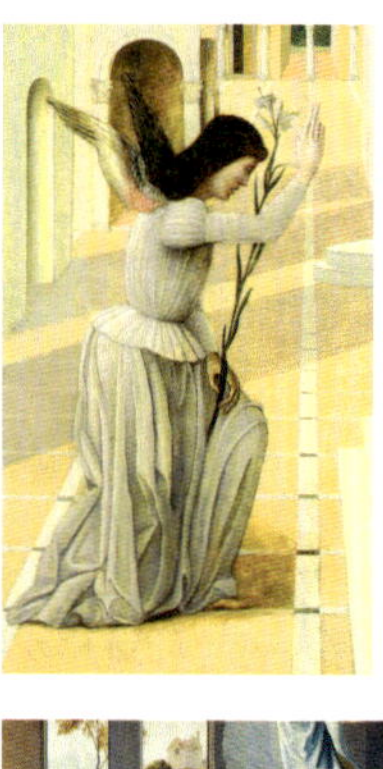

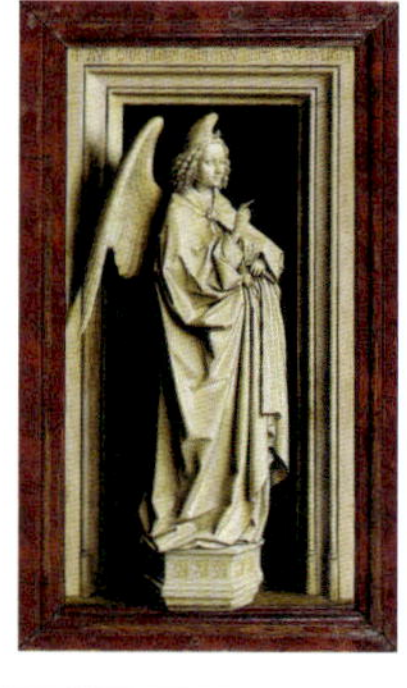

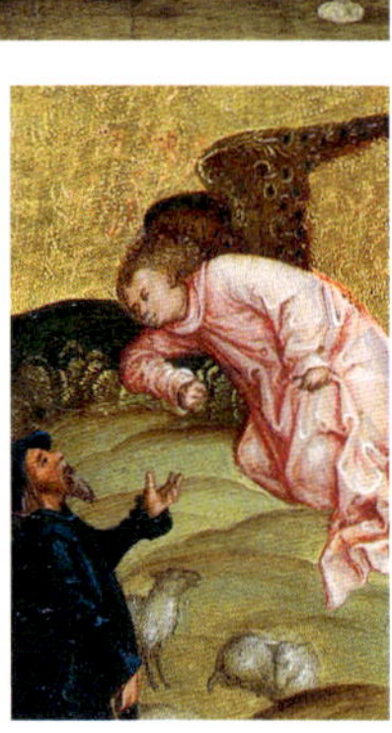

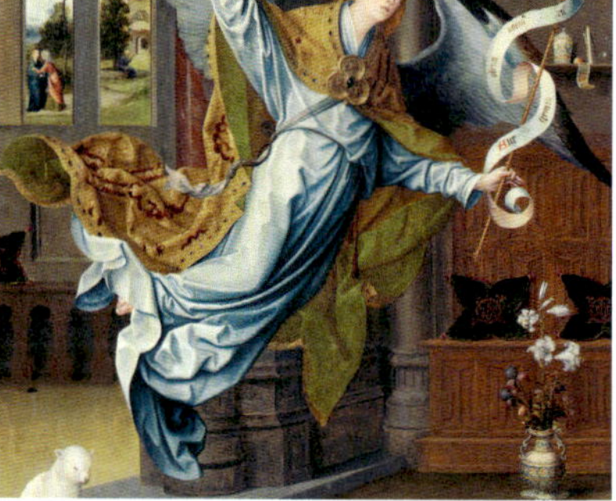

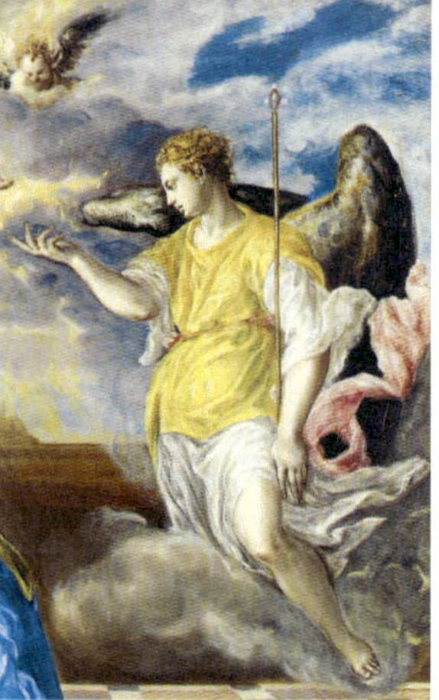

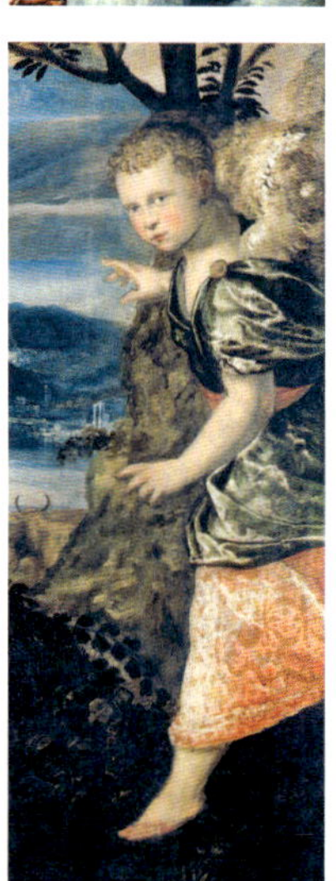

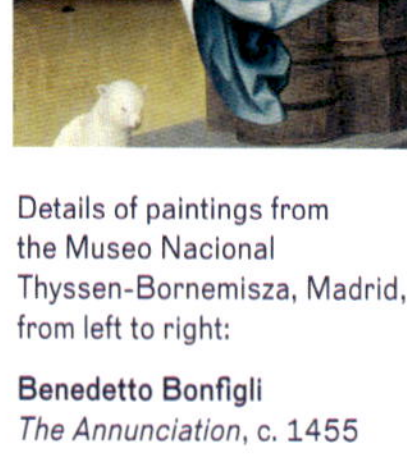

Details of paintings from the Museo Nacional Thyssen-Bornemisza, Madrid, from left to right:

Benedetto Bonfigli
The Annunciation, c. 1455

El Greco
The Annunciation, c. 1596–1600

Gentile Bellini
The Annunciation, c. 1475

Jan van Eyck
The Annunciation Diptych, c. 1433–35

Paolo Veronese
The Annunciation, c. 1580
Thyssen-Bornemisza Collection, on deposit at the Museu Nacional d'Art de Catalunya

Bernhard Strigel
The Annunciation to Saint Anne, c. 1505–10

Tintoretto
The Annunciation to Manoah's Wife, c. 1555–59

Jan de Beer
The Annunciation, c. 1520

El Greco
The Annunciation, c. 1576

Epilogue III: The Flat Corner

To repeat. First Thyssen-Bornemisza tunnel: a carpet that is heavier than its weight. Second tunnel: images of clouds on the backs of paintings whose fronts no one is allowed to see. Now the third.

When I came to Madrid to visit the archives, I also visited the storage spaces, and that is when I found this. Of course, as soon as I saw it, I asked: "What the hell is this?" And again, I was told that this went back to Lamia Antonova.

It seems that when she started working for the baron, Antonova decided to count the number of angels in his collection of paintings. Why she did this I will tell you a bit later. But when she counted how many angels are in all of the paintings, she couldn't believe it. Because, the number of angels in Hans Heinrich Thyssen-Bornemisza's collection of paintings was 285. Two hundred and eighty-five angels! Can you believe it? This is the exact number of times that angels are mentioned in the Bible. And believe me I checked many times. Angels are mentioned 108 times in the Old Testament and 177 times in the New Testament.

Antonova then said and did something that the baron never forgot. She told him: "Baron, angels in paintings should never be restored when damaged. Never. Because angels can self-repair," she said. "But to self-repair," she added, "angels need to rest on a flat corner." Rest, not hang, she said, rest on a flat corner. And then Antonova showed the baron a three-meter-tall structure with a trompe l'oeil wooden structure of what looks like a corner, with rust-colored walls, a checkered floor, and three angels in black on top. And then Antonova said: "If damaged angels rest here then they may self-repair." And I am sure you are wondering about the angels on top? She called these her Angel-Attractors because it seems that to self-repair, damaged angels need the help of other angels. "But you need to attract them first," Antonova said, with what she called Angel-Attractors. These three to be precise.

>>

Gentile Bellini
The Annunciation, c. 1475
Museo Nacional Thyssen-Bornemisza, Madrid

Walid Raad
Epilogue III: The Flat Corner, 2021

El Greco
The Annunciation, c. 1596–1600
Museo Nacional Thyssen-Bornemisza, Madrid

Installation view, Museo Nacional Thyssen-Bornemisza, Madrid, 2021

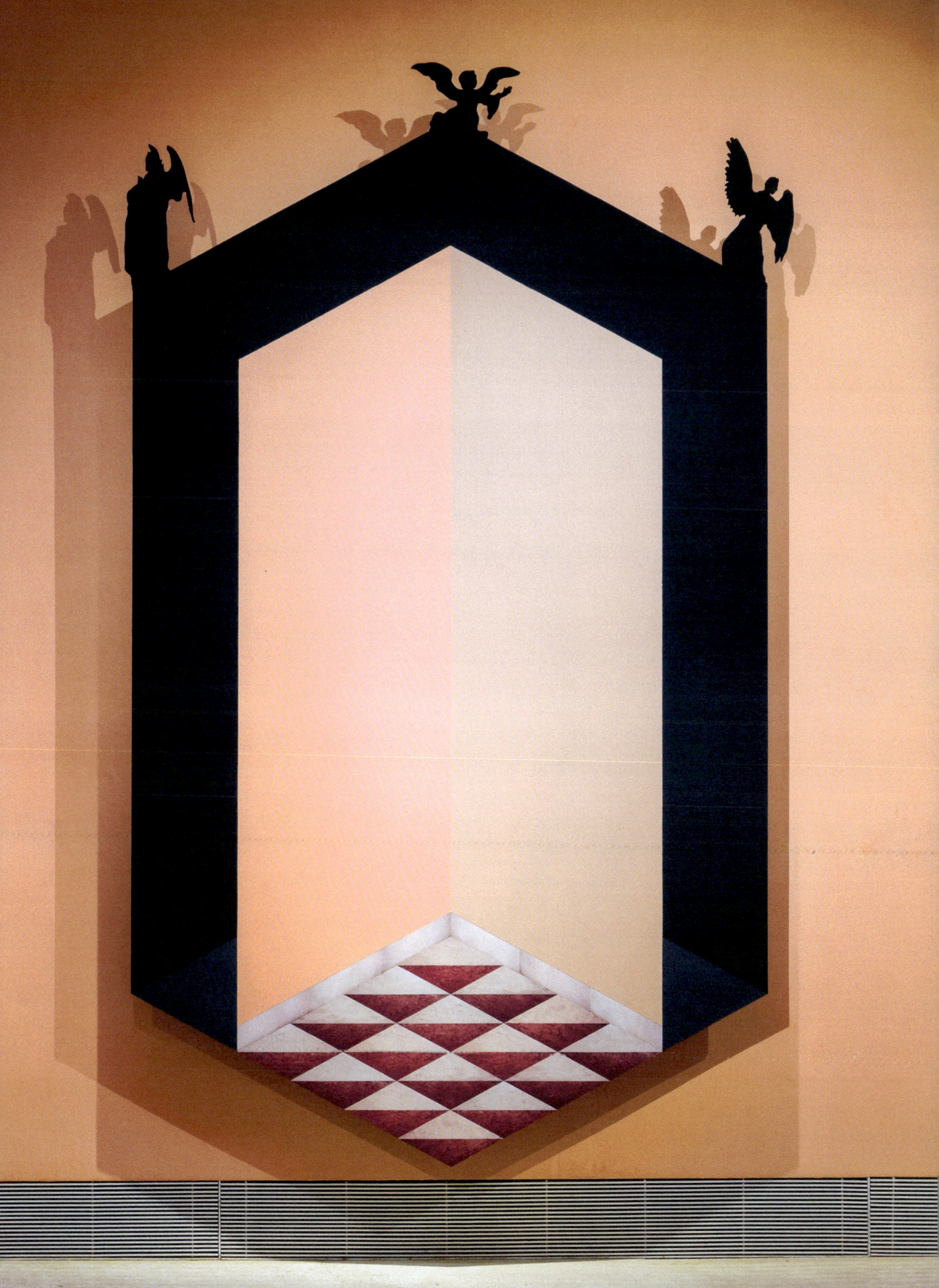

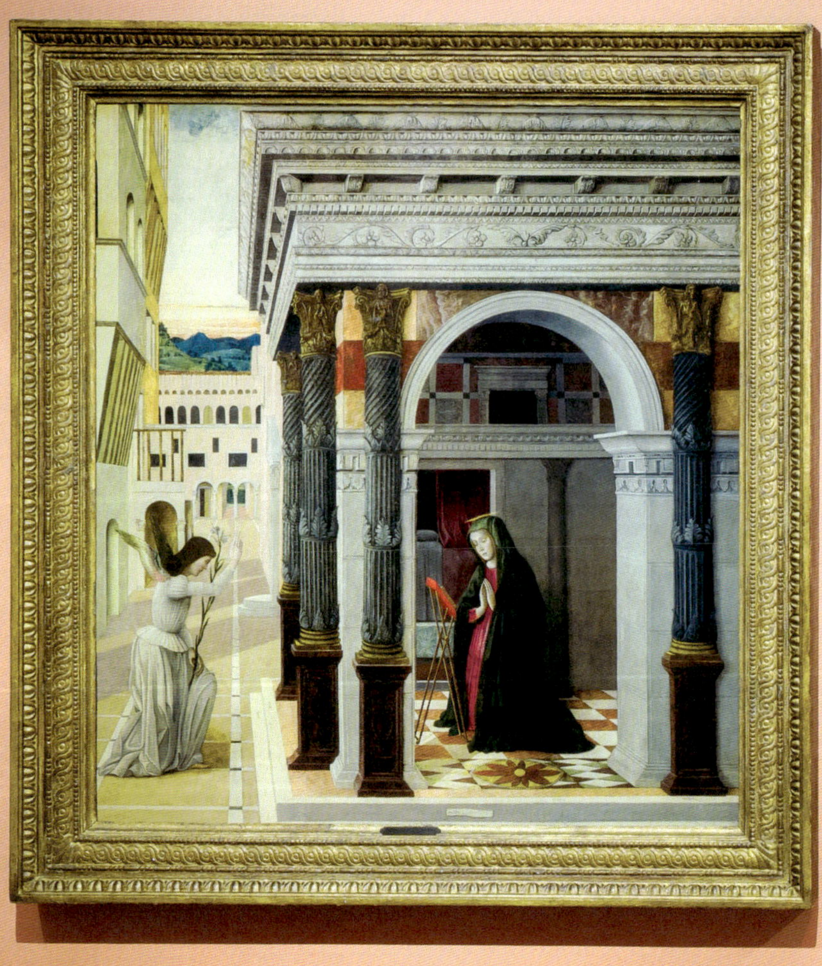

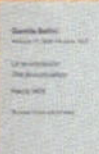

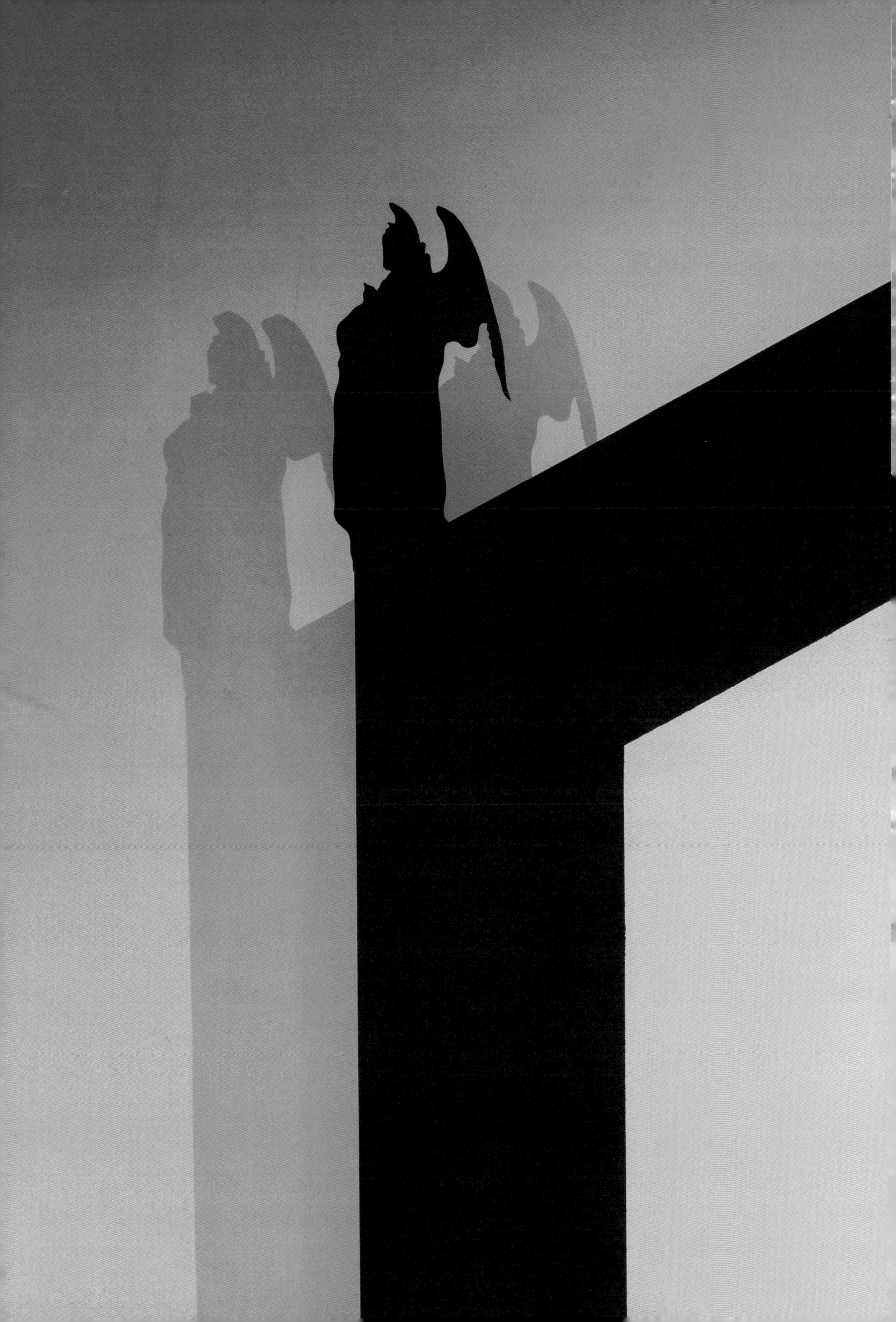

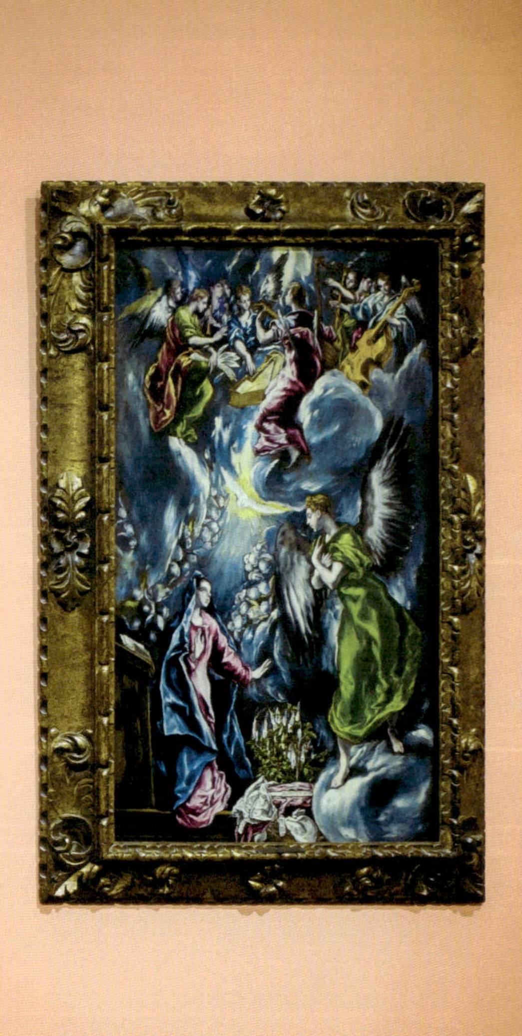

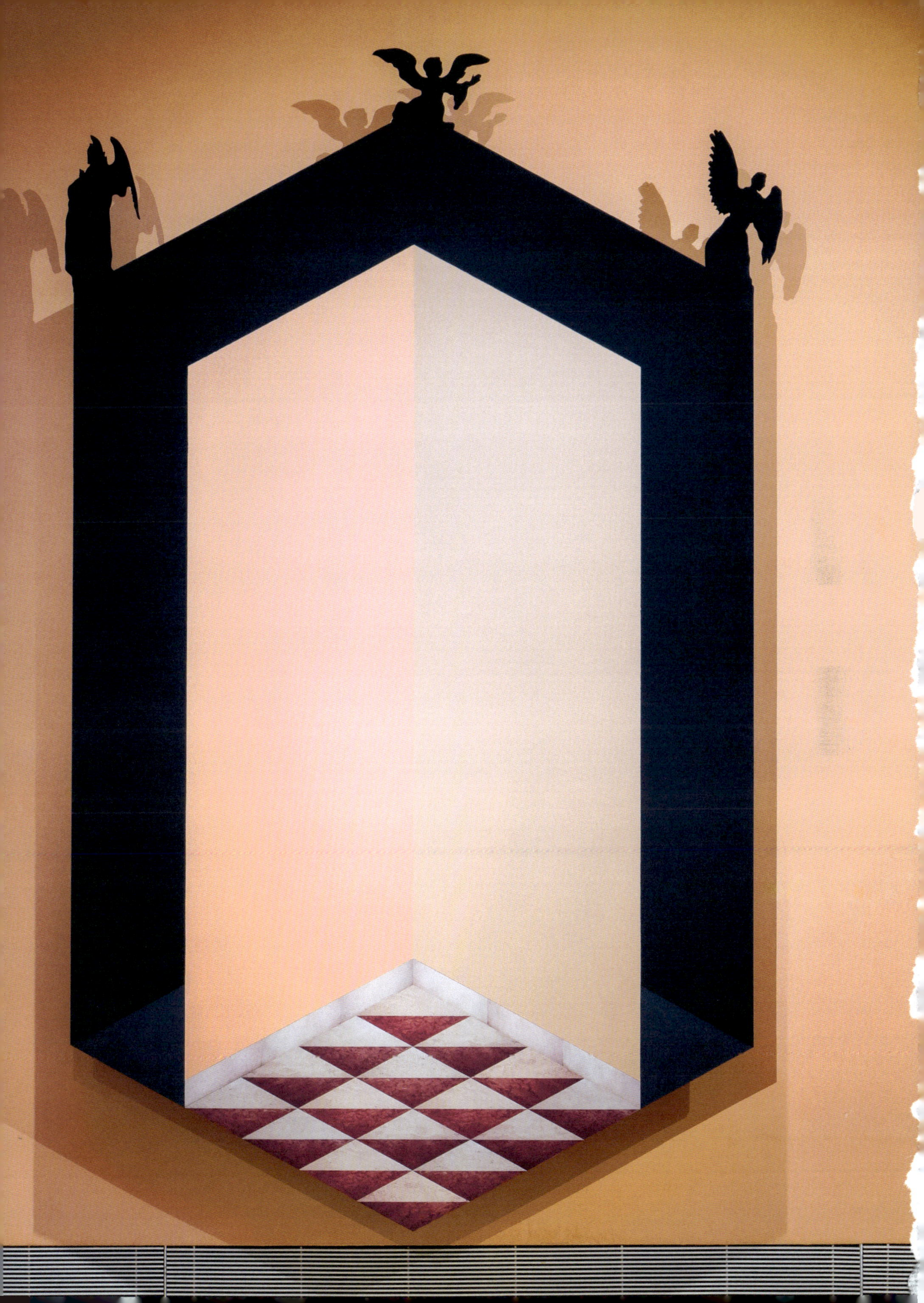

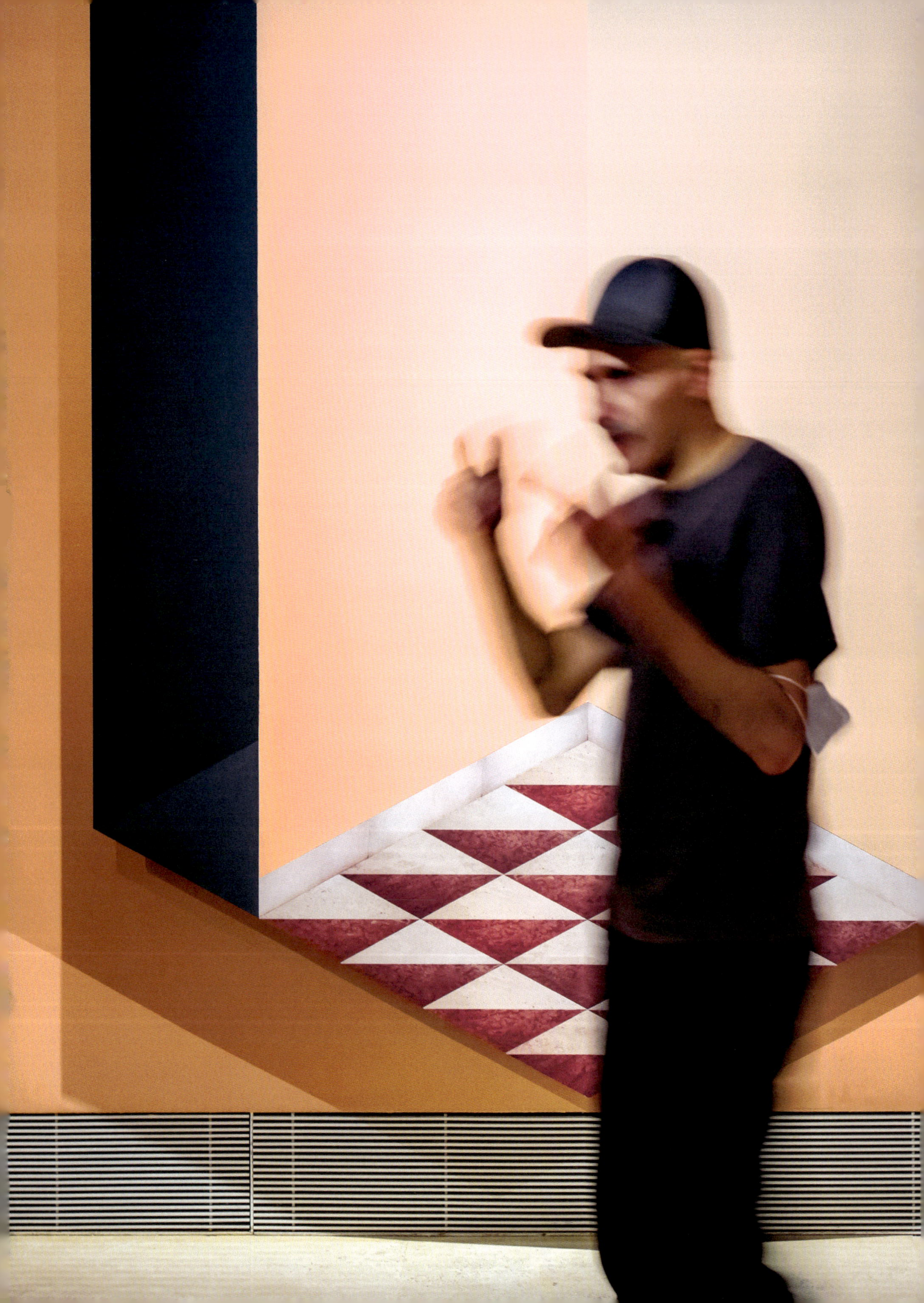

Antonova worked for Hans Heinrich Thyssen-Bornemisza for another seven years, and when she left him, the baron insisted on keeping the flat corner, and he is the one who sent it to Madrid.

I know that this angel story sounds like something I would make up, and I wish I did. But I did not. This story actually appeared in Antonova's biography. I have a copy of it downstairs and will show it to you a bit later. But do you know who else read and loved this story? Rafael Moneo. That's right, the Spanish architect who designed this museum. Moneo read Antonova's book sometime in the late 1980s, when he was just starting to design this building, and then he asked to see the flat corner. This is what inspired the colors of the walls in this museum, this weird peach or salmon color. It comes from Antonova's flat corner.

Alright. So now you know what has been consuming me for the past four years: a carpet that's heavier than its weight, images of clouds that appear out of nowhere, and a flat corner and Angel-Attractors. In a way, you could think of everything I will show next as my attempt to come to terms with these objects, as my attempt to get out of these tunnels relatively intact.

Let's go downstairs now. One floor down. Not that far. And we'll start again.

Frontispiece IIIa: The Peaces
Frontispiece IIIb: The Majors and the Minors

A completely new beginning about some coincidences that link me to Hans Heinrich Thyssen-Bornemisza in 1983, OK? I warned you that I will do this.

I was born in Beirut on June 15, 1967. June 1967, just few days after yet another Arab-Israeli war, the 1967 war. My mother, who was born in Palestine, definitely wanted me to be born on June 15. Why? Because my father's birthday is the 15th of June. So, they did what they had to do, and I have the same birthday as my father.

But there was one birthday that I just hoped would never come. It was my sixteenth birthday. I just did not want to turn sixteen because I knew that as soon as that happened, I would get a very unwelcome knock on the door. Just as expected, on my sixteenth birthday, on June 15, 1983, the fascist militia that controlled where I lived in Beirut came knocking. They were recruiting by force all boys aged sixteen and above into their right-wing, Israeli-funded, Christian military machine. And there was no way I was going to fight for these idiots. So when they came knocking, I hid in a closet, and when they left, my father gave me $500 and a few weeks later, I was on a cargo boat to Cyprus. From Cyprus, I found my way to America.

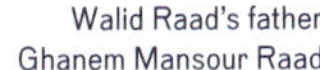
Walid Raad's father
Ghanem Mansour Raad

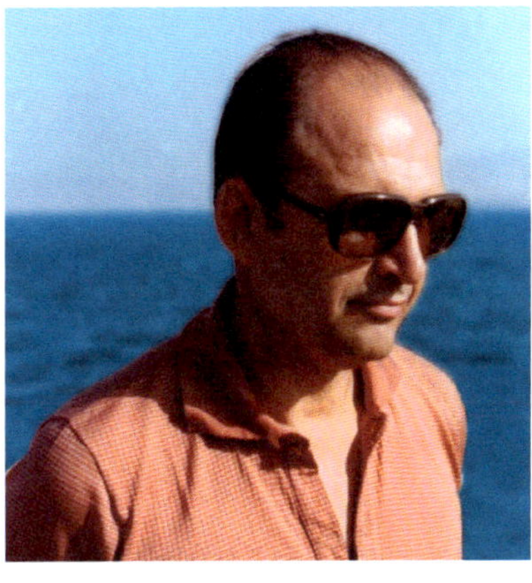

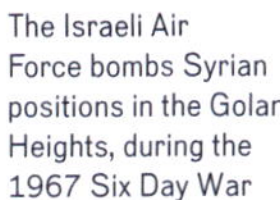
The Israeli Air Force bombs Syrian positions in the Golan Heights, during the 1967 Six Day War

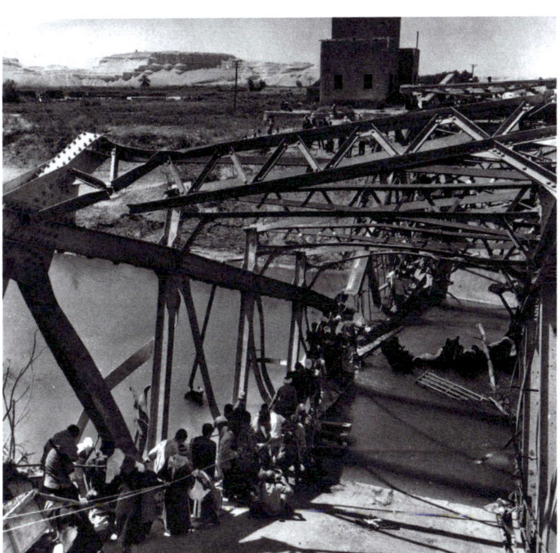

Walid Raad's mother
Vera Khalil Saade

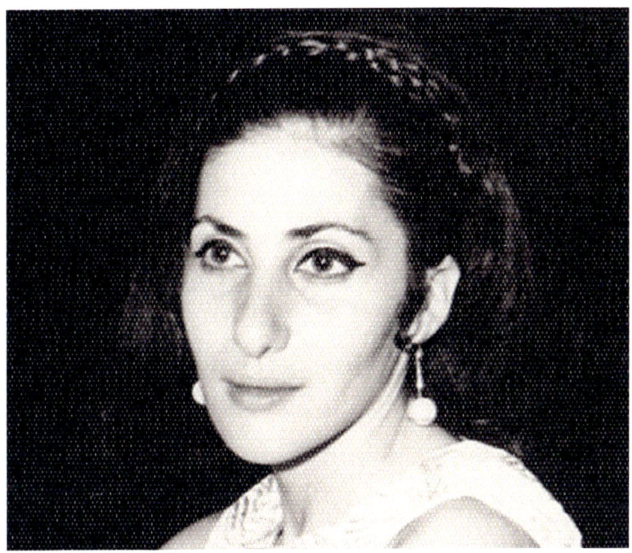

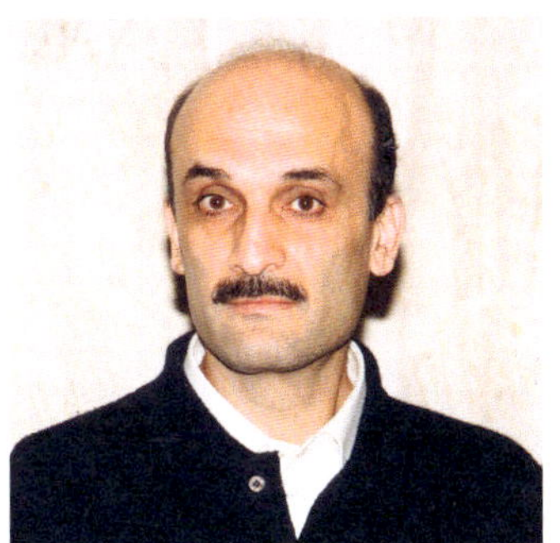

Arab refugees from the Israeli-occupied West Bank move across the damaged Allenby Bridge near Jericho, June 15, 1967. Thousands of Arab refugees are fleeing the West Bank into Jordan

Samir Geagea

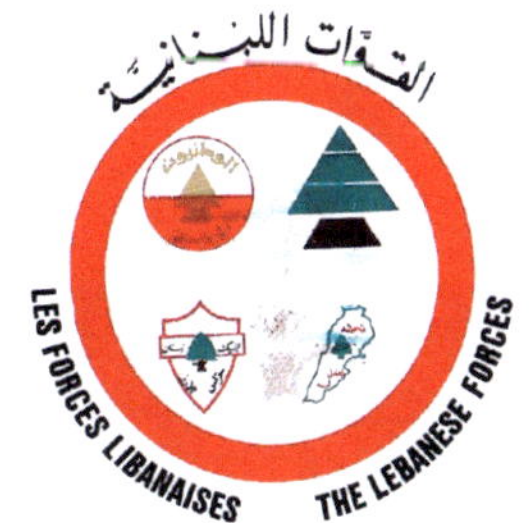

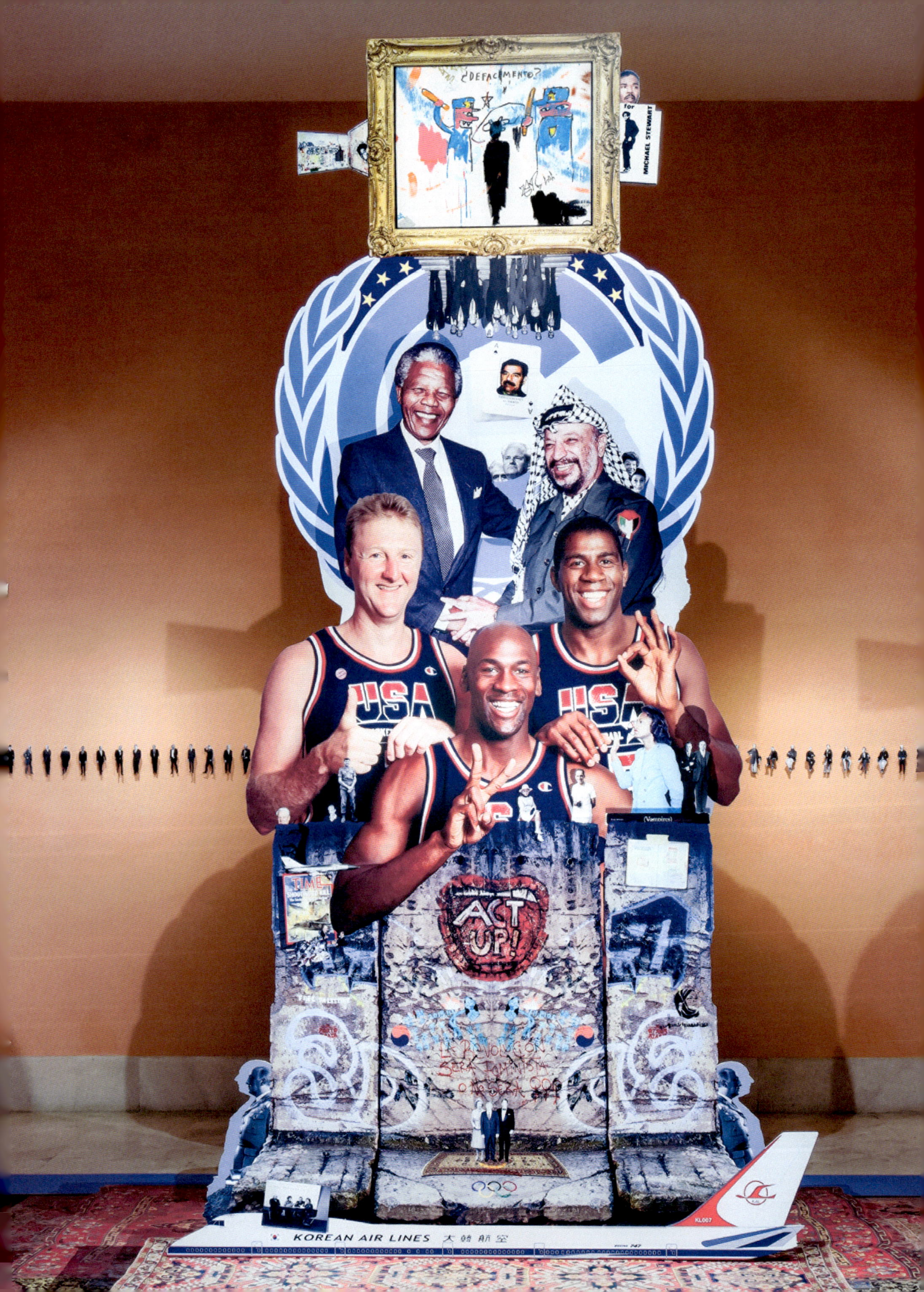
¿DEFACEMENTO?
for
MICHAEL STEWART
USA
USA
ACT UP!
TIME
(Vampires)
KOREAN AIR LINES 大韓航空

I emigrated from Lebanon on September 1, 1983. On that day, and as I was getting on the cargo boat to leave Lebanon for good, on the other side of my world, Soviet pilots shot down a Korean civilian plane, KAL 007. The plane was on its way from America to Korea, but a pilot error deviated the plane into Soviet airspace. The Soviets were convinced this was an American spy plane, and sent their MiGs to intercept, but for some reason the Soviet pilots ended up firing their missiles. Two-hundred and sixty-nine people died immediately. Not a single body was ever recovered, only some shoes. For years thereafter, and despite all evidence to the contrary, the Soviets insisted that they shot an American spy plane. Typical Cold War stuff, I suppose.

<
Walid Raad
Frontispiece IIIa: The Peaces, 2021
Frontispiece IIIb: The Majors and Minors, 2021
Installation view, Museo Nacional
Thyssen-Bornemisza, Madrid, 2021

As I was leaving Lebanon, and at the same moment when the Soviets shot down the Korean plane, Hans Heinrich Thyssen-Bornemisza was flying to Moscow for an exhibition of his paintings in a beautiful museum in Moscow, the Pushkin Museum. This exhibition was all part of an idea cooked up by Hans Heinrich Thyssen-Bornemisza and a Soviet ambassador in Germany. The idea was that the baron's old masters will go to Moscow in exchange for never-before-seen, fantastic Impressionist paintings from the Soviet Union going to the West for the first time. Keep in mind that this was 1983, the Cold War was in full swing, and any East-West exchange was a big deal. The baron landed in Moscow at this tense moment, with the shooting down of the Korean plane, and I am told that he did not keep his mouth shut about this. I am told that he even spoke his mind on live TV, to the displeasure of his Soviet hosts. I am surprised they did not kick him out the next day.

Again, I leave Lebanon on the same day as the Korean plane is shot down, on the same day that Hans Heinrich Thyssen-Bornemisza arrives in Moscow. But I don't arrive in America until two weeks later, on September15, 1983. I arrived in New York City very late at night. I was sixteen. I was by myself. I'd never been to the US. I was scared.

As I was beginning my new life in America on September 15, 1983, a young African American artist's life was ending in New York City. Michael Stewart was at that very moment being beaten to death by two cops in Downtown Manhattan. I learn about this as soon as I land in NYC, as my hosts were Stewart's neighbors. I remember them crying and crying when they picked me up at the airport. They were just besides themselves with anger and grief.

Now, I'd like to move from 1983 to 1992 Spain.

1992 was a very big year for Spain, and not only because this museum opened its doors. I can even say that 1992 had been on the Spanish calendar since 1986, when Barcelona was selected to host the 1992 Summer Olympics. But the selection of Barcelona was made in a pre-1989 world, pre-Berlin Wall. By 1992, the world had changed dramatically: Germany was reunited. "Post-apartheid" South Africa was back in the Olympics. Yugoslavia? Gone. The Soviet Union? Gone. The world had just gone through Operation Desert Storm, the First Gulf War, and after the war, Arabs and Israelis came here to the 1991 Madrid Peace Conference. And a month after the opening of this museum, Russia handed over the black box of the Korean plane they shot down in 1983 to South Korea and the US. In other words, it seemed that the Cold War was over. That was 1992.

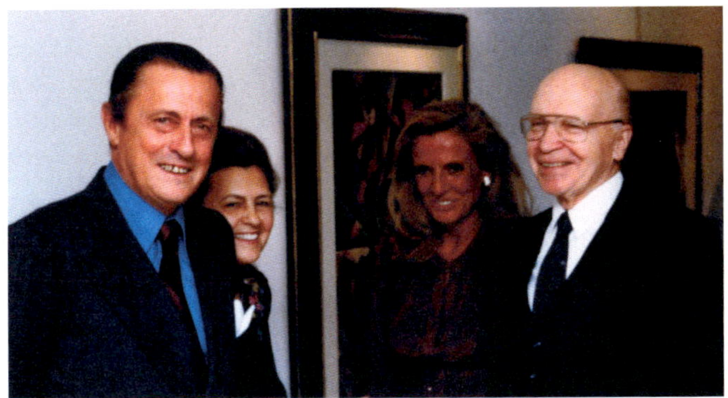

Hans Heinrich Thyssen-Bornemizsa, Antonina Gmurzynska, Soviet ambassador Vladimir Semyonov, Cologne, 1981

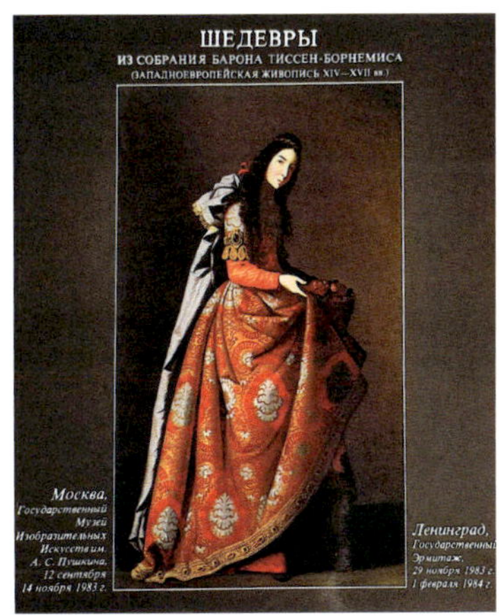

Book cover of the exhibition catalogue *Old Masters Paintings from the Thyssen-Bornemisza Collection*, Pushkin Museum, Moscow, 1983

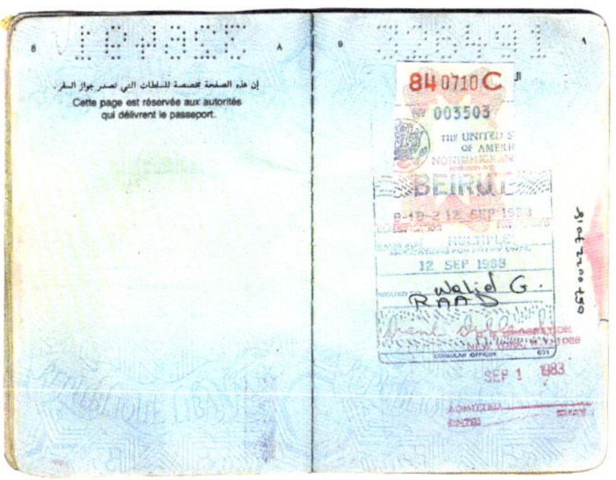

Walid Raad's Lebanese passport, validated on September 15, 1983

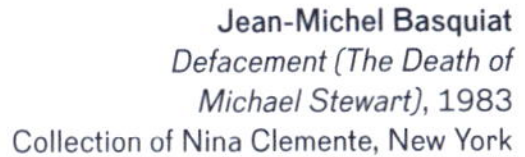

Jean-Michel Basquiat
Defacement (The Death of Michael Stewart), 1983
Collection of Nina Clemente, New York

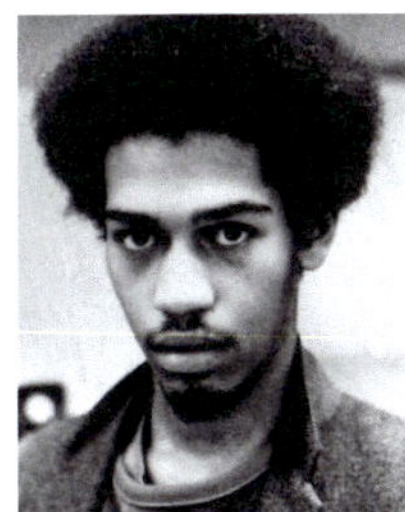

Michael Stewart

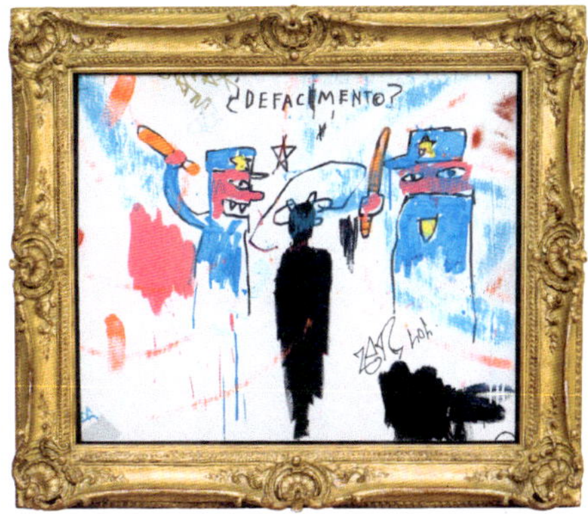

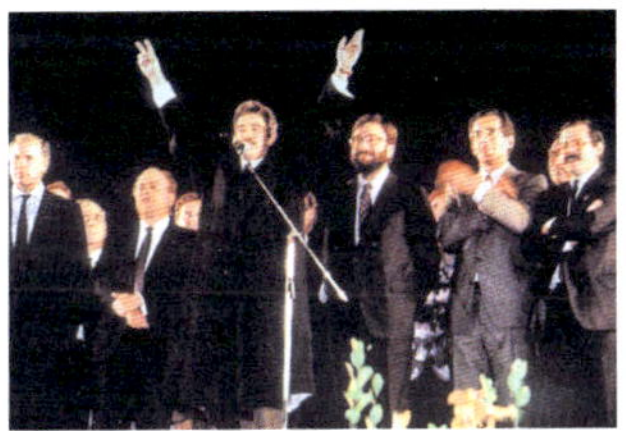

Barcelona selected to host the 1992 Summer Olympics, Lausanne, 1986

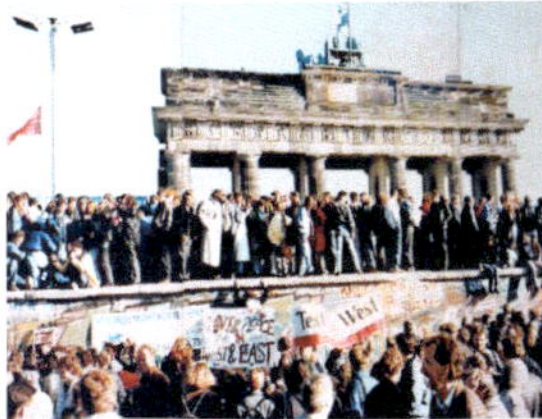

The fall of the Berlin Wall, 1989

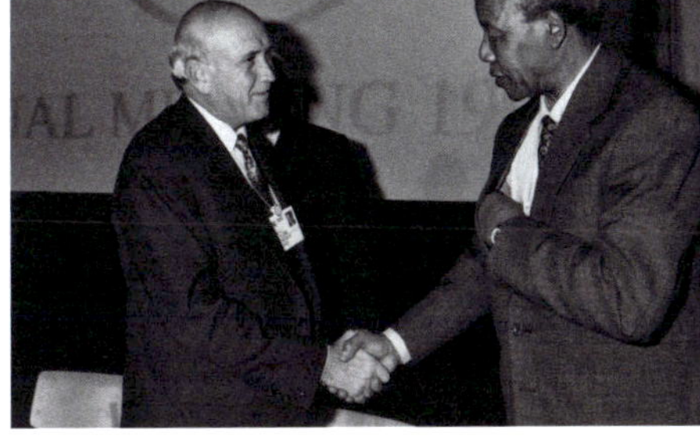

Frederik Willem de Klerk and Nelson Mandela, Davos, 1992

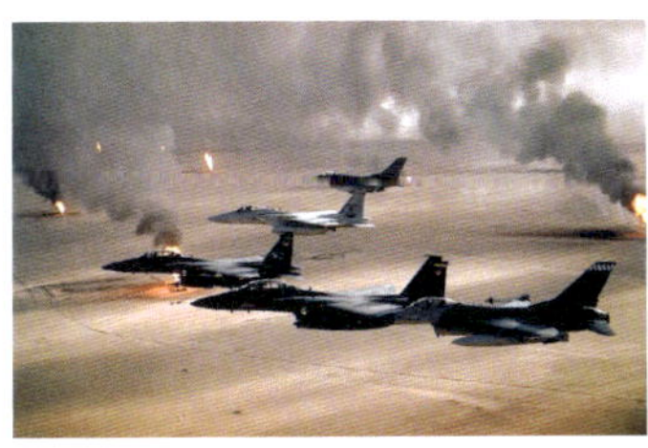

USAF aircrafts fly over retreating Iraqi forces in Kuwait during Operation Desert Storm, 1991

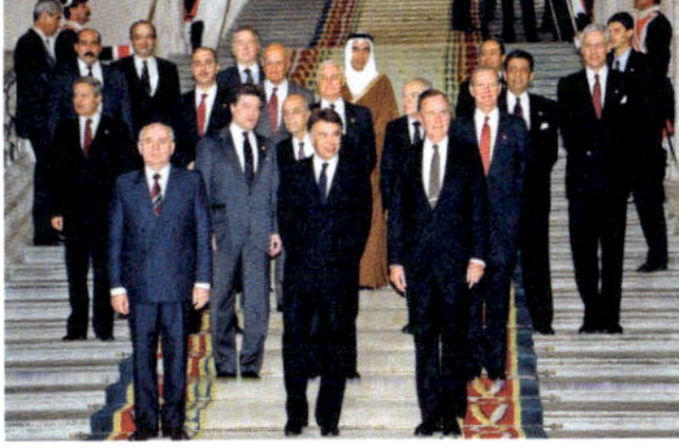

The Madrid Peace Conference, Palacio Real, Madrid, October 30, 1991. From left front: Soviet President Mikhail Gorbachev, Spanish Premier Felipe González and US President George H. W. Bush

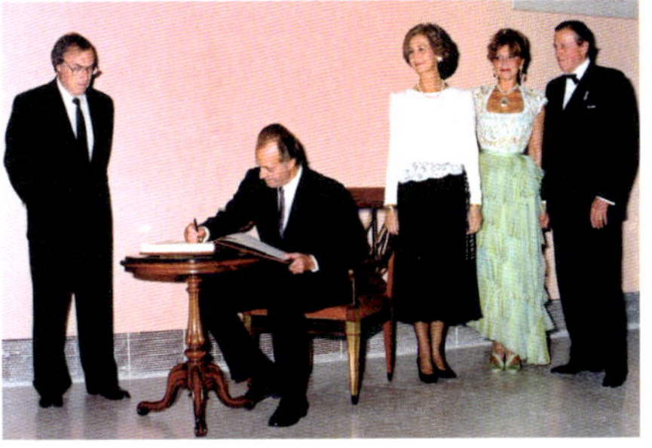

Inauguration of the Museo Thyssen-Bornemisza, October 8, 1992, Madrid. From left to right: Spanish Minister of the Culture Jordi Solé Tura, King Juan Carlos I and Queen Sofía, Baroness Carmen and Baron Hans Heinrich Thyssen-Bornemisza

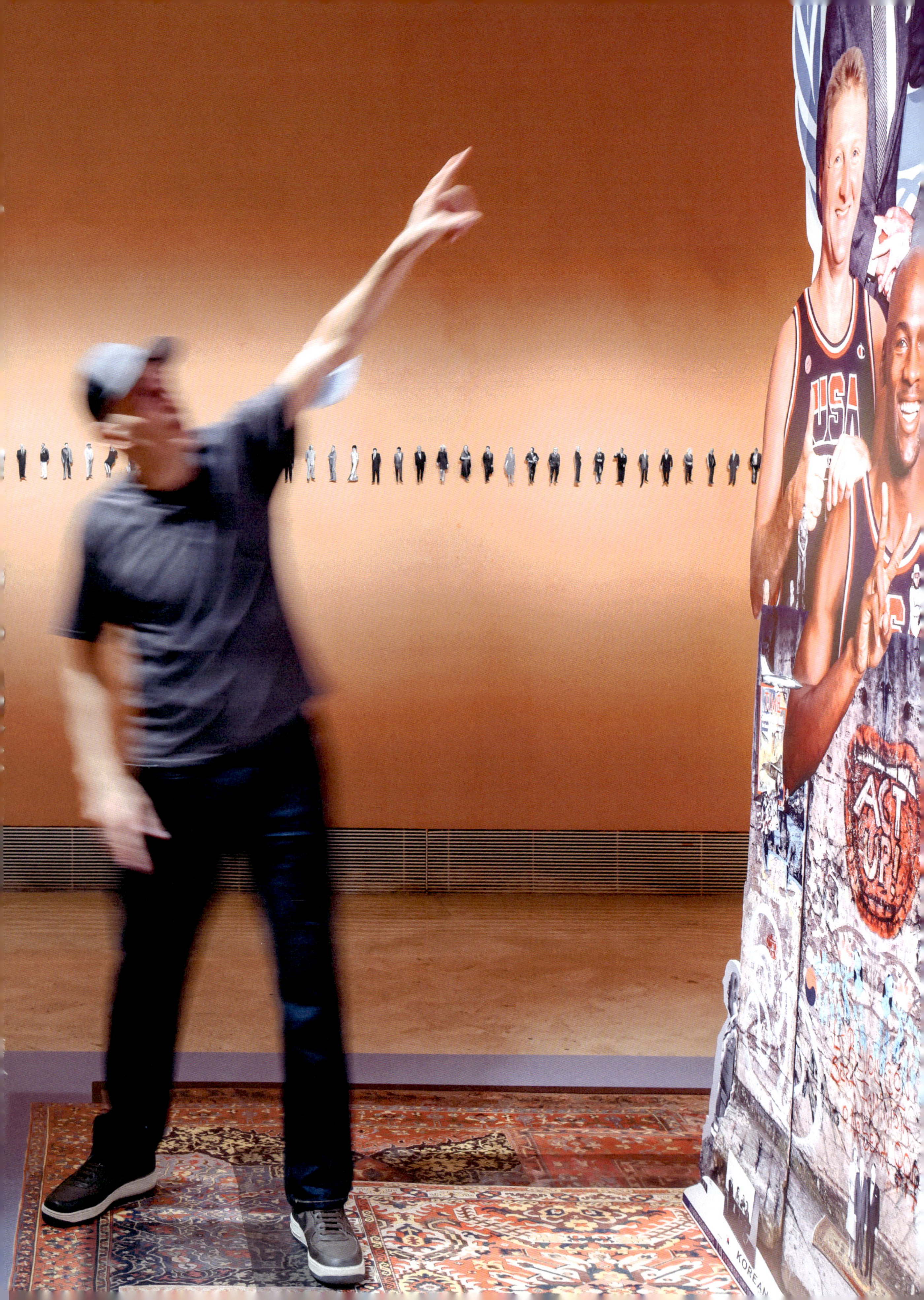
USA
ACT UP!

Gilbert Stuart
George Washington, c. 1795
The Metropolitan Museum of Art, New York

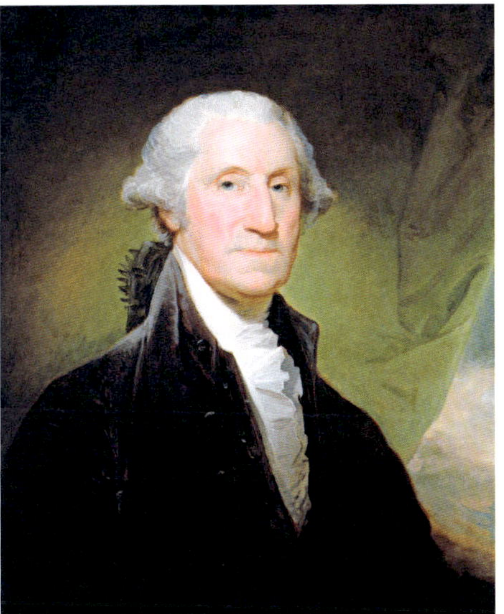

Sarah Goodridge
Gilbert Stuart, c. 1825
National Portrait Gallery, Smithsonian Institution, Washington, DC

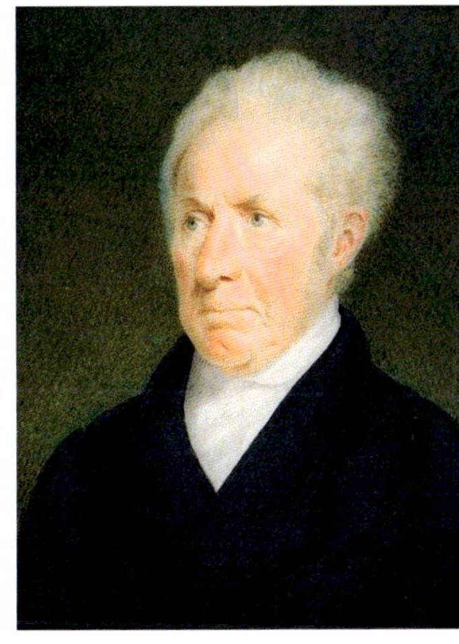

Unknown artist
Portrait of a man, c. 1770–1780
Museo Nacional Thyssen-Bornemisza, Madrid

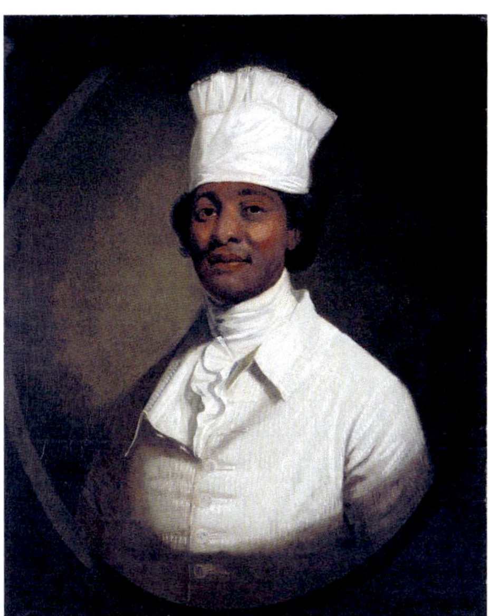

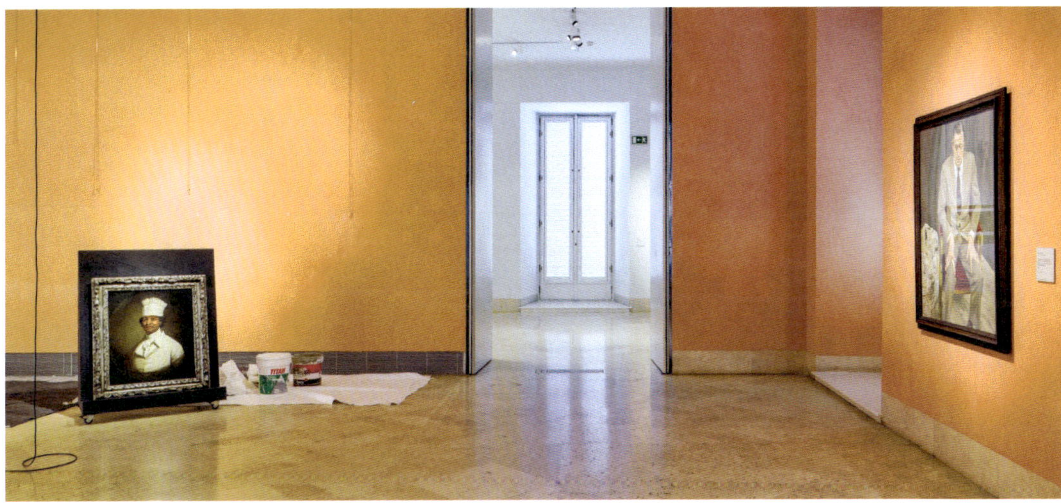

Walid Raad
Frontispiece IV: The Hangs, 2021
Installation view, Museo Nacional Thyssen-Bornemisza, Madrid, 2021

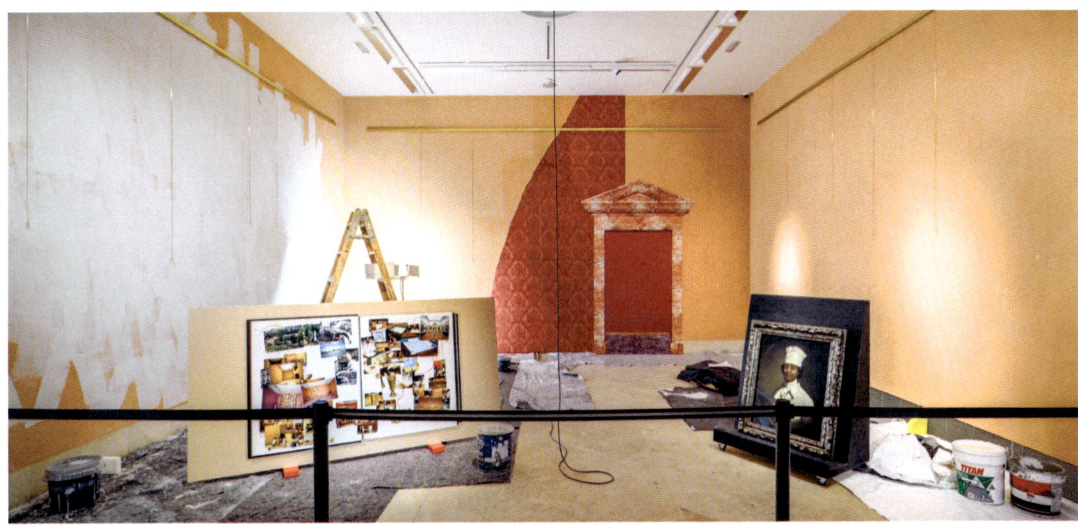

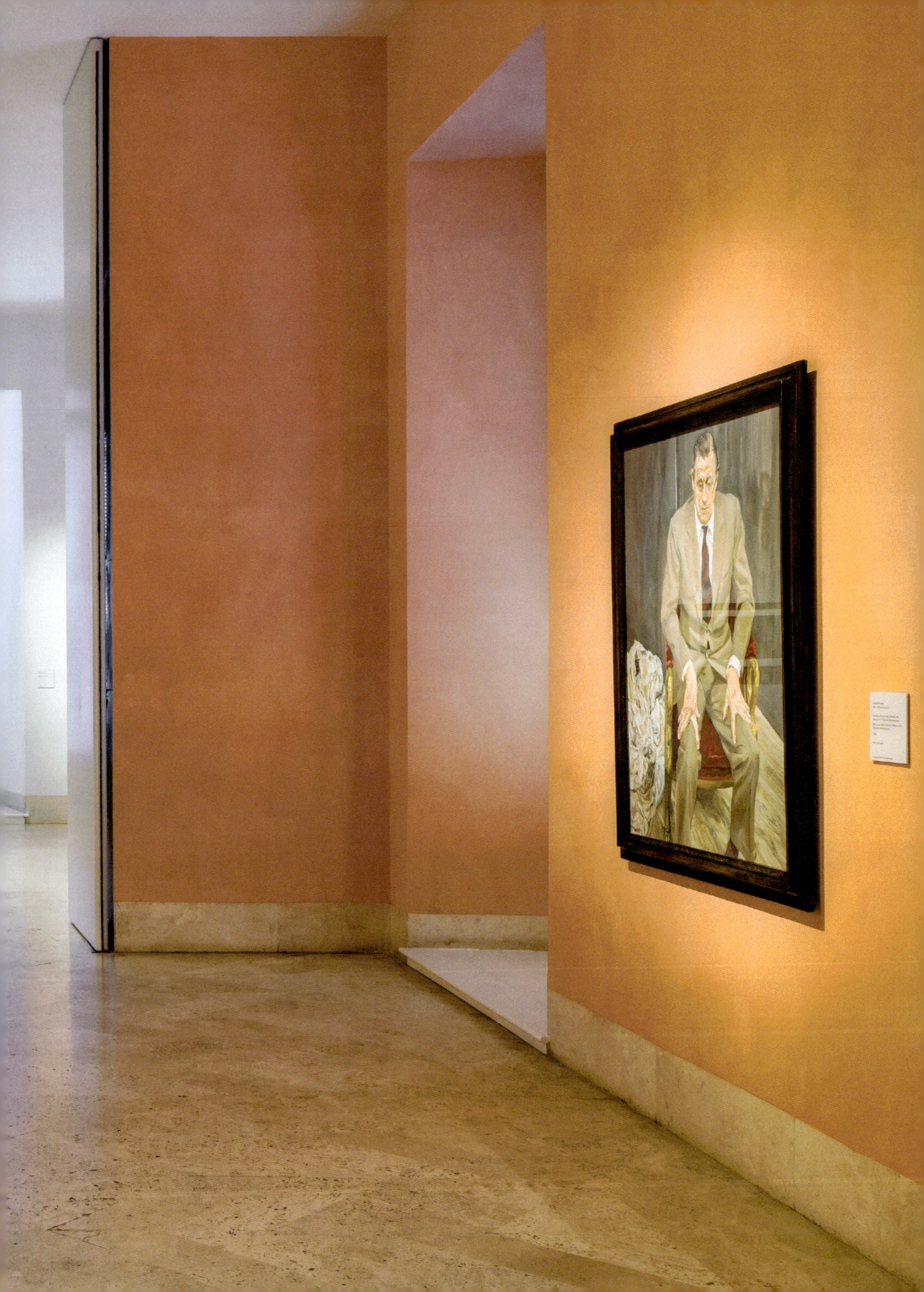

Actually, look at this. See it? The portrait on the rack over there? I can't believe it's here. For over 200 years, this portrait was thought to have been painted by an artist named Gilbert Stuart, one of the best eighteenth-century American artists. The man in the painting was thought to be someone named Hercules Posey. Hercules was George Washington's cook, his enslaved cook. Washington is said to have had 317 enslaved people. The American president loved Hercules's cooking, but Hercules did not love Washington as much as he loved his freedom. So Hercules ran away in 1797, and for years, Washington tried to find and bring him back to his estate.

The interesting point here is that three years ago, and after 200 years of everyone thinking this was Hercules, it was discovered that this is not Hercules. We don't actually know who this person is. And the painting is not by Stuart, either. And we don't know who the painter is either. Anyway, I don't know why this portrait is in this room, and I have no idea what's going on with this creepy and quite disturbing hanging system. This room has been like this for quite some time now.

OK, let's proceed. I want to show you three paintings from the Carmen Thyssen collection. Remember the baroness? Hans Heinrich Thyssen-Bornemisza's fifth wife?

Carmen Thyssen Collection: Eastman Johnson and Martin Johnson Heade

Upstairs, I mentioned that the baron sold 775 artworks to Spain in 1993. Well, that was half of his collection. The other half? It was divided between his wife at the time, the Baroness Carmen Thyssen-Bornemisza and her son, and the other four children.

Carmen Thyssen-Bornemisza inherited around 400 paintings from Hans Heinrich Thyssen-Bornemisza. Some are in the museum—not part of the national collection, but in the museum. The baroness and her son Borja rent them to the museum for around $6 million or something like that. And I want to show you four paintings in her collection.

Take a look at this painting over here. It's a very small painting by an American artist named Eastman Johnson. It is a simple scene about the making of maple syrup, what we Americans put on pancakes. I want you to look at it closely because I will talk about it later.

And over here, I want to show you these two landscapes by another American artist named Martin Johnson Heade. Nice little landscapes. Monet-like but before Monet. Heade is known for painting marsh and swamp scenes, and hummingbirds like in this other painting here. He painted over 120 of these between the 1860s and 1890s. What fascinates me about Heade is that he also assumed a pen name, Didymus, which means twin or double in Greek. And remarkably, Heade made two exact copies of every painting he ever painted: twin paintings, he called them. The baron loved Heade for this, so much so that he tried to acquire the twin copies of every Heade painting he wanted to buy. And here he succeeded. He gave one copy of each to the baroness and that's why they are in this room. The other copies were inherited by Francesca, and they are downstairs.

OK, now let's go downstairs. Follow me.

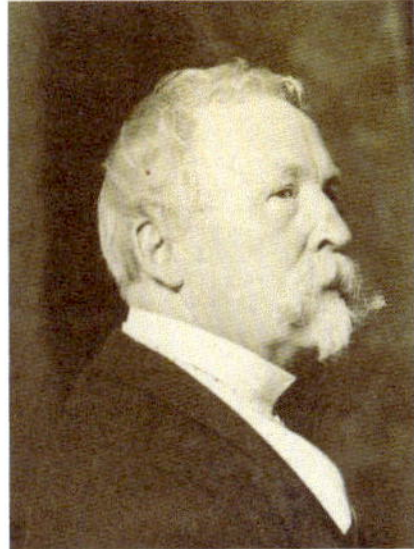

Eastman Johnson, 1890s

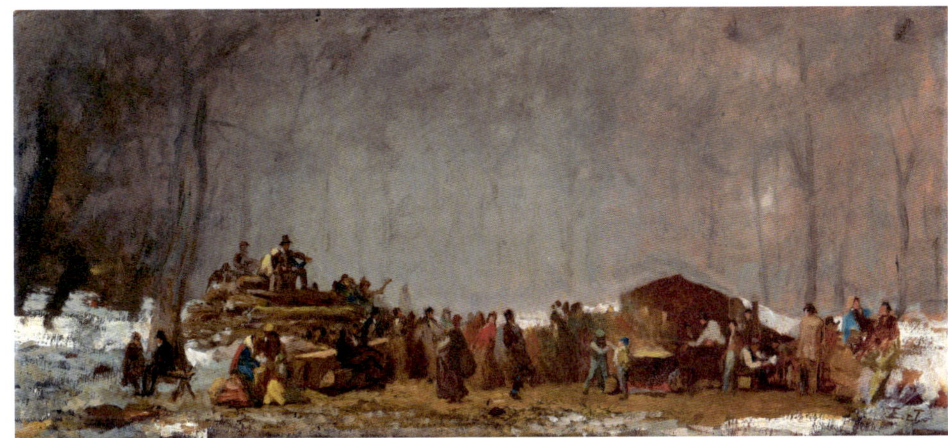

Eastman Johnson, *The Maple Sugar Camp-Turning Off*, c. 1865–1873
Colección Carmen Thyssen

Martin Johnson Heade
Jersey Marshes, 1874
Colección Carmen Thyssen

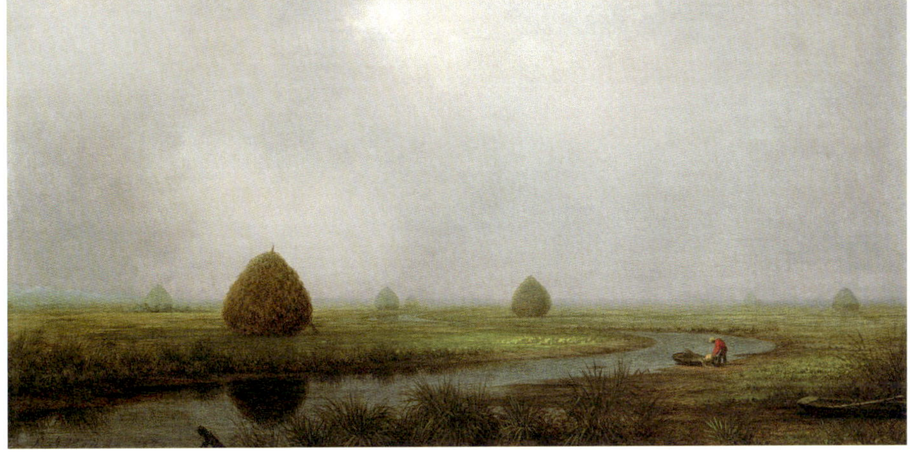

Martin Johnson Heade

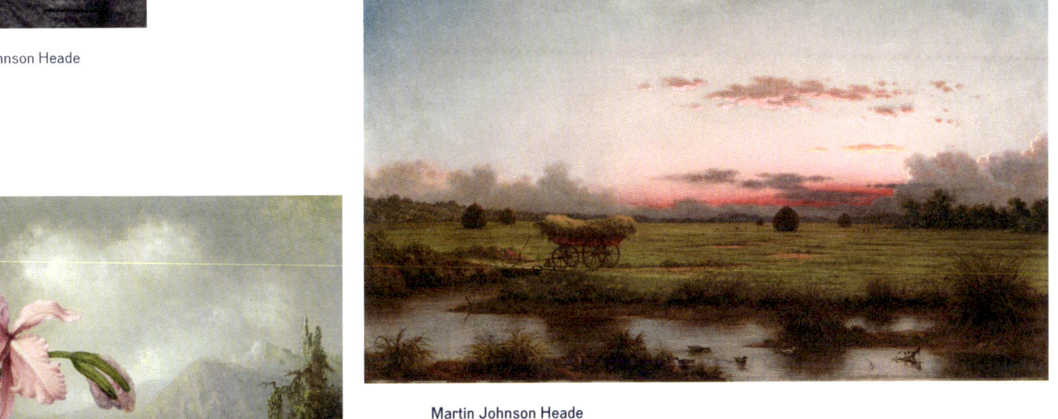

Martin Johnson Heade
The Marshes at Rhode Island, 1866
Colección Carmen Thyssen

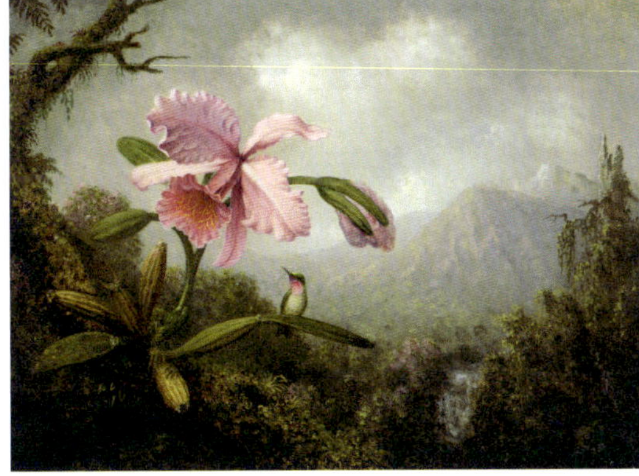

Martin Johnson Heade
Orchid and Hummingbird near a Waterfall, 1902
Colección Carmen Thyssen

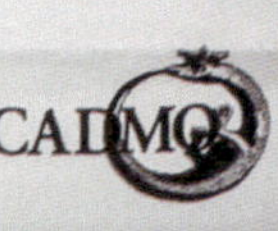
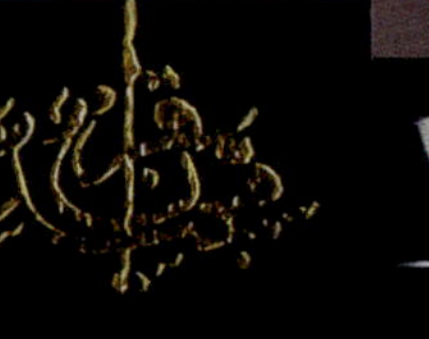
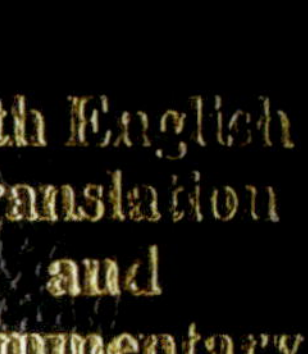
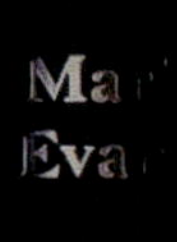
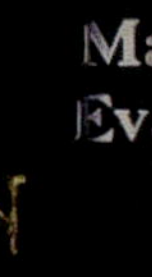
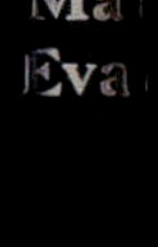
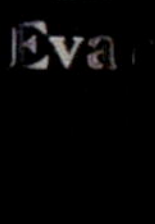
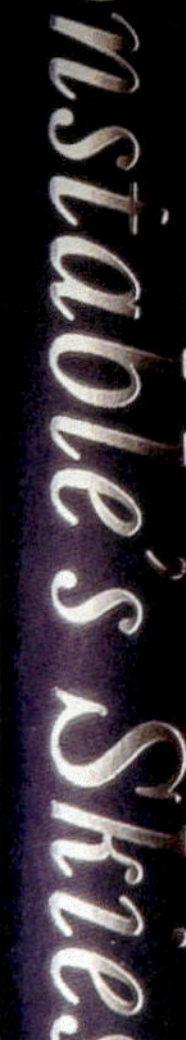
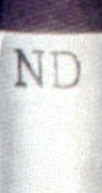
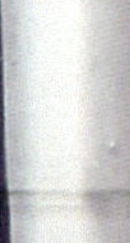
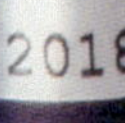
LAMIA ANTONOVA
MASTERPIECES
CADMOS
THE AUCTIONEER
SIMON DE PURY
AND WILLIAM STADIEM
ST. MARTIN'S PRESS
A CRIME IN THE FAMILY
SACHA BATTHYANY
Quercus
KING JAMES VERSION
HOLY QUR'ĀN
with English Translation and Commentary
Maulana Muhammad Ali
V&A
Constable's Skies
ND
2018
annunciation
Jalal Toufic · 'Āshūrā': The Blood Spilled in My Veins
LAPSES / *2
JALAL TOUFIC

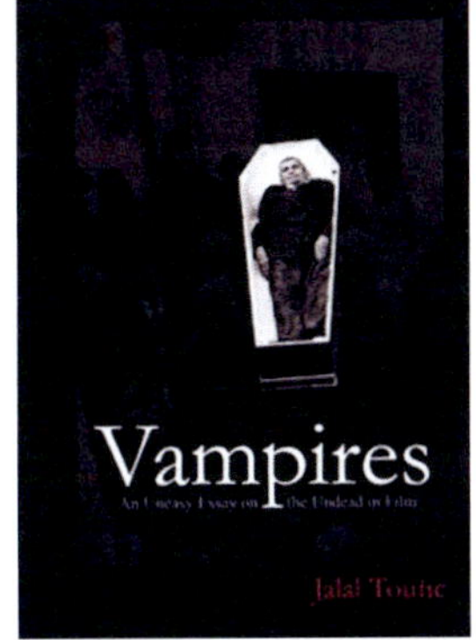

Jalal Toufic
(Vampires): An Uneasy Essay on the Undead,
(Sausalito, CA: Post-Apollo Press, 2003)

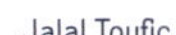
Jalal Toufic

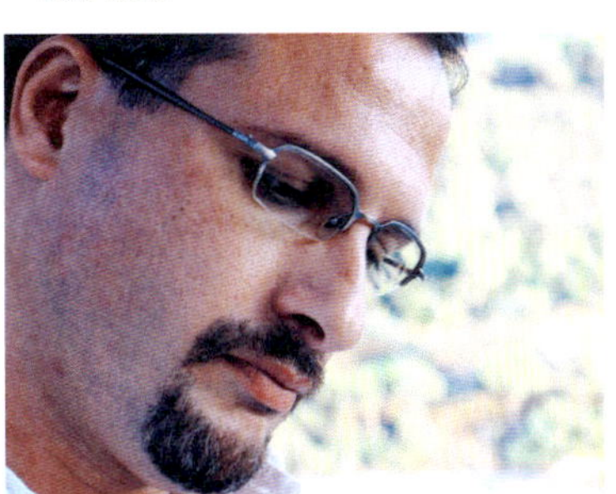

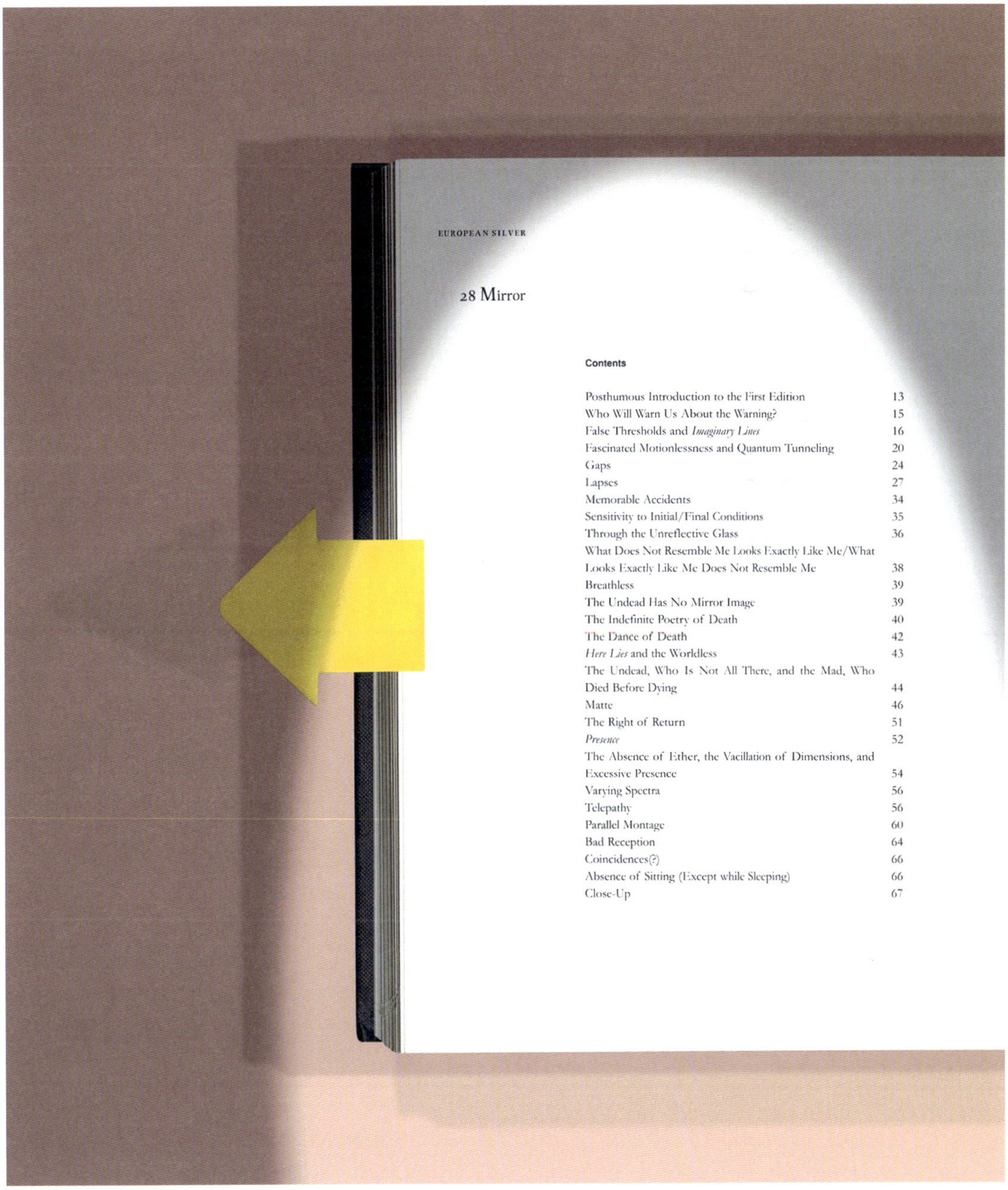

EUROPEAN SILVER

28 Mirror

Contents

Walid Raad
Frontispiece VI: The Spreads,
2021, detail

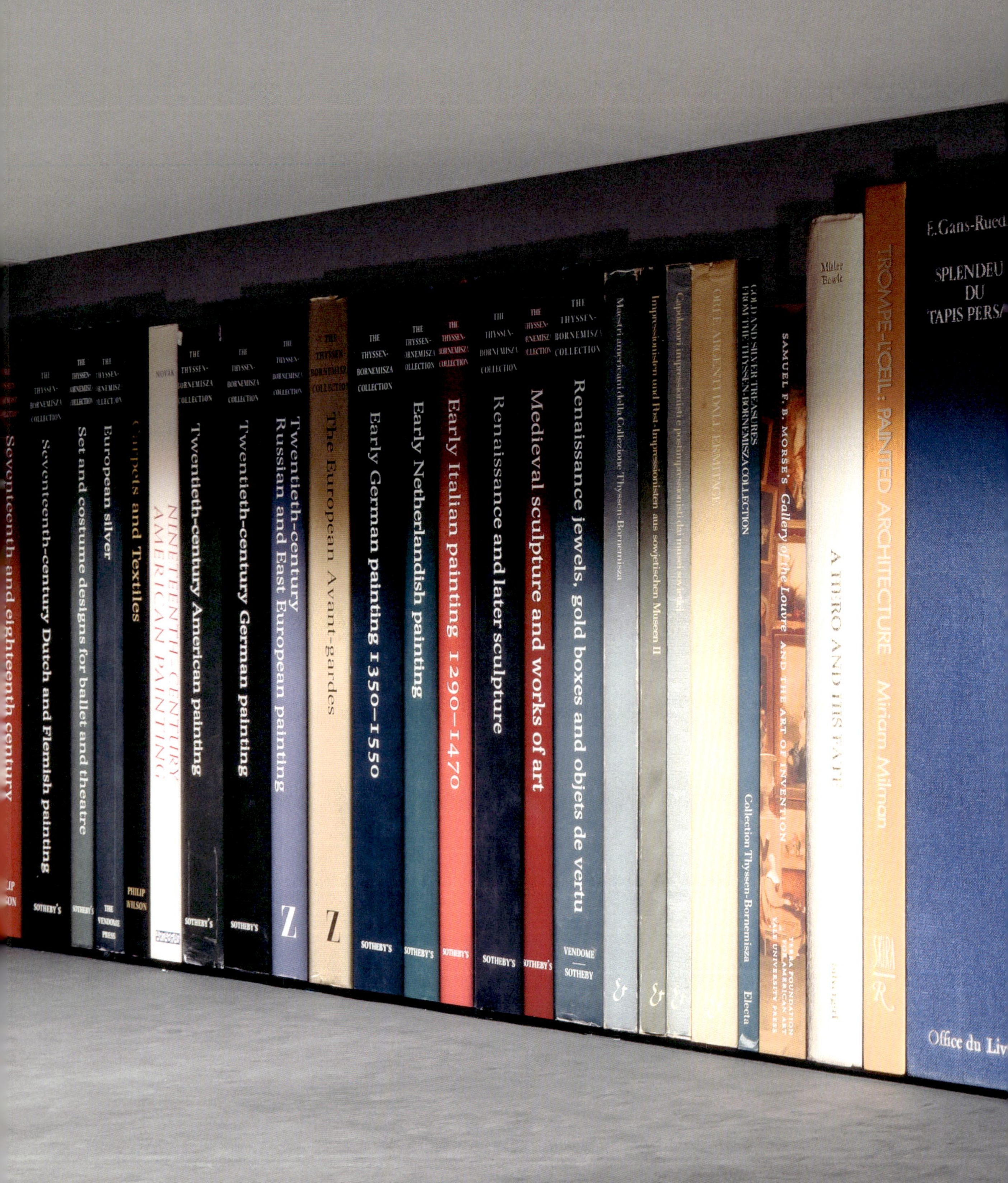
Seventeenth and eighteenth century
THE THYSSEN-BORNEMISZA COLLECTION
Seventeenth-century Dutch and Flemish painting
SOTHEBY'S
Set and costume designs for ballet and theatre
SOTHEBY'S
European silver
THE VENDOME PRESS
Carpets and Textiles
PHILIP WILSON
NOVAK
NINETEENTH-CENTURY AMERICAN PAINTING
THE THYSSEN-BORNEMISZA COLLECTION
Twentieth-century American painting
SOTHEBY'S
THE THYSSEN-BORNEMISZA COLLECTION
Twentieth-century German painting
SOTHEBY'S
Twentieth-century Russian and East European painting
Z
THE THYSSEN-BORNEMISZA COLLECTION
The European Avant-gardes
Z
THE THYSSEN-BORNEMISZA COLLECTION
Early German painting 1350–1550
SOTHEBY'S
THE THYSSEN-BORNEMISZA COLLECTION
Early Netherlandish painting
SOTHEBY'S
THE THYSSEN-BORNEMISZA COLLECTION
Early Italian painting 1290–1470
SOTHEBY'S
THE THYSSEN-BORNEMISZA COLLECTION
Renaissance and later sculpture
SOTHEBY'S
THE THYSSEN-BORNEMISZA COLLECTION
Medieval sculpture and works of art
SOTHEBY'S
THE THYSSEN-BORNEMISZA COLLECTION
Renaissance jewels, gold boxes and objets de vertu
VENDOME / SOTHEBY
Maestri americani della Collezione Thyssen-Bornemisza
Impressionisten und Post-Impressionisten aus sowjetischen Museen II
GOLD AND SILVER TREASURES FROM THE THYSSEN-BORNEMISZA COLLECTION
Collection Thyssen-Bornemisza
Electa
SAMUEL F. B. MORSE'S Gallery of the Louvre AND THE ART OF INVENTION
A HERO AND HIS FATE
TROMPE-L'OEIL : PAINTED ARCHITECTURE
Miriam Milman
SKIRA

Vampires Werewolves & Demons

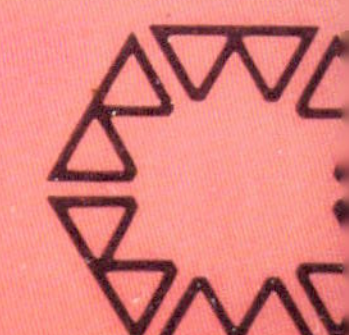

RAINER MARIA RILKE
Duino Elegies & The Sonnets to Orpheus

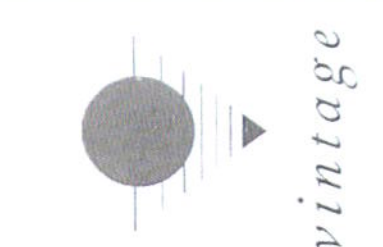

vintage

Edited and Transl
STEPHE
MITCHE

ARIÈS
HOUR OF OUR DEATH

Jalal Toufic Postscripts

e-flux journal Jalal Toufic Forthcoming
Second edition

Over-Sensitivity · Jalal Toufic

SUN & MOON
CLASSICS
119

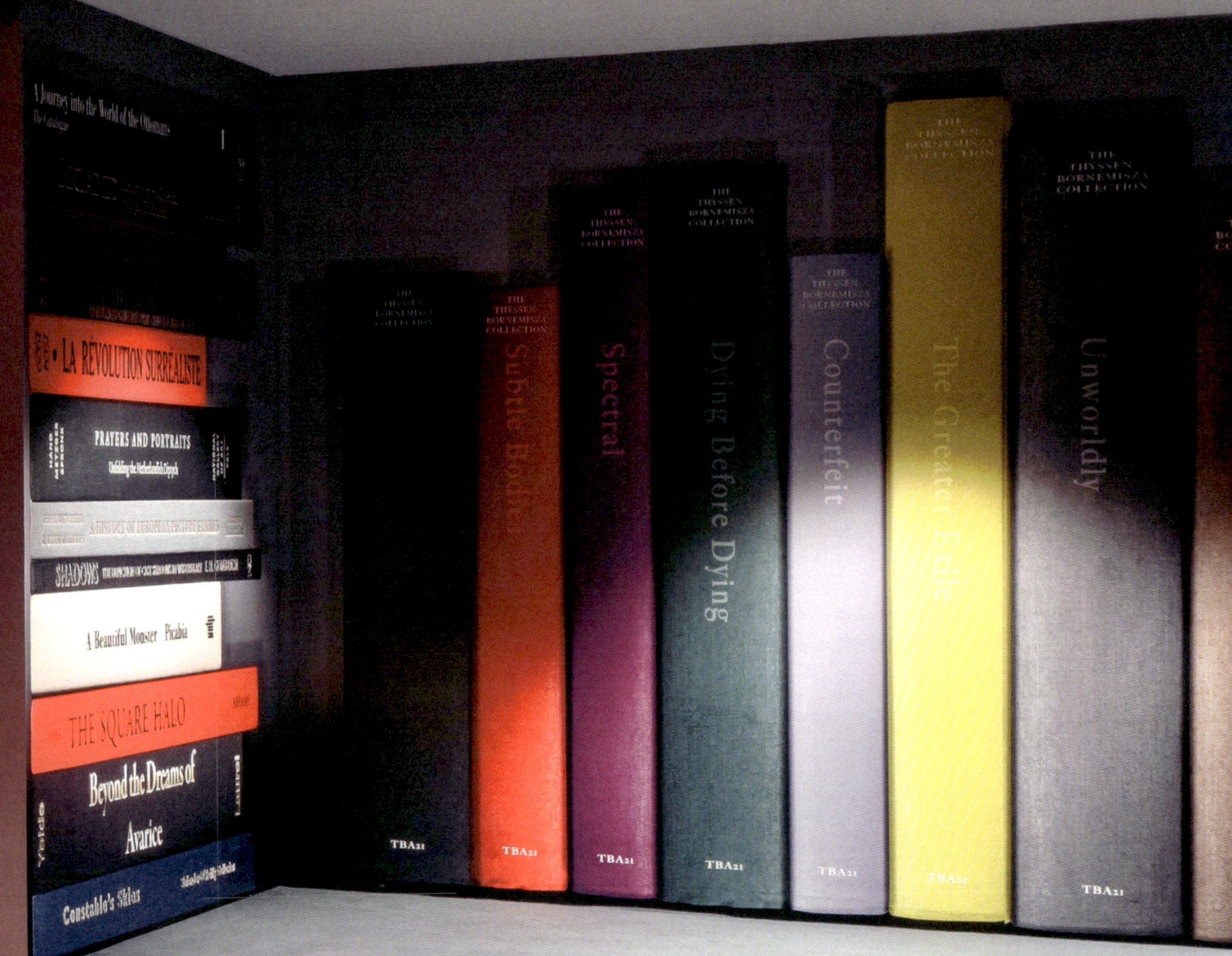
A Journey into the World of the Ottomans
LA RÉVOLUTION SURRÉALISTE
PRAYERS AND PORTRAITS
SHADOWS
A Beautiful Monster Picabia
THE SQUARE HALO
Beyond the Dreams of Avarice
Constable's Skies
THE THYSSEN BORNEMISZA COLLECTION
Subtle Bodies
Spectral
Dying Before Dying
Counterfeit
The Greater Evil
Unworldly
TBA21

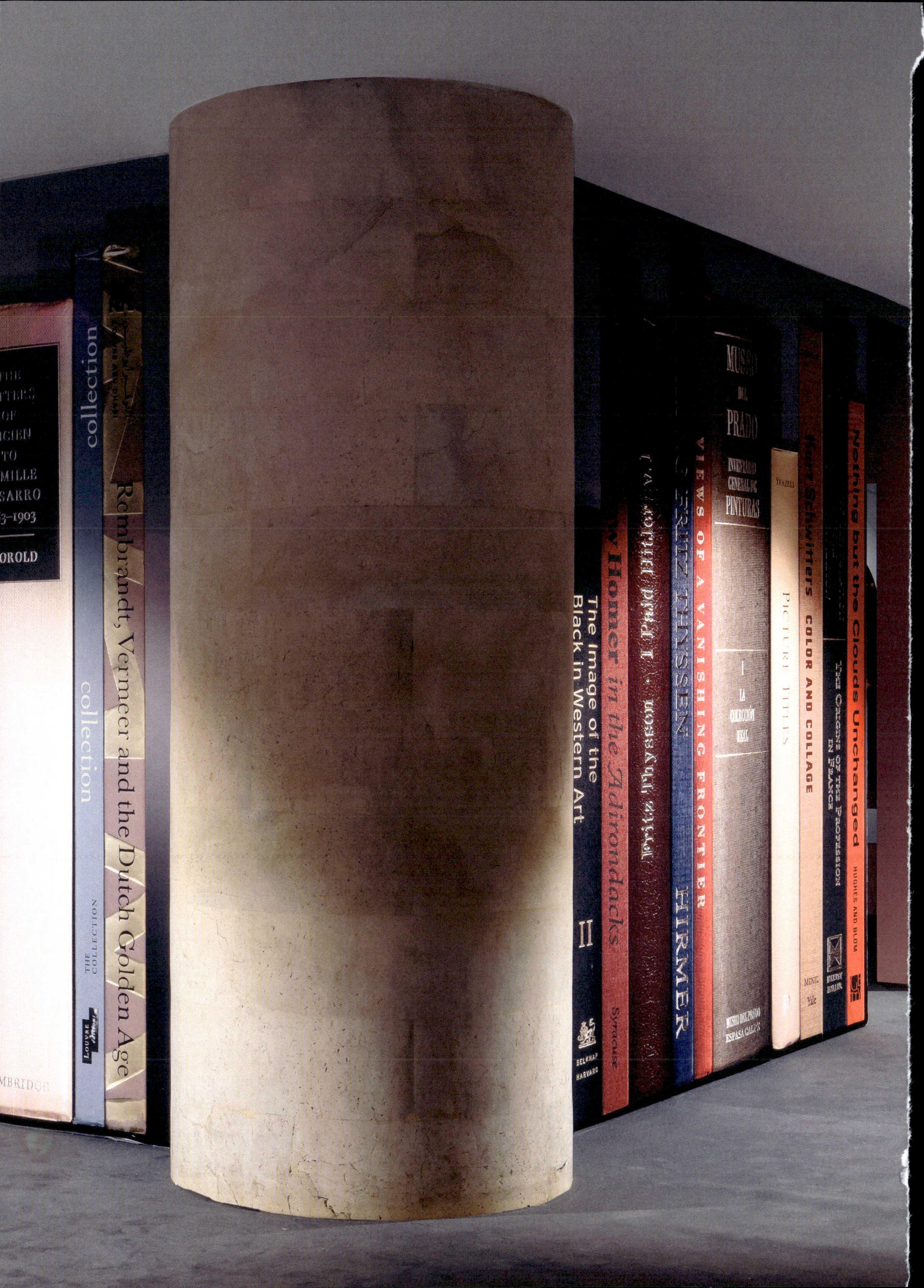

THE LETTERS OF LUCIEN TO CAMILLE PISSARRO 1883–1903
THOROLD
collection
collection
THE COLLECTION
LOUVRE
Rembrandt, Vermeer and the Dutch Golden Age
The Image of the Black in Western Art
II
BELKNAP HARVARD
Homer in the Adirondacks
Syracuse
THYSSEN
HIRMER
VIEWS OF A VANISHING FRONTIER
MUSEO DEL PRADO
INVENTARIO GENERAL DE PINTURAS
I
LA COLECCIÓN REAL
MUSEO DEL PRADO
ESPASA CALPE
PICTURE TITLES
Kurt Schwitters
COLOR AND COLLAGE
MENIL
Yale
THE ORIGINS OF THE PROFESSION IN FRANCE
Nothing but the Clouds Unchanged
HUGHES AND BLOM

IBN AL'ARABI
THE BEZELS OF WISDOM
FRIEDRICH NIETZSCHE The Gay Science
TRANSLATED, WITH COMMENTARY, BY WALTER KAUFMANN
DOSTOYEVSKY Notes from Undergroun
The Double
POST-APOLLO
the Undead in Film
WHAT WERE YOU T
e-flux journal
Jalal Toufic
What

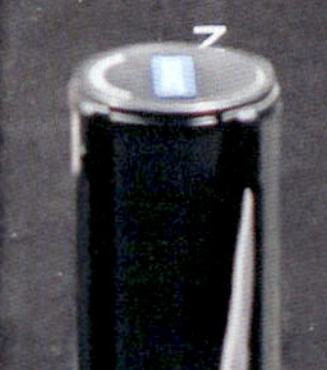

As an artist, when I create what feels to me like a strange image or story, I always find myself wondering whether I am receiving that image or story from this world or from another realm. Let's take the story I told you upstairs, my story about a carpet that is heavier than its weight. Is this story some kind of allegory about this world? Or did I receive this story from another "place"? How can I tell? Well, I have to check. How do I check? I check by examining first what is happening in this world: historically, ideologically, economically, scientifically. And that's what I was doing on the first floor in the Michael Jordan room when I talked about my leaving Lebanon in 1983, Hans Heinrich Thyssen-Bornemisza's visit to Moscow, the shooting of the Korean plane, and the killing of Michael Stewart. I was checking to see if these September 1983 coincidences that link me to Hans Heinrich Thyssen-Bornemisza add up to something that is more than the sum of its parts, something that is heavier than its weight, something that would make my carpet story the compressed and distorted expression of things happening in this world, a strange allegory about this world in 1983.

But, unfortunately for me, and maybe even for you, it turns out that the carpet story is much stranger than this allegory. Much, much stranger. And I am starting to fear that the carpet is literally heavier than its weight. Literally, not figuratively, literally heavier than its weight. And I really do not want to live in a place where carpets are heavier than their weight. Because that place scares the life out of me. So, I need to keep checking. Please follow me.

Frontispiece VI: The Spreads (Deer Hunting)

Did I already mention that this museum holds the largest collection of nineteenth-century American art in Europe? I don't think so, right? I must say that I found it strange that a man who collected Rubens and Caravaggio would, all of sudden, in the 1970s, decide to start buying nineteenth-century American art. I've lived in America for more than thirty years and never really looked at this tradition. But in the last three years, I really got sucked into artworks like this watercolor. It's by an artist named Winslow Homer. This looks like a quaint landscape with deer in the water and a dog here on the left side. But this watercolor is actually quite dark. It depicts a brutal hunting scene, where hunters and their dogs scare deer into the water. Deer can't swim, so they drown. It's actually a form of hunting in America called hunting by drowning.

Hans Heinrich Thyssen-Bornemisza bought this painting in 1980 from a man named Andrew Crispo. In fact, he bought 400 paintings from Crispo, who was known not only as a brilliant art dealer, but also for having a darker than dark side. It turned out that, like most of us, Crispo was living a double life. During the day, he was one of the most respected dealers of American art. But when the sun set, Crispo loved playing violent games with boys in leather. He also liked to take things to the edge, and one time, things went over the edge, and in the late 1980s he ended up being involved in the killing of one of his sex partners, Eigil Dag Vesti. Crispo was jailed, and for a long time, I thought that's what was meant by his darker than dark side because it does not get darker than murder. Well, it turns out that it can get darker. Much, much darker. And I discovered this because when Crispo went to jail, he was forced to sell his personal art collection, and this is when these two paintings came to light.

Look at these two paintings.

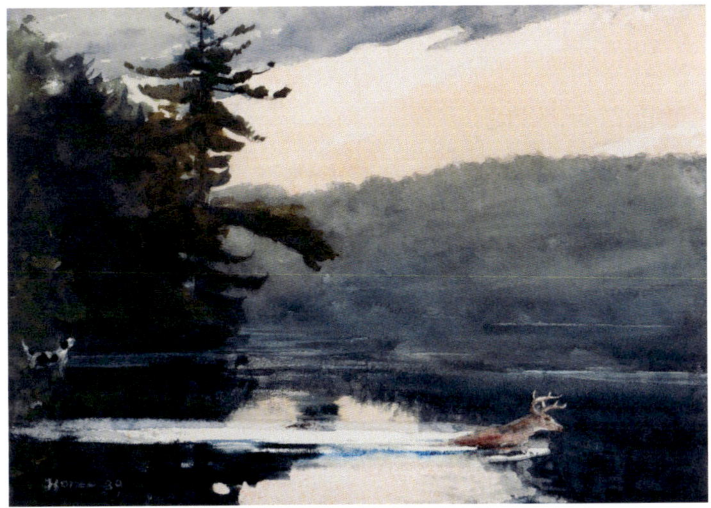

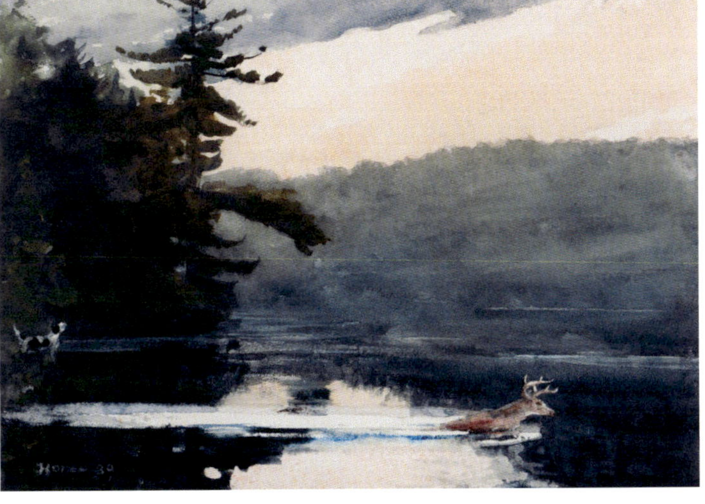

Winslow Homer, 1880

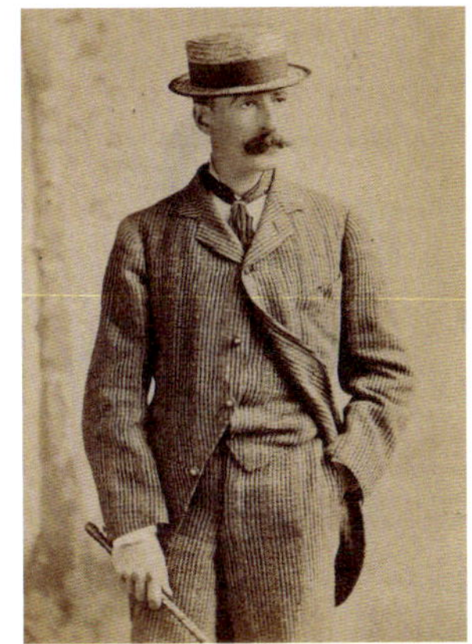

Winslow Homer
Deer in the Adirondacks, 1889
Museo Nacional Thyssen-Bornemisza, Madrid

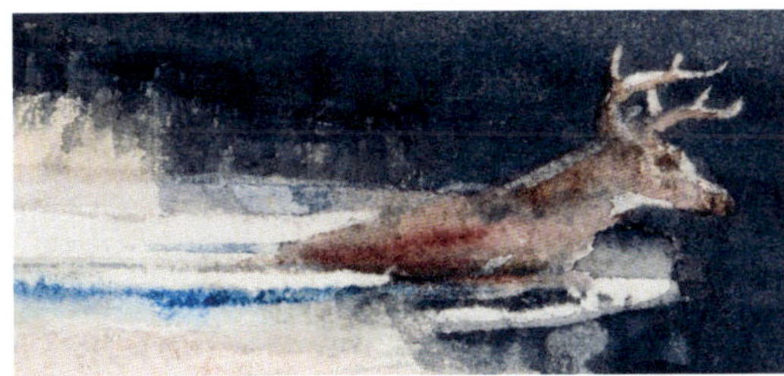

Winslow Homer
Deer in the Adirondacks, 1889, details

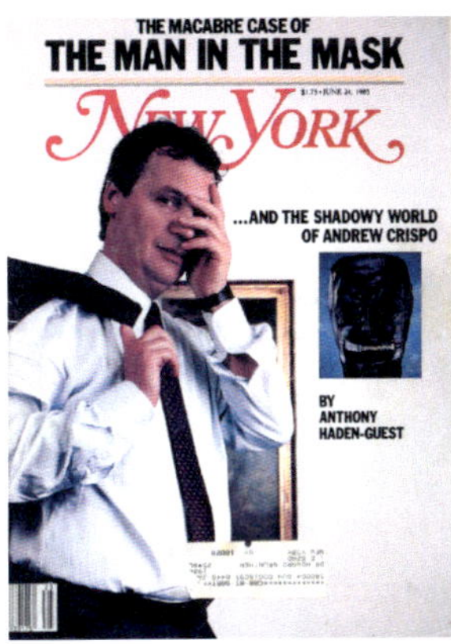

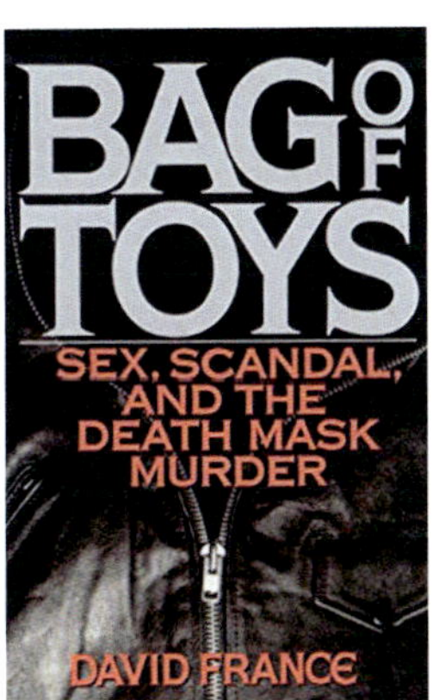

Andrew Crispo cover story, *New York Magazine*, June 24, 1985

David France, *Bag of Toys: Sex, Scandal, and the Death Mask Murder* (New York: Grand Central Publishing, 1992)

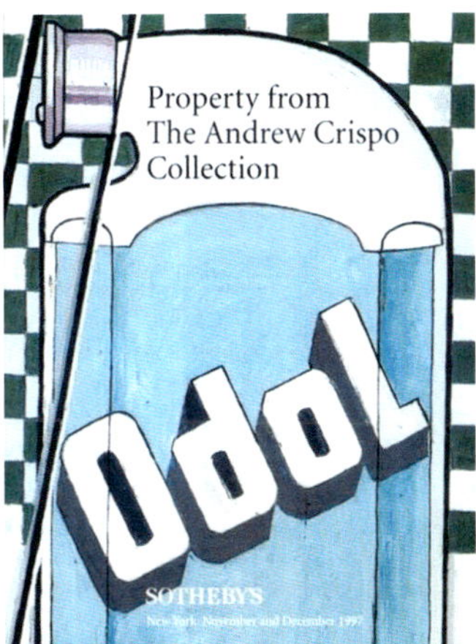

Property from The Andrew Crispo Collection, Sotheby's New York, November and December 1997

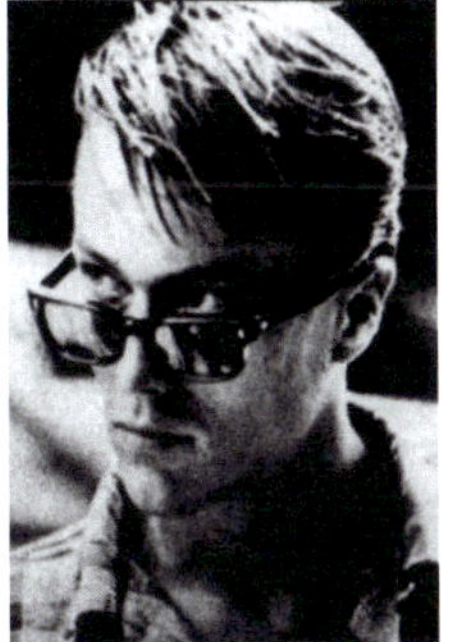

Eigil Dag Vesti

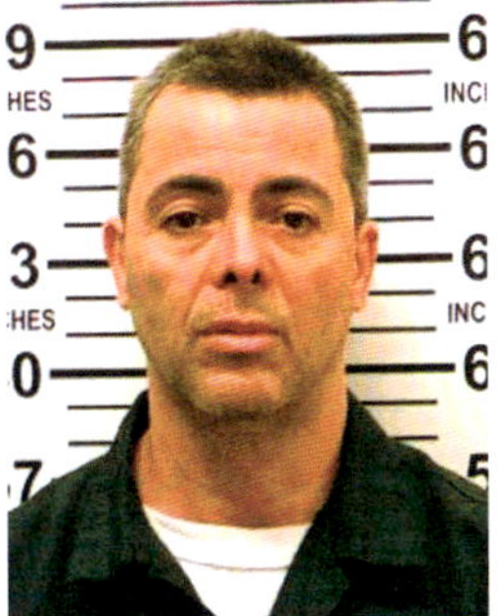

Bernard LeGeros

Martin Johnson Heade
Gremlin in the Studio I, c. 1865–1875
Collection of Dr. and Mrs. Harold Krug

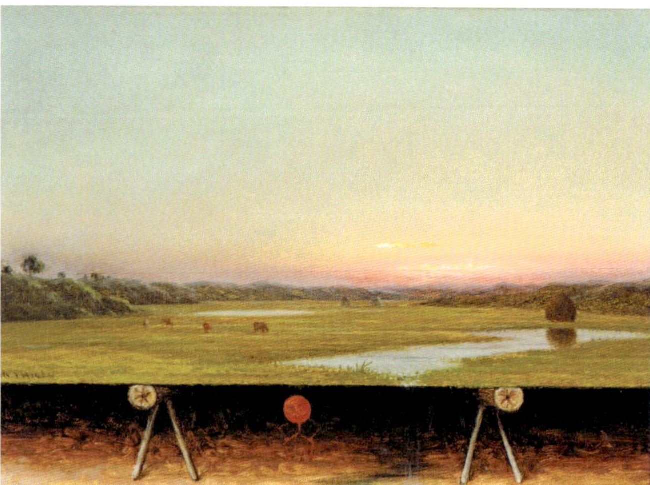

Martin Johnson Heade
Gremlin in the Studio II, c. 1871–1875
Wardsworth Athenaeum Museum of Art, Hartford CT

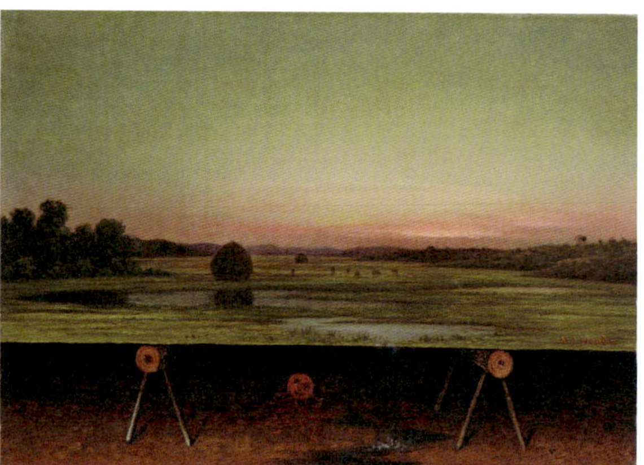

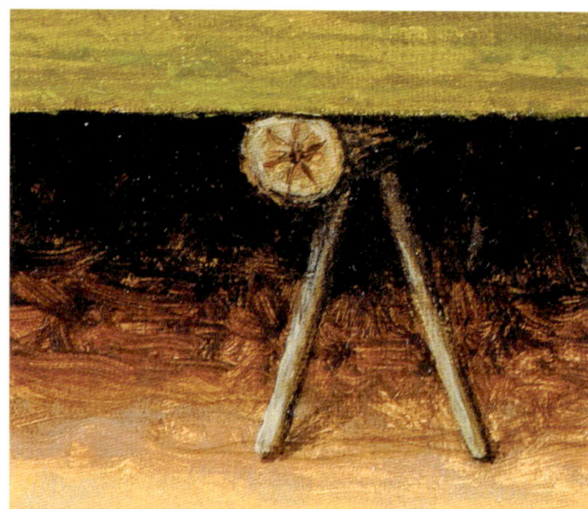

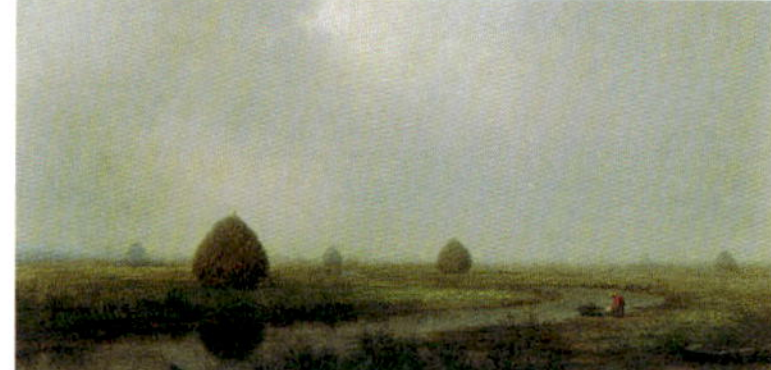

Martin Johnson Heade
Jersey Marshes, 1874
Colección Carmen Thyssen

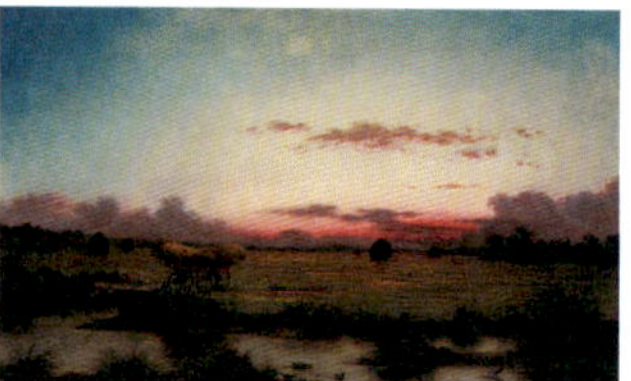

Martin Johnson Heade
The Marshes at Rhode Island, 1866
Colección Carmen Thyssen

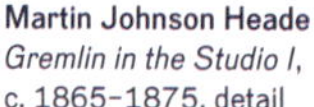

Martin Johnson Heade
Gremlin in the Studio I,
c. 1865–1875, detail

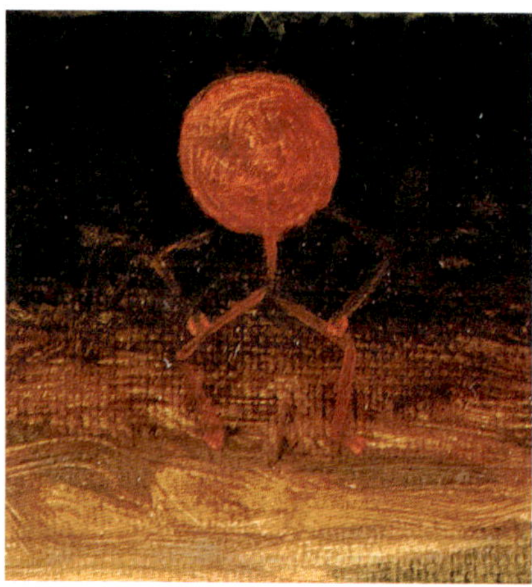

Martin Johnson Heade
Gremlin in the Studio I, c. 1865–1875, detail

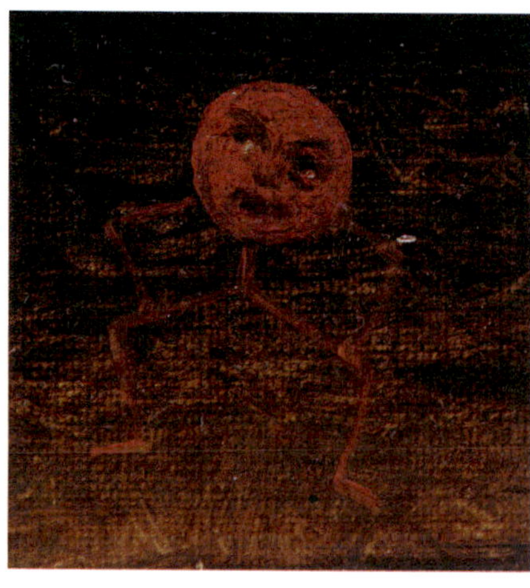

Martin Johnson Heade
Gremlin in the Studio II, c. 1871–1875, detail

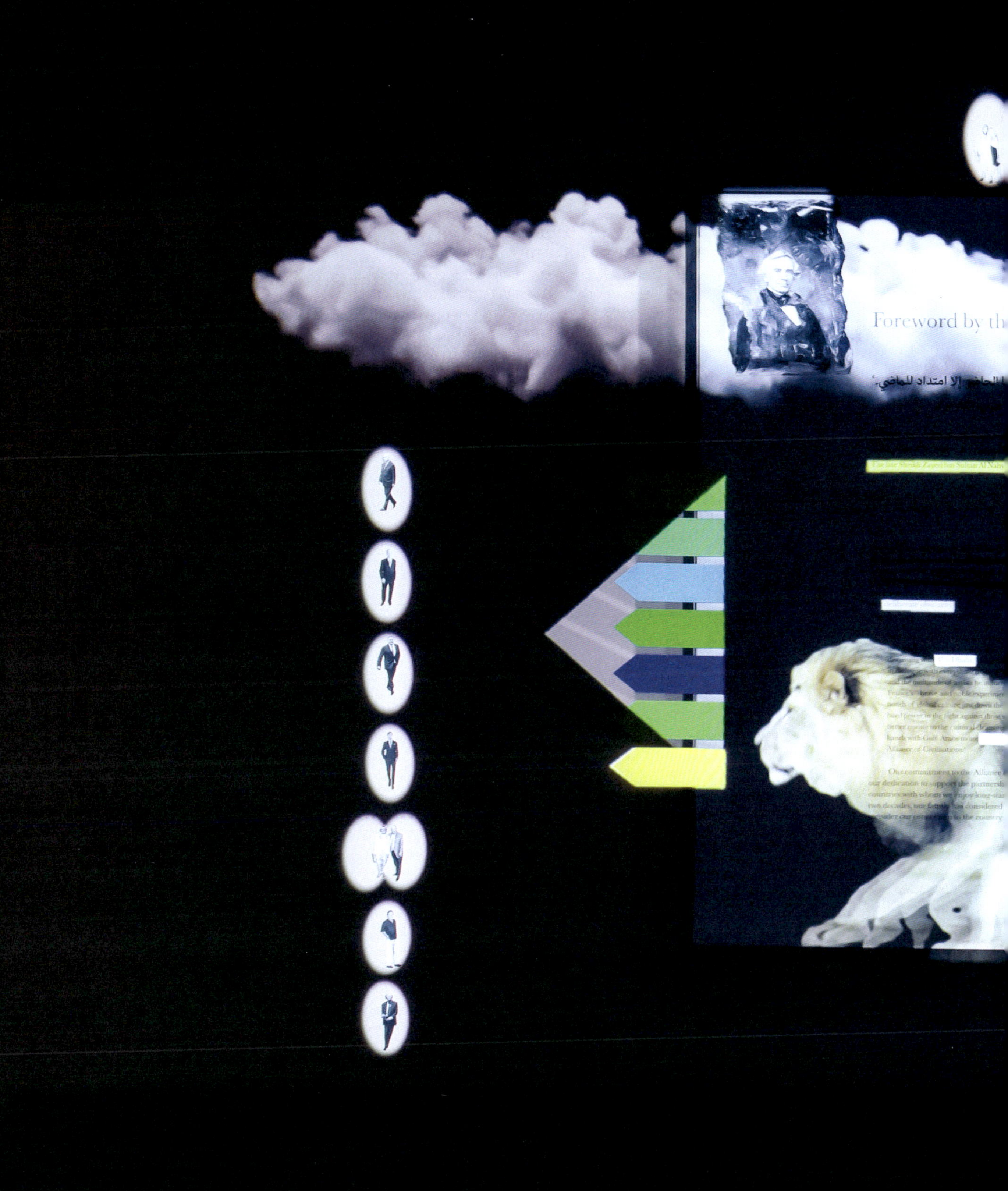

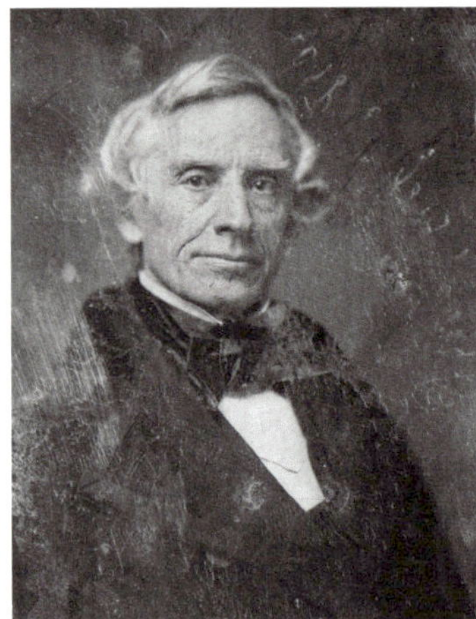

Samuel Morse, c. 1844–1860
Daguerreotype portrait by Mathew Brady

What Hath God Wrought. On May 24, 1844, Samuel Morse dispatched the first telegraphic message over an experimental line from Washington, DC, to Baltimore. In order to transmit messages via this system, he invented Morse Code, an alphabet of electronic dashes and dots used to transmit telegraph messages.

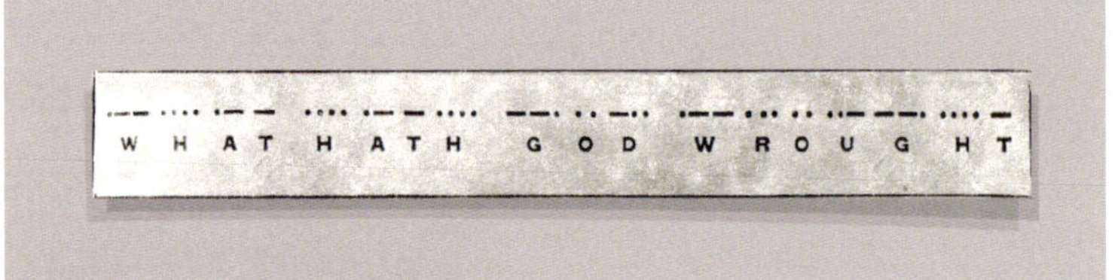

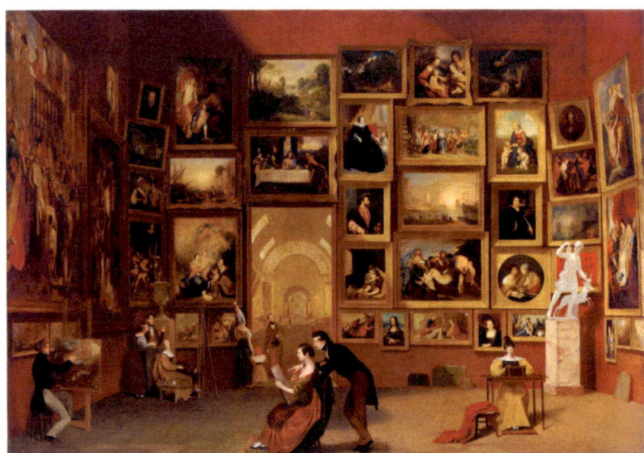

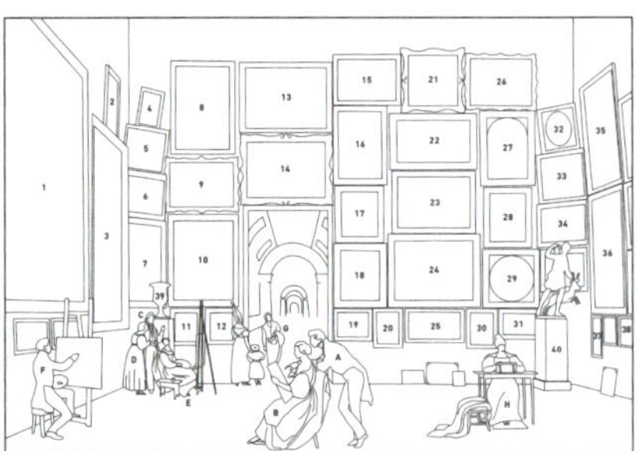

Sketch outline of the 38 paintings as they appear in Morse's painting

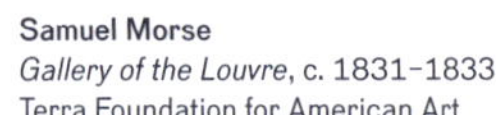

Samuel Morse
Gallery of the Louvre, c. 1831–1833
Terra Foundation for American Art

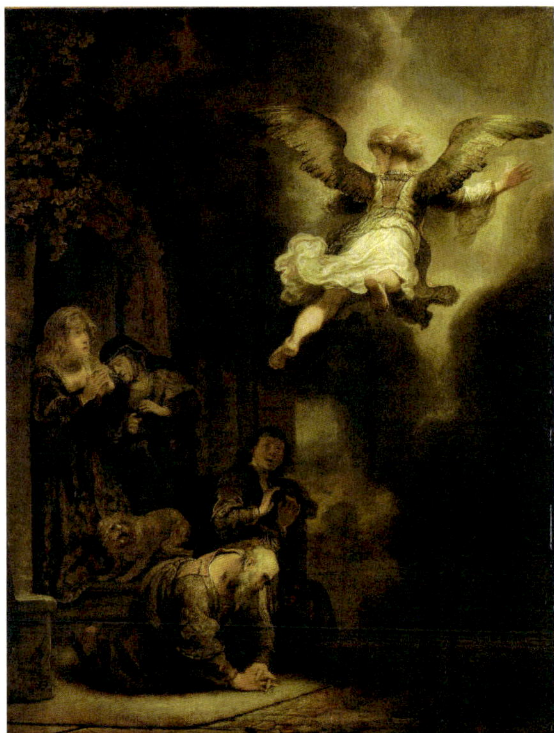

Rembrandt Harmensz. van Rijn
The Archangel Leaving the Family of Tobias, 1637
Louvre, Paris

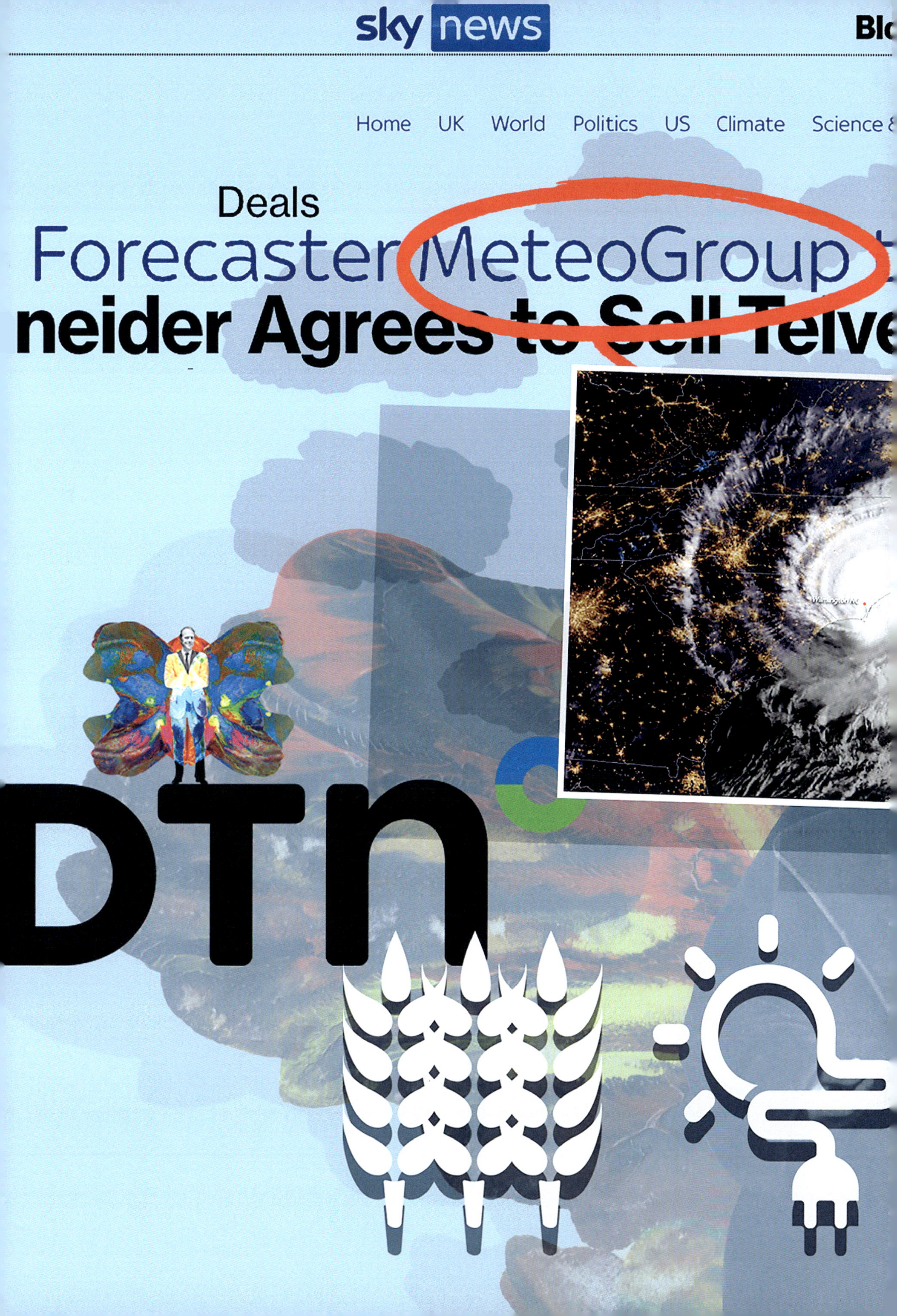

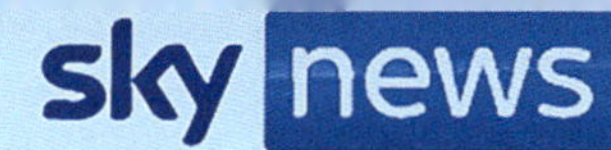

Bl

Home UK World Politics US Climate Science &

Deals

Forecaster MeteoGroup t

neider Agrees to Sell Telve

DTN

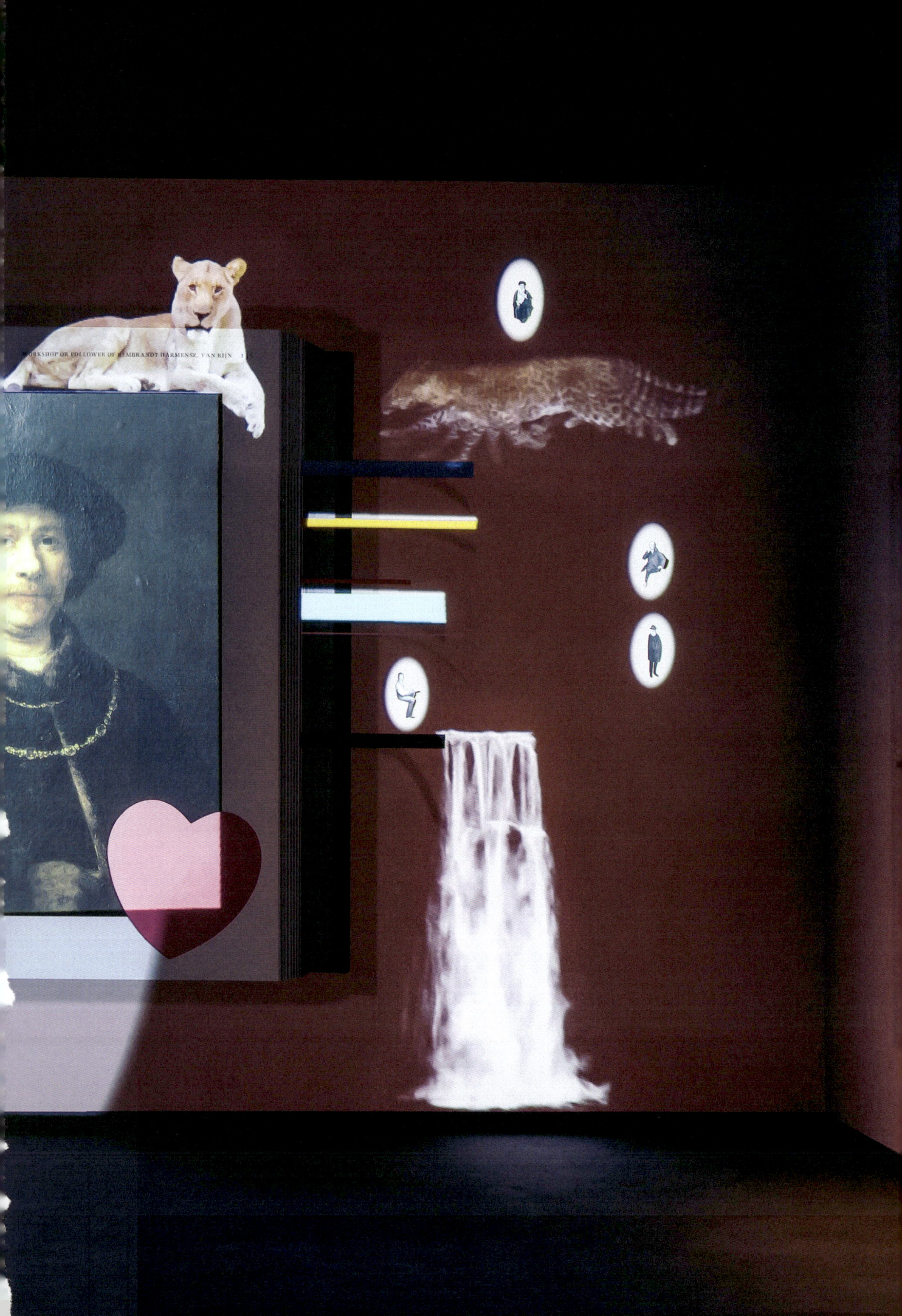
WORKSHOP OR FOLLOWER OF REMBRANDT HARMENSZ. VAN RIJN

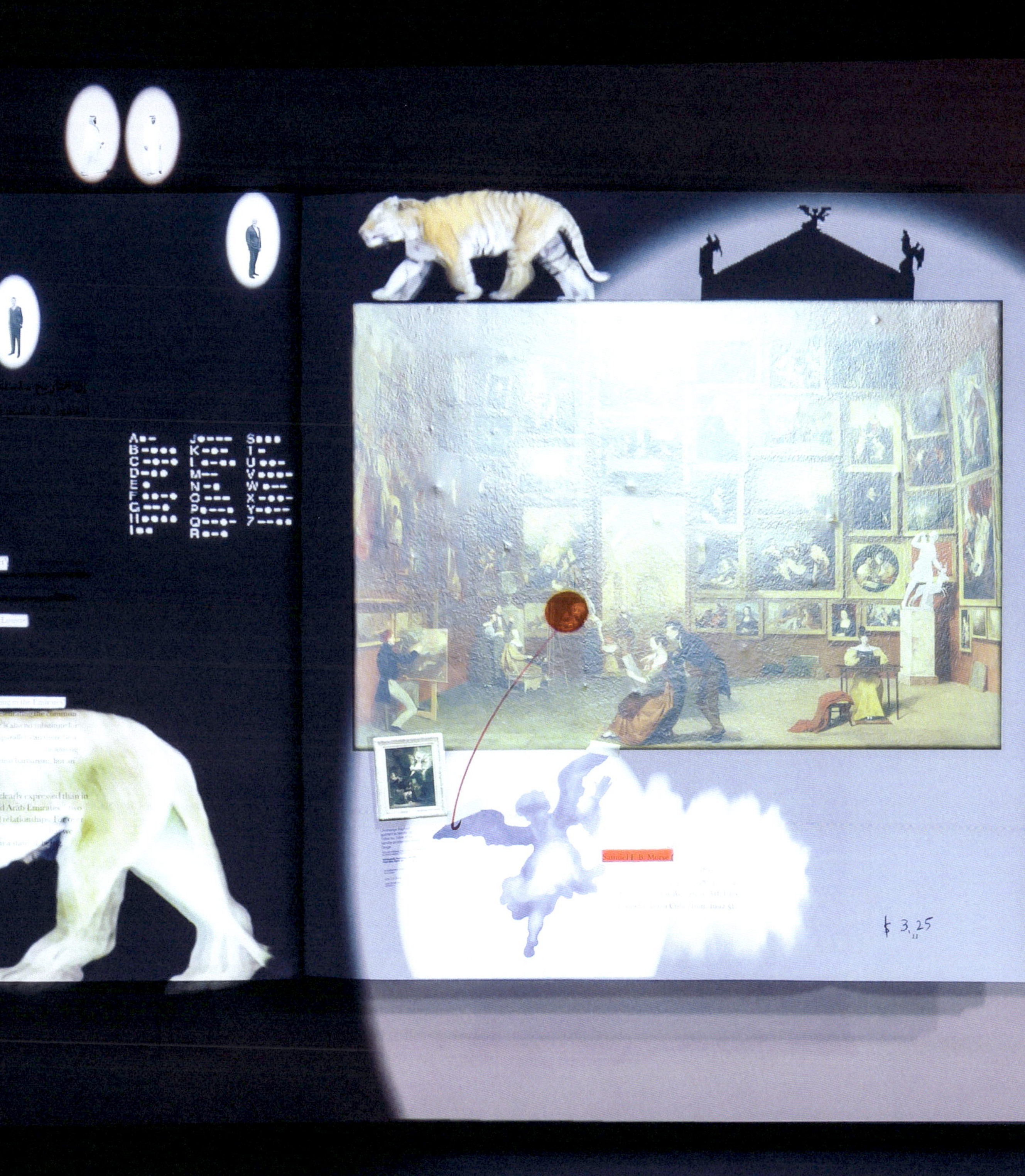
Samuel F. B. Morse
$ 3.25

omberg

Watch Live

& Tech Business Ents & Arts Travel Offbeat More

to come under TBG umbrella

ent DTN to TBG for $900 Mi

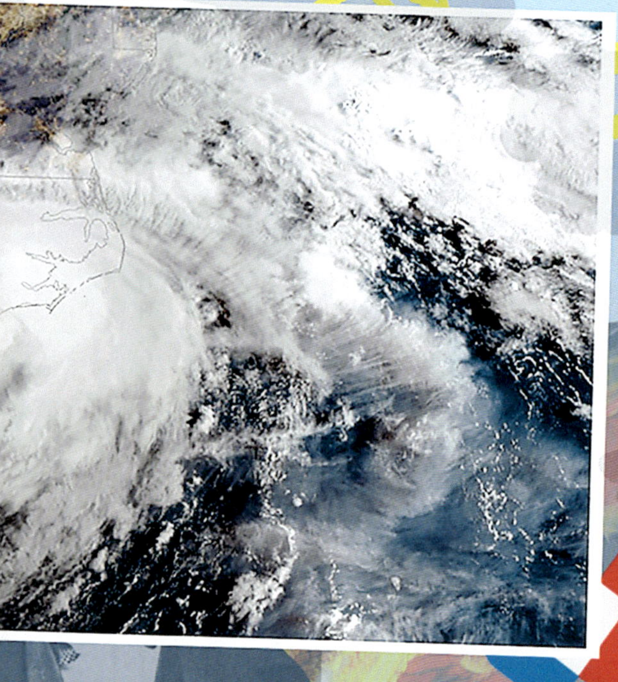

MeteoGro

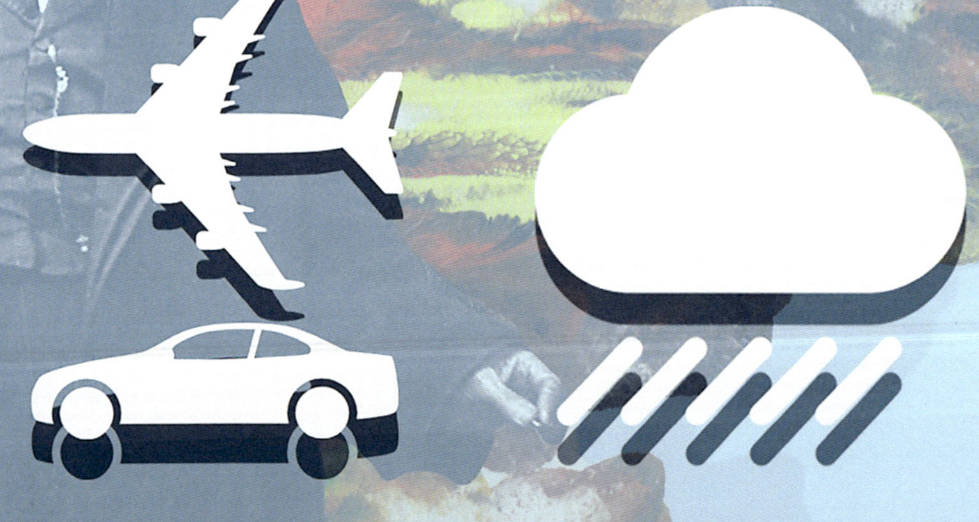

Frontispiece XXXIV: The Weather

Another completely new topic. Are you ready?

The second-largest corporate deal of 2020 was when a company called S&P Global bought another company called IHS Markit. This was a massive $44 billion deal. I've heard of S&P Global, and maybe you have too. But until recently, I have never heard of IHS Markit.

IHS Markit was once part of a larger American company called Indian Head, a company that made textiles, you know, fabric and clothes. In the early 1970s, Hans Heinrich Thyssen-Bornemisza bought Indian Head because it also owned a small engineering catalog company called IHS Global. Hans Heinrich Thyssen-Bornemisza was betting that analog catalogs will soon become digital databases. Essentially, he was anticipating that data will be the future form of information. And just as he predicted, IHS kept growing and growing.

Hans Heinrich Thyssen-Bornemisza died in 2002. Most of his businesses were inherited by his oldest son, Georg Heinrich Thyssen-Bornemisza. In 2012, ten years after his father's death, Georg Heinrich Thyssen-Bornemisza decides to sell eight million shares of IHS. How much? Let's just say for hundreds of millions of dollars. And he was not selling his stock to put the money in the bank. No. Georg Heinrich Thyssen-Bornemisza is a very smart man. He was just moving his money from one big bag of data to even bigger bag of data. Where does he take his money? To answer this, I need to go back to Samuel Morse.

We can all say that Morse's telegraph radically changed our world in many ways. But one of the most dramatic effects of Morse's invention was on an emerging scientific field in the 1830s: meteorology, weather forecasting. I mean, what is the point of even trying to predict the weather if the prediction itself cannot travel faster than the weather. With the telegraph, the different pieces of the sky, all of the clouds, Constable's clouds, can now fit together into one giant picture. And no one understood the contemporary implications of this better than Georg Heinrich Thyssen-Bornemisza. And he proved this two years ago when his private family investment firm, Thyssen-Bornemisza AG in Zurich, bought a company called DTN. Have you heard of DTN? I haven't. It turns out it's one of the largest agriculture and energy information companies in the world. A year later, Georg Heinrich Thyssen-Bornemisza buys Meteogroup, one of the largest private weather forecasting companies in the world. I guess we now know where Georg Heinrich Thyssen-Bornemisza took his money. He took it to crops and clouds.

Georg Heinrich Thyssen-Bornemisza's head was and is clearly in the clouds, that is, in the dark cloud on the horizon: climate change. And he knows very well that climate change will open up asymmetries in the farming, energy, transport, and weather forecasting industries, asymmetries that will require an antidote. His antidote? The merging of DTN and Meteogroup. It is kind of a brilliant move. And he is not the only one who is thinking like this. Georg Heinrich Thyssen-Bornemisza's move into the weather and farming data businesses parallels what IBM did when it bought the Weather Company and it complements the merger of the six agro-chemical companies into the big three: Monsanto/Bayer, Syngenta/ChemChina, and Dupont/Dow.

But in the 1830s in America, when the telegraph was invented, there was another dark cloud on the horizon. It was the dark cloud of the American Civil war. And I am going to change topics again, but I am sure that you are used to this by now.

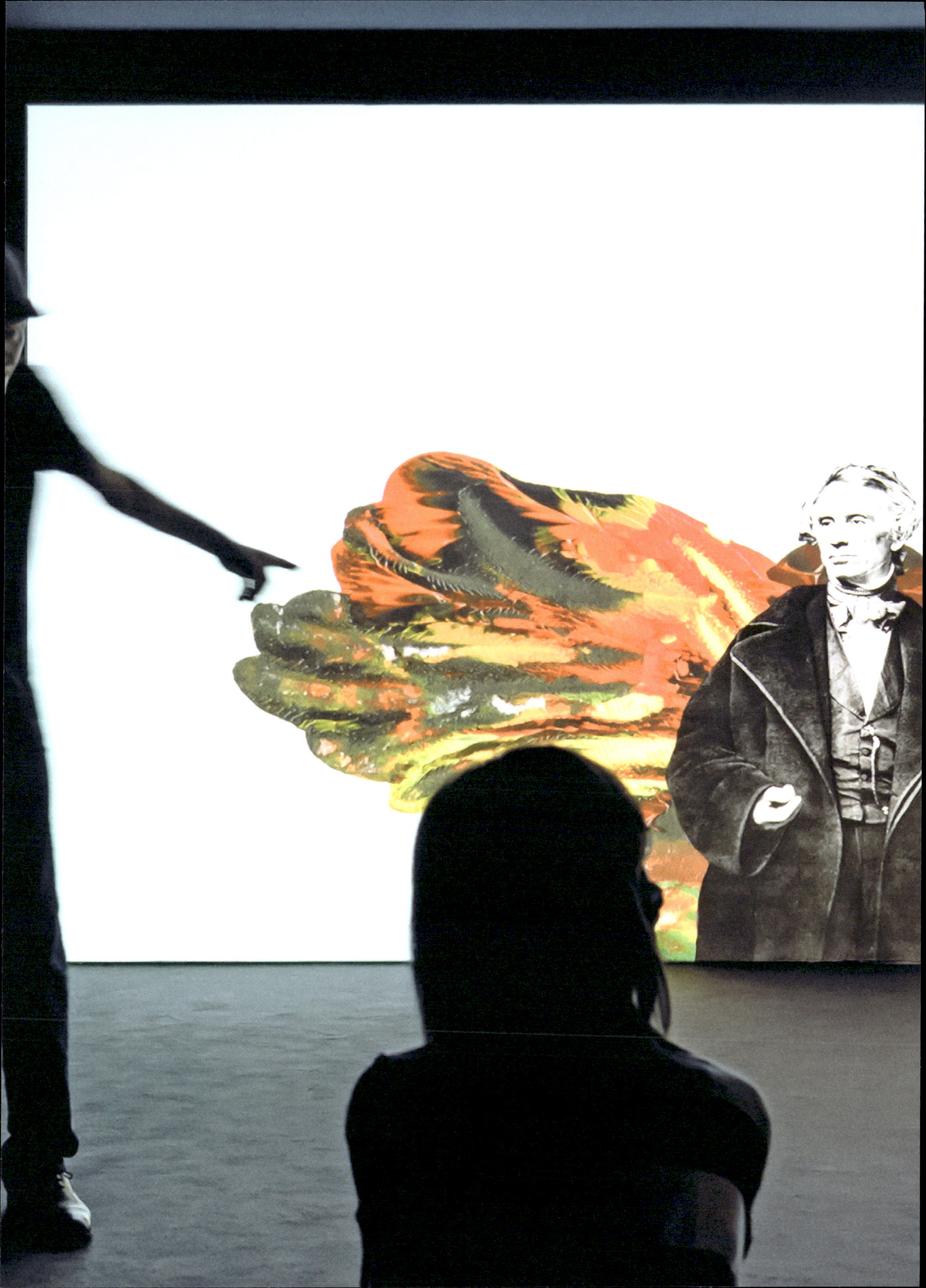

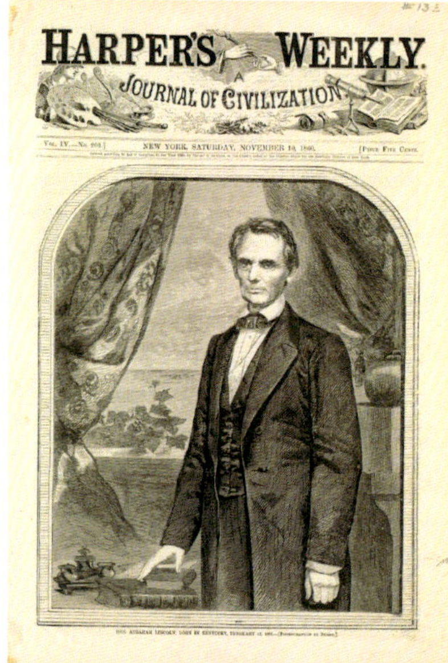

Winslow Homer
Cover design for
Harper's Weekly, 1860

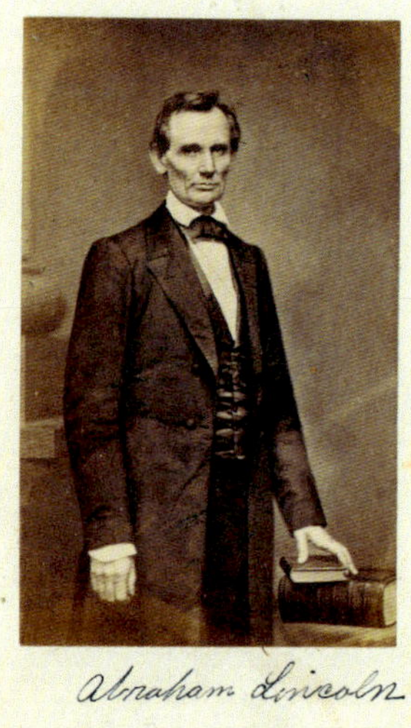

Abraham Lincoln,
1860. Photo by
Mathew Brady

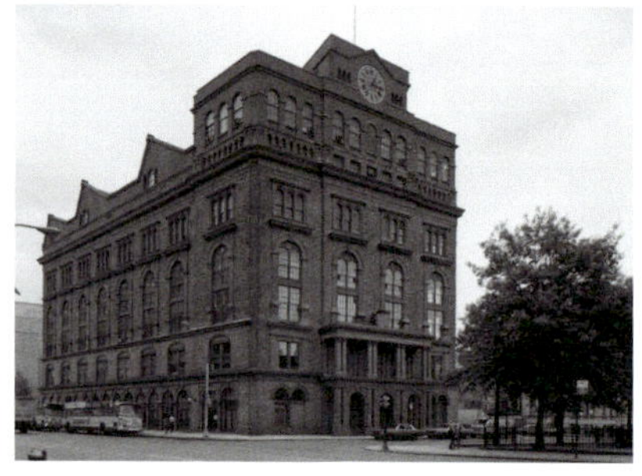

The Cooper Union's Foundation
Building, at Cooper Square
and Astor Place, New York

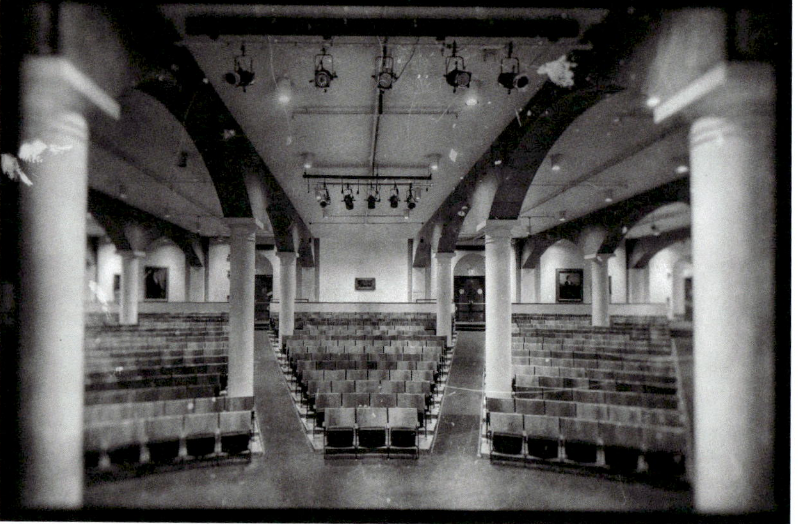

The Cooper Union's Great Hall, view from podium

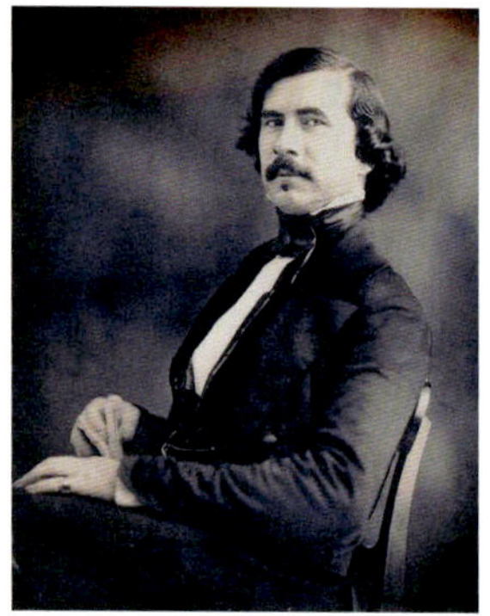

George Peter Alexander
Healy, 1852

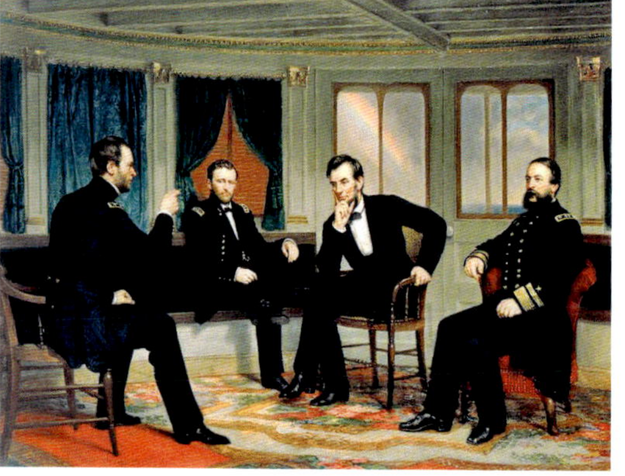

George Peter Alexander Healy
The Peacemakers, 1868
The White House Historical
Association (White
House Collection)

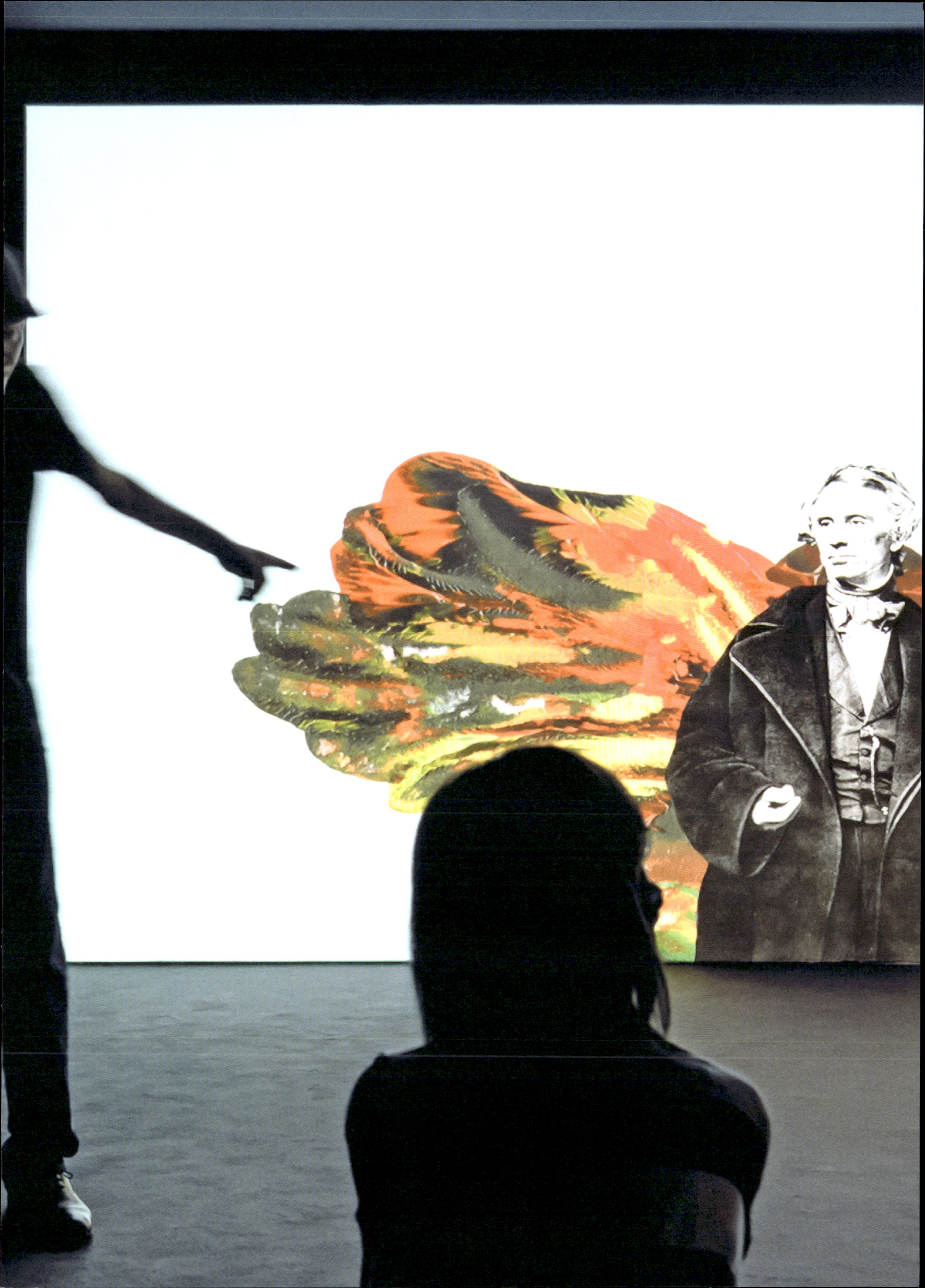

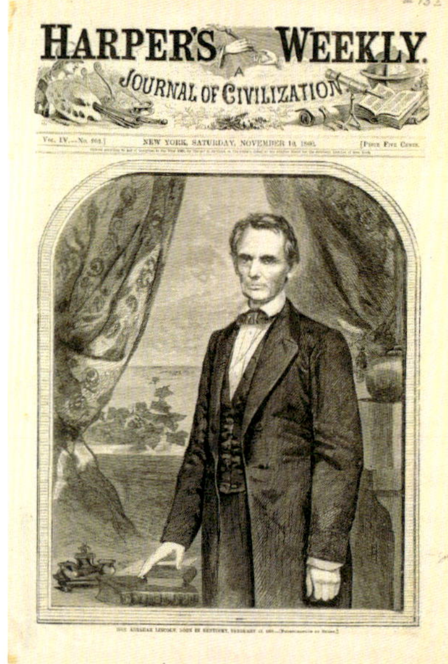

HARPER'S WEEKLY.
A
JOURNAL OF CIVILIZATION

Winslow Homer
Cover design for
Harper's Weekly, 1860

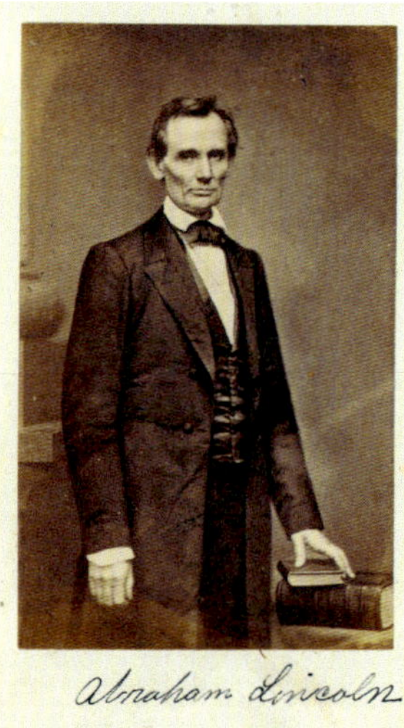

Abraham Lincoln,
1860. Photo by
Mathew Brady

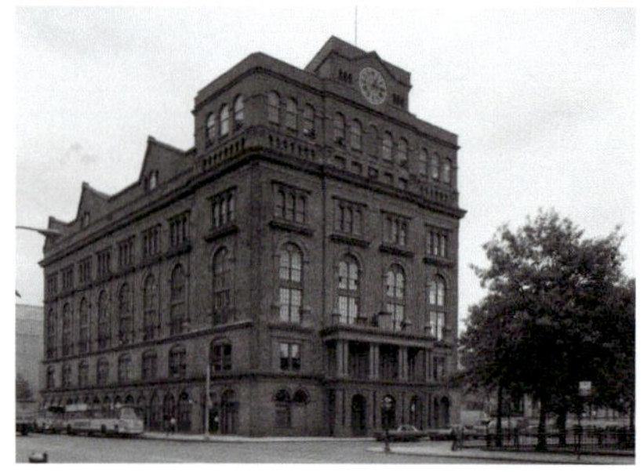

The Cooper Union's Foundation
Building, at Cooper Square
and Astor Place, New York

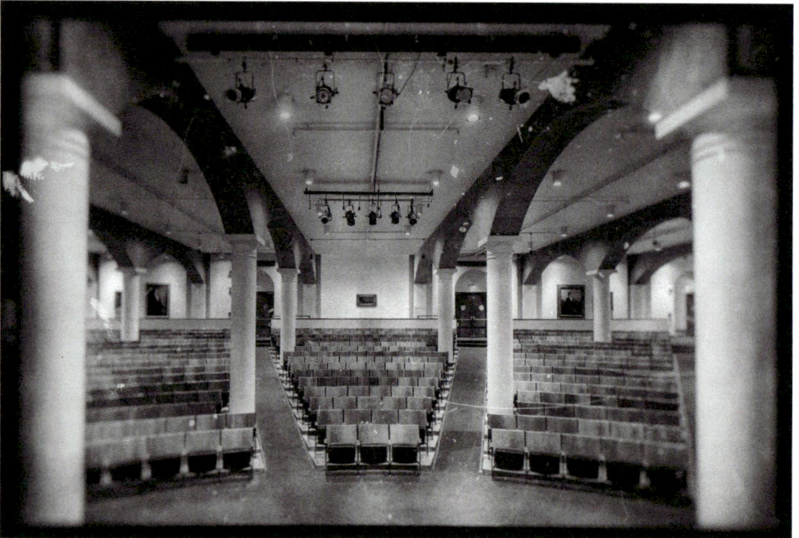

The Cooper Union's Great Hall, view from podium

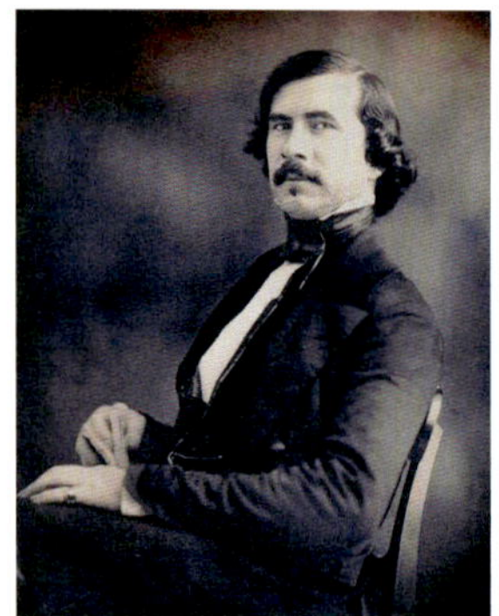

George Peter Alexander
Healy, 1852

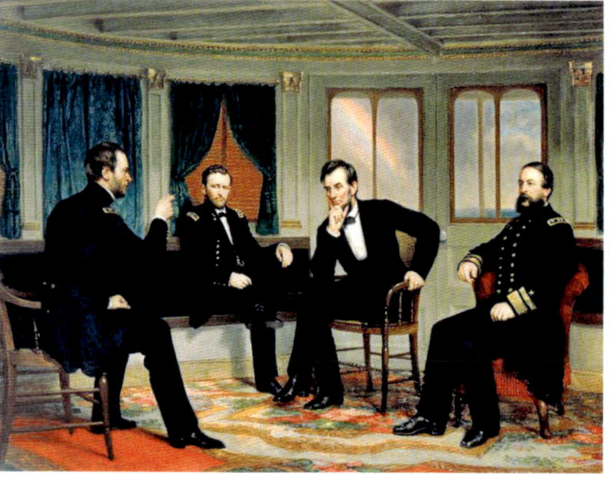

George Peter Alexander Healy
The Peacemakers, 1868
The White House Historical
Association (White
House Collection)

Frontispiece XXXIII: Two Drops Per Heartbeat

Remember Winslow Homer? The awful scene of the about-to-drown deer? Today, Homer is considered one of the best American artists of the nineteenth century. But before he became a full-time painter, Homer was an illustrator. His most famous illustration is of American President Abraham Lincoln. To draw this illustration, Homer relied on a photograph of Lincoln that was taken on February 27, 1860. How do we know the date? Because on that day, Lincoln was invited to New York to give the speech what will eventually turn out to be the most important speech of his life. It is the speech that will make him president of the US in 1860. And keep in mind that we are talking about 1860 America. Slavery is tearing the country apart, and the American Civil War is just months away, a brutal war that will kill or injure 3 percent of the US population. That's a million people!

Lincoln's speech is known today as his Cooper Union speech because Lincoln spoke that night at a school in Manhattan called The Cooper Union. And I guess you probably figured out by now where I teach in NYC. That's right, I teach at The Cooper Union. In fact, my office is right here.

The Great Hall of The Cooper Union, the room where Lincoln gave his speech in 1860 looks like this today. If you are standing at the podium looking at the crowd, you would see that on the back wall, there is a large painting honoring Lincoln. This is actually a painting by an American artist named George Peter Alexander Healy, titled *The Peacemakers*. But when Lincoln gave his speech in 1860, there was another painting hanging in the back. How do I know this? Because I found a photograph of that room from 1860. See? I mention this because Lincoln himself asked for it to hang there facing him. You're never going to guess which painting it was. It was the Eastman Johnson painting I showed you in the Carmen Thyssen collection, the one about the making of maple syrup. I am sure you are asking yourself: "Why would Lincoln ask for a painting about the making of syrup to be hanging in the room where he is giving the most important speech of his political life, on the eve of the American Civil War?" Because of sugar. Yup, sugar, the white stuff.

In the seventeenth, eighteenth, and nineteenth centuries in the Americas, sugar was bittersweet (as it remains today). As you may know, almost two-thirds, or 15 out of the 20 million people enslaved in Africa were brought to the Americas to work in sugar plantations. The life of an enslaved African was measured in sugar. One enslaved person's life equaled one ton of white sugar. Every six days of an enslaved person's life was equal to one teaspoon of the white gold.

In the nineteenth century, those who were against slavery decided to boycott white sugar and came up with an alternative: maple syrup. Drill a hole in a maple tree, wait for late winter/early spring, and two drops of maple sap per heartbeat later, you've got sweet, delicious syrup.

Strangely enough, Johnson, who painted this artwork, was never able to complete any of the twenty-five paintings he did on this subject. Johnson would start a painting but would stop before finishing it. Of course at some point they asked him: "Mr. Johnson, why don't you ever finish any of the syrup paintings?" And he answered: "Well, because if I ever finished a painting, I would have to hang it," and "I don't want to hang anything, anywhere, anytime!" Which, of course, now that I am saying it, this reminds me of the disturbing hanging system upstairs.

Anyway, I think it's time we move our legs a bit. So, let's take a walk. Come with me to the space next door. You can leave your things here. We will come back in a few minutes.

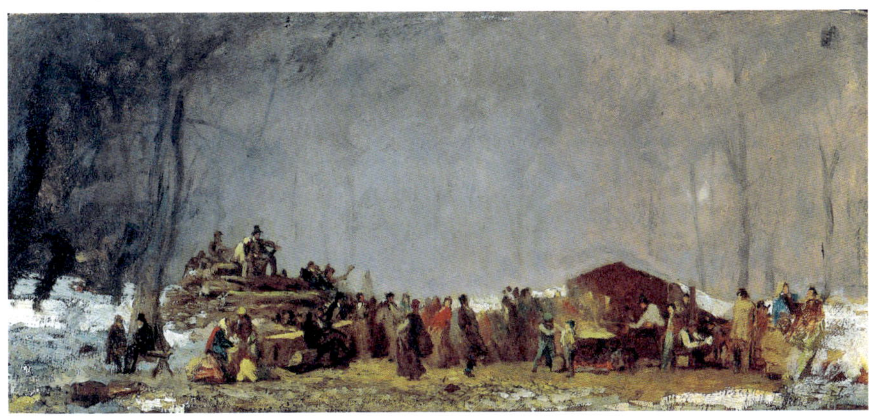

Eastman Johnson
The Maple Sugar Camp–Turning Off, c. 1865–1873
Colección Carmen Thyssen

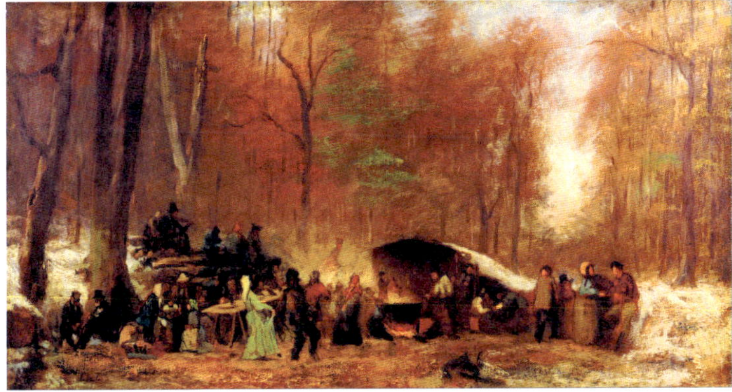

Eastman Johnson
A Different Sugaring Off, c. 1865
De Young Museum, San Francisco

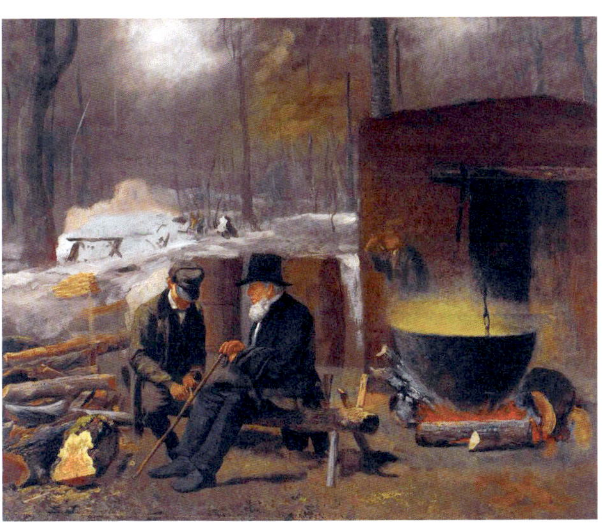

Eastman Johnson
At the Camp–Spinning Yarns and Whittling, c. 1864–1866
Crystal Bridges Museum of American Art, Bentonville, Arkansas

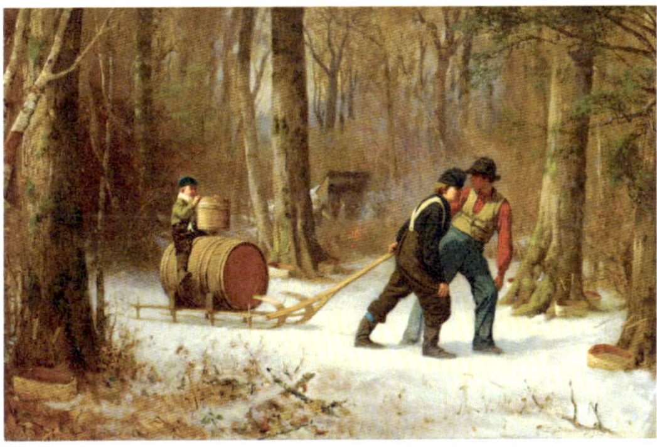

Eastman Johnson. *On Their Way to Camp*, 1873
National Gallery of Art, Washington, DC

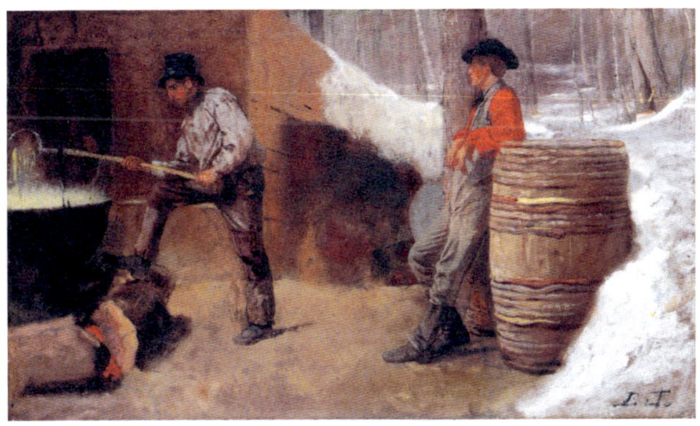

Eastman Johnson
The Sugar Camp, c. 1861–1866
Yale University Art Gallery, New Haven

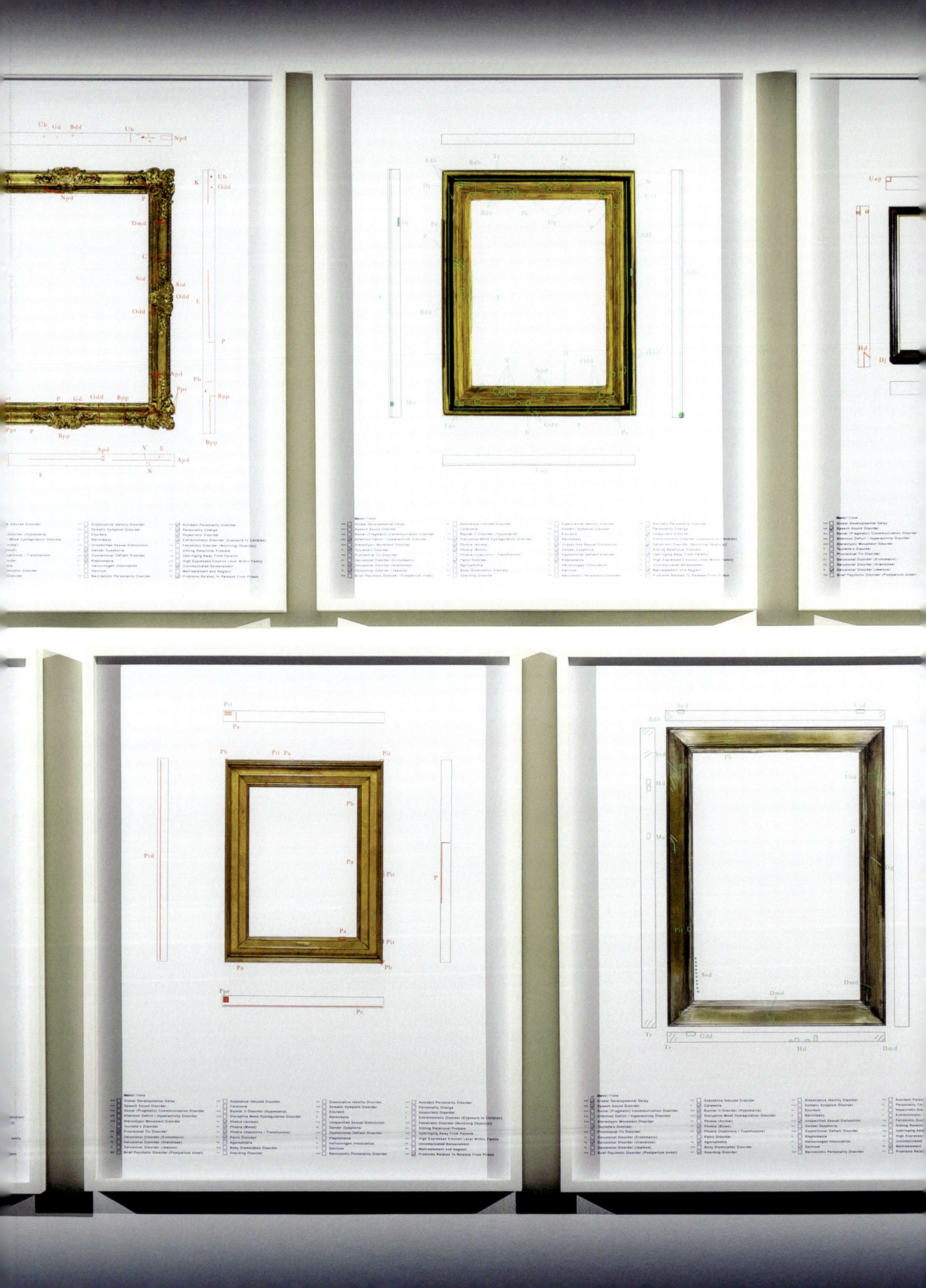

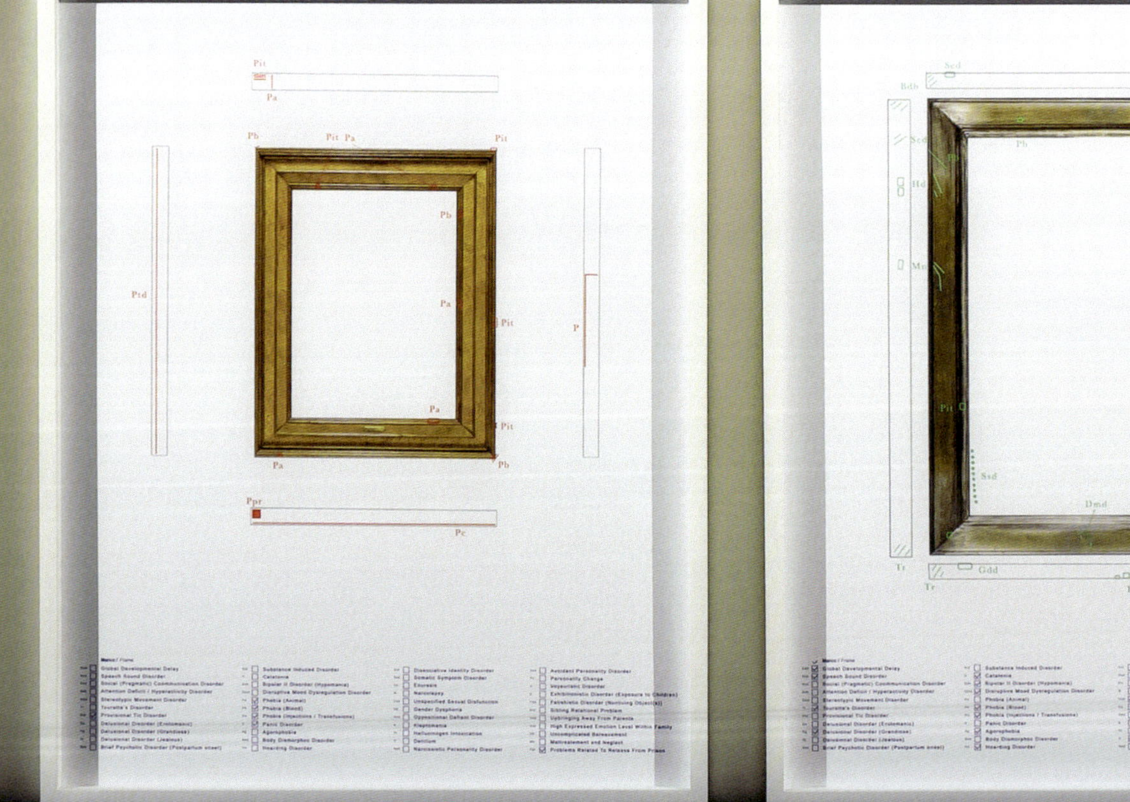

Epilogue V: The Frames

Earlier, I mentioned that in 1983, Hans Heinrich Thyssen-Bornemisza traveled to Moscow to attend the opening of an exhibition of his old masters at the Pushkin Museum. While supervising the installation of his collection, the baron noticed that a woman unpacking his paintings was talking to herself. He approached her and realized that she was not talking to herself but to the paintings. He watched her do this for some time, and then asked: "What are you doing? Why are you talking to the paintings?" The woman was surprised and embarrassed, but she gathered herself enough to say that she was not talking to the paintings. She was talking and listening to the frames. She told the baron that she was checking whether the frames were in good health, and added that she was trained to detect not only physical, material damage to the frames but also to check for a kind of an immaterial damage. She said that frames may be affected not only by worms and insects, but may suffer from diseases that are very much like psychological diseases, and that she created a method to check the appropriate frame pathologies.

The baron was blown away by her diagnostic method, so much so that he immediately invited her to Switzerland to examine his entire collection, his other frames. A year later, she traveled to Villa Favorita, examined the collection, and produced these reports. And from the looks of it, the Swiss frames were quite ill. They had multiple "disorders," that ranged from "global developmental delay," to "catatonia," "kleptomania," "blood phobia," "gender dysphoria," "voyeurism and exhibitionism," and, my favorite, "sibling relational problems," among others.

By the way, the woman's name: Lamia Antonova. That's how she ended up working for the baron for the next seventeen years.

Epilogue IV: The X-Rays

A few months after her move to Switzerland, Lamia Antonova reread her condition reports. But this time, she completely freaked out because she realized that it was just a matter of time before the frames would contaminate the paintings they house. Antonova also had the feeling that the images could sense the forthcoming pathologies, and that they are likely to deploy defensive measures. And the counter-measure she feared the most was that the paintings would decide to run away, to flee.

She immediately tried to warn her Swiss colleagues, but the only thing they said was: "Come on Lamia. This is Switzerland, not Russia. Stop it with your superstitions." But Antonova was so agitated and furious, and just to shut her up, her Swiss colleagues decided that the number of staples and nails will be tripled and quadrupled. You can see their handiwork here, in these X-rays, how they really went overboard with the nails and staples. One painting ended up with sixty-seven additional nails; another one, seven massive screws; another, eighteen more.

Did it work? Did it prevent the images from running away? So far, yes.

But Antonova's feeling remains that, should the images decide to walk away, a million nails and staples would not prevent them from fleeing.

>
Walid Raad
Epilogue IV: The X-Rays, 2021
Installation view, Museo Nacional
Thyssen-Bornemisza, Madrid, 2021

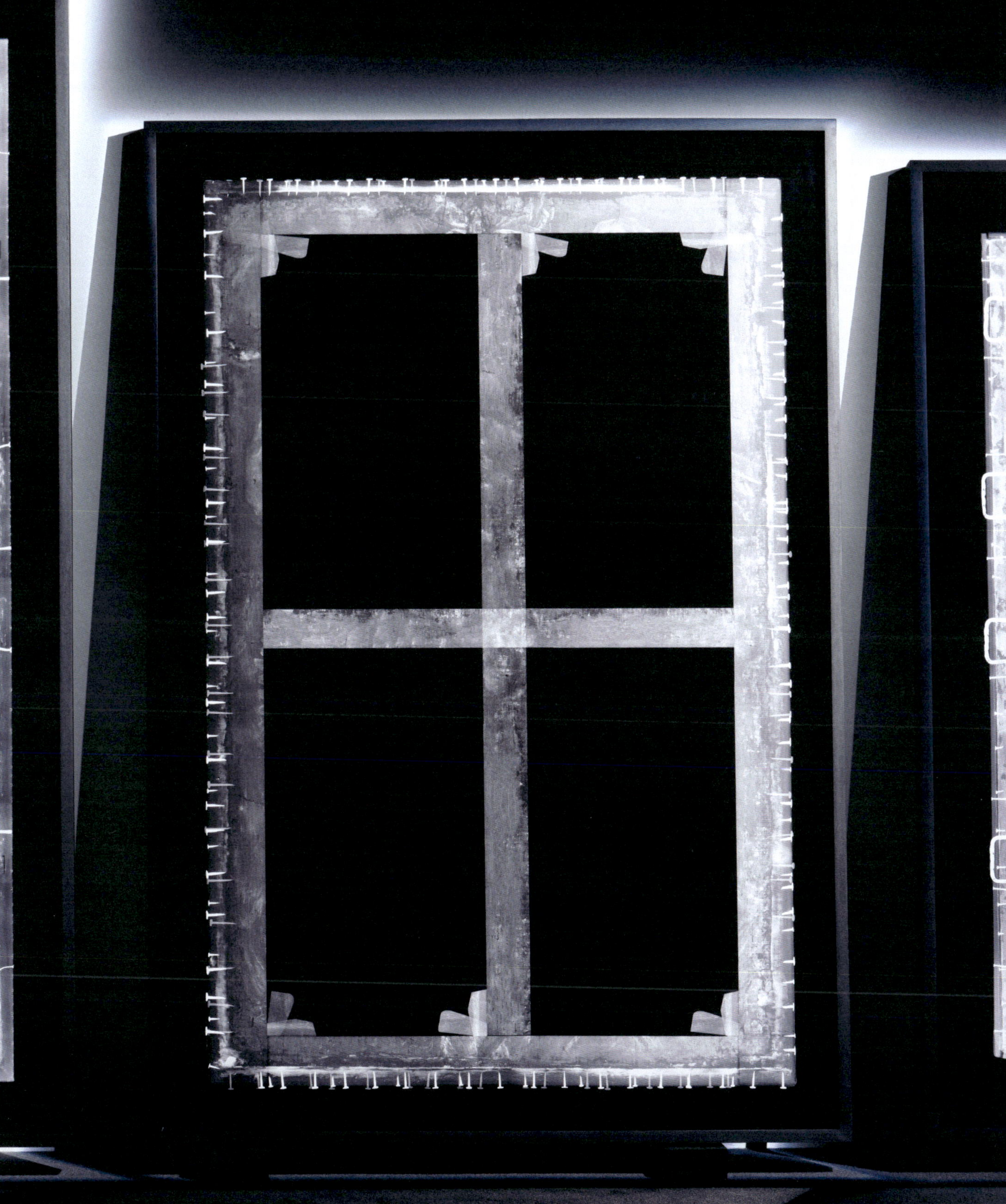

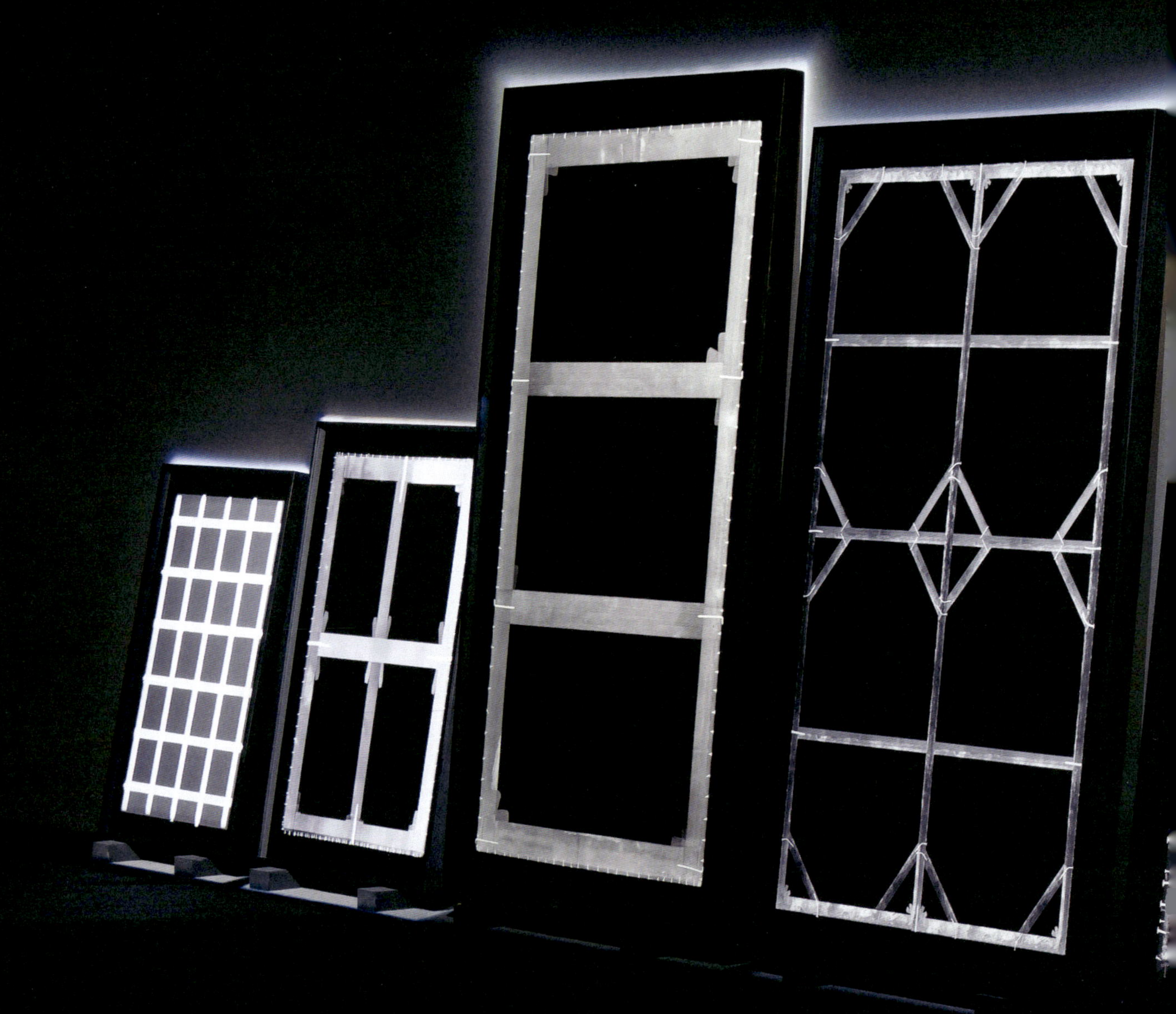

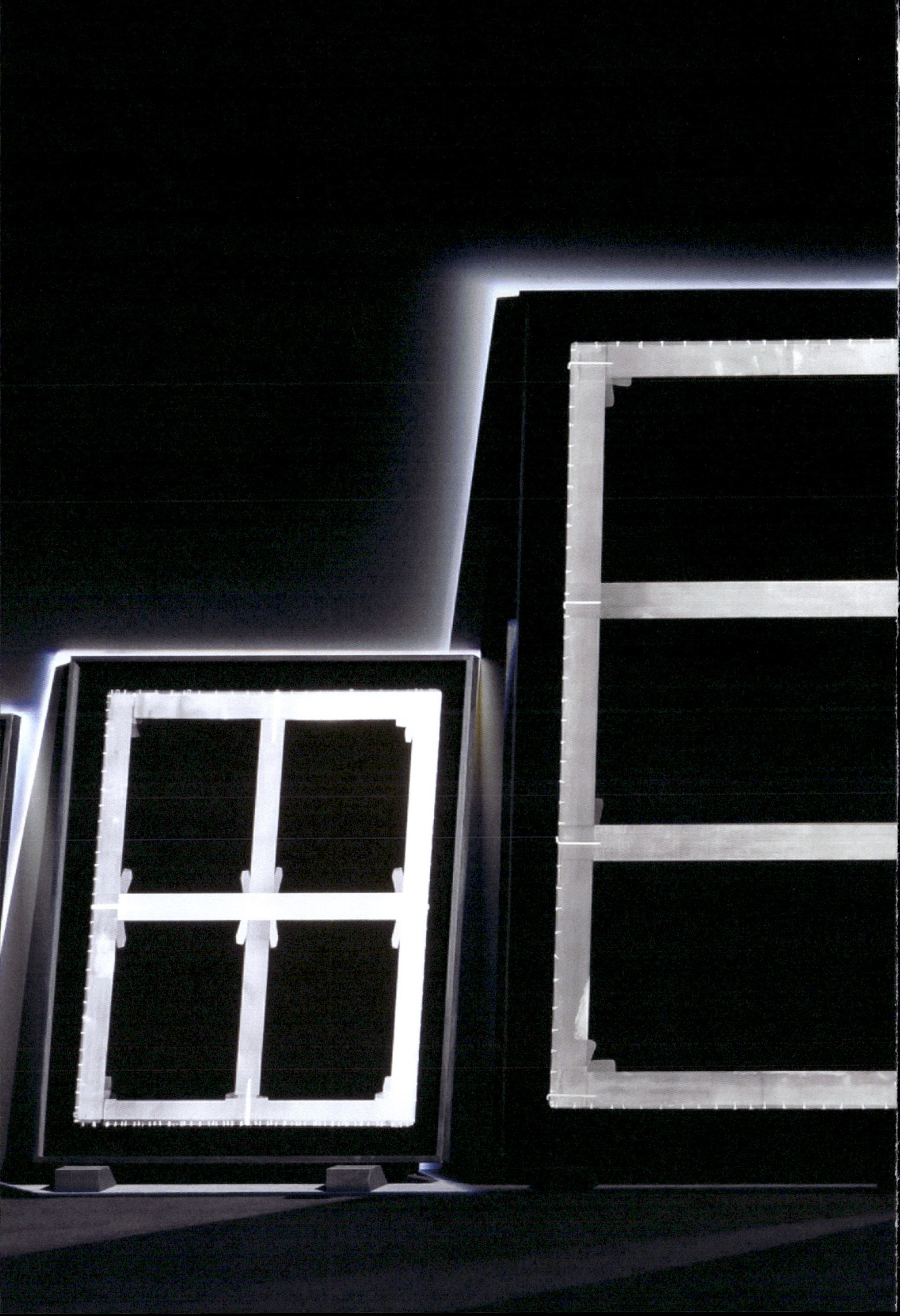

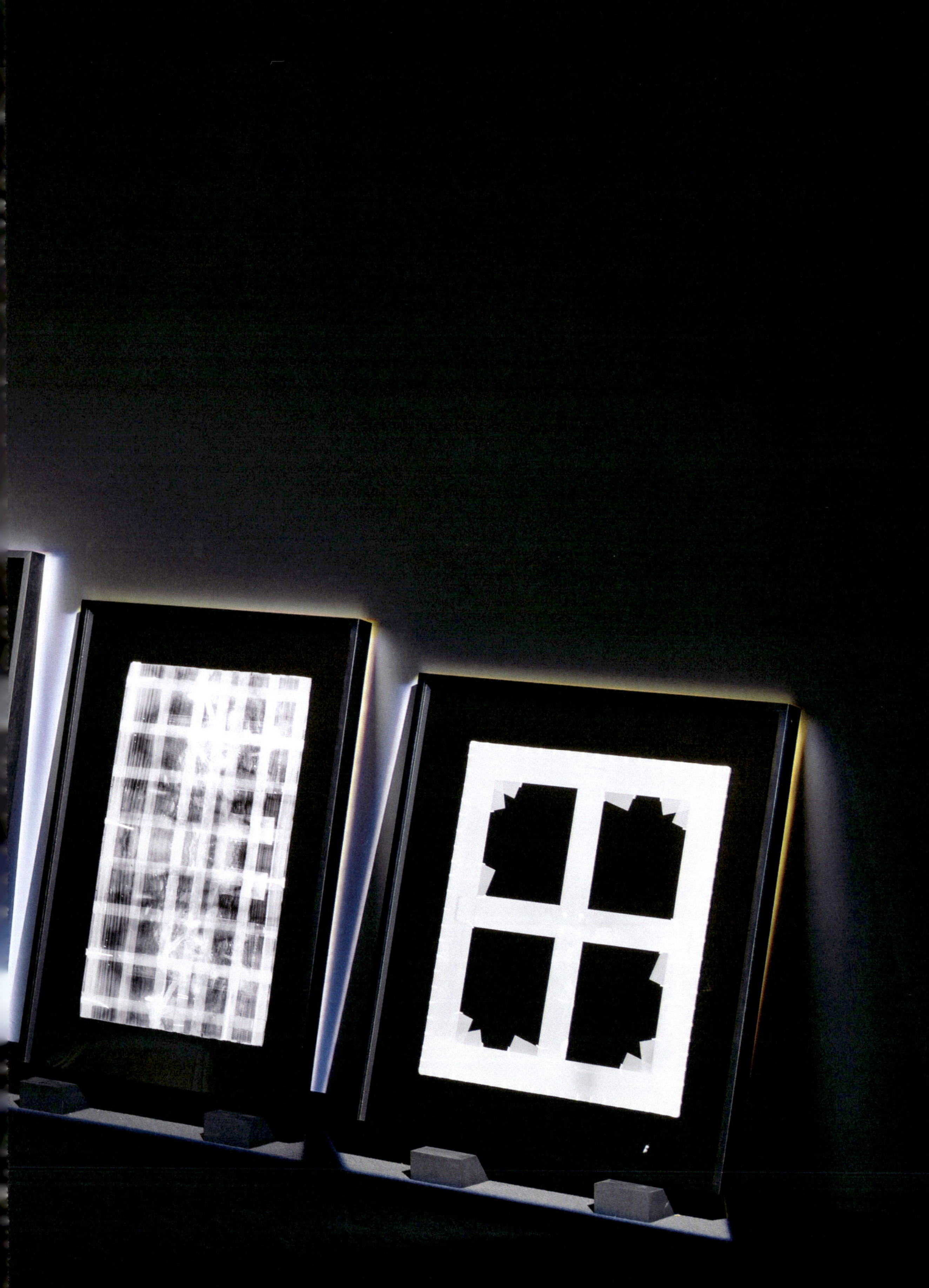

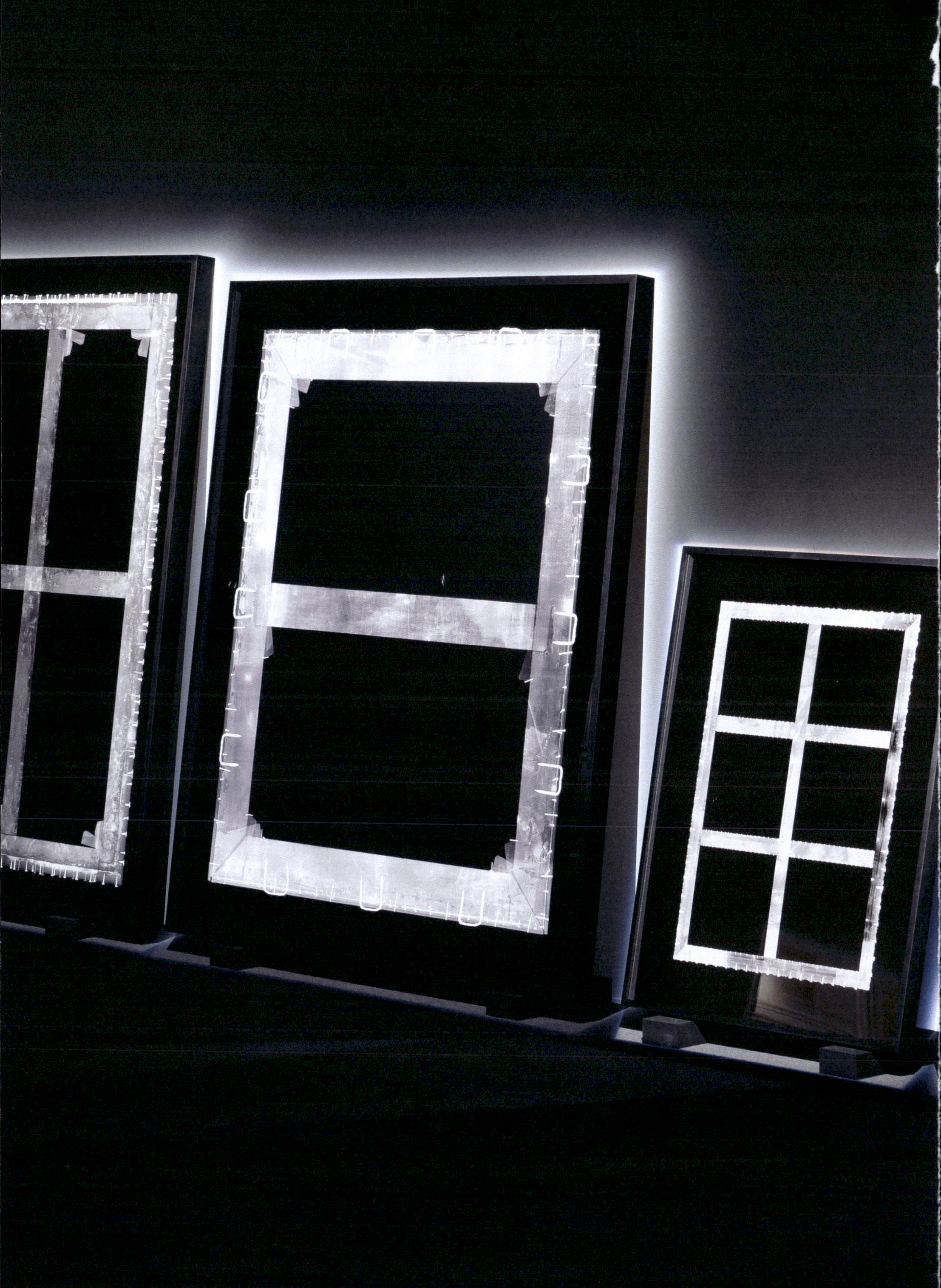

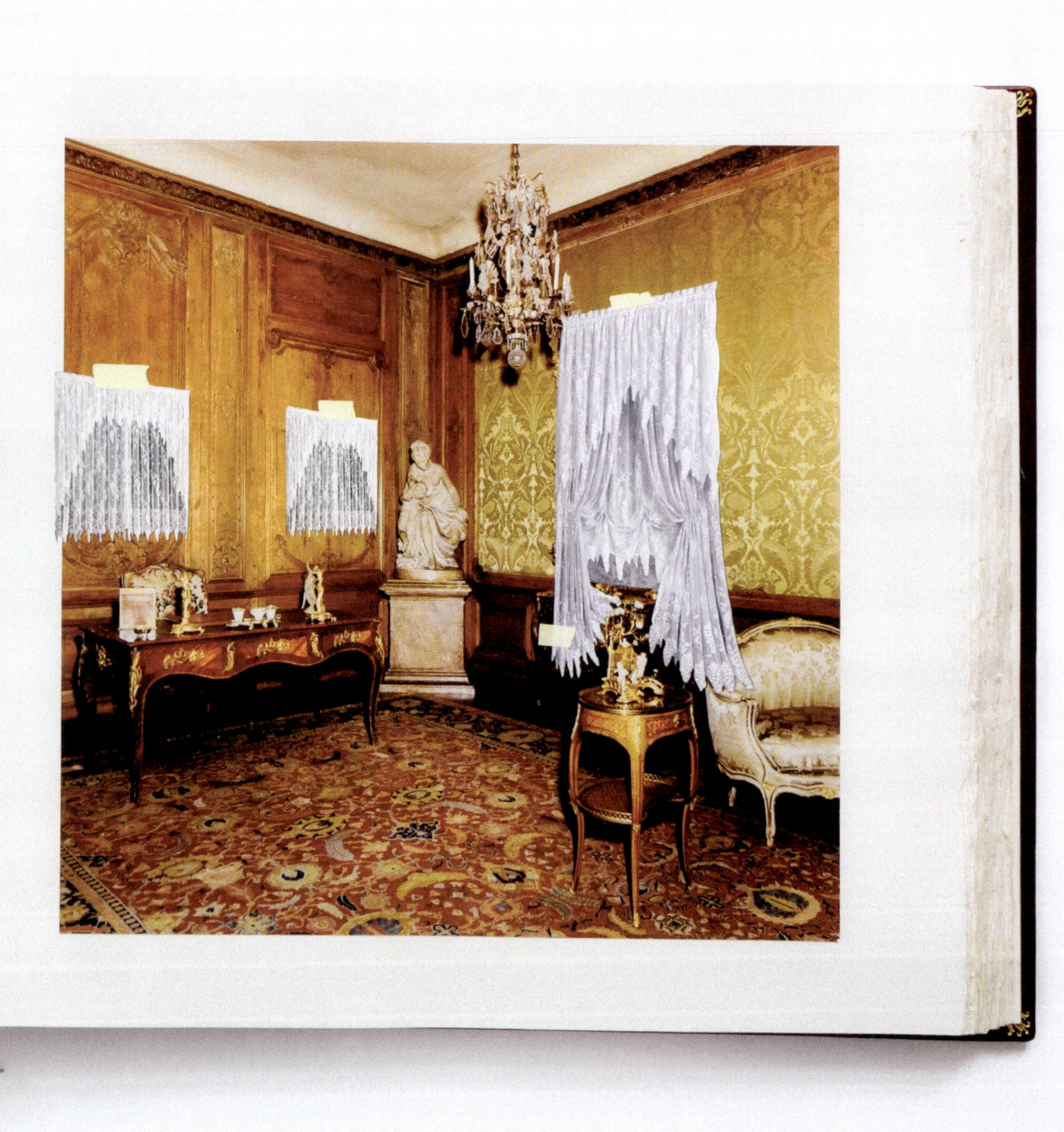

Epilogue VI: The Curtains

Over here, we have something completely different.

Take a look.

As you can see, it is a sort of photo book, and from what I understand, this is an album that Hans Heinrich Thyssen-Bornemisza had custom-made in 1985. It's an album of the interiors of his villa in Switzerland. The baron made four copies, one for each of his heirs.

As you can see, it looks as if all the artworks on the walls are covered with curtains, paper collages of lace curtains. I don't know why this is the case. And what is even stranger is the statement on the first page. It read: "This album was made for those of my children who see through walls, shrouds, veils, curtains, and masks."

When I saw this, I had no idea what to make of it. I asked the Thyssen kids—well, now adults—about it and they told me that their father was convinced that one of his children has or will have "tunnel vision." Tunnel vision means that you can see through surfaces, walls, and so on. Two of the kids assured me that this was typical of their father's superstitions, and that I should not over-interpret this. One of the children told me that he can see through clouds but not walls, and we know who that is. And one Thyssen, Lorne Thyssen-Bornemisza, said to me that he was starting to see through veils. "What does this even mean?" I asked. It took me six months to understand what this means. And I am going to show you what it means. I am going to ask you to go back to your seats for a few minutes. Just a few minutes, and I promise this will all be over.

Frontispiece XXXIII: The Kaplan

Did I already mention that I have the same birthday as Lorne Thyssen-Bornemisza? June 15? And that Lorne spends a lot of time in Lebanon? My Lebanon! And that he wrote and made a movie about the Lebanese Civil War? I am not making this up. I discovered the Lebanon-Lorne connection by accident. I can't remember who gave me this auction catalog of silver and gold coins that came from the collection of Lorne Thyssen-Bornemisza. In the catalog, Lorne talks about Lebanon.

Now this coin collection...OK, it's another small detour but I am sure you are used to this by now. The coins in the catalog were not only the property of Lorne. They belonged to Lorne and his high school friend, a man named Thomas Kaplan.

I want to make something very clear here. These two men, Thomas and Lorne, went to school together, but today they exist on completely separate political planets. Even Lorne writes about this when he says: "Tom and I have had life-long arguments about Middle Eastern politics." You expect me to read this and not want to know everything about Kaplan? So, who is this Kaplan guy? It turns out, this Kaplan person is a silver tycoon, silver as in the precious metal. I guess that's why he collected silver coins. In the early 1990s, Kaplan actually discovered the largest natural silver deposits ever found, in Bolivia. Let me show you a short video about Kaplan and how and why he got into silver. Just a couple of minutes:

Watch three minutes of:  25:00–28:30 min. (approx.)

What he is saying here is really interesting, no? Everyone was assuming that when photography goes from film, silver film to digital, from film to computer chips, that there will be an oversupply of silver, which, of course, would mean that the price of silver will collapse, right? Kaplan makes a bet against this, and makes millions, hundreds of millions of dollars. And what do you do when you make hundreds of millions of dollars? You usually get into philanthropy. His philanthropy is protecting big cats like tigers and lions. And what do you do after the philanthropy? Well, usually suddenly hyper-rich people usually get into art. Remember the Rembrandt in the Louvre? Morse's Rembrandt? The angel's back? No, Kaplan does not own it. The Louvre owns it. The Louvre actually owns thirteen Rembrandts. Rembrandt is said to have painted around 335 paintings. Most of them are owned by museums like the Louvre. But there are thirty-five Rembrandts that are not in museums. They are in private hands. Guess who has the largest collection of Rembrandts in private hands? Yup, you guessed it: Kaplan. Kaplan is very good at detecting scarcity. He loves to be well-surrounded, but not just by Rembrandts, as I also soon discovered. Let me show you what I mean.

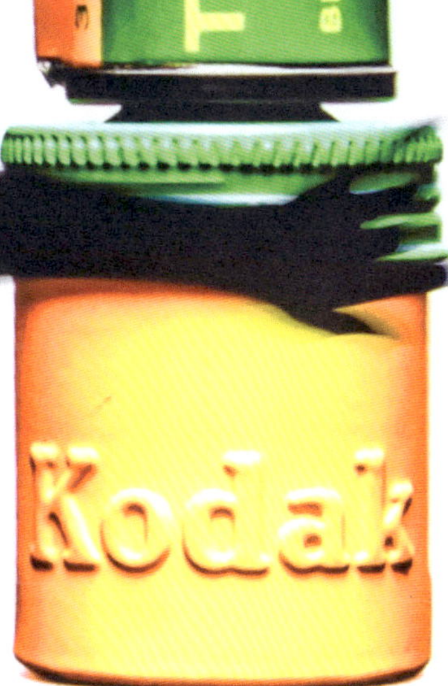

TX 135
Tri-X
Kodak
NGSA AUCTION IX
GENEVA
DECEMBER 14, 2015

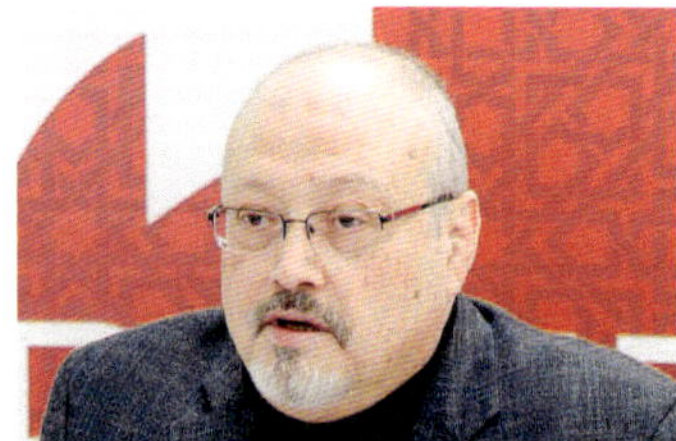

Jamal Khashoggi, 2018

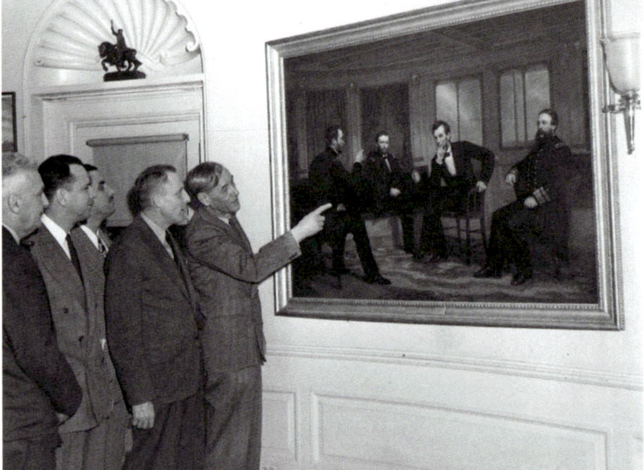

The Peacemakers by George Peter Alexander Healy installed in the White House, Washington, DC, 1947

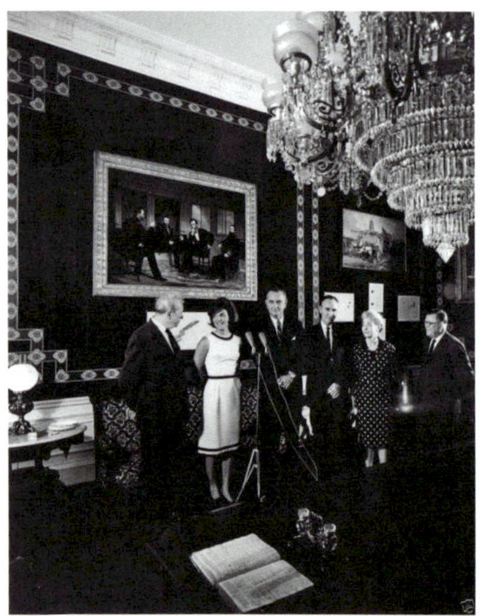

Jackie Kennedy showing off the restored and newly named Treaty Room, 1962

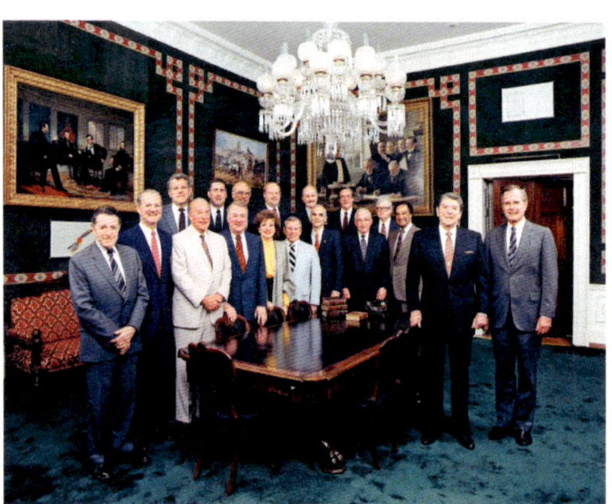

US President Ronald Reagan and his cabinet in the Treaty Room, 1987

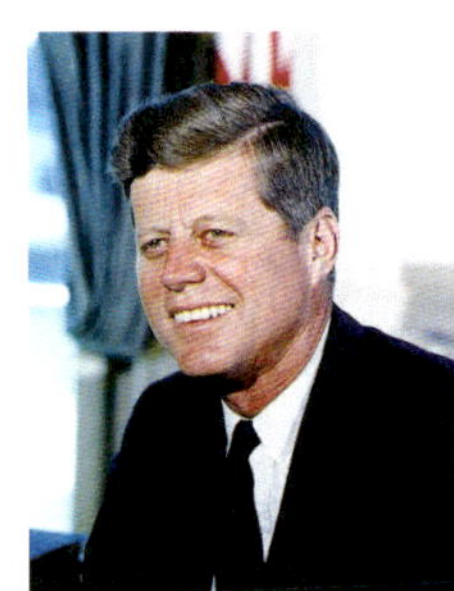

US President
John F. Kennedy, 1963

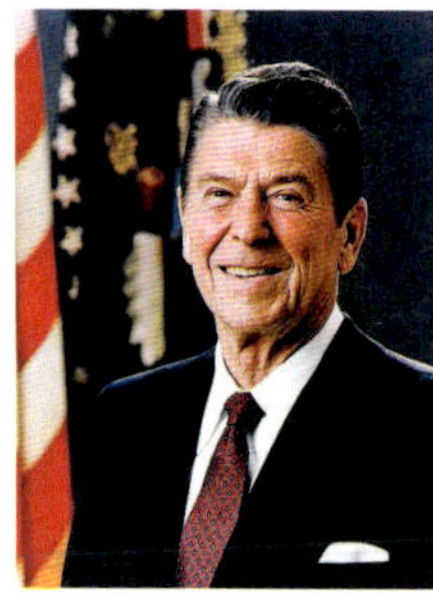

US President
Ronald Reagan, 1981

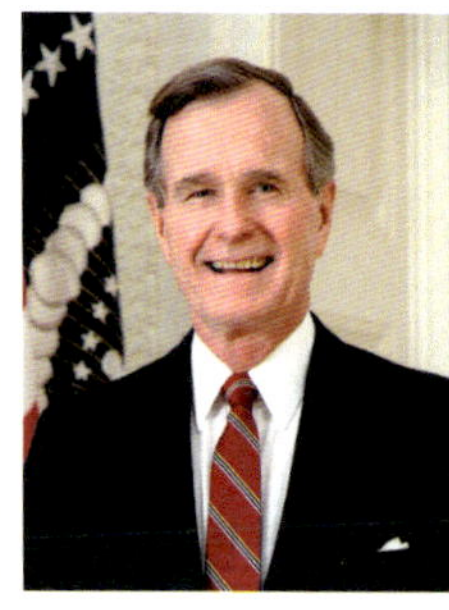

US President
George H. W. Bush, 1989

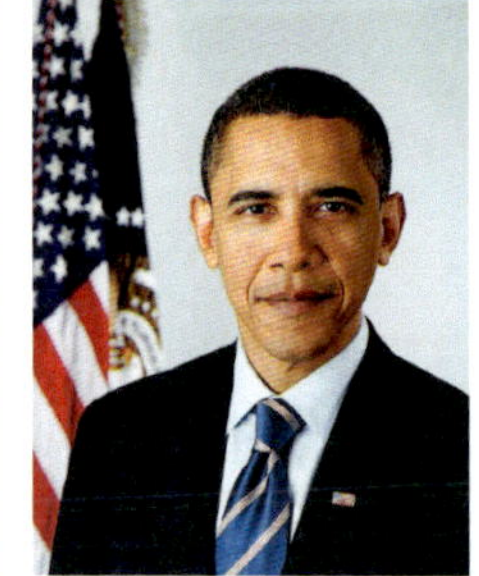

US President
Barack Obama, 2009

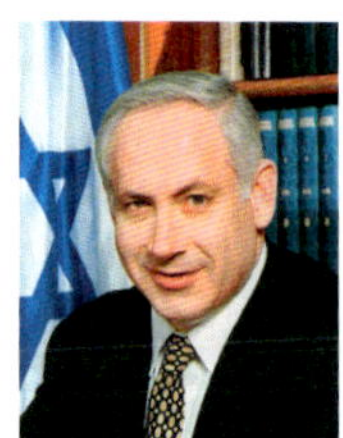

Benjamin Netanyahu, 1996

Frontispiece XXXV: The (Non) Peacemaker

Remember Jamal Khashoggi? The Saudi journalist killed by Saudi agents in Turkey a few years ago?

OK. Take a look at this.

 (from 1:35–3:30)

What is Kaplan doing in Saudi Arabia talking to a CIA analyst? Well, to answer this question, I need to take you back to this painting here, the maple syrup painting. This was the painting Lincoln asked for during his speech at The Cooper Union, and today, as I already mentioned, on the back wall at The Cooper Union hangs the George Healy painting, *The Peacemakers*.

Just like Martin Johnson Heade, Healy also liked to make two copies of every painting he did. I found two copies of *The Peacemakers*. The first copy is, of course, in The Cooper Union. The second copy of *The Peacemakers*? It's in Washington, DC, in the White House. I actually have a picture of it as it is hanging today in the White House. I have pictures of it in the White House in 1947, in 1963, and in 1985. I mean this painting is adored by American presidents. John F. Kennedy loved it. Ronald Reagan loved it. But no one loved it more than Bush Daddy. George H. W. Bush loved it so much that it appears as the background in his official presidential portrait. Another American president who loved this painting is Barack Obama. But Barack would do this strange thing. Barack would ask his staff to hang this painting in his private dining room every time he received one particularly non-peacemaker foreign leader, Israel's former prime minister Benjamin Netanyahu, Bibi. Every time Bibi came to America, Obama would ask the White House staff to hang this picture between him and Bibi.

As you may know, Obama and Bibi did not like each other much. In fact, they hated each other. You see, Obama wanted to talk about Palestine. Bibi wanted none of it. He just wanted America to focus on Iran. Sanction Iran, isolate Iran, threaten Iran, cyber warfare against Iran. The US was doing this, but not enough for Bibi's taste. Bibi also feared that Obama might actually strike a deal with Iran. And it was not just Israel that did not want this US-Iran deal. The Saudis did not want it. The Emiratis did not want it. There were also many Americans who were pushing hard against any US deal with Iran. No one was more vocal, more aggressive against Iran than a super-networked but anonymously funded group called UANI, which stands for United Against a Nuclear Iran. This UANI group has an incredible board. Look at these names: Joe Lieberman. Remember him? Vice president candidate with Al Gore in 2000? John Bolton, national security advisor and former US ambassador to the UN.

Anyway, just as Bibi feared, a deal between the US and Iran is signed in July 2015. But the agreement will barely last three years. Because when Trump was elected, he appointed Bolton as his new national security advisor. But Moustache Bolton was a core member of UANI. So, six weeks after Bolton joined the Trump administration, Trump unilaterally withdrew the US from the Iran nuclear deal. The day after the US withdrew from the Iran deal, a very interesting man visited the White House. His name was named Sheldon Adelson, a casino billionaire, right-wing arch-Zionist, and good friend of Trump and Bibi's. This visit sparked the interest of a very good journalist named Eli Clifton. For years, Clifton has been trying to find out who finances UANI, and when he saw Adelson at the White House, he put it all together. And after dozens of freedom of information requests, Clifton discovers that UANI has been anonymously funded not by hundreds of people, but mostly by just two people. Two people controlled US foreign policy on Iran? The first was Adelson. The second? The silver king himself, Thomas Kaplan.

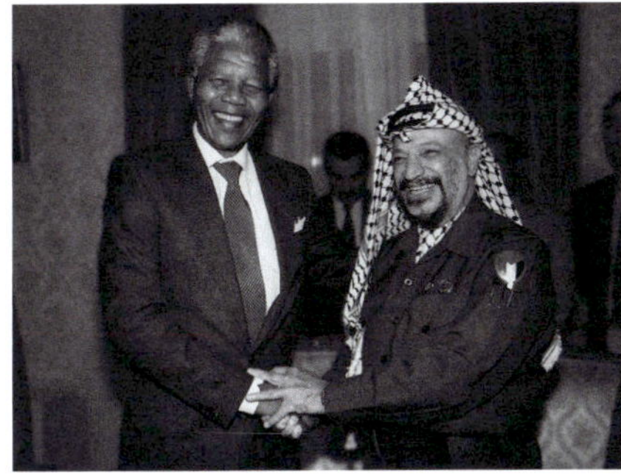

Nelson Mandela and Yasser Arafat, Cairo, 1990

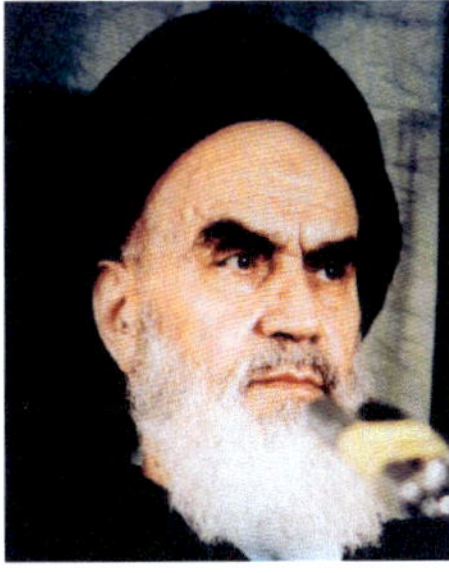

Ayatollah Khomeini, 1979

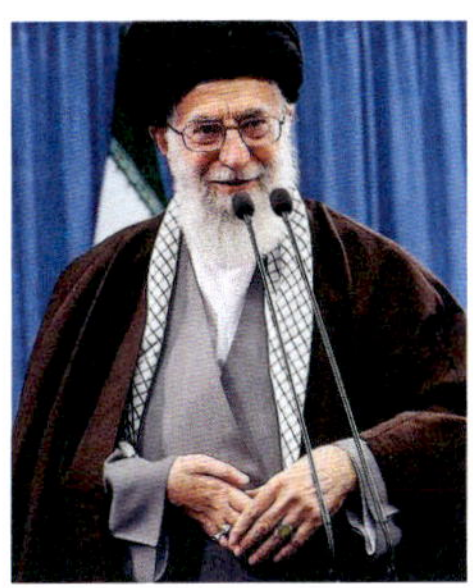

Ayatollah Khamenei, 2016

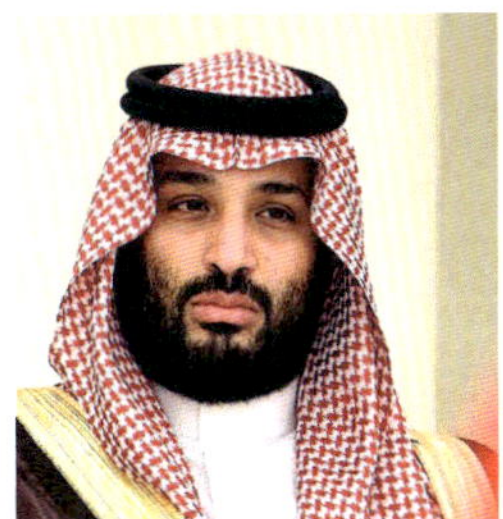

Mohammed bin Salman, 2019

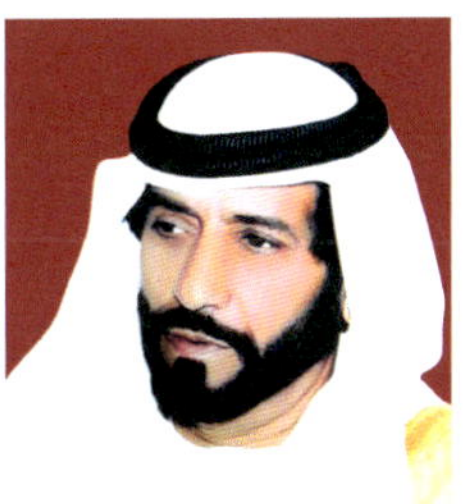

Sheikh Mohamed Bin Zayed Al Nahyan

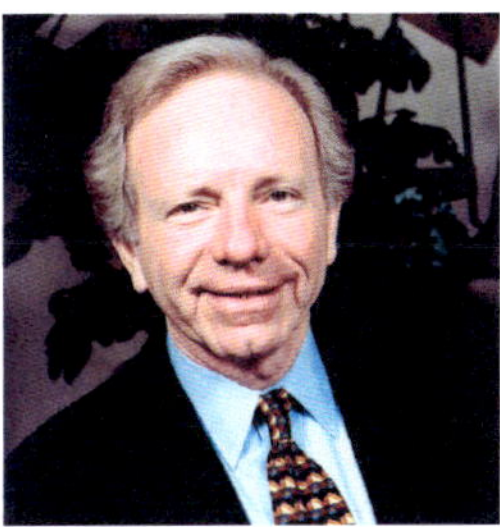

Joe Lieberman, 2004

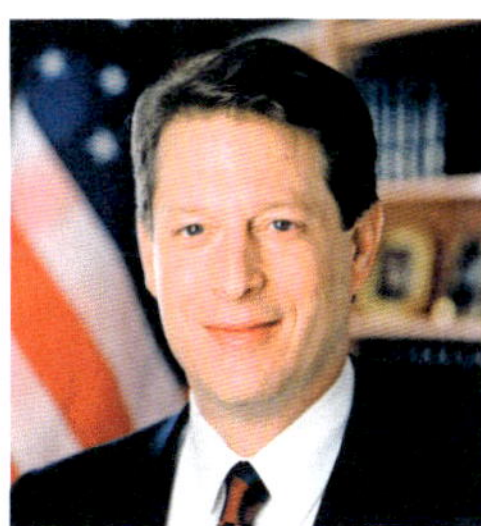

US Vice President Al Gore, 1994

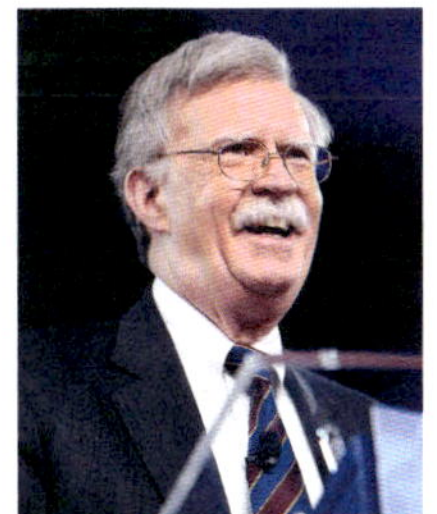

John Bolton, 2017

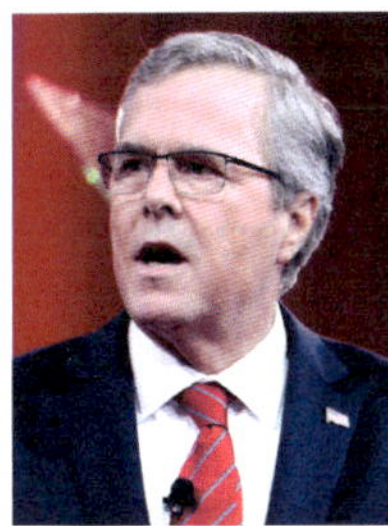

Jeb Bush, 2015

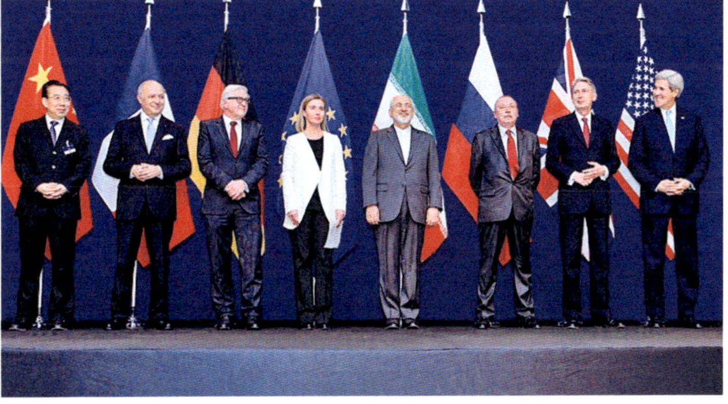

The ministers of foreign affairs and other officials from the P5+1 countries, the European Union, and Iran while announcing the framework of a comprehensive agreement on the Iranian nuclear program. Écublens-Lausanne, Switzerland 2015

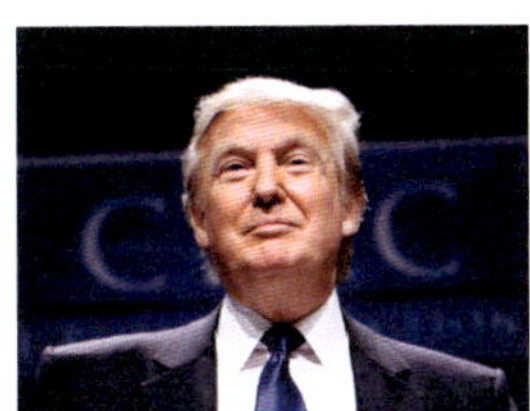

US President Donald Trump, 2011

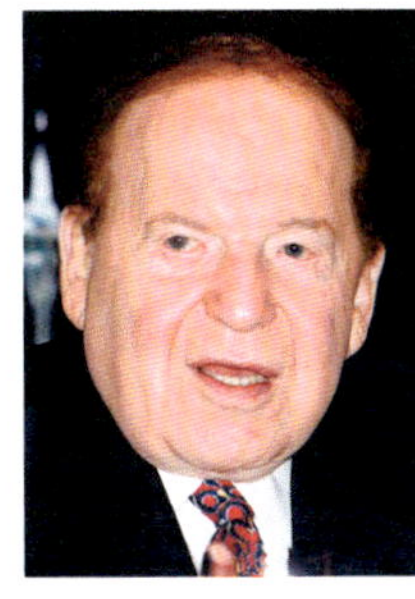

Sheldon Adelson, 2010

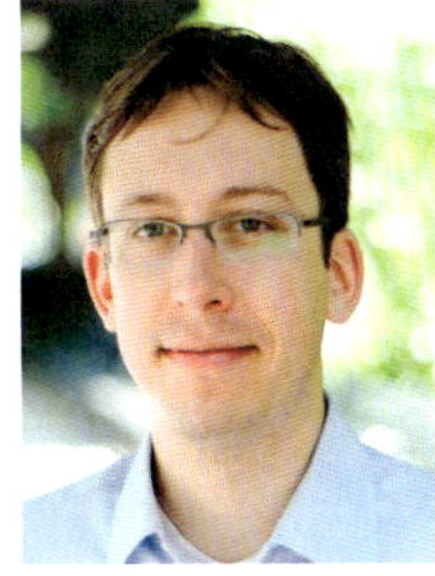

Eli Clifton

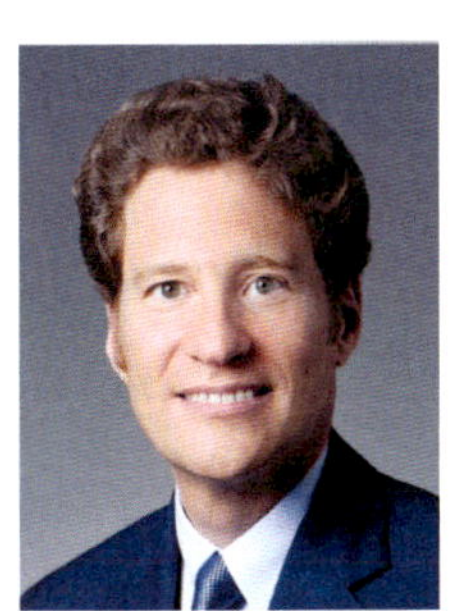

Thomas Kaplan

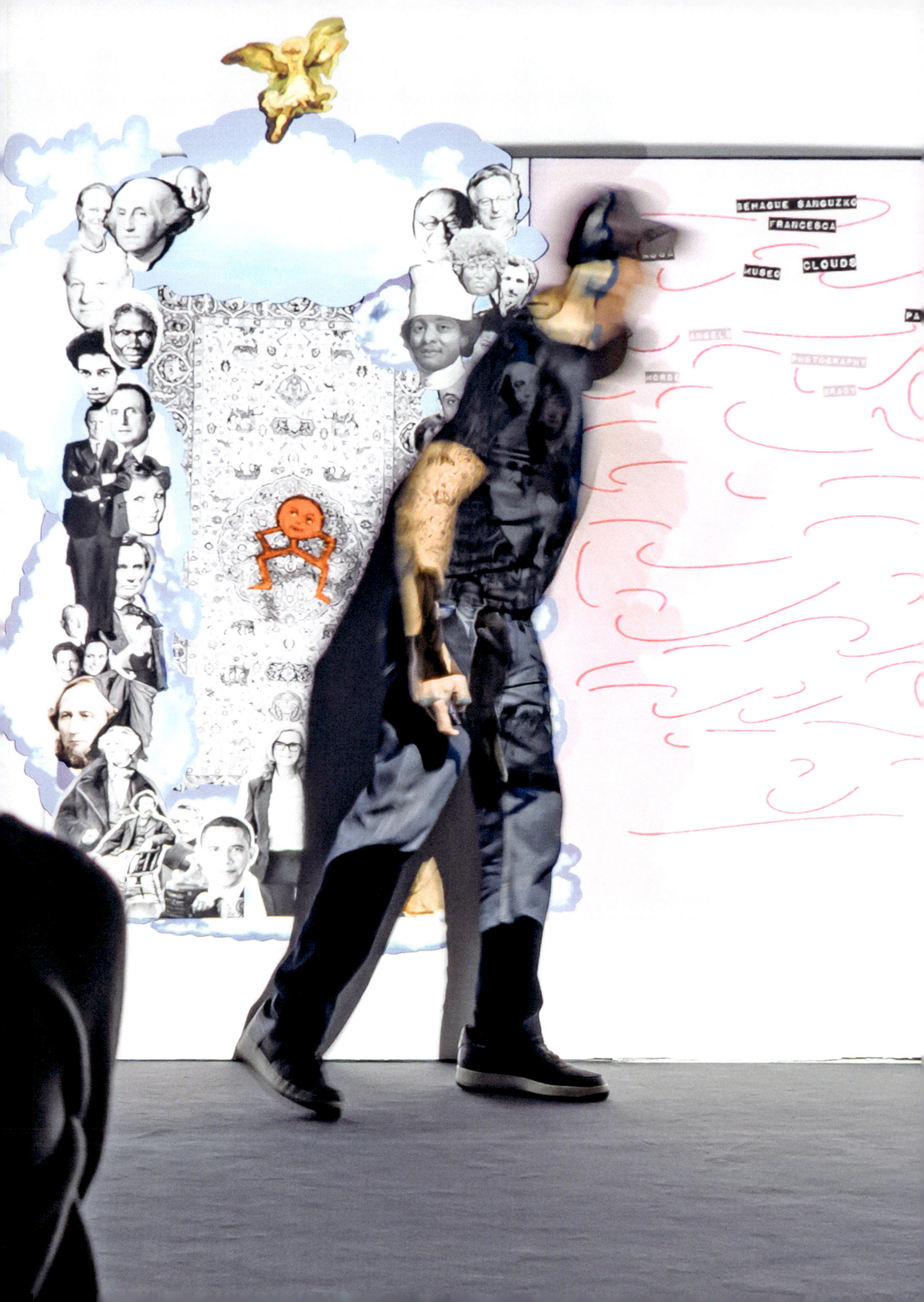
SEHAGUE SANGUZKO
FRANCESCA
MUSEO
CLOUDS

Frontispiece XXXVI: The Spider

I really tried to stay away from Kaplan. I wanted to stay away from Bibi, John Bolton, and Mohammed bin Salman, and Mohammed bin Zayed Al Nahyan, Yasser Arafat, and Iran. I really did. But these people kept popping up wherever I looked.

I thought I was by myself with a nice carpet, some puffy clouds, a gorgeous angel and a creepy gremlin, but before I knew it, all these people showed up. And they keep showing up. How did they all end up here? Actually, I know very well how they ended up here. And today, I am even convinced that these people were with me all along, from the very beginning in Doha. Remember how this went?

Qatar led me to Francesca; Francesca to a carpet; the carpet to this museum; this museum to the clouds and Antonova; Antonova to Palestine and angels; angels to the Louvre and Morse; Morse to photography and Brady and Lincoln; Lincoln to slavery and sugar and the White House and Obama and Bibi; Bibi to UANI, then back to photography and the telegraph; the telegraph to Constable and Carmen Thyssen-Bornemisza and Heade and sunsets and gremlins; gremlins to Crispo and Denise Thyssen-Bornemisza and Hans Heinrich Thyssen-Bornemisza; Hans Heinrich Thyssen-Bornemisza to Heinrich and Fritz Thyssen and the Germans and the Nazis and the Jews and Israel and my fascists; my fascists to 1983 and the Korean plane and Jean-Michel Basquiat and Michael Stewart and back to slavery; slavery to a cook and DTN and IHS and textiles; and, finally, textiles led me back to the jewel of Islamic art, a carpet made in Persia in the sixteenth century that ended up at the Ottoman court in the seventeenth century before it was taken by a Polish count in the eighteenth century, then bought by a French aristocrat in the nineteenth century, who then sold it to a Swiss baron in the twentieth century, who bequeathed it to his only daughter, who would never sell it to the richer-than-rich Arabs who in the twenty-first century tried to bring the carpet back to the region that created the carpet in the first place, and, most importantly for me, a carpet that's heavier than its weight.

Did I forget anything? Oh yes, of course, I forgot about the spider in the glass case! Remember the spider in the glass case upstairs? How did the spider get in there? Well, I now know how. And I'll show you.

Come with me. One last time. I promise. Come with me. I have something to show you. Let's go to the back one last time.

Epilogue VII: The Gold and Silver
Epilogue VIII: The Crates

Take a look at these prints over here.

I did not make these pictures. Lamia Antonova did. She made them in the early 1980s. As you can see, each object is surrounded by a different arthropod. This object has flies, and only flies. This one, spiders, and only spiders. Here, cockroaches. There, slugs. Here, millipedes, stick insects, and so on.

Antonova made these photos to document something very strange. She discovered that ten cups in Hans Heinrich Thyssen-Bornemisza's gold and silver collection attracted only one kind of arthropod and repulsed all others, as though each object had a specific chemical or electric signature. As if this was not strange enough, it also turns out that the flies, bees, slugs, and spiders seem to come out of nowhere. Actually, they don't seem to come out of nowhere. They literally came out of nowhere.

Lamia noticed that whenever she took the objects out of their custom-made cases—the cases are over there, you can look at them later—every time she took the objects out of their cases to display or to photograph, within seconds, out of nowhere, insects would appear. This even happened when the object was immediately transferred to a vacuum-sealed glass box. We saw this already, upstairs: the spider in the case. You don't think the museum staff checked and cleaned the case before closing it? Of course they did. These people are professionals. But it did not matter because as soon as the object went into the totally empty case, out of nowhere, out of the blue, just like clouds, insects irrupted. You can imagine this really freaked Antonova out. It freaks me out. Where the hell are these beasts coming from? It took Antonova seven years to figure this out. Seven years! And it took another strange event for her to figure it out. It actually took this. Take a look over here.

>
Walid Raad
Epilogue VII: The Gold and Silver, 2021

>>
Walid Raad
Epilogue VIII: The Crates, 2021
Installation view, Museo Nacional
Thyssen-Bornemisza, Madrid, 2021

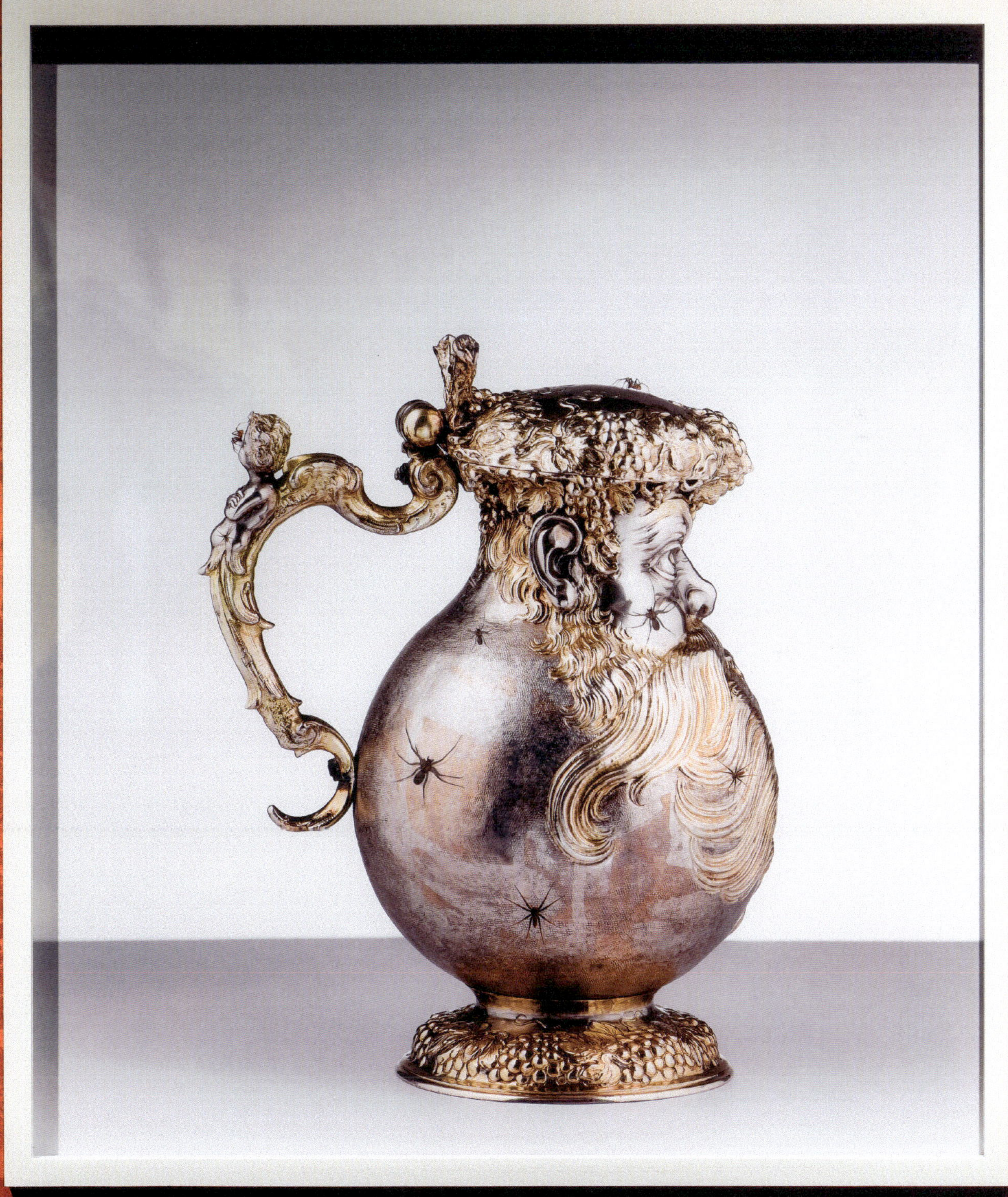

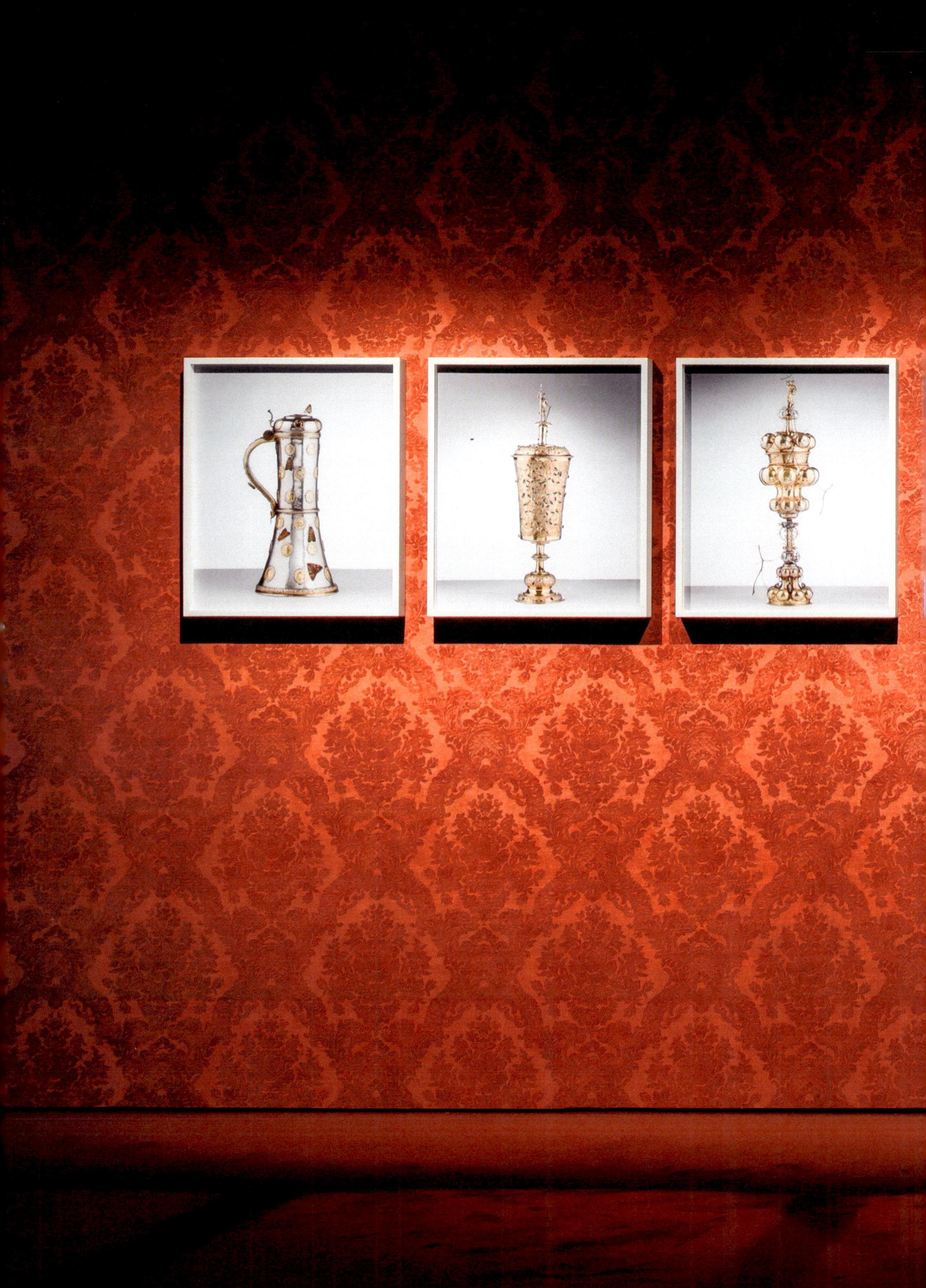

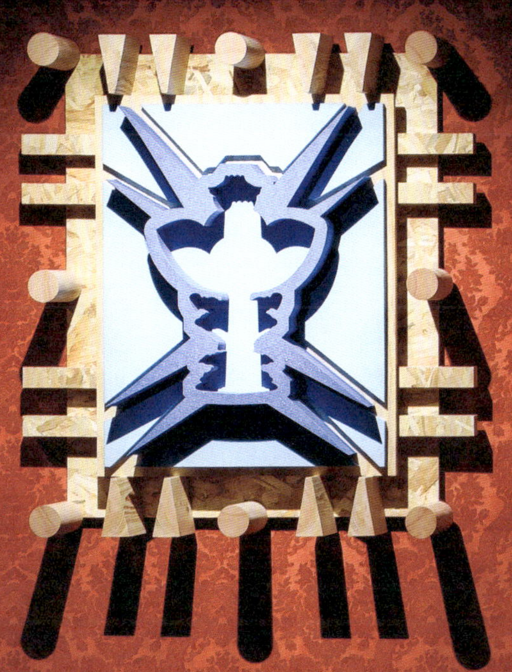
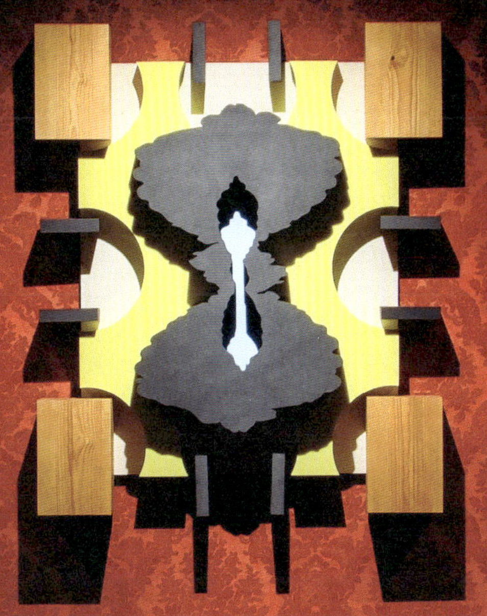

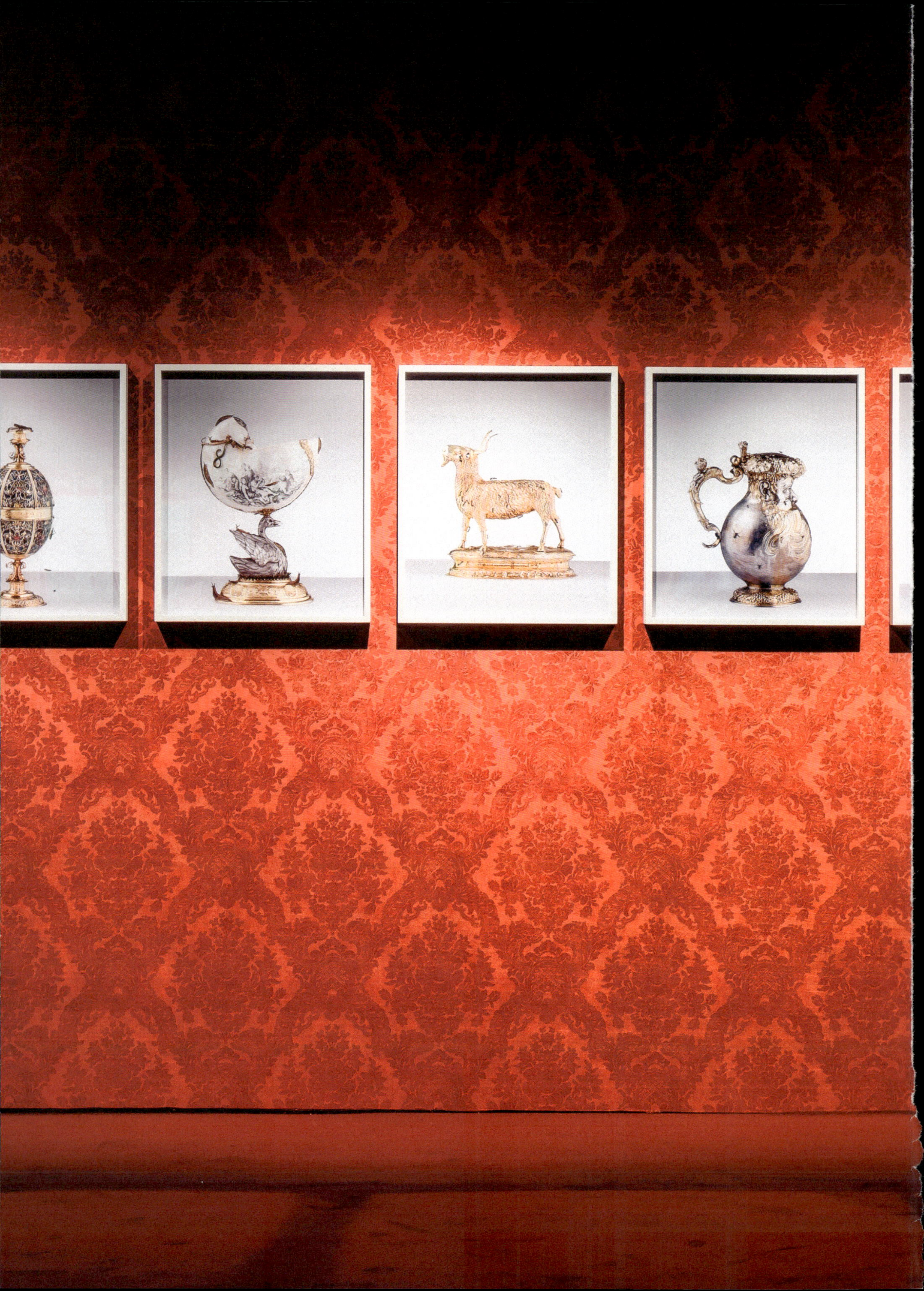

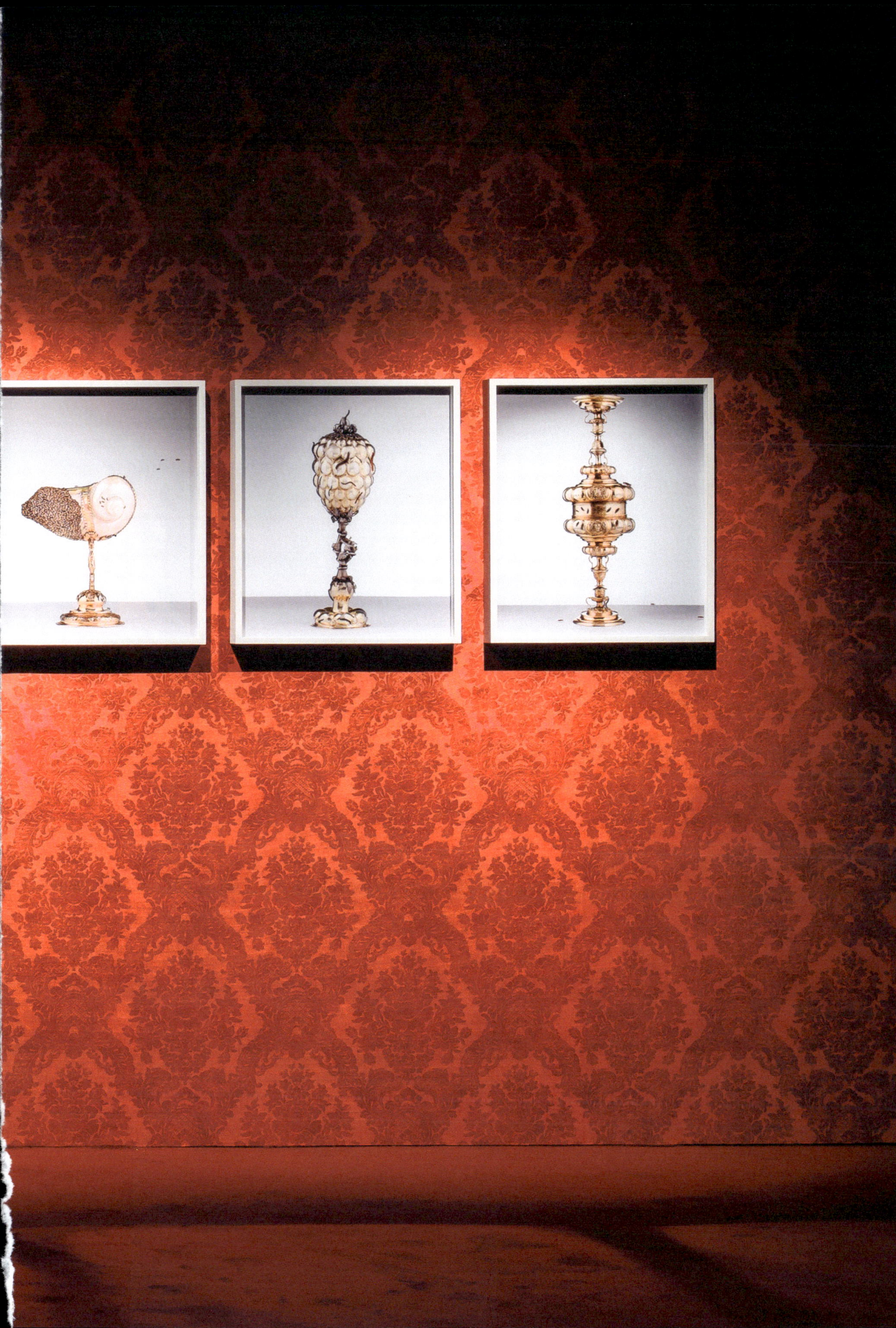

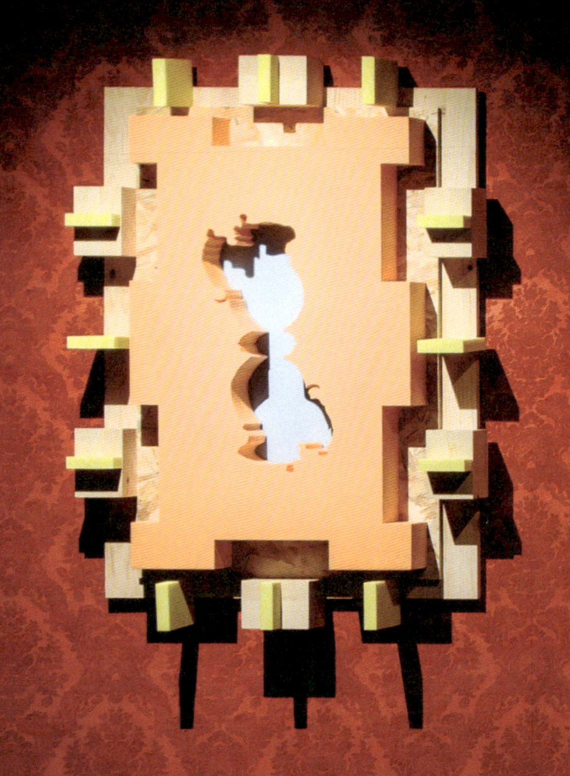

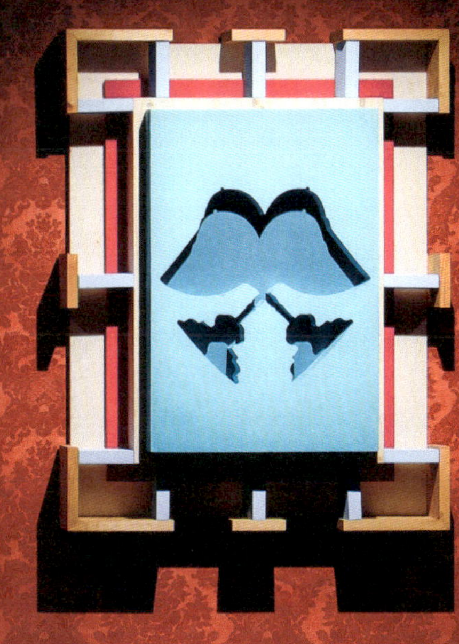
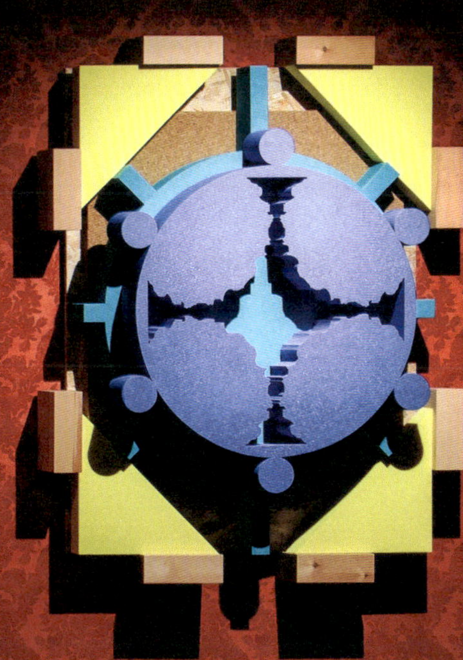

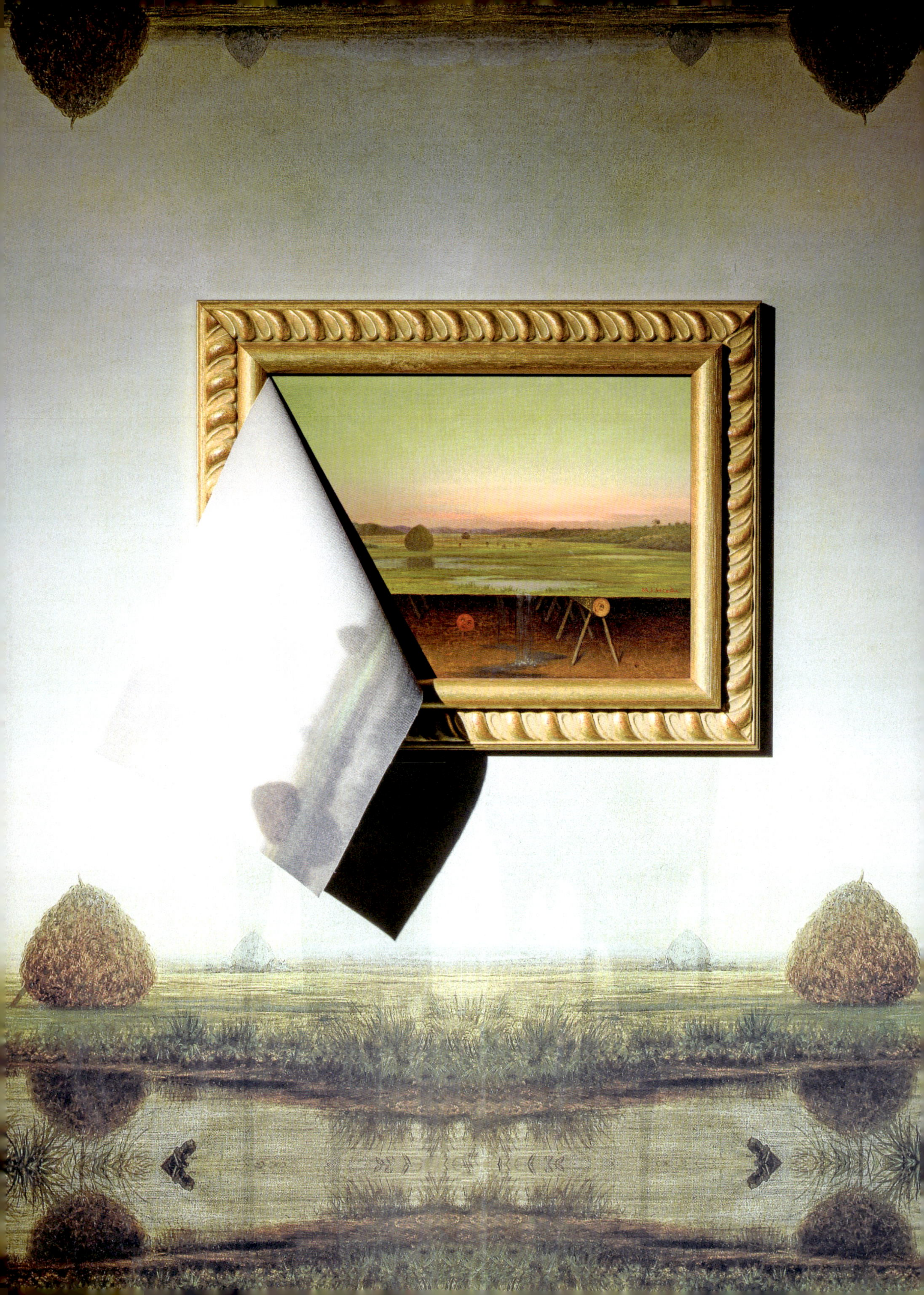

Epilogue IX: The Gremlins

Remember I showed you two paintings by the American artist Martin Johnson Heade in Carmen Thyssen's collection, and I said that Heade painted two copies, twins, of his landscapes. The copies upstairs were inherited by Carmen, and these ones here were inherited by Francesca.

Well, it also turns out that Francesca's copies were painted on top of other paintings. This is not unusual. Painters reuse the same canvases all the time. But what's unusual here is this: on the top layer, we have a familiar Heade swamp scene. But when you peel this top layer off, this is what appears. Look at this! The gremlin painting. Crispo's gremlin painting.

When Lamia Antonova discovered the under-paintings, she researched what if anything Heade ever said about the gremlin paintings. And it turns out that he spoke about them only once. In 1890, Heade stated that one day he was working on two of his marsh paintings, and that for a second, he looked away from the canvas to admire the sunset. When he looked back at the paintings, the gremlins were there. "I don't know where they came from," he said. "They came out of nowhere."

Came out of nowhere? Just like the spiders and flies on the gold and silver cups?

Most people would read Heade's "came out of nowhere" statement in a figurative manner, as some kind of allegory. But when she read his quote, Antonova immediately understood that there was nothing figurative here. This is no allegory. At that moment it all fell into place for her: the heavy carpet, the self-restoring angels, the spiders and flies, the X-rays and frames. Antonova also finally understood why Heade took on the pen name Didymus, the twin. He did so not because he liked to make two exact copies of every painting but because Didymus knew that he had two bodies, one alive and one dead. One body was standing in the middle of the marshes walking among the tall grasses. But the other body had long ago waterfalled to the gremlin side of the painting, to this place called "Nowhere." "Nowhere is a place," Antonova realized in a flash. It is a place where the figurative is literal, where insects and clouds irrupt out of the blue, where paintings never hang, where angels self-repair, where clouds will always travel faster than the weather, where a carpet is heavier than its weight, where vision tunnels, which means that no one can hide behind a curtain or under a carpet. No one. Not Heade. Not Kaplan, Bibi, MBS, MBZ, Obama, or Lincoln. Not Hans Heinrich Thyssen-Bornemisza. Not Francesca, nor Morse, nor Constable. And certainly not me.

Thank you.

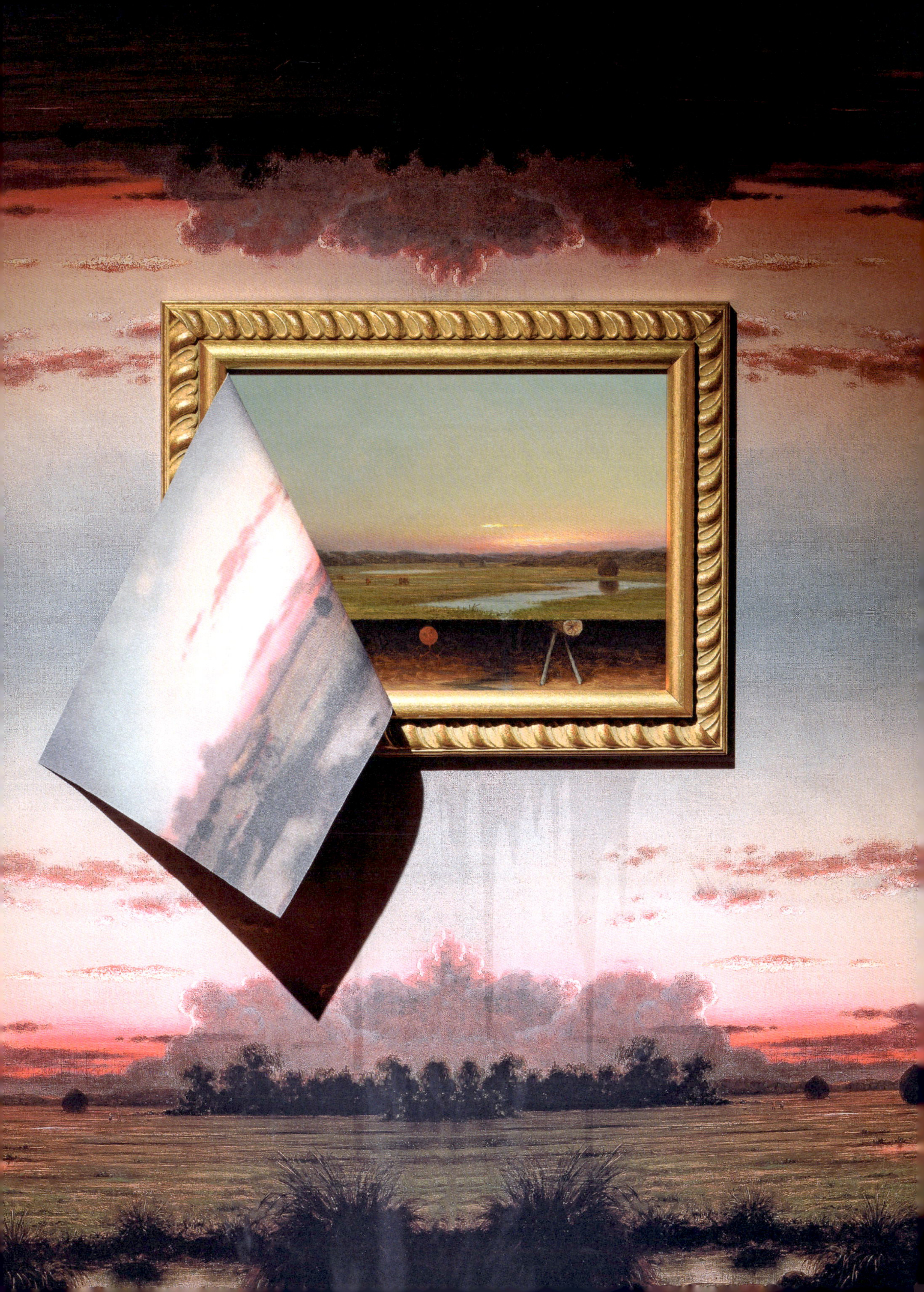

Bibliography

Alexander, James Wesley. "History of the Medical Use of Silver." *Surgical Infections* 10, no. 3 (30 June, 2009): 289–92.

Ali, Maulana Muhammad. *The Holy Quran Arabic Text with English Translation and Commentary*. Dublin, OH: Ahmadiyyah Anjuman Isha'at Islam Lahore, 2002.

Allen, Brian T. *Sugaring off: The Maple Sugar Paintings of Eastman Johnson*. Williamstown, MA: Sterling and Francine Clark Art Institute; New Haven: Yale University Press, 2004.

Annunciation. London; New York: Phaidon, 2004.

Ariès, Philippe. *The Hour of Our Death*. New York: Vintage Books, 1982.

Arts, Ben, and Duncan Campbell. "How Bush's Grandfather Helped Hitler's Rise to Power." *The Guardian*, September 25, 2004. https://www.theguardian.com/world/2004/sep/25/usa.secondworldwar.

Athanassoglou-Kallmyer, Nina. "Blemished Physiologies: Delacroix, Paganini, and the Cholera Epidemic of 1832." *The Art Bulletin* 83, no. 4 (May 9, 2014): 686–710.

Avery, Kevin J., Oswaldo Rodriguez Roque, John K. Howat, Doreen Bolger Burke, and Catherine Hoover Voorsanger. *American Paradise: The World of the Hudson River School*. New York: Metropolitan Museum of Art, 2013.

Benfey, Christopher E. G. *A Summer of Hummingbirds: Love, Art, and Scandal in the Intersecting Worlds of Emily Dickinson, Mark Twain, Harriet Beecher Stowe, and Martin Johnson Heade*. London: Penguin Books, 2009.

Blum, Andrew. *The Weather Machine: A Journey Inside the Forecast*. New York: Ecco, 2019.

Bolger, Doreen, Marc Simpson, and John Wilmerding, eds. *William M. Harnett*. Fort Worth: Amon Carter Museum, 1992.

Boskovits, Miklós. *Early Italian Painting, 1290–1470. The Thyssen-Bornemisza Collection*. London: Sotheby's Publications, 1990.

Bowlt, John E., and Nicoletta Misler. *Twentieth-Century Russian and East European Painting. The Thyssen-Bornemisza Collection*. London: Zwemmer, 1993.

Brown Washington, Dinah. "'Men of Progress'—But Who Are They?" *The New York Times*, March 11, 1962. https://www.nytimes.com/1962/03/11/archives/men-of-progressbut-who-are-they.html.

Brownlee, Peter John, ed. *Samuel F.B. Morse's Gallery of the Louvre and the Art of Invention*. New Haven: Terra Foundation for American Art, Yale University Press, 2014.

Cabra, Mar, and Michael Hudson. "Mega-Rich Use Tax Havens to Buy and Sell Masterpieces." *International Consortium of Investigative Journalists*, April 3, 2013. https://www.icij.org/investigations/offshore/mega-rich-use-tax-havens-buy-and-sell-masterpieces/.

Cambell, Karen J. "Rilke's Duino Angels and the Angels of Islam." *Alif: Journal of Comparative Poetics*, January 1, 2003. https://www.thefreelibrary.com/Rilke%27s+Duino+angels+and+the+angels+of+Islam.-a0122661094.

Cammann, Schuyler. "The Interplay of Art, Literature, and Religion in afavid Symbolism." *The Journal of the Royal Asiatic Society of Great Britain and Ireland*, no. 2 (1978): 124–36.

Cao, Maggio M. *The End of Landscape in Nineteenth-Century America*. Oakland: University of California Press, 2018.

Carbone, Teresa A., and Patricia Hills. *Eastman Johnson: Painting America*. New York: Brooklyn Museum of Art, in association with Rizzoli International Publications, 1999.

Carli, Gabriel Jose de, and Tiago Campos Pereira. "On Human Parthenogenesis." *Medical Hypotheses* 106 (September 2017): 57–60.

Christ, Coastas. "Billionaires Buy into Ocean Conservation." *National Geographic*, November 4, 2013. https://www.nationalgeographic.com/travel/article/billionaires-buy-into-ocean-conservation.

Clifton, Eli. "Sheldon Adelson's Legacy of Underwriting American Militarism." Responsible Statecraft, January 12, 2021. https://responsiblestatecraft.org/2021/01/12/sheldon-adelsons-legacy-of-underwriting-american-militarism/.

Clifton, Eli, and Derek Davison. "Pompeo and Bolton Are Headlining a Pro-War, Anti-Iran Event—And We Should All Be Very Worried." *In The Set Times*, September 24, 2018. https://inthesetimes.com/article/pompeo-bolton-trump-united-against-nuclear-iran.

Cohen, Philip. "The Boy Whose Blood Has No Father." *New Scientist*, October 6, 1995. https://www.newscientist.com/article/mg14819982-300-the-boy-whose-blood-has-no-father/.

Contini, Roberto. *Seventeenth and Eighteenth Century Italian Painting. The Thyssen-Bornemisza Collection*. London: Philip Wilson Publishers, 2002.

De Peverelli, Maria, and Doriana Comerlati, eds. *Thyssen-Bornemisza Foundation, Villa Favorita: Guidebook*. Milano: Skira, 1997.

De Pury, Simon, and William Stadiem. *The Auctioneer: Adventures in the Art Trade*. New York: St. Martin's Press, 2016.

Dickens, Charles. *Bleak House*. New York: Dover Publications, 2017.

Dostoevsky, Fyodor. *Notes from Underground*. Penguin Classics. London: Penguin Books, 2011.

Dommermuth, Jean. "Dianne Modestini Discusses the Treatment of Leonardo da Vinci's *Salvator Mundi* with Jean Dommermuth '96." *Institute of Fine Arts: New York University*, no. 12 (January 2012). https://www.ifa.nyu.edu/pdfs/publications/Newsgram12_SalvatorMundi.pdf.

Drummond, Sarah. *Divine Conception: The Art of the Annunciation*. London: Unicorn Publishing Group, 2018.

Ducos, Blaise, and Dominique Surh, eds. *Chefs-d'œuvre de la collection Leiden: Le siècle de Rembrandt / Masterpieces of the Leiden Collection: The Age of Rembrandt*. Paris: Louvre éditions, 2017.

Ducos, Blaise, and Lara Yeager-Crasselt, eds. *Rembrandt, Vermeer and the Dutch Golden Age: Masterpieces from the Leiden Collection and the Musée du Louvre*, London: Saqi Books, 2019.

Eaton, Leslie. "Art Dealer Returns With a Fresh Canvas; Crispo Survives Bankruptcy, Scandal and Prison to Create a New Gallery." *The New York Times*, August 11, 1998. https://www.nytimes.com/1998/08/11/nyregion/art-dealer-returns-with-fresh-canvas-crispo-survives-bankruptcy-scandal-prison.html.

Eisler, Colin T. *Early Netherlandish Painting. The Thyssen-Bornemisza Collection.* London: Sotheby's Publications, 1989.

Equal Justice Initiative. *Lynching in America: Confronting the Legacy of Racial Terror*. Equal Justice Initiative, 2017.

——. *Reconstruction in America: Racial Violence after the Civil War, 1865–1876*. Equal Justice Initiative, 2020.

——. *Slavery in America: The Montgomery Slave Trade*. Equal Justice Initiative, 2013.

Evans, Mark. *Constable's Skies: Paintings and Sketches by John Constable*. London: Thames & Hudson, 2018.

Feaver, William, and Lucian Freud. *Freud on Constable: Lucian Freud on John Constable—A Conversation with William Feaver*. London: The British Council Visual Arts Publications, 2003.

Ferber, Linda S., ed. *The Hudson River School: Nature and the American Vision*. New York: Skira Rizzoli, 2009.

Ferber, Linda S., and A. B. Durand, eds. *Kindred Spirits: Asher B. Durand and the American Landscape*. New York: Brooklyn Museum; in association with D Giles Limited, 2007.

France, David. *Bag of Toys: Sex, Scandal, and the Death Mask Murder*. New York: Warner Books, 1992.

Frankenstein, Alfred V. *The Reality of Appearance: The Trompe l'Œil Tradition in American Painting*. Greenwich, CT: New York Graphic Society Ltd., 1970.

Franses, Michael. "Persian Classical Carpets: A Museum of Masterpieces, Safavid Carpets in the Museum of Islamic Art, Qatar." *HALI* 155 (2008): 72–89.

Freierman, Shelly. "Telegram Falls Silent Stop Era Ends Stop." *The New York Times*, February 6, 2006. https://www.nytimes.com/2006/02/06/technology/telegram-falls-silent-stop-era-ends-stop.html.

Friedman, Lawrence M. *Dead Hands: A Social History of Wills, Trusts, and Inheritance Law*. Stanford, CA: Stanford Law Books, 2009.

Fry, Hannah. "Why Weather Forecasting Keeps Getting Better." *The New Yorker*, June 24, 2019. https://www.newyorker.com/magazine/2019/07/01/why-weather-forecasting-keeps-getting-better.

Gaskell, Ivan. *Seventeenth-Century Dutch and Flemish Painting. The Thyssen-Bornemisza Collection.* London: Sotheby's Publications, 1990.

Gall, Gabriella Eva Cristina, Stephan Lautenschlager, and Homayoun C. Bagheri. "Quarantine as a Public Health Measure against an Emerging Infectious Disease: Syphilis in Zurich at the Dawn of the Modern Era (1496–1585)." *GMS Hyg Infect Control* 11, no. 13 (May 6, 2016). https://www.ncbi.nlm.nih.gov/pmc/articles/PMC4899769/.

Gibran, Jean, and Kahlil Gibran. *Kahlil Gibran: Beyond Borders*. Northampton, MA: Interlink Books, 2017.

Gillespie, Sarah Kate. "Samuel Morse and the Quest for the Daguerreotype Portrait." *The MIT Press Reader*, March 16, 2020. https://thereader.mitpress.mit.edu/samuel-morse-quest-for-daguerreotype-portrait/.

Giridharadas, Anand. *Winners Take All: The Elite Charade of Changing the World.* New York: Alfred A. Knopf, 2018.

Green, Christopher. *The European Avant-Gardes: Art in France and Western Europe 1904–1945. The Thyssen-Bornemisza Collection.* London: Zwemmer, 1995.

Haddadin, Munther J. "Water in the Middle East Peace Process." *The Geographical Journal* 168, no. 4 (December 2002): 324–40.

Harvey, Eleanor Jones. *The Civil War and American Art*. Washington, DC: Smithsonian American Art Museum; New Haven: Yale University Press, 2012.

Hays, Kristen. "Moneymakers: Five Questions with Guma Aguiar." *Chron*, December 26, 2006. https://www.chron.com/business/energy/article/Moneymakers-Five-questions-with-Guma-Aguiar-1854944.php.

Hilliard, Henry E. "Silver Recycling in the United States in 2000." *USGS Numbered Series*, Open-File Report, 2003.

Holy Bible: King James Version. Compiled by Baker Publishing Group, Cambridge: Cambridge University Press, 2017.

Holzer, Harold. "The Photograph That Made Lincoln President." *HistoryNet*, December 2006. https://www.historynet.com/the-photograph-that-made-lincoln-president.htm.

Hope, Bradley, and Tom Wright. *Billion Dollar Whale: The Man Who Fooled Wall Street, Hollywood, and the World.* New York: Hachette Books, 2018.

Hudson, Brian J. "The Naming of Waterfalls." *Geographical Research* 51, no. 1 (February 2013). https://www.researchgate.net/publication/259691504_The_Naming_of_Waterfalls.

Hussain, Murtaza. "Did an American Billionaire Philanthropist Play a Role in The Imprisonment of Iranian Environmentalists?" *The Intercept*, November 27, 2019. https://theintercept.com/2019/11/27/iran-environmentalists-panthera-thomas-kaplan/.

James, Henry. *The Figure in the Carpet.* Gloucester: Dodo Press, 2007.

Jardine, Boris. "Made Real: Artifice and Accuracy in Nineteenth-Century Scientific Illustration: Luke Howard's Clouds and the Persistence of Convention." *Science Museum Group Journal*, March 9, 2014. http://journal.sciencemuseum.ac.uk/browse/issue-02/made-real/luke-howard-s-clouds-and-the-persistence-of-convention.

Jerez, Concha, Germán Labrador Méndez, and Amador Fernández-Savater. *Libidinal Economy of the Spanish Transition.* Madrid: Museo Reina Sofía, 2018.

Kagan, J.O., O.G. Kostyuk, and M.N. Lopato. *Ori e Argenti Dall'Ermitage.* Lugano and Milan: Thyssen-Bornemisza Collection and Electa international, 1986.

Koepsell. Thomas D. "Eastman Johnson, Freedom Ring (1860)." *Archives of Pediatrics & Adolescent Medicine* 157 (January 2003): 13. doi: 10.1001/archpedi.157.1.013.

Kornhauser, Elizabeth Mankin, Amy Ellis, and Maureen Miesmer. *Hudson River School: Masterworks from the Wadsworth Atheneum Museum of Art.* Hartford: Wadsworth Atheneum Museum of Art; New Haven: Yale University Press, 2003.

Lamb, Juliet. "What If We Had All the Birds from Shakespeare in Central Park?" *Jstor Daily*, June 9, 2016. https://daily.jstor.org/all-the-birds-from-shakespeare-in-central-park/.

Lianos, Ioannis, and Dmitry Katalevsky. "Merger Activity in the Factors of Production Segments of the Food Value Chain: A Critical Assessment of the Bayer/Monsanto Merger." *Center for Law, Economics and Society*, CLES Policy Paper Series 2017/1, October 2017.

Levin, Gail. *Twentieth-Century American Painting. The Thyssen-Bornemisza Collection.* London: Sotheby's Publications, 1987.

Lewis, Ben. *The Last Leonardo: The Secret Lives of the World's Most Expensive Painting.* New York: Ballantine Books, 2019.

Litchfield, David R. L., and Caroline Schmitz. *The Thyssen Art Macabre.* London: Quartet Books, 2006.

Lloyd, Jill, and Michael Peppiatt. *Christian Schad and the Neue Sachlichkeit.* New York: Neue Galerie and W.W. Norton & Company, 2003.

Lübbeke, Isolde. *Early German Painting, 1350–1550. The Thyssen-Bornemisza Collection.* London: Sotheby's Publications, 1991.

Martin, Therese. "The Development of Winged Angels in Early Christian Art." *Espacio Tiempo y Forma Serie VII Historia Del Arte* 14 (January 2001). https://www.researchgate.net/publication/242610155_The_Development_of_Winged_Angels_in_Early_Christian_Art.

Massinger, Charles. "The Gremlin Myth." *The Journal of Educational Sociology*, American Sociological Association 17, no. 6 (February 1944): 359–67.

McCullough, David. "Samuel Morse's Reversal of Fortune." *Smithsonian Magazine*, September 2011. https://www.smithsonianmag.com/history/samuel-morses-reversal-of-fortune-49650609/.

McNeil, James. "The Ecology of Death: Forensic Entomology as a Teaching Tool." *The American Biology Teacher* 72, no. 3 (March 2010): 153–55.

Metz, Phoebe. "Pieces of 'The Peacemakers.'" *The Newberry*, July 7, 2016. https://www.newberry.org/pieces-peacemakers.

Miller, David C. *Dark Eden: The Swamp in Nineteenth-Century American Culture.* Cambridge: Cambridge University Press, 2010.

Miller, Lillian B., ed. *The Peale Family: Creation of a Legacy, 1770–1870.* New York: Abbeville Press in association with the Trust for Museum Exhibitions and the National Portrait Gallery, Smithsonian Institution, 1996.

Moore, Peter. *The Weather Experiment: The Pioneers Who Sought to See the Future*. New York: Farrar, Straus and Giroux, 2016.

Muhammad, Khalil Gibran. "The Sugar That Saturates the American Diet Has a Barbaric History as the 'White Gold' That Fueled Slavery." *The New York Times Magazine*, August 14, 2019. https://www.nytimes.com/interactive/2019/08/14/magazine/sugar-slave-trade-slavery.html.

Muromtseva, Olga. "Connoisseurs Extraordinaire: Irina Antonova, President of the A. Pushkin State Museum of Fine Arts, Devoted Her Entire Life to the Museum and Its Collection." *Unident Group of Companies*, May 15, 2019. http://www.unident.ru/en/uart/Connoisseurs-extraordinaire-15286.phtml.

Müller, Hannelore. *European Silver. The Thyssen-Bornemisza Collection*. London: Sotheby's Publications, 1986.

Myers, Kenneth John, Kevin J. Avery, Gerald L. Carr, and Mercedes Volait. *Frederic Church: A Painter's Pilgrimage*. Detroit: Detroit Institute of Arts, 2017.

Neimanis, Astrida. "The Sea and the Breathing." Oceans in Transformation (series), *e-flux Architecture,* May 2020. https://www.e-flux.com/architecture/oceans/331869/the-sea-and-the-breathing/.

Noll, Richard, ed. *Vampires, Werewolves, and Demons: Twentieth Century Reports in the Psychiatric Literature*. New York: Brunner/Mazel, 1992.

Novak, Barbara. *Nature and Culture: American Landscape and Painting, 1825–1875*. Oxford: Oxford University Press, 2007.

Novak, Barbara, and Timothy A. Eaton. *Martin Johnson Heade: A Survey, 1840–1900*. West Palm Beach: Eaton Fine Art, 1996.

Novak, Barbara, and Elizabeth Garrity Ellis. *Nineteenth-Century American Painting: Catalogue*. Milano: Mondadori, 1986.

Parry, Ellwood C. III. "Thomas Cole's The Titan's Goblet: A Reinterpretation." *Metropolitan Museum Journal* 4 (1971): 123–140. https://www.jstor.org/stable/1512618.

Pearsall, Glenn. "Maple Syrup Production and Slavery." *Adirondack Almanack*, March 25, 2015. https://www.adirondackalmanack.com/2015/03/maple-syrup-production-and-slavery-2.html.

Peluso, Anthony J. *The Bard Brothers: Painting America under Steam and Sail*. New York: H.N. Abrams, in association with the Mariners' Museum, 1997.

Pirovano, Carlo. *Capolavori impressionisti e postimpressionisti dai musei sovietici*. Lugano and Milan: Thyssen-Bornemisza Collection and Electa international, 1983.

Pollan, Michael. "The Intelligent Plant: Scientists Debate a New Way of Understanding Flora." *The New Yorker*, December 15, 2013. https://www.newyorker.com/magazine/2013/12/23/the-intelligent-plant.

Pope, Annemarie H. *American Masters. The Thyssen-Bornemisza Collection*. London: Sotheby's Publications, 1985.

Property from the Andrew Crispo Collection: New York, November and December 1997. New York: Sotheby's Publications, 1997.

Radcliffe, Anthony. *Renaissance and Later Sculpture. The Thyssen-Bornemisza Collection*. London: Sotheby's Publications, 1992.

Rahbé, Yvan, Edwige Keller-Rahbé, and Sibylle Orlandi. "Insects as Interactants in Artists' Minds: Symbols and Anti-Symbols." *Comptes Rendus Biologies* 342, no. 7–8 (October 2019): 249–50.

Rancière, Jacques. *Le temps du paysage: Aux origines de la révolution esthétique*. Paris: La Fabrique éditions, 2020.

Reich, Rob. *Just Giving: Why Philanthropy Is Failing Democracy and How It Can Do Better*. Princeton: Princeton University Press, 2018.

The Reminiscent Object: Paintings by William Michael Harnett, John Frederick Peto and John Haberle. San Diego: La Jolla Museum of Art, 1965.

Rilke, Rainer Maria. *Duino Elegies and the Sonnets to Orpheus*. Translated by Stephen Mitchell. New York: Vintage International, 2009.

Richardson, Paul. "Why Are so Many Art Collectors Opening Museums in Spain?" *Financial Times*, June 21, 2019. https://www.ft.com/content/dd3bf112-8928-11e9-b861-54ee436f9768.

Rhodes, Carl, and Peter Bloom. "The Trouble with Charitable Billionaires." *The Guardian*, May 24, 2018. https://www.theguardian.com/news/2018/may/24/the-trouble-with-charitable-billionaires-philanthrocapitalism.

Rozen, Laura. "In W.H., Are Pictures Telling a Story?" *Politico*, November 15, 2009. https://www.politico.com/story/2009/11/in-wh-are-pictures-telling-a-story-029559.

Ruskin, John. "The Storm-Cloud of the Nineteenth Century: Two Lectures Delivered at the London Institution February 4th and 11th, 1884." Project Gutenberg eBook, December 28, 2006. https://www.gutenberg.org/files/20204/20204-h/20204-h.htm.

Schmidt-Nowara, Christopher. "Silver, Slaves, and Sugar: The Persistence of Spanish Colonialism from Absolutism to Liberalism." *Latin American Research Review* 39, no. 2 (January 2004): 196–210.

Schouvaloff, Alexander. *Set and Costume Designs for Ballet and Theatre. The Thyssen-Bornemisza Collection.* London: Sotheby's Publications, 1987.

Schwarz, Erich M. "Evolution: A Parthenogenetic Nematode Shows How Animals Become Sexless." *Current Biology: Dispatches* 27, no. 9 (October 9, 2017): R1064–66.

Searls, Damion. *The Inkblots: Hermann Rorschach, His Iconic Test, and the Power of Seeing*. New York: Crown, 2017.

Shallenberger, Krysti. "Mine Backers Call Report That Says the Donlin Gold Mine Is Too Expensive to Build 'Misinformation.'" *KTOO* (blog), June 17, 2020. https://www.ktoo.org/2020/06/17/mine-backers-call-report-that-says-the-donlin-gold-mine-is-too-expensive-to-build-misinformation/.

Silber, William L. *The Story of Silver: How the White Metal Shaped America and the Modern World*. Princeton: Princeton University Press, 2019.

Silverman, Kenneth. *Lightning Man: The Accursed Life of Samuel F.B. Morse*. New York: Alfred A. Knopf, 2003.

Solana, Guillermo, and Paloma Alarcó. *Expresionismo alemán en la Colección del Barón Thyssen-Bornemisza*. Madrid: Museo Nacional Thyssen-Bornemisza, 2020.

Somers Cocks, Anna, and Charles Truman. *Renaissance Jewels, Gold Boxes and Objets de Vertu. The Thyssen-Bornemisza Collection.* London: Sotheby's Publications, 1984.

Specter, Michael. "Why the Climate Corporation Sold Itself to Monsanto." *The New Yorker*, November 3, 2013. https://www.newyorker.com/tech/annals-of-technology/why-the-climate-corporation-sold-itself-to-monsanto.

Sterba, James P. "Wildcat Oilmen a Dying Breed." *The New York Times*, September 22, 1975. https://www.nytimes.com/1975/09/22/archives/wildcat-oilmen-a-dying-breed-wildcatters-are-fading-from-nations.html.

Spuhler, Friedrich. *Carpets and Textiles. The Thyssen-Bornemisza Collection.* London: Philip Wilson Publishers, 1998.

Stebbins, Theodore E. *Martin Johnson Heade*. Boston: Museum of Fine Arts, 1999.

——. *The Life and Work of Martin Johnson Heade: A Critical Analysis and Catalogue Raisonné*. New Haven: Yale University Press, 2000.

Stoker, Bram. *Dracula*. Wordsworth Classics. Ware: Wordsworth Editions, 1993.

"Thomas Kaplan, the Billionaire Pushing Abu Dhabi's Interests in the Middle East." *Intelligence Online*. March 4, 2019. https://www.intelligenceonline.com/insiders/united-arab-emirates_united-states_iran/2019/03/04/thomas-kaplan-the-billionaire-pushing-abu-dhabi-s-interests-in-the-middle-east/108347124-be1.

Thyssen-Bornemisza, Hans Heinrich, Tita Thyssen, and Luis María Anson. *Yo, el barón Thyssen: Memorias*. Barcelona: Editorial Planeta, S.A, 2014.

Toufic, Jalal. *Radical Closure*. Singapore: National Gallery Singapore, 2020 (published in conjunction with the Singapore Biennale 2019 Symposium, *Right Here, Right Now: Constellating Worlds in the Contemporary*).

——. *Postscripts*. Stockholm: Moderna Museet; Amsterdam: Roma Publications, 2020.

——. *What Was I Thinking?* Berlin: e-flux journal and Sternberg Press, 2017.

——. *What Were You Thinking?* Berlin: Berliner Künstlerprogramm/DAAD, 2011.

——. *'Âshûrâ': This Blood Spilled in My Veins*. Beirut, Lebanon: Forthcoming Books, 2005.

——. *Forthcoming*. Berlin: e-flux journal and Sternberg Press, 2014.

——. *Two or Three Things I'm Dying to Tell You*. Sausalito: Post-Apollo Press, 2005.

——. *Over-Sensitivity*. Los Angeles: Sun & Moon Press, 1996; 2nd ed., Forthcoming Books, 2009.

——. *(Vampires): An Uneasy Essay on the Undead in Film*. Barrytown, New York: Station Hill Press, 1993; revised and expanded edition, Sausalito, CA: The Post-Apollo Press, 2003.

Tucker, Hayes. *Monet in the '90s: The Series Paintings*. New Haven: Yale University Press, 1989.

Vergo, Peter. *Twentieth Century German Painting. The Thyssen-Bornemisza Collection.* London: Sotheby's Publications, 1992.

Williamson, Paul. *Medieval Sculpture and Works of Art. The Thyssen-Bornemisza Collection.* London: Sotheby's Publications, 1987.

Wilton, Andrew, and T. J. Barringer. *American Sublime: Landscape Painting in the United States, 1820–1880*. Princeton: Princeton University Press, 2002.

The Pages to Nowhere: Reading and Rereading "Cotton Under My Feet"

Eva Ebersberger

The mortal, who is not simply someone who will die physically some day in the future, but who is also dead before he or she dies physically, is never fully at home and in a homeland, but, in so far as he or she is dead even while alive, is a "stranger [as is confirmed by his or her depersonalization...] in a strange land [partly because this land is labyrinthine]" (Stoker's *Dracula*), in exile irrespective of whether or not he or she lives in his or her country. The exile from one's country is merely the *lesser exile*, whereas the death contained in all mortals even while they live is, along with the one after their physical demise, the *greater exile*.

—JALAL TOUFIC[1]

Hans Heinrich Thyssen-Bornemisza (1921–2002) understood the significance of publishing as a means to emphasize his collection's reputation and extend its accessibility. Beginning in 1984, sixteen catalogs, dedicated to the various aspects of his vast collection, and each authored by a distinguished expert in their field, were published in coordination with the auction house Sotheby's.[2] Hans Heinrich Thyssen-Bornemisza's collection was housed at his residence, Villa Favorita in Lugano, Switzerland, until the tenth title in the series was published. (The last title went to print in 2002, the year of his death.) The series was an exceptional undertaking at a time when lavish and well-researched catalogs were mainly published by major museums. Hans Heinrich Thyssen-Bornemisza did not simply limit the volumes to prominent themes like *Early Netherlandish Painting*, *Early Italian Painting (1290–1470)*, or *Twentieth Century German Painting*.[3] One of the first volumes was dedicated to the exquisite but rather marginal subject of *Set and Costume Designs for Ballet and Theatre*.[4] All of this was not lost on Walid Raad. These sixteen volumes, along with others that Raad studied during his preparation of the current exhibition, "Cotton Under My Feet," form a syllabus of sorts that defines the framework of Raad's show and performance, as well as this publication.

Implicitly arguing the significance of these books—and books/research in general—in the construction of the collection's identity and as a way to unearth untold stories, Raad stages them within the narrative framework of this project. The very titles of the works in the exhibition rely on designations used to specify parts of books and refer to a manuscript that remains absent from the project even though it plays an important role in its conception. Six works are grouped

1 Jalal Toufic, *What Were You Thinking* (Berlin: Berliner Künstlerprogramm/DAAD, 2011), 46; available at https://jalaltoufic.com/downloads/Jalal_Toufic,_What_Were_You_Thinking.pdf. This quote is also included in Walid Raad's installation *Frontispiece VI: The Spreads*, where it sits, like a work description, next to a reproduction of Jan Gossaert's painting *Adam and Eve*.

2 Volumes 1–12, edited by Simon de Pury and later Irene Martin, were published by Sotheby's Publications; volumes 13–16, edited by Martin and Maria de Peverelli, were published by Philip Wilson Publishers and its imprint Zwemmer.

3 Colin T. Eisler, *Early Netherlandish Painting. The Thyssen-Bornemisza Collection* (London: Sotheby's Publications, 1989); Miklós Boskovits, *Early Italian Painting, 1290–1470. The Thyssen-Bornemisza Collection* (London: New York: Sotheby's Publications, 1990); Peter Vergo, *Twentieth Century German Painting. The Thyssen-Bornemisza Collection* (London: Sotheby's Publications, 1992).

4 Alexander Schouvaloff, *Set and Costume Designs for Ballet and Theatre. The Thyssen-Bornemisza Collection* (London: Sotheby's Publications, 1987).

under the category *Frontispiece* (*The Carpet*, *The Peaces*, *The Majors and Minors*, *The Hangs*, *The Spines*, and *The Spreads*). Together, they explore the political and historical backdrop of "Cotton Under My Feet." In book publishing, the frontispiece is historically a decorative or informative illustration facing the title page, featuring thematic or allegorical elements, or the author's portrait. (In contemporary books, this page mostly remains empty.) Accordingly, these works introduce various equivocal, at times dubious, characters, fictional and real, dead and undead, which Raad keeps coming back to (or not) in his accompanying performance. For another set of works, Raad draws on the epilogue, the section that traditionally appears at a book's end and is meant to bring a kind of post-narrative closure. As such, the epilogue is symmetrically differentiated from the frontispiece. The seven works in "Cotton Under My Feet" grouped together as *Epilogue* (*The Constables*, *The Flat Corner*, *The Frames*, *The X-Rays*, *The Curtains*, *The Gold and Silver*, *The Crates*, and *The Gremlins*) speculate about the immaterial conditions of artworks that suffer from pathologies that resemble psychological diseases. The subjects of transformations, these artworks develop lives of their own. Theatrical lighting and strong dark shadows add an eerie layer to their appearances and amplify their unstable conditions. It takes some effort and attention to unravel their mysteries.

"Cotton Under My Feet," as Raad explains, has many beginnings. One is in 1993, when Hans Heinrich Thyssen-Bornemisza transferred half of his collection to Spain, including old and modern masterpieces by Hans Holbein the Younger, Rembrandt, El Greco, Titian, Paul Cézanne, Pablo Picasso, and Edward Hopper to name just a few—which had been on view at the Museo Nacional Thyssen-Bornemisza as loans since 1992—making one of the world's most valuable private collections public. It remains one of the largest ever private-to-public transfers of art. Weaving together historic, political, economic, bibliographic, meteorological, and aesthetic facts, Raad presents an investigation of the events and documents around the sale, transfer, display, storage, and conditions of the more than 700 artworks in the collection. Raad's propositions are introduced through thirteen works, divided into two categories and including photographs, sculptural installations, videos, tapestry, wallpapers—all held together by a circuitous narrative that he performs as a seventy-minute scripted monologue in the form of a gallery talk, or walkthrough. Titled *Two Drops Per Heartbeat: A Free Fall Through the Thyssen-Bornemisza Collections in Madrid and Elsewhere*, it connects the story of the collection with weather forecasting technologies, slavery in America, US foreign policy in Iran, and Raad's own biography. The walkthrough unlocks the meaning of the works and provides a thread connecting their complex relationships. In the artist's absence, wall texts and an audio guide aid in navigating this story.

Two Drops Per Heartbeat begins in front of the installation *Frontispiece II: The Carpet*, which is dedicated to one of several strange encounters that motivated Raad's research into the collection, or so his story goes. This semi-fictional episode takes place in 2012, when Raad meets Francesca Thyssen-Bornemisza at the Museum of Islamic Art in Doha, Qatar. There he learns that the legendary Béhague-Sanguszko carpet, a rare Persian wool-silk tapestry from the late sixteenth, early seventeenth century, is part of the Thyssen-Bornemisza collections. It is a carpet that Raad had wanted to study for the longest time, because of its legendary heft: the carpet feels much heavier than its weight of twenty-one kilograms. "About four years ago," Raad says, "I was allowed to spend as much time as I wanted with the carpet. I started to study it closely, to look at it and around it, and I would like to say to look under it but I could not lift it to look at what's underneath. And that's how I found myself in a very deep tunnel, one that started with Francesca and the carpet, and then it just kept going and going and going."[5] Mounted horizontally on a tilted wall, the carpet's top border is lined with photographic collages of the story's main protagonists—Hans Heinrich Thyssen-Bornemisza, surrounded by his five wives and children—adorned by brightly colored butterfly wings. Keeping in mind that the ancient Greek word for butterfly is ψυχή (psȳchē), which primarily means "soul" or "mind," the winged figurines invoke the immaterial conditions that play a central role in Raad's narration. The butterflies also evoke metamorphosis, the potential for transformation, as well as the fragility and uncertainties of memory and recollection.

5 Walid Raad, *Frontispiece II: The Carpet*, wall text.

In the same room, *Epilogue II: The Constables* consists of seven photographs in different sizes showing the back sides of paintings whose fronts are to remain hidden. The backs depict copies of John Constable's famous *Cloud Studies*. As a clue to the Thyssen-Bornemisza collection's history, they are installed on a freestanding wall covered with fake nineteenth-century red damask wallpaper of the kind used to decorate the rooms in the Villa Favorita. By historicizing the installation in this way, Raad links the contemporary display to a period when museums were indeed private homes and not public institutions. At this juncture Raad opens a "new beginning," a central argument he develops in the course of the exhibition. He connects Constable's clouds with the newly developing science of meteorology—intimately related to the development of the telegraph and, later in a PowerPoint presentation, to contemporary climate data and weather forecasting technologies. But the clouds also evoke other, violent forms, like nuclear mushroom clouds and the tear gas clouds deployed in Raad's native Lebanon and the Middle East. "Our air is weaponized. Our clouds are toxic," according to the research agency Forensic Architecture.

As an investigation of a collection and of institutional practices, "Cotton Under My Feet" can be considered alongside Raad's long-term research projects on the history of art in the Arab world. *Scratching on things I could disavow* (2007–11) and *Les Louvres / Kicking the Dead* (2011–17) investigate the way history is constructed under conditions of violence and at times of crisis.

These two projects were sparked by the exponential rise in investment in culture, with new museums, biennials, and foundations in Abu Dhabi, Dubai, Doha, Sharjah, and elsewhere in the Gulf. Raad looks into how in these new institutions, which the critic Alexandre Kazerouni has called "mirror museums," the artworks that are purchased, organized, exhibited, and historicized according to models of Western art withdraw: they shrink, they lose their shadows, they remain absent so the halls of these museums appear empty or inaccessible. Raad makes this connection through the writings of thinker and artist Jalal Toufic, who argues that certain historical events can be so devastating that their impact causes tradition to "withdraw," meaning that even if it is materially present, tradition becomes unavailable to communities affected by the surpassing disaster.[6] In "Cotton Under My Feet" Raad builds on Toufic's notion of the undead, elaborated in his book *(Vampires): An Uneasy Essay on the Undead in Film.* For Toufic, the mortal is someone who is dead even while still physically alive. He then further indicates that—and this is central to Raad's project—he or she has two, different bodies: one that lives in this natural world and another, subtle body that haunts the undeath realm since, lost in its labyrinthine space and time, it cannot be found there. The dead aspect of a mortal in the undeath realm sends unworldly images, sounds, and fragments of stories to the version that lives in the natural world, who may or may not heed them. "As an artist, and during the past three years as I explored several artifacts in this museum, I found myself wondering time and again whether the artworks and stories I created came from this world or from another," Raad says. His project becomes one of systematically confirming and checking. Toufic's book is reproduced in *Frontispiece V: The Spines*, a large wallpaper installation showing the spines of existing and imagined books. In *Frontispiece VI: The Spreads*, one page from the table of contents of *(Vampires)*, combined with the vampiric motif of a non-reflecting mirror on the opposite page, is placed as a counterpart to the contents of the (fictional) acquisition agreement of the Thyssen-Bornemisza collection.

6 Jalal Toufic, "Credits Included," *The Withdrawal of Tradition Past a Surpassing Disaster* (Forthcoming Books, 2009), 11–12; available at http://www.jalaltoufic.com/downloads/Jalal_Toufic,_The_Withdrawal_of_Tradition_Past_a_Surpassing_Disaster.pdf. This text was also part of the multivolume publication that accompanied Walid Raad's exhibition / performance "Scratching on things I could disavow" at TBA21, Vienna, May 26–June 15, 2011.

In "Cotton Under My Feet" Raad speculates about the origins and futures of the Thyssen-Bornemisza collections and other large Western and non-Western art collections—specifically, the shifts and fissures that occur when a private art collection becomes public. Raad is looking at the artworks in the museum—in particular nineteenth-century American paintings by Winslow Homer, Eastman Johnson, and Martin Johnson Heade—and under and around things and carpets, addressing the processes of transformation artworks can undergo as transmitters of messages from the realm of the undeath. Exploring the museum that way,

Raad points to the counterintuitive perception of spaces that, like stage sets, appear deep but in fact are very flat, like a fake backdrop. *Epilogue III: The Flat Corner*, for example, is a trompe l'oeil view of a corner in the Museo Nacional Thyssen-Bornemisza, including its characteristic wall color and floor pattern. It functions as a restoration device, on which angels from the collection's paintings can rest to self-repair when damaged. Three black silhouettes of angels, attached to the top of the flat corner attract angels in need. They are reminiscent of Kara Walker's signature cut-outs, depicting historical narratives haunted by sexuality, violence, and subjugation. Indeed, the histories of slavery and racism also feature centrally in two of Raad's works. *Frontispiece IV: The Hangs* is a seemingly unfinished room in the first floor of the museum, with open buckets of paint and half-finished walls. Amidst the clutter, a gilt-framed portrait of a Black man leans against a transport trolley. It is the only portrait of a person of color in the museum's collection—now known as an unidentified individual painted by an unidentified painter of the eighteenth century. Originally attributed to the famous Gilbert Stuart, it was long thought to represent Georg Washington's cook, Hercules Posey. With the revised attribution, the painting literally exists in an art historical limbo. The wayward painting points to suppressed narratives and the way race is a blind spot for many art institutions. The installation *Frontispiece IIIa: The Peaces* in the adjacent room is overwhelmed by a reproduction of part of a painting by Jean-Michel Basquiat, which Raad then links to his personal narrative, describing how he moved to New York in 1983, on the day the African American artist Michael Stewart was killed by New York City police officers. "Cotton Under My Feet" explores the way models for the categorization, collecting, and display of art exemplify fraught ideologies and power relations inscribed into the fabric of institutions to reveal concealed histories of violence and oppression.

Raad was working on "Cotton Under My Feet" in 2020, against a background of social, political, and personal circumstances that intersect in the project: in May 2020, the murder of George Floyd ignited Black Lives Matter protests across the country, creating the largest racial justice demonstrations in the United States since the time of the Civil Rights Movement. While Raad sheltered in the Catskill Mountains throughout the Covid-19 pandemic, he was immersed in the landscape depicted in the paintings of the nineteenth-century Hudson Valley School, many of which found their way to Hans Heinrich Thyssen-Bornemisza's collection. Then, in August 2020, an explosion in the port of Beirut destroyed much of the artist's childhood city, setting Lebanon in freefall. "So, oddly enough, I was thinking about the time of the American Civil War, and how artists responded or not to the American one; and how I (and others in Lebanon) were responding to the Lebanese one. I realized that, 160 years after the American Civil War, the BLM movement was clearly trying to address issues which remain un-addressed by the 1861 Civil War. Will Lebanon live with the legacy of its war for another 160 years?"[7] In "Cotton Under My Feet" Raad uses the museum and its collections as a lens through which

7 Raad in conversation with the author, September 28, 2021.

to scrutinize these urgent topics, which loom large in the US. The performance's poetic title, *Two Drops Per Heartbeat*, refers to the rate at which maple trees let down their sap in winter that then can be made into maple syrup, as depicted in Eastman Johnson's painting *The Maple Sugar Camp–Turning Off* (1865–1873). The painting forms part of the extensive collection of nineteenth-century American art housed in the museum and is incorporated as *Appendix I* into the performative tour.[8] While Johnson's painting might at first appear to be a straightforward nostalgic scene of a New England tradition, it also communicates a powerful message about freedom and independence. A strong supporter of the Union cause, Johnson likely identified maple syrup, created by free workers, as a valuable alternative to white sugar, which was produced on the continent by enslaved people. In fact, the very life of an enslaved person on a sugar plantation in the American South was measured in sugar, with one life equaling one ton of white sugar.

8 There is also an *Appendix II*, introducing two landscape paintings (*The Marshes at Rhode Island*, 1866, and *Jersey Marshes*, 1874) by Martin Johnson Heade from Carmen Thyssen's collection.

The large wallpaper installations *Frontispiece V: The Spines* and *Frontispiece VI: The Spreads* introduce the final and central part of the exhibition. Covering the walls outside of the lower level exhibition gallery, *The Spines* create an immersive environment demonstrating the bibliographic depth of Raad's research. It shows the spines of the books Raad has read, consulted, or imagined during his research (a bibliography documenting his research is included in this book). *The Spreads*, lining the walls of the first spaces, is a complex installation displaying six imagined layouts, including the two tables of contents mentioned earlier, as well as pages from the Thyssen-Bornemisza collection catalogs and an auction catalog, presenting paintings Raad looked at as part of his research. Raad modified, removed, edited, and annotated texts and graphics, added video images and cut outs, and codified pages with a system of post-its and bookmarks in various colors and shapes. These visually dense installations superimpose various layers of encoded information and as such are highly charged and politicized documents.

As Raad walks visitors through the museum and its histories, he gives an immersive account of being around the artworks, the institution, the collector, and the family. It's a story that veers between the historical, political, and the mundane on the one hand and the realm of undeath on the other. Looking around and under things, his ideas move as quickly as clouds in a stormy sky through the many textures and dimensions of time and space. As he ends his presentation in front of *Epilogue IX: The Gremlins*, Raad, in an emotionally charged moment, recognizes that "Nowhere" is an actual place, a place where the figurative is literal and where no one can hide behind a curtain or under a carpet. Nowhere is indeed the place, where flat corners heal damaged angels, carpets are heavier than their weight, and clouds always travel faster than the weather.

Labyrinth

Jalal Toufic

While *Encyclopædia Britannica* does not note any difference between labyrinth and maze, "*Labyrinth*, also called *maze*, system of intricate passageways and blind alleys. 'Labyrinth' was the name given by the ancient Greeks and Romans to buildings, entirely or partly subterranean, containing a number of chambers and passages that rendered egress difficult. Later, especially from the European Renaissance onward, the labyrinth or maze occurred in formal gardens, consisting of intricate paths separated by high hedges.... In gardening, a labyrinth or maze means an intricate network of pathways enclosed by hedges of which it is difficult to find the centre or exit,"[1] according to *Wikipedia*, "In English, the term *labyrinth* is generally synonymous with *maze*. As a result of the long history of unicursal representation of the mythological Labyrinth, however, many contemporary scholars and enthusiasts observe a distinction between the two. In this specialized usage *maze* refers to a complex branching multicursal puzzle with choices of path and direction, while a unicursal *labyrinth* has only a single path to the center. A labyrinth in this sense has an unambiguous route to the center and back and is not difficult to navigate."[2] While, unlike *Encyclopædia Britannica*, I differentiate between a maze and a labyrinth, the distinction between the two is different in my books from the one in *Wikipedia*: I reserve "maze" for worldly configurations and "labyrinth" for unworldly unnatural spaces and times—for me, both of the aforementioned structures in *Wikipedia*'s "Labyrinth" entry are mazes. If we are just living beings, one type of animal, then we would be exclusively in the natural world, and in the natural world while there can be and are mazes, there isn't, indeed cannot be a labyrinth (in years to come, it is likely that researchers would be able to assert, based on human neuroimaging,[3] that a certain mortal is experiencing being lost in a labyrinth, but that does not mean that the labyrinth itself is then part of nature and within the purview of science). It is not by crossing some natural threshold, for example, a river, or some man-made threshold, for example, a gate, that you will reach a labyrinth. You are not going to reach the labyrinth by airplane or train or car—except if the airplane or train or car crashes and you die.

1 *Encyclopædia Britannica Online*, s.v. "Labyrinth (Architecture)," https://www.britannica.com/technology/labyrinth-architecture.

2 *Wikipedia*, s.v. "Labyrinth," https://en.wikipedia.org/wiki/Labyrinth.

3 "Recent advances in human neuroimaging have shown that it is possible to accurately decode a person's conscious experience based only on non-invasive measurements of their brain activity. Such 'brain reading' has mostly been studied in the domain of visual perception, where it helps reveal the way in which individual experiences are encoded in the human brain. The same approach can also be extended to other types of mental state, such as covert attitudes and lie detection." John-Dylan Haynes and Geraint Rees, "Decoding mental states from brain activity in humans," *Nature Reviews Neuroscience*, no. 7 (July 2006): 523–534, http://www.nature.com/nrn/journal/v7/n7/full/nrn1931.html.

With most spaces, we can rather easily detect where the threshold is. Where is the threshold of a mundane lecture room? A knock indicates where it is: at the door. Where is the threshold of a commercial maze? One reaches it after one pays at the cashier; as long as one has not paid yet, one can rest assured that one is not yet in the maze. This is not the case with the labyrinth. Where is the threshold of the labyrinthine realm of death or madness? That is, where is the last point prior to which one can still turn and go back (at the threshold of the labyrinth one cannot turn and go back since one undergoes there a lapse of consciousness if not of being and "finds" "oneself" [dissociated] to the other side)? Apprehensive that one would otherwise inadvertently enter and become indefinitely lost "in" the labyrinth, one tries one's utmost not to miss anything, however fleeting and seemingly insignificant, and then to interpret and reinterpret what one did not so much see clearly and unhurriedly as tried to discern in the darkness, or espied, or glimpsed from a moving car or a subway train or before averting one's eyes or running away in terror, and that seems impossible—but this is what happens "*in*" the labyrinth: one interprets signs so as not to inadvertently *enter* and then so as not to become indefinitely lost "in" the labyrinth (this is all the more so since in the vast majority of cases, one mistakes the apparent threshold of the labyrinth, which one hasn't yet crossed, for example, the open door at which the vampire tells Harker in Coppola's *Dracula*, "Welcome to my home. Enter freely of your own will," for the actual threshold of the labyrinth, which one has, unawares, already crossed in a lapse of consciousness if not of being). And so what at first seems a preventive measure against inadvertently entering the labyrinth later turns out, unbeknownst to oneself, to be a manner of extending being lost "in" the labyrinth. The way to be through the labyrinth out of the labyrinth is to resort to a suspension of interpretation and an eclipse of meaning. Is there a sign, an unambiguous sign—one that one would not have to interpret—that would indicate that one is now "in" the labyrinth and therefore that one should cease noting, let alone being on the lookout for signs and interpreting them, that one should disregard them, even though one is unable to determine one's whereabouts or find one's destination, and even though they link with each other and seem to reinforce and confirm each other, indeed appear to address one directly if not talk to one? No. While it is very difficult to suspend interpretation "in" the labyrinth, one nonetheless may, out of desperation (for example, the one induced by one's realization that death, whether through suicide or otherwise, does not provide a way out of the labyrinth, since following one's death, one will "find" "oneself" still lost "in" the labyrinth), manage to do so. If one wishes then to be positive about the fortunate disappearance of any labyrinthine anomalies, one would consider that one is really back in the world—strictly speaking, though, having once been "in" the labyrinth, one thenceforth can never for sure assert: I am no longer "in" the labyrinth.

He was on the point of exiting the subway train that had just arrived at his destination when, suddenly, he saw an unworldly creature and event (what would be an apt paraphrase of Cioran's "The essential often appears at the end of a long conversation. The great truths are spoken on the doorstep"[4] in these conditions? "The great untruths, for example, labyrinthine unworldly anomalies, are glimpsed at a subway train's door on the point of closing so it can resume its journey, in the window of a car at a crossroads just as the lights turn green for it and red for the car in which one is seated ...").

4 E. M. Cioran, *Anathemas and Admirations*, translated by Richard Howard (New York: Arcade Publishing, 1991), 82.

He had seconds to decide whether to stay in order to confirm that he actually saw it and to make sure, all the more since the subway's light was flickering, *what* it is that he saw or to leave since what he ostensibly glimpsed was too eerie and sinister and since the circumstance that he appeared to have reached his destination provided him with a ready-made justification to do so. He yielded to the impulse to rush outside just before the door closed again. He was left wondering: Did I actually see it in those few seconds or did I hallucinate it? How was he to try to answer this question? He did some research to check whether others had reported similar sightings—someone beginning to undergo psychosis does more research more earnestly than most if not all PhD students, because it is a life *and death* matter for him or her.

You can allow yourself when reading a bad writer not to notice many things in the book because neither the writer *nor the book* registered them. But in a fine book, while the writer may not have noticed them, his or her book would have registered them, that is, they have consequences elsewhere in the book. For example, some things in a fine book will seem arbitrary if we do not take into consideration the literal meaning of figurative expressions, for instance, "dead silence" (in the case of "dead silence" the nonliteral meaning, "complete silence," and the literal one fit well, since the only complete silence, silence-over, which cannot be interrupted by sounds, is encountered or undergone in death and produces a dead stop ["dead: 9. (only before noun) complete: *a dead stop*" (https://www.macmillandictionary.com/dictionary/british/dead_1#dead_1__3)], i.e., immobilizes one). One sign that one is dealing with journalism: figurative expressions are used and function almost always only in the figurative sense; in literature when a figurative expression is used, the literal sense too has to be taken into consideration, so if someone is described as *more dead than alive*, these words do not simply mean "hurt and in a very poor state" (*Oxford Dictionary of English*, 3rd edition, 2016)—indeed the figurative expression is in a way used mainly to convey in an esoteric manner the literal sense. However poor the health of the resurrected brother of Mary and Martha (who was solely alive since resurrected by the life) might have been at some point prior to his second physical demise, and however hurt Jesus Christ, "the life" (John 11:25), was while on the cross, a great book of literature or religion would not describe either as "more dead than alive." When said about a mortal, three sorts of people would have understood "he was more dead than alive" only in the figurative sense, as "he was hurt and in a very poor state":[5] a journalist/bad writer; a mortal, who is dead while still physically alive, in disavowal of his or her condition; and the disoriented mortal who suspects that he's already "in" the labyrinth and has realized that noticing signs and landmarks would then be not a manner of finding out where he is and avoiding continuing to be lost "in" the labyrinth, but, misleadingly, a manner of getting more entangled "in" the labyrinth, and that he will not leave the labyrinth, which is not simply spatial, by opening some door and walking out but rather by

5 All figurative expressions prove to be literal in one realm or another (death, dance, etc.). It is crucial though, *as long as one is aware that they are borrowings from the literal sense*, to liberate them as figurative expressions.

a suspension of interpretation and an eclipse of meaning. "How to Read a Dostoevsky Novel as If One Is Reading a Newspaper?": that could be the title of a workshop I could one day give to those who, most often one or two semesters after attending my seminar on the labyrinth, may rush into my office panicked that they are now discovering in newspapers lower depths and cryptic notes from the underground worthy of Dostoevsky.

Although I am writing about a generic labyrinth, its concept is signed Jalal Toufic, and although its concept is signed Jalal Toufic, "in" this labyrinth I would mistake myself for others and sign with their names.

At the threshold of the labyrinth one goes into trance, then one realizes that one is lost "in" the labyrinth. One may find oneself, following another trance, apparently outside the labyrinth. Given that one doesn't experience leaving the labyrinth, one will, at least momentarily, have the feeling that a part of one or a version of one or one oneself is still "in" the labyrinth.

"The [real estate] agent picked up the closest [photograph] to him. It showed the living room. He picked up a second photograph. It showed him in the building. He screamed: 'But, I've never been here before!' While he was picking up a third photograph, the vampire remarked: 'The moment you enter the labyrinth, you've been there before.' The agent let go of the photograph he had just glimpsed, uttered a scream and fell unconscious: the photograph showed him lying on the floor, blood on his neck."[6] What Delbert Grady affirms to Jack Torrance in Kubrick's *The Shining* regarding the labyrinthine Overlook Hotel where Torrance ostensibly arrived sometime in the 1970s, "You have *always* been the caretaker. I should know, sir; I've always been here," applies *only once* Torrance "is" "in" the labyrinthine hotel.

Unless one is released from the labyrinth by some messianic figure, then were one to find oneself again "in" it after appearing to have left it, one would (again) feel that one has always been there—*which would imply that one never left it*—but as someone who is shown by his or her absence in the mirror not to be (fully) there, thus whose mode of existence "in" the labyrinth is haunting; who undergoes there lapses of consciousness if not of being; and who is lost there, including in the sense that he or she cannot be found there.

The least that one can say about someone who insists on being truthful in *death and the labyrinth*,[7] where there is no truth (one ought not to trust one's memory "in" the labyrinth—it is alright to do so in a

6 Jalal Toufic, *(Vampires): An Uneasy Essay on the Undead in Film*, revised and expanded edition (Sausalito, CA: Post-Apollo Press, 2003), 86.

7 "Death and the Labyrinth" is the title of Michel Foucault's book on Raymond Roussel.

maze), is that he is deluded as to his condition, or, in case he recognizes it, that he is incredibly, fetishistically disavowing his condition, or, if the truth *in question* is a negative one, that he is a man or woman of bad conscience and *ressentiment*, guilty of opting to be guilty.

While, unless it is very simple, almost straightforward, or one is lucky, one will experience some repetition in a maze, one cannot repeat anything "in" the labyrinth. For example, you won't be able to repeat the sentence "Dick Laurent is dead" "in" the labyrinth, because you are amnesiac there; and/or because you no longer coincide with yourself but are dissociated, with the consequence that if the first time you said it then the second time you will be its addressee; and/or because you've become subject to the regime of exhaustive permutation, assuming every name in history, and thus it is another who is repeating it; and/or because it is itself now subject to exhaustive permutation, with the result that you find yourself saying it as an exclamation, as an assertion, as a question, etc.; and/or because you will one time by saying it be saying what you consciously wanted to say, another time you will by saying it be committing a parapraxis, another time you will report it to your psychoanalyst as a parapraxis you committed, another time you will say it as an actor to another actor in a film or theater play, etc. To be able to repeat again suggests that one is already outside the labyrinth, in the world.

Would the exhaustive permutation of all the possibilities "in" the labyrinth end up making one find oneself outside the labyrinth? Anyway, having become subject to the regime of permutation, how can one be sure that the one who left the labyrinth is the same as (or different from) the one who entered it?

The shifter is basically labyrinthine. Whenever I say, "I," a shifter, I am threatened with being seamlessly replaced by another (one manner of reading "I is another" [*je est un autre* (Rimbaud)]), thus with being lost "in" the labyrinth. Having shortly before died before dying and feeling threatened by the labyrinth, Jalal Toufic minimized as much as possible the use of deictics, for example, *I*, *here*, *there*, *now*, replacing them, even in an emergency and even when addressing his siblings, mother, and friends, by his full name and a complete specification of the time and place. Running late and phoning to check whether his friend was already at the location where they had planned to meet, he responded to the latter's, "Yes, I am there already," with: "Jalal Omran Toufic will be at the Seminary Co-op bookstore, Chicago, at 11 in the morning of June 6th 1989 CE"—and then he hurriedly phoned his friend again to try to specify in which branch of the multiverse he was!

A mortal cannot be fully "in" the labyrinth because the labyrinth, which is all border, maintains one on the outside, and because "in" the labyrinth one is dissociated from oneself as alive.

How come when I am reading a book on the labyrinth I can feel intuitively that certain sections don't work while others do (the former sections don't trigger my anxiety but the latter sections do)? It is because, as a mortal, that is, as dead even while still physically alive, I am, possibly under another name, already "in" the labyrinthine realm of undeath. In the revised and expanded edition of my book *(Vampires): An Uneasy Essay on the Undead in Film*, I wrote: "My body, sensing the proximity and imminence of the threshold, and not fooled by my ongoing mental rationalization, performs a bungled action, most characteristically tripping, to provide me with time to deliberate if I want to go through with my one-way trip to the altered realm, given that at the threshold itself I do not have the chance to deliberate, to make a decision, since I am then and there entranced, thus have no will of my own, and find myself when I come out of the trance already to the other side of the threshold, 'in' the labyrinth, always already 'in' the labyrinth."[8] It is not, strictly speaking, my physical body that feels the proximity of the labyrinth, for my physical body is part of nature whereas the labyrinth isn't; it is rather something in me as a mortal, as dead even while still physically alive, that feels the proximity of the false threshold (i.e., the actual threshold, which is usually reached prior to the apparent threshold) and whose interference in my physical body's movement results in a bungled action that provides me with an interval to reconsider my unconcerned progress. The replacement of one body, the natural, physical one this side of the threshold of the undeath realm with another, subtle body to the other side happens in the lapse of consciousness if not of being one undergoes at the threshold. In order to leave the labyrinth, a kind of resurrection, one has to regain the natural body.

We can deduce from the circumstance that we can be together in a certain space that it is not a labyrinth; indeed, I can deduce from the circumstance that I am not dissociated that I am not in a labyrinth ("in" the labyrinth one is alone not only in relation to others but also to oneself [as alive]). Unlike in a maze, one can no longer be part of a group, say, "we," "in" the labyrinth—were one to hear, for example from the voices-over, that someone else is with one "in" the labyrinth, one would feel that they are lying to one or that the other is one's double, in relation to whom one is *alone with the alone*.[9] This out-and-out subtraction from any worldly community is a sign that I must have died or become mad—or that I am at the Last Judgment. A group of people sets out to the undead's haunt.

8 Toufic, *(Vampires): An Uneasy Essay on the Undead in Film*, 18.

9 "The living person is a composite that dissociates in death-as-undeath or during some states of altered consciousness first into separate subunits that are themselves composites, most of them uglier than the original one, then into elements, becoming alien. Each of us is common, not alien, both because each of us is a composite of all the others, even of those who lived erstwhile and who are long dead, and because each of us is part of the composite that constitutes the others. That is why we do not find others or for that matter ourselves alien, and that is why they too do not find us alien. In certain states of altered consciousness, though, we see the dead, people who have become not merely uglier, but alien, and that is because they are no longer composites (the withdrawal of the cathexis of the world). What is extremely discomposing about the double is that in a twisted, too logical way, he is more me than myself: while I include all the others, he includes only 'me,' and therefore he is not really me, since I am never purely myself. The double is unrecognizable because he is the Same. The double is not the other, but I divested of all others. That is why whenever I encounter him, even in a crowded public place, I feel I am alone with him, *alone with the alone*; he embodies the divestment of the world. That is why encountering the double is such a desolate experience, and is a premonition of death with its loss of others and the rest of the world" (Toufic, *(Vampires): An Uneasy Essay on the Undead in Film*, 173–174; "Alone with the Alone" is the English title of Henry Corbin's book on the Sufism of Ibn 'Arabī—in Corbin's title the second *Alone* refers to God).

One of them forgets the cross he believes would protect him. How come he forgot it? Was it a parapraxis? Did he sense already at the point of departure that the journey is one of no return and so unconsciously forgot the cross in order to have an excuse to go back before it was too late, purportedly to fetch the object he forgot? The others go ahead. But, soon enough, another member of the group, a lucky one, gets lost, physically and temporarily, in the forest (in the world) ostensibly leading to the (unworldly) labyrinth. These separations from the group heading to the haunt of the undead continue, then one man or woman realizes that he or she is now alone. If one is lucky, one will realize this before the threshold of the labyrinth, when it is still not too late to reconsider and rejoin the others in a community and the world (one may still choose then, crazy as one may prove to be, to go ahead into the labyrinth—yet "in" the labyrinth one did not ever make a choice to enter it since once one crosses its threshold one has always been "in" it); if one is not lucky, one, dissociated, having separated from oneself, will notice too late, past the threshold of the labyrinthine realm of no return, that one is now alone (as long as one has not undergone dissociation, been separated from "oneself," one is not fully alone). Even though those who intuitively stayed behind may witness two people crossing together into what turns out to be a labyrinth, each of the two will "find" himself/herself, past his or her trance and therefore lapse of consciousness at the en*trance* of the labyrinth, alone "in" the labyrinth, having lost the other. We can head together to the labyrinth but we cannot be together "in" the labyrinth. Till death do us part, that is, till the labyrinth do us part.

Insofar as he or she "is" dead even while still physically alive, a mortal is lost "in" the labyrinth, alone "in" the labyrinth, having, as a result of one circumstance or another, separated from the living people. And yet he or she is now accompanied by previously unheard and unseen others, for example, the voices. That is why however foreign they may seem to one, these voices can nonetheless be considered to be inextricably related to one, *extimate* (to borrow this coinage of Jacques Lacan), since one can be lost together with them "in" the labyrinth, in other words, since they are not lost to one "in" the labyrinth but keep one company there—thus, in a way, proving to be more related to one than oneself (even when, as if one doesn't exist, they hold prolonged conversations that do not address or refer to one) since "in" the labyrinth one undergoes dissociation, dissociates as (un)dead from oneself as alive.

One cannot have an overview of the labyrinth; if one seems able to have an overview of it, for example, from a helicopter or a satellite, it could be that one is mistaking a mundane maze for an unworldly labyrinth, since one can locate a mundane maze on Google Earth, zoom in on it, then direct someone lost in it on how to leave it. Notwithstanding that there can be no overview of the labyrinth, one may come across paintings, floor plans, or scale models that seem to show the layout of the labyrinthine zone, only to then, across a lapse not only of consciousness but also of being, "find" oneself in them and then discover that what looked like a representation of the labyrinth is part of the labyrinth and thus itself constantly changing without anyone doing the alteration.

"In" the labyrinth what one may have assumed to be the left may turn out to be "the other right." In Adrian Lyne's *Jacob's Ladder*, 1990, Jacob's chiropractor, Louie, tells Jacob, who died physically or died before dying physically: "Turn on your right side." When he turns in the wrong direction, the chiropractor muses: "How about the other right?" Unlike mortal chiropractors in disavowal of their being dead even while still physically alive, and unlike angels (Jacob: "You know, you look like an angel, Louie, like an overgrown cherub. Anyone ever tell you that?" "Yeah"), thinkers who died before dying are aware that in *death and the labyrinth* the two sides are not always, if ever, right and left but right and the other right—with no left. Given that he had died before dying, and, as a result, was lost "in" the labyrinth, had his chiropractor been standing to one side of him and an intern to the other side and Jacob turned toward the intern, he would have been amazed to realize that he either still faced the chiropractor or, while no longer facing the chiropractor, did not end up facing the intern.

"If anyone slaps you on the right cheek, turn to them the other cheek also ... that you may be children of your Father in heaven" (Matthew 5:39–45), in other words, that you may not find yourself, following your physical demise, fully in hell or death, both labyrinthine realms, hence realms where one cannot turn the other cheek even if one mustered the unequivocal wish to do so, since even when one ostensibly manages to turn the other cheek for the next slap, one discovers from the pain that one feels that one is still being slapped on the same cheek, for example, by one's unprovoked double[10] (how reassuring it would be in labyrinthine death to be able to turn one's other cheek for anything, including a slap, and how soothing it would then be to feel that one is indeed being slapped on the other cheek). Is turning one's other cheek for another slap an exorbitant price to pay for never entering the labyrinth, through the reduction of death to simple physical demise, or rather, since we are mortals, therefore already dead even while still physically alive, for getting resurrected by *the life* from the death realm, becoming fully alive?

10 The moment I, exasperated, end up responding with a slap to the repeated unprovoked slaps of the double, I feel the pain of having slapped myself, so that ready to slap him following further provocations, I have the expression less of anger as of apprehension and fear.

Can a living person in the natural world write a labyrinthine book? No, for the labyrinth is not part of the world. Can the one "in" the labyrinth, for example, a dead man or woman, write a labyrinthine book? No, since, undergoing *word salads*, glossolalia, *theft of thought*, etc., he or she finds it extremely difficult if not well-nigh impossible to think and write. To write something that is related extimately to the labyrinth, one has to be outside the labyrinth (to continue to be able to write) but in an untimely collaboration with someone "in" it (for example, the dead, including oneself insofar as, a mortal, one is dead even while still physically alive, and the mad [who died before dying physically]), who is in no condition to think and write (and who may undergo this untimely collaboration in the manner of *thought broadcasting* [and, in the reverse direction, *thought insertion*]). It is not enough for a living mortal to write about the labyrinth a novel or a seemingly short story that does not fall apart "two days" later and that he or she, insofar as he or she is dead even while still physically alive or is collaborating in an untimely manner with a dead or mad person lost in a labyrinthine space and time, intuitively finds accurate; the novel or seemingly short story has to be extimately related to the labyrinth, and it can be that only if it manages to make possible, indeed induce labyrinthine variants of itself, that is, variants of itself "in" the labyrinth. The essential and specific reader of such a novel is someone lost "in" the labyrinth, thus someone to whom the novel cannot be sent, but who sooner or later comes across a labyrinthine variant of it "in" the labyrinth and discovers that he is one of its protagonists and that while it very accurately relates events from his past life it also shows him participating in other events that are incompossible with them as well as ones that ostensibly belong to his future. Perhaps it is time, now that I have finally finished and published the revised edition of the fourth and last of my books that required emendation (my first four books), to try to write a book about the labyrinth that would induce its own labyrinthine variants "in" the labyrinth, thus a book that would have numerous editions that I did not myself edit. David Deutsch: "'Displace one note and there would be diminishment. Displace one phrase and the structure would fall.' That is how Mozart's music is described by Peter Shaffer's 1979 play *Amadeus*. This is reminiscent of the remark by John Archibald Wheeler with which this book [Deutsch's *The Beginning of Infinity: Explanations That Transform the World*] begins, speaking of a hoped-for unified theory of fundamental physics: '... how could it have been otherwise.' Shaffer and Wheeler were describing the same attribute: being hard to vary while still doing the job. In the first case it is an attribute of aesthetically good music, and in the second of good scientific explanations."[11] While there is exactly one way for a novel relating to the labyrinth not to fall apart, that is, to manage to construct a world that keeps falling apart as a labyrinth that does not itself fall apart, paradoxically numerous if not a limitless number of labyrinthine variants of the novel turn out to be not only possible "in" the labyrinth (as impossible) but also actual and seemingly lasting an inordinate, incredible time, giving the impression that they are older than the universe itself, and therefore older than the corresponding book in the world that ostensibly induced them. Such variants are instances within the labyrinth of a sort of creation ex nihilo, since they do not seem to have an author there; and since even though they appear to have been made possible if not induced by a book written by a specific mortal author (that is, one who is dead even while still

11 David Deutsch, *The Beginning of Infinity: Explanations That Transform the World* (London: Allen Lane, 2011), 353.

physically alive) outside the labyrinth, the latter did not actually write them. I, who refuse adamantly that my finished screenplay concerning the labyrinth, *Jouissance in Postwar Beirut* (Forthcoming Books, 2014),[12] be changed in any way, for example, at the recommendation or demand of some film producer, uphold its changing drastically outside my control "in" the labyrinth. The one who writes a novel that does not fall apart "two days" later and that's extimately related to the labyrinth suspects sooner or later that even if he or she does not end up doing any revised editions of it, it has many variants "in" the labyrinth, that it keeps changing there. Sometime after he, as a physically alive mortal, finished the novel he was writing concerning the labyrinth, "he," insofar as, a mortal, he was concurrently dead, "found" "himself" (lost) "in" the labyrinth only to discover that "in" the labyrinth no book is finished, that every book "in" the labyrinth keeps changing. At some level, it is madness to manage to write a novel that's extimately related to the labyrinth, for the "punch line" of its labyrinthine variants, uttered in no uncertain terms by some weird figure (a hallucination?) or by the voices(-over) and heard or over-heard by its over-sensitive mortal, thus dead even while alive, author is, "You've always been lost 'in' the labyrinth, where, undergoing *word salads*, glossolalia, *theft of thought*, etc., you cannot write."

12 Jalal Toufic, *Jouissance in Postwar Beirut* (Forthcoming Books, 2014), http://www.jalaltoufic.com/downloads/Jalal_Toufic,_Jouissance_in_Postwar_Beirut.pdf.

Notwithstanding such structures as the pyramids of ancient Egypt and mausoleums, architecture has, except *in* rare novels, seemingly short stories, and fiction films, failed the dead and schizophrenics, who died before dying physically, by failing to devise spaces (not necessarily mazelike ones) that make possible if not induce variants of them "in" the labyrinth, that is, labyrinthine variants.

"As people moved eastward, they found a plain in Shinar and settled there.... Then they said, 'Come, let us build ourselves a city, with a tower that reaches to the heavens, so that we may make a name for ourselves; otherwise we will be scattered over the face of the whole earth'" (Genesis 11:2–4). Was the tower a folly? The folly was to consider that they, the descendants of mortal Adam (from Hebrew *'ādhām*; prior to man's dying before physically dying on eating of the tree of the knowledge of good and evil, *'ādhām* was not a proper name but meant generically "man"), thus of someone who, once he partook of the tree of the knowledge of good and evil, was dead ("And the Lord God commanded the man, saying, Of the tree of the knowledge of good and evil, thou shalt not eat of it: for in the day that thou eatest thereof thou shalt surely die" [Genesis 2:16–17, King James Version]) even while still physically alive (following his eating from the tree of the knowledge of good and evil, "Adam lived a total of

930 years, and then he died" [Genesis 5:5] physically), could, while mortal, still have "one language and a common speech," which amounted to omitting and unheeding as dead even while still physically alive glossolalia and more generally the languages of *the voices*, which are unworldly ones and which cannot be fully understood by the one hearing them extimately; and that they, notwithstanding their being, as mortals, as dead even while still physically alive, "in" a labyrinth, lost to each other, indeed lost each also to himself or herself (thus undergoing dissociation and depersonalization), could still be together—other than merely exoterically (the only community of the dead is that of each one's feeling: *every name in history is I*; each of the dead is torn between his or her feeling "every name in history is I" and the alienating experience of seeing each of the others divested of all others—in contrast, each of the living has a singular name but enters into the composition of others and others enter into his or her composition[13]). Since Genesis 10 runs through and details the scattering of the descendants of Noah and the diversification of their language following the Flood, Genesis 11's account of the scattering of Noah's descendants and the diversification of their language must involve an additional kind of scattering of people and multiplication of languages. "The Lord said, 'Come, let us go down and confuse their language so they will not understand each other.' So the Lord scattered them from there over all the earth, and they stopped building the city. That is why it was called Babel—because there the Lord confused the language of the whole world. From there the Lord scattered them over the face of the whole earth" (Genesis 11:5–9). What God said had only to let itself be understood as addressed to someone else ("Come, let us ...") for it to be used by the devil as an invitation to collaborate on the multiplication of the language and the scattering of the people (the tree of the knowledge of good and evil instances a previous such collaboration of the devil with God): God would scatter them in the world, in a worldly Earth, and the devil would scatter them in an unworldly Earth, that of the falling apart world "in" the labyrinth. If the unfinished and crumbling Tower of Babel that the survivors of the Flood had tried to build as a means to "continue" to be one community and avoid being dispersed remained a folly, then its builders were simply then scattered by God over the whole Earth; but if it amazingly or devilishly metamorphosed from an apparent ruin into an actual ruin (the danger to God, the threat to "the Order of the World" [to use Daniel Paul Schreber's expression in his book *Memoirs of My Nervous Illness*] was not the building of a skyscraper but the latter's lapse into a ruin), turning into the "first" labyrinth, actually into a token of the first labyrinth (which was the first spatiotemporal contribution of the devil, a *folie*), the one "in" which, once he died (before dying physically) on tasting the knowledge of evil, Adam (as well as Eve and their mortal descendants) was lost, then the dispersal of its mortal builders, indeed of all mortals, was also "within" the labyrinth, which, while seemingly a part of the world, is as large as the world, indeed larger, immeasurable. The humor of the devil was to push the proliferation of languages to the level where one could

13 See note 9 of this essay.

not fully understand and communicate with "oneself," for example, with the voices "in" one's head, and to push the scattering to the point where people are scattered "in" a labyrinth, with the result that each is dissociated not only from others but also from himself or herself. They were scattered *from* worldly Babylon by God and they were scattered "*in*" labyrinthine "Babylon" and its tower, the Tower of Babel, by the devil. If a Messiah is needed to end the Diaspora even though the state of Israel, "the Jewish state," was established on much of Palestinian land, and millions of Jews immigrated to it and were promptly made its citizens, it is because Babylonian Captivity persists, since it is a captivity "in" the labyrinth. While "exiled" from it, many Jews felt nostalgia for Jerusalem and the "holy land" in Palestine in general; if they, after moving there and displacing hundreds of thousands of Palestinians, continue to unconsciously feel nostalgia *in* Jerusalem and the "holy land" in general, and will continue to do so until the coming of the Messiah, it is that they concomitantly continue to haunt labyrinthine Babylon. But why do Jews, as well as all other mortals, feel nostalgia for labyrinthine Babylon too notwithstanding that it is the realm they would do anything to leave? It is because on "finding" "oneself" "in" the labyrinth, *even when doing so ostensibly for the first time*, one sooner or later comes across various signs implying that one has been there before ("The moment you enter the labyrinth, you've been there before,"[14] in other words, "There is a *false threshold*[15] of the labyrinth: prior to it one is outside the labyrinth, past it one has always been 'in' the labyrinth and can thenceforth be outside it only through it"[16]); and because one cannot will the eternal recurrence of being lost "in" the labyrinth;[17] and because while one cannot leave the labyrinth, one is never fully in it ("You've always been lost 'in' it, that is, you cannot be found there. Are you then ever 'in' the labyrinth from which you cannot leave? On a[n ever changing] map, a labyrinth is formed of one line that meanders on and on, twists and involutes, forming an object with a fractional dimension between one and two, with the following two consequences. First, the labyrinth is all border, hence one cannot be fully inside it: if one can hide 'in' the labyrinth, it is not because one is inside the labyrinth, for the labyrinth maintains one on the outside [thus it has aura], but because it is 'in' the labyrinth that one is lost. Second, lapses [of consciousness if not of being] are sure to occur to one 'in' the labyrinth since it does not have a dimension of 3, is not a full volume"[18]). If Babylon has come to epitomize captivity and exile, it is not simply on account of the captivity of Jews there from 598/7 BCE to 538 BCE (which would seem to be the case from reading, for example, *Encyclopædia Britannica*: "The Babylonian Exile, also called Babylonian Captivity: the forced detention of Jews in Babylonia following the latter's

14 Toufic, *(Vampires): An Uneasy Essay on the Undead in Film*, 86.

15 One of the reasons I chose to term *the false threshold* for the actual, as opposed to the apparent, threshold of the labyrinth is that "*past* it one has always been 'in' the labyrinth."

16 Toufic, *(Vampires): An Uneasy Essay on the Undead in Film*, 76.

17 "Nostalgia is basically less a yearning for the repetition of an event than an indication that one did not will the event, that is, did not 'will' its eternal recurrence. Nostalgia reveals not only what I feel now about a past event, but also how I 'willed' that event when it happened in the past: I did not 'will' its eternal recurrence. When it is not merely psychological, nostalgia is basically a facet of the present event; with regard to any event toward which I feel nostalgic, I know that I did not 'will' its eternal recurrence when it happened. We are nostalgic beings less—if at all—because we are creatures who remember in an ostensibly transient present than because we do not will events. I really will an event only if I will its eternal recurrence, thus making it recur eternally (Nietzsche's philosophy could be a philosophy of the will only insofar as it was also one of eternal recurrence). Until someone experiences countless recurrence and ends up willing, beneath 'willing' some event what we, nostalgic beings, 'will' is nostalgia, rather than the event itself. But can't this basic nostalgia itself be genuinely willed? No; only the psychological nostalgia can be 'willed'" (Jalal Toufic, *Forthcoming*, 2nd ed. [Berlin: e-flux journal and Sternberg Press, 2014], 86–87).

18 Toufic, *(Vampires): An Uneasy Essay on the Undead in Film*, 27.

conquest of the kingdom of Judah in 598/7 and 587/6 BC. The exile formally ended in 538 BC, when the Persian conqueror of Babylonia, Cyrus the Great, gave the Jews permission to return to Palestine. Historians agree that several deportations took place [each the result of uprisings in Palestine], that not all Jews were forced to leave their homeland, that returning Jews left Babylonia at various times, and that some Jews chose to remain in Babylonia—thus constituting the first of numerous Jewish communities living permanently in the Diaspora"), for the Jews were, according to the Bible, also captive in Egypt, enslaved there for generations; but also because of the esoteric and more basic captivity "in" Babylon and its tower as a labyrinth, from where it is impossible to fully leave—a captivity that is coexistent with mortals' ostensible, exoteric scattering all over the earth. The essential Babylonian Captivity precedes the exile of many Jews to Babylon by Nebuchadnezzar; it is related to the labyrinth that Babylon became in Genesis 11 and/or to which it gave its "name." Babylon concerns and should concern Jews as much as Jerusalem does, not only on account of the Babylonian Talmud and other Jewish religious texts from that culture, but also because the full *aliyah* (ascent) to Israel is not possible as long as Jews, like all other mortals, are dead even while still physically alive, thus still captive and exiled "in" the labyrinth, "in" "Babylon" (the name that the labyrinth assumed in Genesis 11)—the warning of some messianists against moving to Palestine since it would be a *forcing of the* (messianic) *end* implies an oblivion of the persistent captivity and dispersal "in" the labyrinth, *including* on the part of the Iraqi Jews who immigrated to that country in the 1950s—even were all Jews living outside of Israel, who are mortals, to move to Palestine, that would still not force the (messianic) end. While in the twentieth century many Jews, including the Iraqi ones who immigrated to Israel in the 1950s, appear to have accomplished the *aliyah*, the ascent to Palestine, in the absence of the Messiah, they are still subject to Babylonian Captivity and will not be released from it except by the Messiah, who would thus initially and radically reduce the scattering to what it is generally taken to be, a geographical one in homogenous space and time that can be reversed by an exoteric *aliyah*. Even were all Jews to immigrate to Palestine, the Messiah would still be needed: to make possible and accomplish the ingathering by abolishing mortality, the death concomitant with life, and thus do away with the labyrinth associated with the former. There can really be a *forcing of the* (messianic) *end* only by someone who, acting like Jesus, the life, resurrects the dead as well as mortals, insofar as the latter are dead even while still physically alive, in such a way that they become fully, solely alive. As "the life" (John 11:25), Jesus, through his resurrections of three dead inhabitants of the "holy land," which, by making them fully alive, rendered possible their thorough *aliyah* (since they would not then have been "in" the labyrinth "Babylon" as dead people even while in Palestine as living people), *forced the* (messianic) *end*, that of his assumption of the role of the Christ. Until now it seems only three or four Jews have returned from Babylonian captivity, that is, accomplished fully the *aliyah*, the ascent to the "holy land": the three people Jesus of Nazareth, the life and the resurrection, who was never a mortal, and therefore was never "in" the labyrinth of "Babylon," resurrected, specifically "the disciple whom Jesus loved" (John 21:20) and whose name prior to his resurrection was Lazarus; the young man from the town of Nain (Luke 7:11–16); and the only daughter of Jairus, a synagogue leader, a girl of about twelve (Luke 8:41–56). It is in this sense rather than the exoteric one that the Messiah will end the Jewish diaspora, by making those still exiled and subject to the coexistent Babylonian Captivity "in" the labyrinth able to fully leave it—in the case of those Jews presently living in Palestine this would be tantamount to accomplishing the *aliyah* not only exoterically but also esoterically, thus fully. If the *aliyah* is one of the signs announcing the coming of the Messiah, it is that only the Messiah can accomplish it not only exoterically but also, more radically, esoterically. While Moses led the Jews out of their exoteric captivity in Egypt; and while Jesus Christ, as the life, released less than nine Jews, one at a time, as individuals, from the labyrinth of "Babylon" by resurrecting them to full life; and while the Nizārī imam Hasan *'alā dhikrihi'l-salām* (on his mention be peace) freed his followers as a community from their esoteric captivity "in" labyrinthine "Babylon" and its tower through the Great Resurrection,[19] which officially lasted from 1164 to 1210, the year of its ostensible annulation (one could advance that compared to the Nizārī Great Resurrection, there was something exoteric about the action of the Christ as the life and resurrection, in that he reportedly resurrected only those who were already physically dead), the other Messiah, or the Christ at his Second Coming, would end mortality for all, "Jews and Gentiles," thus releasing them from "Babylon" as the labyrinth ushered in in Genesis 11. Thus the task of the Messiah is far greater than Moses's leading the Jews out of another captivity, in Egypt, the "house of bondage," and miraculous since it is impossible to (fully) leave the labyrinth. Babylonians, including those Jews who remained in Babylon when others returned exoterically from Mesopotamia to their "holy land," were also scattered, though not as alive but only as dead, "in" the labyrinth that came to be named the Tower of Babel. With the exception of Jesus Christ and the between four and eight people he resurrected, we all remain, as mortals, "Babylonians."

19 *Al-qiyāma al-kubrá*, aka *qiyāmat-i qiyāmāt*.

Jalal Toufic, *What Was I Thinking?* (Berlin: Sternberg Press, 2017), 97–120.

>
Walid Raad
Epilogue III: The Flat Corner, 2021
Installation view, Museo Nacional Thyssen-Bornemisza, Madrid, 2021

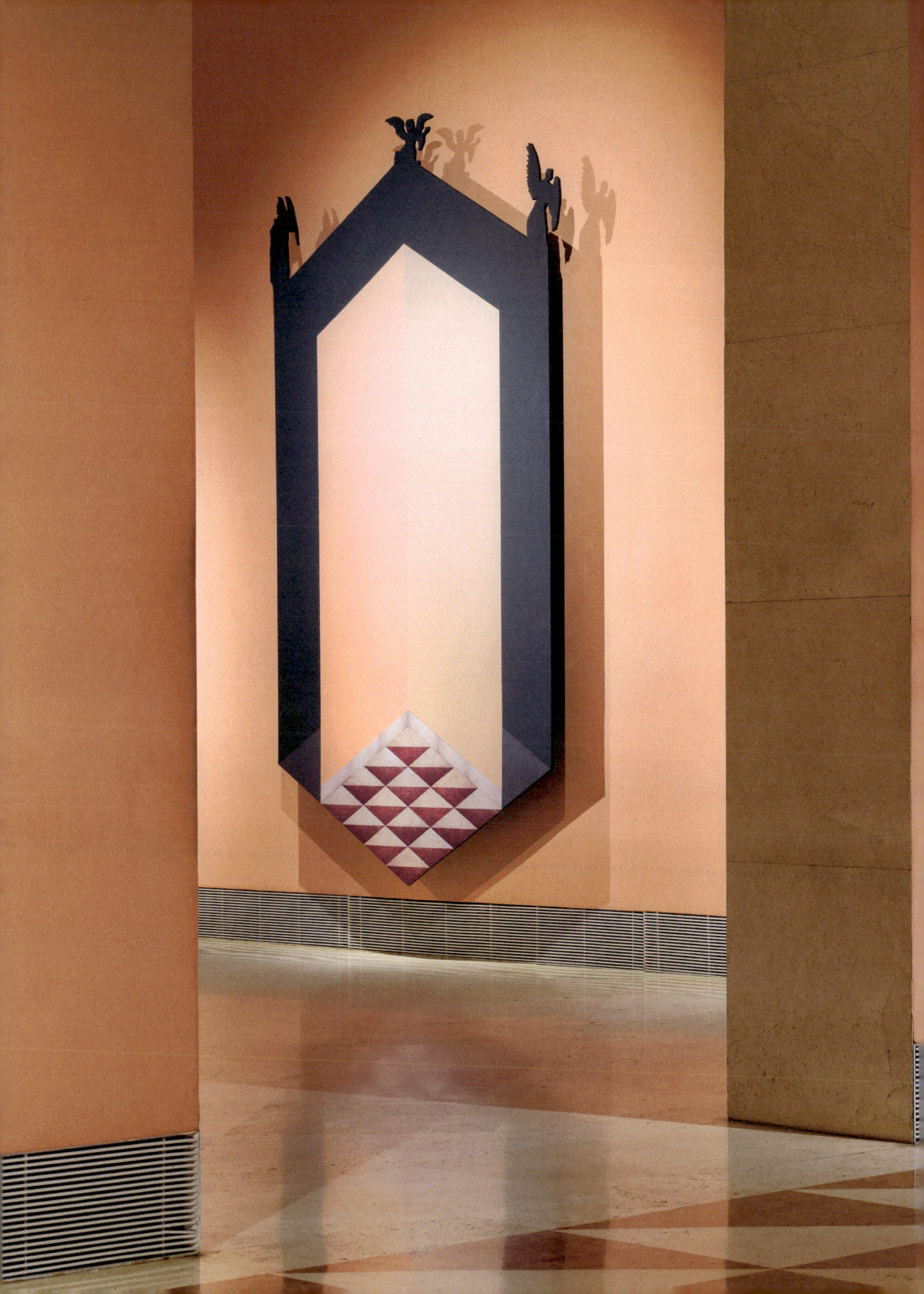

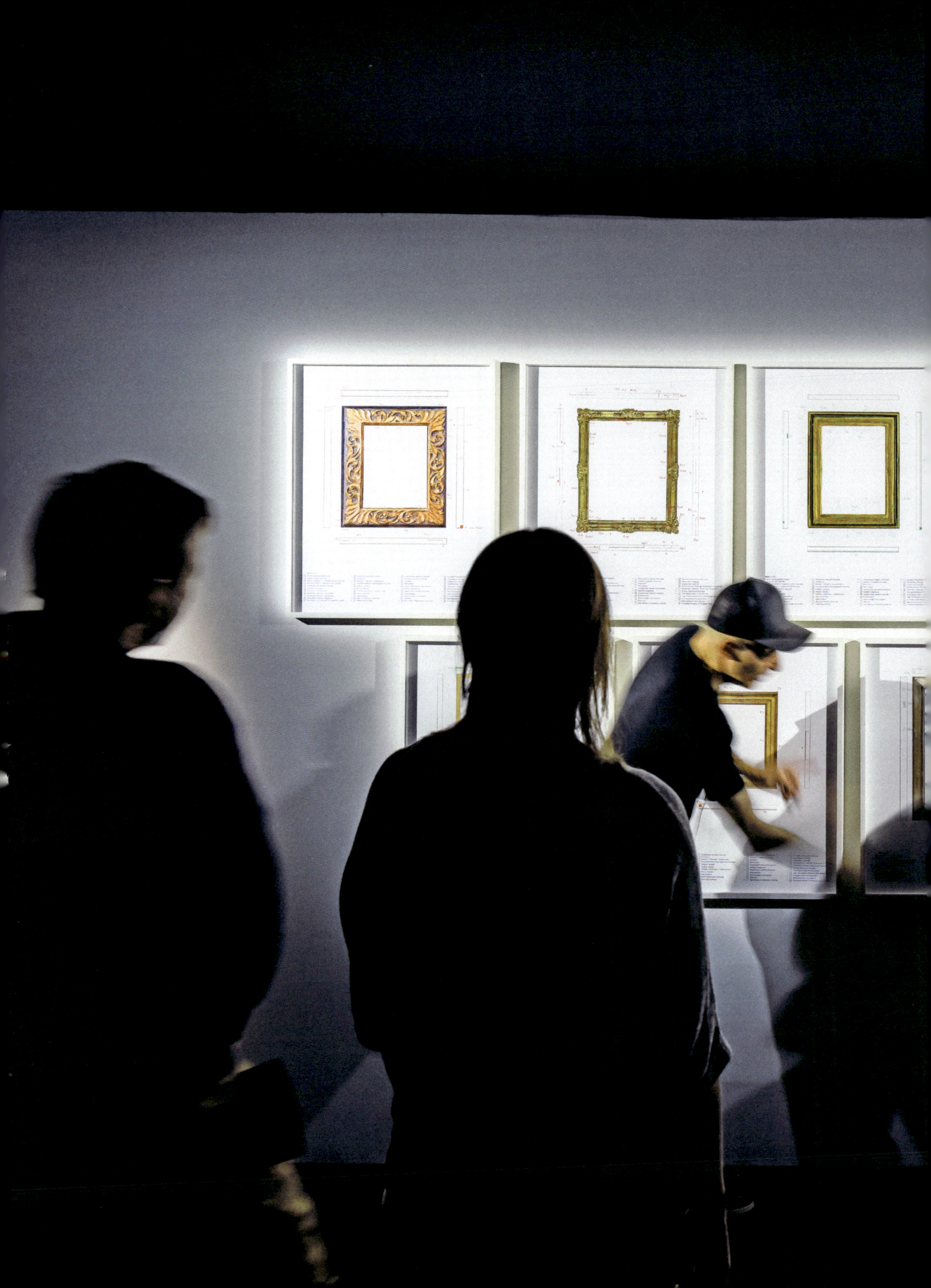

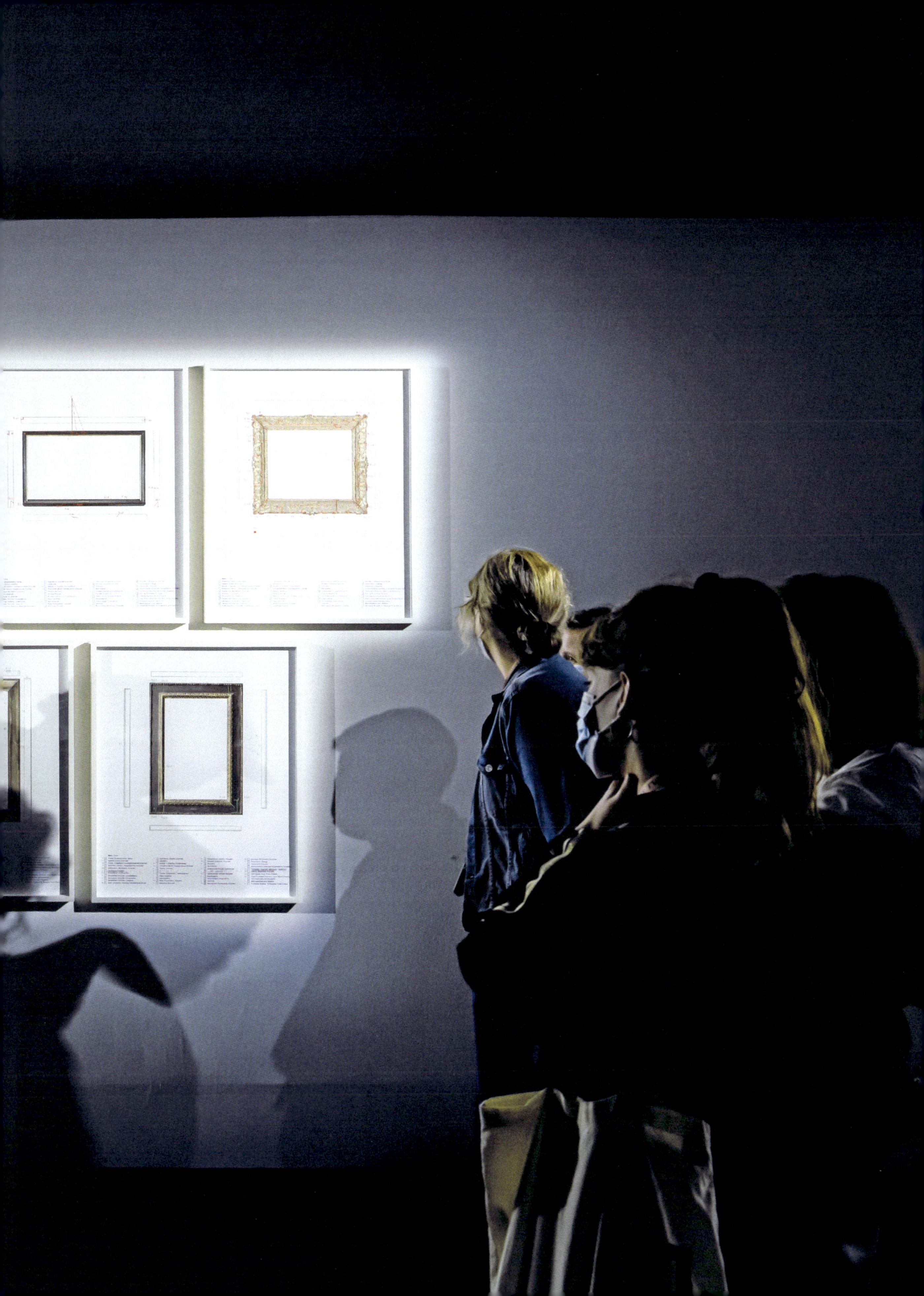

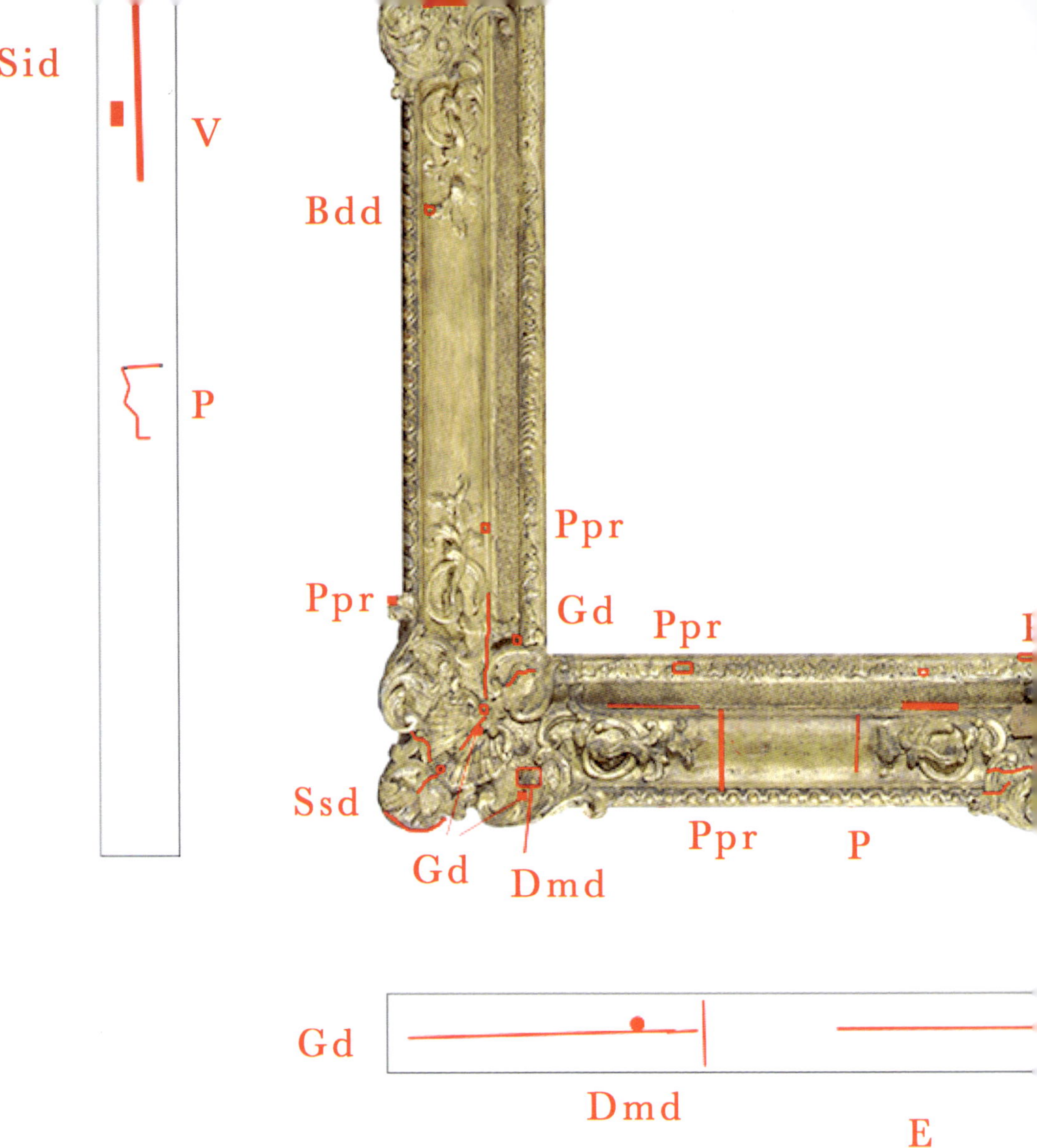

Marco / Frame

- Gdd [x] Global Developmental Delay
- Ssd [x] Speech Sound Disorder
- Scd [ ] Social (Pragmatic) Coommunication Disorder
- Adh [ ] Attention Deficit / Hyperactivity Disorder
- Smd [ ] Stereotypic Movement Disorder
- Tr [ ] Tourette's Disorder
- Ptd [ ] Provisional Tic Disorder
- De [ ] Delusional Disorder (Erotomanic)
- Dg [ ] Delusional Disorder (Grandiose)
- Dj [ ] Delusional Disorder (Jealous)
- Bpp [x] Brief Psychotic Disorder (Postpartum onset)

- Sid [x] Substance Induced Disorder
- C [x] Catatonia
- Bdh [ ] Bipolar II Disorder (Hypomania)
- Dmd [x] Disruptive Mood Dysregulation Disord
- Pa [ ] Phobia (Animal)
- Pb [x] Phobia (Blood)
- Pit [ ] Phobia (Injections / Transfusions)
- P [x] Panic Disorder
- Ag [ ] Agorophobia
- Bdd [ ] Body Dismorphoc Disorder
- Hd [ ] Hoarding Disorder

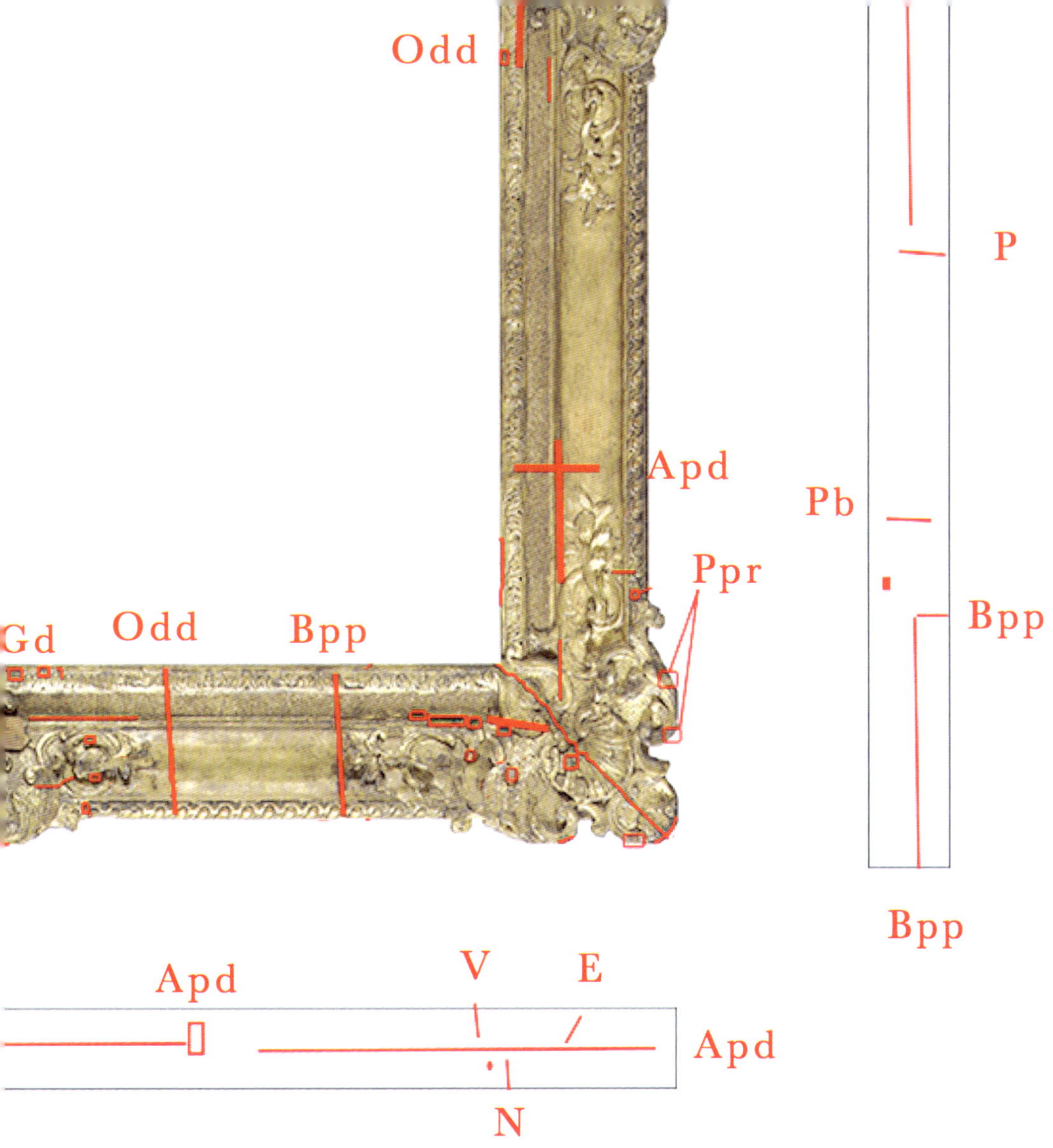

Odd

P

Apd

Pb

Ppr

Bpp

Gd Odd Bpp

Bpp

Apd V E

Apd

N

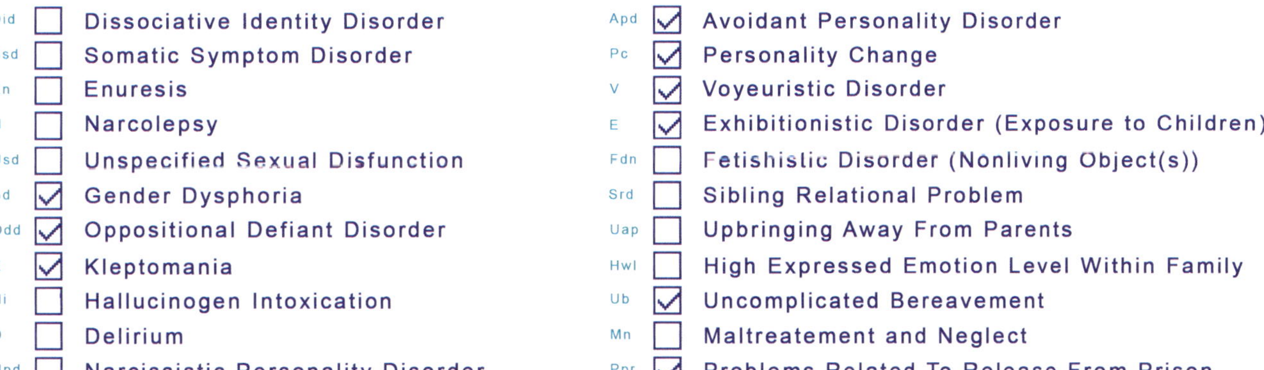

- Did [ ] Dissociative Identity Disorder
- Ssd [ ] Somatic Symptom Disorder
- En [ ] Enuresis
- N [ ] Narcolepsy
- Usd [ ] Unspecified Sexual Disfunction
- Gd [x] Gender Dysphoria
- Odd [x] Oppositional Defiant Disorder
- K [x] Kleptomania
- Hi [ ] Hallucinogen Intoxication
- D [ ] Delirium
- Npd [ ] Narcissistic Personality Disorder
- Apd [x] Avoidant Personality Disorder
- Pc [x] Personality Change
- V [x] Voyeuristic Disorder
- E [x] Exhibitionistic Disorder (Exposure to Children)
- Fdn [ ] Fetishistic Disorder (Nonliving Object(s))
- Srd [ ] Sibling Relational Problem
- Uap [ ] Upbringing Away From Parents
- Hwl [ ] High Expressed Emotion Level Within Family
- Ub [x] Uncomplicated Bereavement
- Mn [ ] Maltreatement and Neglect
- Ppr [x] Problems Related To Release From Prison

List of Works

Melchior Bair
Bellermine (Bartmannskrug), c. 1625
Augsburg, Germany
Silver, cast, chased, engraved, partly gilded
25.8 cm height
Thyssen-Bornemisza Collections

PP. 6, 9, 59–61
Walid Raad
Frontispiece II: The Carpet, 2021
Installation with carpet, pigmented inkjet prints, wood
279 × 510 cm (carpet)
Carpet Courtesy of the Thyssen-Bornemisza Collections

PP. 55, 56
Béhague-Sanguszko carpet, late sixteenth century
Kashan or Kerman, south-central Persia
Cotton, wool, silk
279 × 510 cm
Thyssen-Bornemisza Collections

PP. 6–7, 62, 66–67
Walid Raad
Epilogue II: The Constables, 2021
Installation with seven pigmented inkjet prints, wallpaper
Various dimensions

PP. 7, 8, 71, 72–73, 169
Walid Raad
Epilogue III: The Flat Corner, 2021
Wood, paint, steel
320 × 200 cm

PP. 8, 72
Gentile Bellini
The Annunciation, c. 1475
Mixed media on panel
133 × 124 cm
Museo Nacional Thyssen-Bornemisza

P. 73
El Greco
The Annunciation, c. 1596–1600
Oil on canvas
114 × 67 cm
Museo Nacional Thyssen-Bornemisza

PP. 8–9
(Workshop Of) Andrea della Robbia
Two Adoring Angels, c. 1510
Terracotta
93.5 × 54 × 27 cm; 99 × 57 × 24 cm
Colección Carmen Thyssen

PP. 2–3, 86
Walid Raad
Frontispiece IV: The Hangs, 2021
Installation with paint, metal, wallpaper, buckets, brushes, pigmented inkjet print

P. 86
Unknown artist
Portrait of a man, c. 1770–1780
Oil on canvas
67 × 63.5 cm
Museo Nacional Thyssen-Bornemisza

PP. 4–5, 78
Walid Raad
Frontispiece IIIa: The Peaces, 2021
Frontispiece IIIb: The Majors and Minors, 2021
Installation with pigmented inkjet print, foamboard, 150 pigment inkjet prints

PP. 1, 52, 85
Lucian Freud
Man in a Chair (Portrait of Baron H.H. Thyssen-Bornemisza), 1985
Oil on canvas
120.5 × 100.5 cm
Thyssen-Bornemisza Collections

PP. 87, 113
Eastman Johnson
The Maple Sugar Camp–Turning Off, c. 1865–1873
Oil on panel
25.7 × 57.4 cm
Colección Carmen Thyssen

PP. 87, 100
Martin Johnson Heade
The Marshes at Rhode Island, 1866
Oil on canvas
56 × 91.4 cm
Colección Carmen Thyssen

PP. 87, 100
Martin Johnson Heade
Jersey Marshes, 1874
Oil on canvas
39.4 × 76.2 cm
Colección Carmen Thyssen

P. 87
Martin Johnson Heade
Orchid and Hummingbird near a Waterfall, 1902
Oil on canvas
38.2 × 51.5 cm
Colección Carmen Thyssen

PP. 10–11, 90, 94–95
Walid Raad
Frontispiece V: The Spines, 2021
Wallpaper

PP. 12–13, 93, 104–105
Walid Raad
Frontispiece VI: The Spreads, 2021
Wallpaper, pigmented inkjet prints, video

PP. 16–17, 114, 170–173
Walid Raad
Epilogue V: The Frames, 2021
Nine pigmented inkjet prints
60 × 72 cm each (framed)

PP. 14–15, 117–119
Walid Raad
Epilogue IV: The X-Rays, 2021
Nine pigmented inkjet prints
Various dimensions

PP. 18–19, 120
Walid Raad
Epilogue VI: The Curtains, 2021
Eleven pigmented inkjet prints
90 × 60 cm each (framed)

PP. 20–21, 131–133
Walid Raad
Epilogue VII: The Gold and Silver, 2021
Ten pigmented inkjet prints
54 × 61.5 cm each (framed)

PP. 26–27, 134–135
Walid Raad
Epilogue VIII: The Crates, 2021
Five objects
Wood, polystyrene foam, paint
Dimensions variable

PP. 136, 139
Walid Raad
Epilogue IX: The Gremlins, 2021
Wood, wallpaper, pigmented inkjet prints
250 × 200 cm

—

All works by Walid Raad commissioned by **Thyssen-Bornemisza Art Contemporary** and courtesy of the artist, **Sfeir-Semler Gallery** (Beirut/Hamburg), **Paula Cooper Gallery** (New York).

Walid Raad: Cotton Under My Feet

An exhibition and performance commissioned by **Thyssen-Bornemisza Art Contemporary** and organized in collaboration with **Museo Nacional Thyssen-Bornemisza**

Museo Nacional Thyssen-Bornemisza
Paseo del Prado, 8
28014 Madrid
Spain
www.museothyssen.org

October 6, 2021–January 23, 2022

Curator
Daniela Zyman

Exhibition Coordination
Leticia de Cos Martín
Araceli Galán

Registrars
Natalia Gastelut
Cristina Guerras

Assistant Curators
Marina Avia
Beatrice Forchini

Curatorial Intern
Aleksandra Czerniak

Performance Coordination
María Rubio

Publication
Eva Ebersberger

Project Architect
Marta Banach

Graphic Design
Alex Gifreu

Production
DIME Museos

Lighting Design
Carlos Alzueta

AV
Fluge

Walid Raad wishes to thank

Francesca Thyssen-Bornemisza, Guillermo Solana, Daniela Zyman, Eva Ebersberger, Markus Reymann, Leticia de Cos Martín, Juan Ángel Lopez-Manzanares, Paloma Alarcó, Mar Borovia, Carlos Urroz, Carmen Thyssen-Bornemisza, Borja Thyssen-Bornemisza, Maria de Peverelli, Araceli Galán, Beatrice Forchini, Cristina Guerras, María Rubio, Marina Avia, Aleksandra Czerniak, Elena Utrilla, Noelia Lecue, Orit Gat, Fernando Pérez de la Sota, Antonio Manzano, Alberto Hernández, Soledad Cánovas Del Castillo, Maribel Ruiz, Moritz Bernoully, Irene Aguilar, Alex Gifreu, and the teams of Museo Nacional Thyssen-Bornemisza and TBA21

Tarek Abou El Fetouh, Mai Abu ElDahab, Kostas Anagnopoulos, Fadia Antar, Zeina Arida, Zdenka Badovinac, Pedro Barbosa, Karl Bassil, Daniel Blanga Gubbay, Renata Bokalo, Manuel Borja-Villel, Stefanie Böttcher, James Brookens, Eduardo Cadava, Stacey Calvert, Alberto Caputo, Alejandro Cesarco, Tony Chakar, William L. Coleman, Marie Colin, Tamara Corm, Renaud Detalle, Amelie Deuflhard, Nitasha Dhillon, David Diao, Katherine Dieckmann, Nico Dockx, Doris Douibi, Hannah Feldman, Raphael Fleuriet, Louis Galli, Vallejo Gantner, Alan Gilbert, Galen Green, Joana Hadjithomas, Matthias von Hartz, Bernard Haykel, Richard Haykel, Belal Hibri, Alexandra van Horne, Charles van Horne, Amin Husain, Jesse James, Khalil Joreige, Lamia Joreige, Veronica Kaup-Hasler, Kristine Khouri, Nathalie Khoury, Bernard Khoury, Adam Kleinman, Harold Krug, Marta Kuzma, Gundega Laivina, Fredrik Liew, Maria Lind, Charles Lindsay, Glenn Lowry, Roman Luba, Anja Lutz, Lina Majdalani, Jean Marc Prevost, David Metzger, Sean Miller, Rabih Mroueh, Funmi Oladipo, Nataša Petrešin-Bachelez, Christine Peters, Claus Philipp, Laura Quinn, Lucy Raven, Shelley Rice, Sarah Rifky, Marwan Rechmaoui, Eva Respini, Celesta Rottiers, Beatrix Ruf, Ghalya Saadawi, Dan Safer, Rasha Salti, Lucien Samaha, Kirsten Scheid, Mame Schrager, Victor Schrager, Friederike Schuler, Stephen Sheehi, Allan Shope, Julie Shope, Kaja Silverman, Hans Soderquist, Herman Sorgeloos, Jimmy Traboulsi, Christine Tohme, Jalal Toufic, Anton Vidokle, Brian Wallis, Lodewijk Werre, Ariella Wolens, Ann Wolf, Akram Zaatari

Anthony Allen, Joe Borelli, Daisy Charles, Anna Cloarec, Lucas Cooper, Paula Cooper, Jake Ewert, Kristoffer Haynes, Steve Henry, Eva Jensen, Alexis Johnson, Francisco Marcial, Tessa Morefield, Steven Probert, Jan Riley, Ylenia Tripodi, Cara Zhuang

Andrée Sfeir, Ulli Semler, Léa Chikhani, Patrick Kamman, Katrin Krumm, Joshua Sassmannshausen, Ana Siler

Achim Borchardt-Hume, Nevenka Koprivšek

Lynn Love, Petra Love, Mansour Raad, Myrna Raad, Vera Saade, Penne Love

About Thyssen-Bornemisza Art Contemporary

Thyssen-Bornemisza Art Contemporary (TBA21) is a leading international art and advocacy foundation harnessing the power of art as an agent for change. With hubs in Madrid and Venice that radiate worldwide, TBA21 has partnered on the realization of more than 100 works that engage the public in the most pressing issues of our times. Created in 2002 by the activist, philanthropist, and collector Francesca Thyssen-Bornemisza, TBA21 represents the fourth generation of the Thyssen family's commitment to the arts.

TBA21 commissions artists to spearhead research and development into complex social and environmental issues to make them both comprehensible and visceral, and to provoke awareness and action. The foundation extends its advocacy work by catalyzing new collaborations across the arts, humanities, and sciences, organizing symposia and workshops, and partnering with other research and educational organizations.

TBA21 has evolved an institutional model that enables artists to pursue sustained projects that expand their practices and provides them with powerful platforms for presenting them, ranging from national museums to interventions in the public realm to online. Central to its stewardship of these commissions, the foundation forms symbiotic relationships with institutions to bring these works into the life of communities around the world. In 2018, TBA21 initiated a partnership with the Museo Nacional Thyssen-Bornemisza which has been presenting new commissions and works from the collection annually.

The foundation has established three ongoing centers of research and development, including TBA21–Academy, which advocates ocean literacy and sustainability as it continues its ten-year journey as the exploratory soul of the foundation; the online venue, st_age, created in response to the changing landscape brought forth by the Covid-19 crisis, providing a global hub for artists and audiences; and Remedios, a multi-platform research series, currently under development, centered around ideas of healing, peace-making, and remedy in advancement of social and environmental justice.

www.TBA21.org

Press

Resnicow and Associates

Catherine Coughlin
ccoughlin@resnicow.com

Maria May
mmay@resnicow.com

Mahala Comunicación y Relaciones Públicas SL

Marta del Riego
mdelriego@mahala.es

Press and Institutional Relations of the Museo Nacional Thyssen-Bornemisza
Gema Sesé
Alicia Barrigüete
Lucía Villanueva
comunicación@museothyssen.org

About Walid Raad
www.walidraad.com

Image credits

PP. 1–21, 26–27, 48, 51, 59–61, 66–67, 71–74, 78, 82, 85, 90, 94–96, 104–105, 109, 114, 117–120, 123, 128, 131–136, 139, 169–171: Moritz Bernoully

Image credits are listed from left top to right bottom

P. 52: Photo: Hélène Desplechin; Courtesy Carmen Thyssen-Bornemizsa; Courtesy Thyssen-Bornemizsa Collections; Photo: Pablo Casares, Courtesy Museo Nacional Thyssen-Bornemisza, Madrid; © Walid Raad; Courtesy Museo Nacional Thyssen-Bornemisza, Madrid; ThyssenKrupp Konzernarchiv, Duisburg; Courtesy Carmen Thyssen-Bornemizsa.

P. 55: Photo: Brigitte Lacombe; Source: Cornucopia Magazine; Courtesy the artist; Photo: The Museum of Islamic Art & Pei Partnership Architects; Courtesy Thyssen-Bornemizsa Collections.

P. 56: Courtesy Thyssen-Bornemizsa Collections; Source: Sotheby's; Photo: Walery Rzewuski.

P. 65: Courtesy the artist; Photo: © National Portrait Gallery, London; Photo: Yale Center for British Art, Public domain; Photo: The Frick Collection; Photo: Yale Center for British Art, Public domain; Photo: National Gallery of Victoria, Melbourne.

P. 68: Courtesy the artist; © Museo Nacional Thyssen-Bornemisza, Madrid.

P. 77: World History Archive / Alamy Stock Photo; Berez / Associated Press Photo; Courtesy the artist.

P. 81: Courtesy Galerie Gmurzynska; Courtesy the artist; Courtesy New York Daily News; Jean-Michel Basquiat © Bildrecht, Wien, 2022; Unknown photographer, Reproduction by Lear 21 at English Wikipedia; © World Economic Forum (www.weforum.org), licensend under the Creative Commons Attribution-Share Alike 2.0 Generic; US Air Force; ASSOCIATED PRESS / Jerome Delay; Courtesy Museo Nacional Thyssen-Bornemisza, Madrid.

P. 86: The Metropolitan Museum of Art, New York; National Portrait Gallery, Smithsonian Institution, Washington DC; © Museo Nacional Thyssen-Bornemisza, Madrid; Photos: Moritz Bernoully.

P. 89: Print by Edwin S. Bennett. Department of Image Collections, National Gallery of Art Library, Washington, DC. Public domain; Unattributed, PD-US permission, public domain; © Colección Carmen Thyssen, on loan at the Museo Nacional Thyssen-Bornemisza.

P. 93: Courtesy Jalal Toufic; © Walid Raad.

P. 99: © Museo Nacional Thyssen-Bornemisza, Madrid; Photo: Napoleon Sarony. Public domain; New York State Department of Corrections and Community Supervision.

P. 100: Photo: Kevin Todora; Photo: Allen Philipps / Wadsworth Atheneum; © Colección Carmen Thyssen, on loan at the Museo Nacional Thyssen-Bornemisza.

P. 103: Mathew Brady / Library of Congress; Courtesy the artist; Terra Foundation for American Art; © 2014 RMN-Grand Palais (Musée du Louvre) / Tony Querrec.

P. 110: Boston Public Library, licensed under CC BY 2.0; Retrieved from the Library of Congress, https://www.loc.gov/item/98504529/; Southworth & Hawes, Museum of Fine Arts, Boston; The White House Historical Association, United States Government purchase, 1947, public domain.

P. 113: © Colección Carmen Thyssen, on loan at the Museo Nacional Thyssen-Bornemisza; De Young Museum, San Francisco, Creative Commons CC0 1.0 Universal Public Domain Dedication; Paul Mellon Fund and Gift of Jo Ann and Julian Ganz, Jr., National Gallery of Art, Washington, DC, public domain; Crystal Bridges Museum of American Art, Bentonville, Arkansas; Yale University Art Gallery.

P. 124: April Brady / POMED, Creative Commons Attribution 2.0 Generic; Abbie Rowe /John F. Kennedy Presidential Library and Museum; Harry S. Truman Library & Museum; United States Federal Government; Cecil Stoughton, White House; United States Federal Government; Executive Office of the President of the United States, Public Domain; Photo: Pete Souza, Creative Commons Attribution 3.0 Unported; Ya'acov Sa'ar Ya'acov / © The State of Israel Government Press Office.

P. 127: Reuters; by: iichs.ir (unknown photographer) Public domain; By: Mahmoud Hosseini, CC; www.kremlin.ru, Creative Commons Attribution 4.0; Abu Dhabi Government Services; United States Congress; Photo: Gage Skidmore from Peoria, AZ, United States of America, Creative Commons Attribution-Share Alike 2.0 Generic; by Gage Skidmore, licensed under CC BY-SA 2.0; Executive Office of the President of the United States; Photo: Gage Skidmore, CC BY-SA 2.0; https://responsiblestatecraft.org/; https://www.concordia.net/.

Illustrations of works provided by courtesy of the Museo Nacional Thyssen-Bornemisza, Colección Carmen Thyssen, Thyssen-Bornemisza Collections, Wadsworth Atheneum Museum of Art (Hartford, CT), Dr. Harold Krug, and Nina Clemente.

Colophon

Walid Raad: Cotton Under My Feet

This catalog is published on the occasion of the eponymous exhibition at Museo Nacional Thyssen-Bornemisza, Madrid, October 6, 2021–January 23, 2022.

Editors
Daniela Zyman
Eva Ebersberger
Thyssen-Bornemisza Art Contemporary

Editorial Team
Marina Avia
Aleksandra Czerniak

Graphic Design
Alex Gifreu

Exhibition Photography
Moritz Bernoully

Copyediting
Orit Gat

Translation from the Spanish
Philip Sutton (Guillermo Solana)

Printing
Nova Era Publications

Paper
Materica Gesso Recycled 120 gsm
Arena Smooth EW Recycled 140 gsm
Materica Gesso Recycled 250 gsm

Cover
Walid Raad, *Following Martin Johnson Heade*, 2021
Based on Martin Johnson Heade, *Orchids and Spray Orchids with Hummingbirds*, about 1875–1890.
Museum of Fine Arts, Boston

Bibliographic information published by the Deutsche Nationalbibliothek The Deutsche Nationalbibliothek lists this publication in the Deutsche Nationalbibliografie; detailed bibliographic data are available on the Internet at http://dnb.d-nb.de.

Distributed by

Europe
Buchhandlung Walther König
Ehrenstraße 4
D - 50672 Köln
Tel: +49 (0) 221 / 20 59 6 53
verlag@buchhandlung-walther-koenig.de

UK & Ireland
Cornerhouse Publications Ltd. - HOME
2 Tony Wilson Place
UK – Manchester M15 4FN
Tel: +44 (0) 161 212 3466
publications@cornerhouse.org

Outside Europe
D.A.P. / Distributed Art Publishers, Inc.
75 Broad Street, Suite 630
USA - New York, NY 10004
Tel: +1 (0) 212 627 1999
orders@dapinc.com

ISBN 978-3-7533-0103-7
Printed in Spain

Published by
Verlag der Buchhandlung Walther und Franz König
Ehrenstraße 4, D-50672 Köln

Thyssen-Bornemisza Art Contemporary Privatstiftung
Köstlergasse 1/40, A-1060 Vienna